# The Arlington Meeting
## January 1968

© **Truth Publications, Inc. 2025. Second Printing.** All rights reserved. No part of this book may be reproduced in any form without prior written permission from the publisher.

ISBN 10: 1-58427-064-0
ISBN 13: 978-158427-064-5

First Printing: 1969

Truth Publications, Inc.
CEI Bookstore
220 S. Marion St., Athens, AL 35611
855-492-6657
sales@truthpublications.com
www.truthbooks.com

## *Publisher's Statement*

A few words might be in order explaining how these speeches were reduced to written form. Some of the main speeches were read from manuscript. But others had to be transcribed from tape.

The transcription of these manuscripts was not done under the most propitious circumstances. Conditions over which we had no control resulted in four different transcribers being employed. The manuscripts taken from the tape were sent, as had been agreed beforehand, to the speakers. However, some of the speakers were nearly a year in returning their corrected manuscripts.

The manuscripts were delivered to me as having been corrected. I did not attempt to compare each sentence with the tape. However, several proofings of the manuscripts were made.

It is almost certain that some mistakes were made, but if they were made, they were made inadvertently. We hope no serious mistakes were made in transcription and type setting. The long delay by some of the speakers in returning the corrected manuscripts precluded the advisability of sending galley proofs and page proofs, as we would have liked to have done. So under circumstances which were not quite ideal, we have done the best we could.

Cecil Willis
Cogdill Foundation
P. O. Box 403
Marion, Ind. 46952

## *Team Arrangement for Arlington Discussion*

*Norman W. Starling—Coordinator*

| Team No. 1 | Team No. 2 |
|---|---|
| Jimmy H. Allen | James W. Adams |
| L. H. (Buster) Dobbs | Roy E. Cogdill |
| Lewis G. Hale | Melvin Curry |
| Alan E. Highers | Harold Fite |
| Bill J. Humble | Clinton D. Hamilton |
| Hulen L. Jackson | Stanley J. Lovett |
| Roy H. Lanier | Harry Pickup Jr. |
| Reuel G. Lemmons | Franklin T. Puckett |
| Gus Nichols | Dudley Ross Spears |
| Hardeman Nichols | William Floyd Thompson |
| Johnny Ramsey | Robert F. Turner |
| Eldred Stevens | Bryan Vinson Sr. |
| J. D. Thomas | W. L. Wharton Jr. |

## *The Arlington Meeting — A Foreword*

Unity among the people of God is a solemn responsibility of Christians second in importance only to the obligation to preserve, proclaim, and defend the word of God. Strife and consequent division among God's people are at once abominable in the sight of God (Proverbs 6:16-19) and destructive of the happiness and vitality of the church of the Lord. Where such division obtains, any sincere, scriptural move toward a restoration of unity could only be pleasing to God, hence should be viewed with delight and encouraged with joyful anticipation on the part of God's people thus divided. Any such move is fraught with significance and merit.

Perhaps no meeting between dissident groups among the churches of Christ in our time has received more publicity, good and bad, than the meeting conducted at Arlington, Texas in January of 1968. What began, in the minds of those who conceived it, as a single, constructive step on the long, painful road from open division back to New Testament unity among the Lord's people became, in the minds of many, a "denominational, ecumenical movement convened by self-appointed delegates to settle brotherhood problems."

What the Arlington meeting *actually was* is simply stated. It was a meeting between two groups of sincere brethren of opposing views relative to church organization, work, and cooperation. The men of each group were men of ability and stature among the brethren who shared their concepts and practices. The immediate purpose of the meeting was to discuss from a Bible point of view the issues which divide us, and to do this in a spirit of mutual respect for each other and deep concern for the truth of God and the unity of his people. It was thought that a meeting limited in attendance to the participating speakers and conducted in the relaxed and informal atmosphere of a private location would be more conducive to a rational, restrained, brotherly probing of our differences than a public confrontation would afford, hence the meeting took place at a private camp owned by brethren near Arlington, Texas. Most of the participants ate and slept on the premises and between sessions of the discussion associated freely with one another forming new acquaintances and renewing old ones. We met, therefore, not as enemies seeking the accolades of polemic victory, but as alienated brethren sorrowfully, yet hopefully, seeking for Bible answers to the issues which divide us.

It was the hope of those who conceived the idea of such a meeting that it might have the immediate effect of encouraging a restoration of all but extinct communication between us. At this point, we had all but written each other off as hopeless cases going our separate ways as two distinct bodies of people. It was also hoped that such a meeting might promote a better understanding of what each of us actually believed and practiced and thus bring into sharp focus the issues which would have to be resolved before we could "be agreed and walk together."

The ultimate aim was, of course, the restoration of unity and fellowship among brethren throughout the world. However, it was never the thought or hope of those who arranged the Arlington meeting that such could or would be accomplished in a single meeting of this kind. It was rather hoped that this meeting would lead to others of like nature as well as public meetings throughout the world and that thereby, step by step, Christian by Christian, and congregation by congregation, a fractured brotherhood might be mended and that once again there might be a single body of happy, militant people united on the solid foundation of Divine truth and vitally knit together by a mutual love and a common faith and practice.

This book contains an accurate publication of the principal speeches delivered at the Arlington meeting. The reader will observe that the arrangement was not strictly a *debate* situation. There were five topics discussed involving the major problems now obtaining among churches of Christ. There were five major speakers each of whom came with a prepared speech on his assigned topic. There were five *major* sessions and five *minor* sessions. Each major speaker delivered his prepared speech of forty-five minutes length in each major session, then had the privilege of a fifteen minutes rebuttal.

Each major session was followed by a minor session on the same topic in which three men from each group spoke for fifteen minutes each on the subject of the preceding major session. There was also in this session a period of thirty minutes in which there were questions and answers and short speeches by as many speakers as could be crowded into that period of time. The speeches in these sessions of questions and answers are not included in the book. Their deletion was mutually agreed upon by both groups to reduce the size of the book and its resultant price upon publication.

The reader of the book is advised that each speaker in the discussion represented no one but himself, hence is solely responsible for his own statements. Each man spoke his own convictions without regard to what others, even of his own group believed or practiced, hence no statements of one man are by virtue of group association to be charged to another. Neither are the views expressed by any of the participants in the discussion necessarily the views of the publishers of the book.

In committing this book to the reading public, the publishers hope and pray that it will be the means of exciting renewed interest in a careful study of Bible teaching on the subjects with which it deals and which today divide brethren into opposing camps. It is their hope and prayer that it will encourage a further restoration of communication between these two camps of alienated brethren, and a revitalization of the desire to find common, scriptural ground on which they can stand and work together in the cause of Jesus our Lord. Also, it is the hope and prayer of the publishers that the book will be successful in dispelling any misgivings that brethren may have had relative to the essential nature of the Arlington meeting.

The publication of the book has been delayed far beyond what was originally contemplated. This was due to a series of unfortunate occurrences over which the publishers had no absolute control. They hereby tender their sincere apologies and ardently hope that the delay may not measurably affect the interest of the reading brethren in its contents so as to materially hinder the good it otherwise would have accomplished. May the God of all grace bless this book to the advancement of his truth, to the promotion of unity among his people, and therefore, to his own eternal glory.

                James W. Adams,
                1102 N. Mound Street,
                Nacogdoches, Texas   75961

                Reuel Lemmons
                Box 610
                Austin, Texas

## Introductory Remarks

### Norman Starling

We are at one of the most crucial periods in the history of our nation. Abroad there exist war in Vietnam, piracy on the high seas, threats of new aggression in Korea. At home, civil disobedience, lawlessness, crime. In spite of the sincere efforts of some to solve these problems, insufficient progress has been made, for it is evident that Hanoi does not really want to talk peace, that the Soviets will not be guided by reason, and that many Americans fail to work for peace and harmony at home. These difficult times make us aware that although man has lived on the earth for thousands of years, he still has not learned how to live in peace with his neighbor.

Such a failure to live in peace should not characterize my brethren. Is it not fitting and right, then, when brethren in the family of God differ, when fellowship has been impaired—and even broken—that the lines of communication be re-established? What better way is there for brethren of divergent views to be united in spirit than to meet together to discuss earnestly, prayerfully, and humbly the differences that exist? It is my conviction, brethren, that we are twenty years late with this meeting.

For a century or more, we have pled with people of this nation to be restored to God's perfect way. We have entreated men to be just Christians and to accept Christ as the authority for their religious practices. We have proclaimed that all men can be reconciled in the one body through the cross and that Christ prayed that His followers might be one. We have upheld Paul's plea for unity in mind and in judgment. We have warned that division is devilish, carnal, and that they who practice division cannot inherit the Kingdom of God. Sadly, this great plea has been adopted by less than two per cent of the people of this country. The fault is not in the plea, but perhaps in our own failure to heed it ourselves, for a great brotherhood, born out of a burning passion for unity, is now divided.

Thanks be to God, brethren, that you are willing to do what you can to restore unity in that brotherhood. Thanks be to Him that you have come together to discuss His Word with those with whom you differ in a sincere effort to achieve unity in the Family, as it pleases God.

In addition to our primary motive to please God in our unity, we also feel the need of the strength that only unity can bring. Brethren, we have a common foe: atheism, communism, modernism, liberalism, Catholicism, denominationalism, the social gospel. If there has ever been a time in the history of Israel when we need one another, it is now. I am convinced that greater unity between us is possible. We all believe that the New Testament of our Lord Jesus Christ is our rule of faith and practice. We believe the Bible is the inspired word of God. We believe in undenominational Christianity. It may be that one of our primary problems is in determining what God binds and what God looses. I do not believe that there is one soul here tonight who desires to bind where God has not bound nor to loose where God has not loosed. We need, then, to deal with this problem.

All of us have appealed to our religious friends in trying to convince them of God's truth by asking the question, "Is there any infallibly safe way a human being can pursue?" We believe that with the Bible we can show any honest, humble person the safe course to pursue in the midst of religious strife and confusion. Surely in overcoming the confusion that exists in the church today, there is likewise an infallibly safe course to pursue without sacrificing truth or conscience. If this is a valid contention, brethren, why not seek the safe way? At least this is a good place to begin.

The proper attitude toward one another is indispensable, not only in maintaining the proper relationship to God, but in the solution to our problems. Before Paul gave the plan for religious unity, he described the spirit that must characterize the children of God. Paul said, "I therefore, the prisoner in the Lord, beseech you to walk worthily of the calling wherewith you were called, with all lowliness, and meekness, with long-suffering, forbearing one another in love." Remember these words, brethren: "Love the brotherhood." "He that loves his brother abideth in the light. We know we have passed out of death into life, because we love the brethren. He that loveth not abideth in death, beloved, let us love one another, for God is love. Beloved, if God so loved us, we ought also to love one another and this commandment have we from Him: that he who loveth God love his brother also." Love for each other does not imply a compromise of truth nor a participation in unscriptural actions. But to love one another does mean that we "suffer long"; that is patience. To love one another does mean that kindness characterizes our speech and our actions. Paul said "Love envieth not"; it is full of generosity. "Love vaunteth not itself, is not puffed up"; it is full of humility. "Love does not behave itself unseemly"; it is courteous. Love "seeketh not her own"; it is unselfish. Love "is not easily provoked"; it manifests good temper. Love "thinketh no evil"; it is guileless. Love "rejoiceth not in iniquity, but rejoiceth in the truth"; it is sincere. May that spirit abound in our hearts and therefore in our words, brethren, so that we can solve and resolve some of the differences that exist tonight.

Our plea for decades has been, "Where the Bible speaks, we speak; where the Bible is silent, we are silent. In matters of faith, unity; in matters of opinion, liberty; in all things, love." By each man's complete allegiance to that plea, our discussions will be fruitful. God will be honored; His children will rejoice; and His kingdom will be made stronger. May God help us.

## *Introductory Statement*

### James W. Adams

Brother Reuel Lemmons and I agreed to make opening statements before we began this series of studies. We had a meeting of this kind at Buchanan Dam last April. Nine of us participated in it. It was somewhat different from this discussion in that we had no formal agenda. We simply told each other what we found wrong with each other. These differences were then discussed back and forth in an informal way. All of us kept our tempers and we got along splendidly. When we were not arguing with one another in the regular sessions, we played dominoes and otherwise enjoyed each other's company. Everything worked out so well that we hoped another meeting might result in further progress.

In reference to the matters which shall be the subject of discussion in this meeting, we feel that there has been an almost complete breakdown of communication between those with whom I stand identified in this discussion and those with whom Brother Lemmons stands identified. We further feel we can never make any progress toward unity or understanding until we can restore communication with one another. With this in view, we have planned this meeting as a more formal discussion of the questions which divide us.

This is not a debate in the ordinary sense of that expression. The men who make the principal speeches in this meeting will come with speeches already prepared—for the most part in manuscript form. There will be rebuttals. They will constitute the only characteristic which this discussion will have in common with an ordinary religious debate.

We have agreed, and our chairman will emphasize this at greater length, that this will be a *Bible discussion.* So many of our debates have been marred by charges and counter charges:

"You did this at such a place, and this or that occurred at this place or that." We all agreed that this discussion would be strictly a Bible discussion of the subjects under consideration. All of us profess to believe the Bible to be the word of God. We should all be willing for the Bible to settle our differences and problems. We can never get together until there is a common understanding among us of what the Bible teaches on these subjects. It is our hope that our hope for a Bible discussion will not be marred in this discussion, that each speaker will confine himself strictly to a discussion of his subject from a Bible point of view.

Furthermore, we made the agreement that there would be no personal reflections of any kind upon anyone, that everyone would be treated with absolute fairness, and that we would recognize one another as brethren. Of course, we recognize that you think we are wrong, and we believe you are wrong. We would not be here if this were not so. Yet, we recognize each other as brethren. Each one of us comes into this meeting with the understanding that all of us are sincere in that for which we are contending. Hence, we shall not only recognize one another as brethren, but as sincere brethren, each person honestly contending for what he believes to be the truth.

We believe that all of us are big enough men and that we have enough respect for the Lord to engage in a discussion of this kind in this spirit and attitude. With reference to the results, we have qualified hopes. Some people ask us, "What do you hope to come from this?" I answer, "I do not know actually." They ask, "How much good do you think will be accomplished?" I answer, "I do not know." But, neither do I know the answer to this question when I stand up to preach. I honestly do not know how much good will come from this meeting, but it is certainly never wrong for brethren who profess to serve a common Lord in a common cause to sit down and discuss their differences with one another in the spirit and attitude which we have suggested for this meeting. We hope this will be a pleasant time for all of us and that it will be a discussion such as will glorify God and benefit His cause in the world.

## Introductory Remarks

### Reuel Lemmons

These meetings are of special interest to me because I love the brotherhood and I love the fellowship of every one of you.

I believe that there is room in the scriptures for fellowship between many more of us than are exercising that fellowship today. I believe that many diversities of opinions enlarge themselves into issues causing needless divisions in the body of Christ. All of us agree that the scriptures teach that the body of Christ is essentially and organically one.

I think we love truth; I believe every man here loves the truth and I expect one of us loves it about as much as the other. I grant to every one of you the same sincerity and the same loyalty to the Lord that I think I have myself, and it is our hope that out of such meetings as this, as we know each other better and understand each other's positions better, there may grow a mutual respect among us; and that, if differences do have to exist, at least respect for each other can continue.

I don't believe there can be real unity in the body of Christ until we believe the same things. I believe the restoration principle that "in matters of faith there must be unity" is as binding today as it has always been. I believe that in opinions there must be liberty. And while all of us may be guilty, at times, of preaching our opinions when we think they are law, here we have an opportunity to bring these issues to sharp focus and to weed out the things that are pseudo-issues, and get down to the real bone of contention, if there is one. Loving the scriptures as all of us do, I believe we can come to some agreement on what the truth is.

I had a very small part in the first of these meetings and I was gratified beyond expectation at the good that came out of it. I felt that the distance between me and some of my brethren was not nearly so great after those three days as it was before. I think all of us agreed that the differences were not nearly so great as we had thought they were, and that basically we excluded the same specifics and included the same generics. We just arrived at the conclusion in a different manner. I guess as long as people are human there will be some differences among us. These existed between disciples in the first century, and some room for differences is allowable even within the faith, but I hope that through meetings like this we can draw closer to each other at the same time we're drawing closer to the Lord; and that out of this meeting there may come an amelioration of the sharp, caustic feelings and sayings that have characterized some past writings and preaching among us.

I honestly believe that we have a good chance of doing the unusual and closing a breach and narrowing a gap in the body of Christ. I hope that everybody is here with the intention and fervent prayer that we will come closer together and not be farther apart when these meetings are over. I hope that we will personally pray God's guidance upon our efforts to bind up a wound.

## How to Establish Bible Authority

### Roy E. Cogdill

I am happy to be here to engage in this discussion. I will forego any personal remarks, and take for granted that all of you know that my attitude toward you personally is what a Christian's attitude should be. If it is not, you call it to my attention and I will gladly correct it. I am interested, so far as I know my own heart, in only one thing and that is in serving God so that I can go to heaven after awhile. If this is not the desire of my heart, I have deceived myself for a good many years. This is my primary interest personally and, of course, I want to help everyone else that I can to go to heaven. This is the reason I have been engaged all of these years in preaching the gospel of Christ. I am grateful for the opportunity that is mine to discuss the question of "How to Establish Bible Authority." I will use the forty-five minutes that have been allotted to say all that I can on this very vital theme and will quit when the time is gone, whether I am finished or not.

First of all, I would like to give you a definition of what I believe to be the real meaning of authority. "The principal

---

ROY E. COGDILL—*Author of several perennial best sellers in the field of*

*Bible study books; debater; evangelist for the Par Avenue congregation in Orlando, Florida; special lecturer at Florida College, Temple Terrace, Florida; widely used in gospel meetings throughout the nation.*

Bible word for authority is 'Exousia.' Important material from the essay in Kittel's 'Worterbuch' on 'Exousia' (II, 559ff.) will be found in Geldenhuys, 'Supreme Authority' (pp. 15-16 et passim). Geldenhuys says the word expresses *'the idea of an all-inclusive authority, in the sense of the freedom and the power to command and to enforce obedience, and to have possession of,* and rule and dominion over' "(p. 16). *(The Pattern of Authority* by Bernard Ramm, p. 17) The idea of authority is then simply the right to command and to expect or demand and require obedience.

We proceed with the first proposition——*The Necessity for Authority In Religion.* Authority in religion is necessary, for the nature and being of deity dictate it. Sovereignty belongs to deity. By right of creation, omnipotence, omniscience, love, mercy, and grace toward humanity this is true. Then, second, the nature of man requires authority in religion—some sort of a standard of authority in religion. He cannot provide it for himself. (Jer. 10:23) The word of God says that the way of man is not in himself. And yet his need for redemption and for divine provision in the interest of his redemption, and his accountability unto God as a responsible creature, certainly mean that he needs some standard of authority in religion that he can understand and by which he can be governed and guided through faith in what the Word of God has revealed and teaches. In the third place, reconciliation with God is impossible without authority. Provisions must be made by the God of heaven for man's redemption. A knowledge of these provisions and terms or conditions must be made known to man in order that he might comply with them. A standard of right and wrong is essential and necessary. Truth and error must be distinguished so that people can understand and can recognize what God would have them do in order that they might enjoy the proper relationship with God and among men. It is impossible to please God without a knowledge of His will. So, the will of God must be revealed in order that our efforts may be directed toward being pleasing to God, and this ought to be the major objective of our hearts.

*Authority must be objective, however, not subjective.* It must come from without. James talks about the implanted or the engrafted word which is able to save your souls. This is a revealed word, a revealed message from God, Himself, for the purpose of guiding men and women in harmony with His will. Authority must have an object and must be free from subjectivism. It must find its origin outside of the individual. Authority cannot exist upon the basis of a religious experience, upon the basis of just thought, upon the basis of aspirations and unclouded reason, or upon the basis of the instincts and pure conscience of man. These cannot and will not establish authority for any of us. For men to do that which they hold to be right in their own sight is to destroy any standard, and God condemned that upon the part of Israel in the long ago. (Deut 12:8) It denies accountability toward God and responsibility toward their fellow man.

*God is sovereign by right of creation and possession.* All authority inheres in God for this reason. As the Word of God reveals, "The earth is the Lord's and the fullness thereof." (I Cor. 10:26) It belongs to God, David declared, in Psalms 44: 1-2, that God rules over it and that all power and authority emanate from the Father, that all powers or authorities upon this earth have been ordained of God and that apart from God there is no power and there is no authority. He is the one God unto whom all should ascribe glory and majesty and dominion and power forever. Paul on Mar's Hill in the city of Athens said that God who made the world and everything in it, being Lord of heaven and earth, since He Himself gives to all men life and breath and everything, and He made from one every nation of men to live on the face of the earth, having determined allotted periods and the boundaries of their habitations, that they should seek God in the hope that they might feel after Him and find Him, for He is not far from each of us. (Acts 17) In Romans 9:20-21, Paul raises the question. "But who, are you, a man, to answer back to God? Will what is molded say to its molder, Why have you made me thus? Has the potter no right over the clay, to make out of the same lump one vessel for beauty and another for menial use?" (Revised Standard Version)

*God, then, is the object in religion.* He is "I AM THAT I AM." (Exodus 3:14). Religion cannot be determined anymore by subjective wish than can science. In physical anthropology the human body is the source of all data. In chemistry, all theories must be submitted to the facts of chemistry. The object of science is to discover or convey to the scientist by experimentation and exploration these facts that exist in the various fields. In religion the reverse is true. Knowledge in religion comes through the self-revelation of God Almighty. In Christianity, the authority principle is the triune God in self-revelation. God is the true God or the God of Truth. He that cometh from God is above all. He that cometh from heaven is above all. "He that received His testimony hath set to his seal that God is truth." (John 3:31-34) And then in Romans 3:4, Paul said, "Let God be true, but every man a liar. As it is written, that thou mightest be justified in thy sayings and mightest overcome when thou are judged." Paul wrote to the Thessalonian brethren and expressed to them his gratitude for the fact that they had turned from their idols to serve the living and the true God. The Bible declares that God's judgments are according to truth. In Romans 2:2, we are assured that the judgment of God is according to truth against such things. And then in Revelation 16:7, "And I heard another out of the altar say, Even so, Lord God almighty, true and righteous are thy judgments." So God's judgments are according to truth and God's word is truth. It is the only standard of truth that there is. Jesus said, "Sanctify them through thy truth; Thy word is truth." And in Psalms 31:5, the Psalmist said, "Into thy hands I commit my spirit; Thou hast redeemed me, O Lord God of truth." God's will is right in any matter and His word is truth. "He is the rock, His work is perfect, for all His ways are judgment: a God of truth without iniquity; just and right is He." (Deut. 32:3-4) Then in Psalms 19, "The judgments of the Lord are true and righteous altogether." So Peter said, "Whether it be right in the sight of God to hearken unto you more than unto God, judge ye. For we cannot but speak the things which we have seen and heard." (Acts 4:19-20)

*The standard of authority in religion, then, is the self-revelation of Jehovah and His will.* The objects of science convey their properties to the scientist in a number of ways. In religion the knowledge of the object is conveyed to the subject by revelation. If God is the object in religion, and is known only as He reveals Himself, there can be no rational objection to the authority in a divine revelation or of the recognition of a divine revelation as the standard of authority. I would like to emphasize the fact, then, that God can be known only as He reveals Himself. Paul declared, "Great is the mystery of godliness." (I Tim. 3:16) And he said again in I Corinthians 2:7, "We speak the wisdom of God in a mystery, even the hidden wisdom which God ordained before the world unto our glory." Again in I Corinthians 2:10, "But God has revealed them unto us by His Spirit, for the Spirit searcheth all things, yea, the deep things of God." In Romans 1:17 Paul declares that the righteousness of God has been revealed unto us in the gospel of Christ from faith—(from the faith)—in order to faith (in our hearts). We have God's standard of righteousness and God's standard of authority in religion in God's Word. In Romans 11, Paul declares, and I believe this should be the sentiment of our hearts, verses 33 and 34, "O, the depth of the riches, both of the wisdom and the knowledge of God. How unsearchable are His judgments, and His ways past finding out. But who has known the mind of the Lord or who has been his counselor?" Isaiah promised that God would teach us of His ways. (Isaiah 2:3) In Hosea 8:12 God said, "I have written unto them the greater things of my law, but they have been counted as a strange thing." Our attitude, then, toward the word of God and toward that which God has revealed in His word, our willingness to accept it at face value, to put our faith and trust and confidence in it, and to stand upon it and be guided by what we know it to say and teach, certainly is the way to please God and win not only His approval now but the hope of eternal life in the world to come.

The modern scientist does not feel restricted because nature is determined. The orderliness and the uniformity of nature is still a major premise to the scientist. The goal of science is to bring as much of the phenomena of the universe as they can learn under general laws. The scientist, therefore, should not, nor should anyone else, be surprised to find that the domain of the spirit is structured for him by divine revelation. "Rather than the spirit world, or the spiritual world, be a chaos of cults, a Babel of religious confusion, or a quaking jelly of subjectivism, it is structured by the certain and the true knowledge of God, which is revealed in His will." (Ramm, *The Pattern of Authority*, p. 24)

*God speaks and has revealed Himself through His Son, Jesus Christ.* In Hebrews 1:1, Paul declares that God speaks to us through His Son Jesus Christ. In Matthew 11:27, Jesus thanked the Father that He had hidden these things from the wise and the understanding and had "revealed them unto babes." Then he said, "For no man knoweth the Son but the Father, neither doth any man know the Father, but the Son and him to whomsoever the Son wills to reveal Him." Therefore, all I can know about God and all I can know about the will of God and all I can know about what is right, and all I can know about the truth, I have to learn from the Word of God. I have to learn all of it from what God, Himself, has said.

Jesus Christ, the messenger of God to men today, is the true minister of the truth of God. Paul declares it in Rom. 15:8, "Now I say that Jesus Christ was the minister of the circumcision for the truth of God to confirm the promises made unto the Father." John 1:14 declares that He is full of grace and truth, and in the same chapter the Apostle affirms that Christ is life and that life is the "light of men." Paul tells us that Christ is the "light of the knowledge of the glory of God" that was manifest first in the face of Jesus Christ, revealed in his own personality, the mystery of godliness manifested in the flesh, and that it has been revealed to us through the earthen vessels (the apostles) by whom divine revelation was made in New Testament days. This "light of the knowledge of the glory of God" then is found only in the Gospel of Christ.

Jesus evidenced that he had complete reverence for the Word of God——the sort of an attitude toward God and His word that you and I need to emulate—that he had no message of his own, for He said, "I have not spoken of myself, but the Father which sent me, He gave me a commandment what I should say and what I should speak, and I know that His commandment is life everlasting." In John 8:25, "I have many things to say and to judge of you that He that sent me is true and I speak to the world those things which I have heard of Him . . . But as My Father hath taught me, I speak these things." Jesus Christ, then, in this dispensation, has been given all authority. He announced it when he had been raised up from the dead, "All authority is given unto me, both in heaven and on earth." It had been prophesied by Moses that a prophet the Lord God would raise up from among his brethren like unto him and he said, "Unto him must ye give heed in all things and it shall come to pass that the soul that does not hearken to the words of that prophet shall be cut off from among the people." (Deut. 18:15). So, God's message is delivered to the world today, and all that we know about what God wills and authorizes or about our duty to God or how to please Him has been revealed through Jesus Christ our Lord. James says in chapter 4, and verse 12, "There is one law giver." Paul said in 2 Cor. 10:5, "Casting down imaginations and every high thing that exalteth itself against the knowledge of God and bringing into captivity every thought to the obedience of Christ."

*But the Holy Spirit is the divine agent in the work of revelation.* Every word that Jesus used in John 14:16, 26, and 16:13-15 in promising the Holy Spirit to the apostles indicated that His work and mission would be that of divine revelation. That he will *teach* you all things; that he will *remind* you of all things that I have spoken unto you; that He will *guide* you into all truth; that He shall *speak* unto you those things that He shall hear and that He shall *show* unto you the things to come. Jesus promised that He would guide the apostles into *all* the truth. Moreover the Spirit had no message of His own. John 16:13 "For He shall not speak of Himself, but whatsoever He shall hear, that shall He speak." Jesus received the message from the Father and the Holy Spirit revealed the message that had been given him by the Father.

*The apostles of our Lord have places of authority in the Kingdom of God.* They were selected, schooled, and trained by the Lord. They were permitted, during the three and a half years of His personal ministry, to hear what He taught, to see how He lived, and the miracles that He performed. The apostle John said, "That which was from the beginning, which we have heard, which we have seen with our eyes, which we have looked upon, and our hands have handled, of the Word of Life" (I John 1:1). This qualified an apostle. Not only were they eye and ear witnesses of Jesus Christ, but in addition, Jesus said, "Ye shall receive power after that the Holy Ghost is come upon you and ye shall be witnesses unto me both in Jerusalem, and in all Judea, and in Samaria, and unto the uttermost parts of the earth." (Acts 1:8). He commissioned them as His ambassadors to speak with binding authority. Matthew 16:19, "I will give unto you the keys of the kingdom of heaven: and whatsoever thou shalt bind on earth shall be bound in heaven: and whatsoever thou shalt loose on earth shall be loosed in heaven." He made the same statement to all the apostles in Matt. 18:18. In I John 4:6 John said, "He that heareth us knoweth God. He that heareth us not knoweth not God." So, we must be willing, in order to know God and to know what the will of God is, to hear the apostles of our Lord. They are His ambassadors. Paul said he had given unto them the ministry of reconciliation. The word of reconciliation was delivered into their hands and they could say, "We beseech you in Christ's stead." (2 Corinthians 5:18-20).

He also indicated that they would be the Supreme Court in the church of God, the judges of spiritual Israel. "In the regeneration when the Son of Man shall sit upon the throne of His glory, ye also shall sit upon twelve thrones, judging the twelve tribes of Israel." (Matt. 19:28) This was not fleshly Israel but spiritual Israel, the church of our Lord. The apostles were set in the church. (I Corinthians 12:28). As apostles in the church of the Lord, they were infallibly guided by the Holy Spirit, so that they made no mistakes, either as to revelation of God's mind or of the inspired words that were delivered unto them or chosen for them by the Holy Spirit with which that revelation was conveyed. Paul affirmed that the message which he preached was revealed by the Spirit of God. He said, "We have received not the spirit which is of the world but the Spirit which is of God that we might know the things freely given us of God." And again, "Which things we speak, not in words which man's wisdom teacheth, but in words which the Spirit teacheth, combining spiritual things with spiritual." (I Cor. 2: 12-13).

In the great commission of Matt. 28, Jesus limited their authority, however, to that which He had taught them. The force of an apostolically approved example in the New Testament rests upon the fact that they were limited in teaching the church to that which Jesus Christ had commanded. He said, "All authority is mine, both in heaven and on earth, go ye therefore and teach all nations, baptizing them into the name of the Father and of the Son and of the Holy Spirit, teaching them (those whom you baptize—the church) to observe all things whatsoever I have commanded you." Beyond that they dared not go. They were limited to that message which Christ had received from the Father and which He had delivered unto them. Jesus said, "He that receiveth you receiveth me, and he that rejecteth you rejecteth me, and he that rejecteth me rejecteth Him that sent me." (Matt. 10:39; Luke 10:16) I cannot reject the message preached by the apostles without rejecting the authority of Jesus Christ. To receive any message not preached by Him is to stand condemned. John said, "He that goeth onward and abideth not in the doctrine of Christ hath not God." (2 John 9-11) That which was revealed unto them has been delivered unto us in the scriptures. Paul said, "By revelation he made known unto me the mystery as I wrote afore in few words, whereby when ye read ye may understand my knowledge in the mystery of Christ which in other ages was not made known unto the sons of men as it is now revealed unto His holy apostles and prophets by the Spirit." (Eph. 3:3-6) So we can read what they wrote and learn what they taught and what the will of God therefore is.

Jude tells us that one of the greatest obligations resting upon the soul of any man who will serve God is to *contend earnestly* for the faith—"epi-agonize" for the faith. There is no greater duty that you and I owe to God. I must love my brother to the point that I would do him no wrong and all of the good that I could do for him, but this should not keep me from differing with him when he is wrong and it should not soften down my love for the truth so that I would be willing to effect any kind of a compromise with error. I used to have some differences with my mother. I know she loved me. I never did question it in my life. She usually resolved our differences, and without any great difficulty, though she did it sometimes in a rather painful way to me. Let me tell you something. Do not ever doubt or question the attitude of one, though he may differ with you, that is trying to contend for what he believes the Word of God teaches. He is the best friend you have. For if he should have the truth and you reject it, it would be your soul that would pay the penalty. We need to recognize that we must first of all respect the Word of God Almighty above every other consideration on earth. The man who does not do it cannot enjoy the favor of God or the proper relationship with God.

I have some charts to illustrate some of the things that I want to say. Perhaps they can set forth what I want to present better than I could without them.

CHART NO. 1 *illustrates the order of divine authority.* God is supreme in authority, the sovereign of all power and over the whole universe. Jesus Christ exercises authority that has been delegated to Him by the Father. The Holy Spirit, through the Apostles and the prophets of the New Testament day, revealed the word that Christ received from God and delivered it to the world in the Scriptures as God revealed His mind to the Spirit, and as the Spirit inspired the apostles and prophets by selecting even the words by which God's will was made known.

Our faith comes by hearing this Word of God. (Rom. 10: 17) The realm of faith lies within that of divine revelation. All that I have the right to believe (and it does not matter from what other source I might learn it), I must believe because it is that which God has revealed and stated plainly enough in His word that I can understand what God would have me know. Paul said, "Having received the same spirit of faith, according to that which is written, I have believed, and therefore do I speak." (2 Cor. 4:13) The scriptures are the truth. They are all of the truth. They claim this. (John 16:13) They are the Word of truth, (2 Cor. 6:7) and the truth of Christ, (2 Cor. 11:10) and the way of truth. (2 Peter 2:21) Sanctification of the Spirit and belief of the truth are the effects of gospel preaching. (2 Thess. 2:13) "The fruit of the Spirit is in all goodness and righteousness and truth." (Eph. 5:9) Jesus said, "Thy word is truth." (John 17:17) The Psalmist said, "The sum of thy word is truth." (Psalms 119:160) All of God's testimony must be heard.

I raise the question now, *"How may I determine whether or not a thing is within the scope of divine authority?"* Let me suggest that can be determined by whether or not it comes from God or man. Where did it originate? Let us look at

*Chart No. 2.* Here you have on one side divine revelation and on the other side, human reason. But the way of man is not in himself. Paul said, "All scripture is given by inspiration of

God, and is profitable for doctrine, for reproof, for correction, for instruction in righteousness: that the man of God may be perfect, thoroughly furnished unto all good works." Over on one side you have the truth, and Jesus drew the line between truth and error, as distinguished by the fact that one came from God and other from man. He said in Matthew 16:13, when he came into the coast of Caesarea Philippi, "Whom do men say that I the Son of Man am?" They said, "Some say that thou are John the Baptist: some, Elias; and others, Jeremias, or one of the prophets." One answer was as good as another, for all of them were dictated by human reason or of their own thinking and therefore were their own conclusions, and though one of them was as good as another, all of them were wrong and none of them was any good at all. So the Lord said, "But whom say ye that I am?" Simon Peter answered and said, "Thou art the Christ, the Son of the living God." Jesus said, "Blessed art thou, Simon Barjona; for flesh and blood hath not revealed it unto thee, but my Father which is in heaven." Truth came from God and error from man. This is the dividing line between truth and error! Does it come from man or God?

Blackboard Illustration No. 1.

---

Matthew 16:13-18

| FROM GOD | OR | FROM MAN? |
|---|---|---|
| | | Some say: |
| "Thou art the Christ, | | |
| | | John, the baptist. |
| the Son of the Living | | |
| | | Jeremiah |
| God." | | |
| | | Elijah |
| | | |
| | | One of the prophets. |

The line of separation between what men say and what God says is the line of distinction between truth and error.

---

When they raised the question with Jesus again, "By what authority doest thou these things?" Jesus answered that if they were interested in authority and honest in their inquiry he would ask one question of them, "The baptism of John, whence was it? from heaven or from men?" Now brethren, that is the way to settle the question of authority. If it came from God, then it is in the Word of God. If you can not find it taught in the Word of God, then you know that it did not come from God but from man and therefore there is no divine authority for its practice.

---

Blackboard Illustration No. 2.

Matthew 21:23-27.

FROM GOD          OR          FROM MAN?

THE BAPTISM OF JOHN ???

By whose authority? Where did it originate? These are factors determining man's duty toward anything.

---

When you cannot put your finger on the passage that teaches it, then you should be able readily to reach the conclusion that it did not come from God. Paul affirms that only the Holy Spirit can know and reveal the mind of God. (I Cor. 2: 10-11) What the Spirit has not revealed cannot therefore be the will of God.

Jesus drew the line of distinction again between that which comes from men and that which comes from God. In Matthew 15 he was dealing with the traditions of the elders and the right to bind and loose or exercise authority in religious mat-

Blackboard Illustration No. 3.

Matthew 15:1-20

| FROM GOD | OR | FROM MAN? |
|---|---|---|
| "Honour thy father and mother" | | "be it corban" (It is given rather as a gift unto God) |
| | | "Wash your hands when you eat bread" (Bound by the traditions of the elders) |

The traditions of men make void the commandments of God whether they bind where God has not bound or loose where God has bound.

---

ters. (Blackboard Ill. No. 3) The Jews had practiced, by the traditions of the elders, the washing of hands before they ate, as a religious rite. They condemned Jesus because He would not observe this human tradition and did not teach his disciples to do so. When they raised the question with him, he said, "Why do ye also transgress the commandment of God by your tradition?" He declared to them again, "Thus have ye made the commandment of God of none effect by your tradition." Human tradition in religion always conflicts with the commandments of God and Jesus condemned them in worship and service to God. He further declared, "Every plant which my heavenly Father hath not planted shall be rooted up."

In Matthew 7:22-23, in the judgment scene which Jesus pictured, he said, "Many will say to me in that day, Lord, Lord, have we not prophesied in thy name? and in thy name cast out devils? and in thy name done many wonderful works? And then will I profess unto them, depart from me, ye that work iniquity, I never knew you." We must be able to find what we teach and practice in the Word of God. It must be found there in language plain enough that we can understand what the will of the Lord is. Our faith must rest in God and in the power of God and the revelation of God rather than in the wisdom of man. We do not need someone to tell us what God meant by what He said. The Catholics try to do that. God has said it plainly enough that if I will honestly approach His word and hear all the testimony, free from my own ideas, opinions, and preconceptions, I can learn what the will of the Lord is for myself. Is it then within the scope of divine revelation? If it is, it can be practiced in the name of Jesus Christ. If it is not in the scope of divine revelation, then to put the name of Jesus to it is to be guilty of spiritual forgery. I have no right to do a thing in the name of Jesus Christ that He has not taught. Neither does anyone else! So let us emphasize again, a thing must be taught in order to be authorized. If it is not taught, then it is not authorized, and if it is not authorized, then it cannot be done by faith. If it is not done by faith, then it is wrong. Paul taught, you remember, that faith comes by hearing and hearing by the Word of God.

## The Sufficiency of SCRIPTURE
### II TIM. 3:14-17.

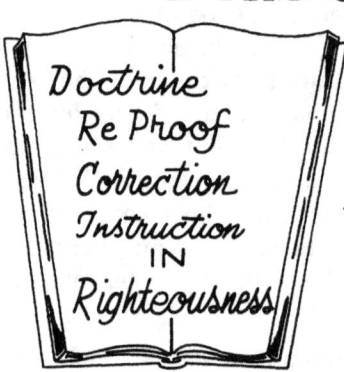

Doctrine
Re Proof
Correction
Instruction
IN
Righteousness

1. INSPIRATION of GOD.
2. WISE UNTO SALVATION.
   ABLE
3. THROUGH FAITH.
4. THAT MAN OF GOD MAY BE PERFECT.
5. THROUGHLY FURNISHED UNTO EVERY GOOD WORK.

CHART NO. 3. We are affirming, as we have suggested, the sufficiency of the Scriptures. The Scriptures are profitable for doctrine. I do not need any other doctrine than that which I can read in the Word of God in language plain enough to understand.

I do not need anything to reprove that which is wrong or to correct any error or false doctrine or with which to instruct anybody in the righteousness of God but the plain, simple Word of God, without additions or subtractions, and with no human philosophy connected with it. The Scriptures have been given by the inspiration of God. In the Scriptures the Holy Spirit has revealed the mind of God in words of the Spirit's own choosing. These Scriptures are able to make us wise unto salvation through the faith that is in Christ Jesus, that the man of God may be perfect, complete, throughly, perfectly, completely furnished unto every good work. This affirms and we must accept the complete sufficiency of the Scriptures.

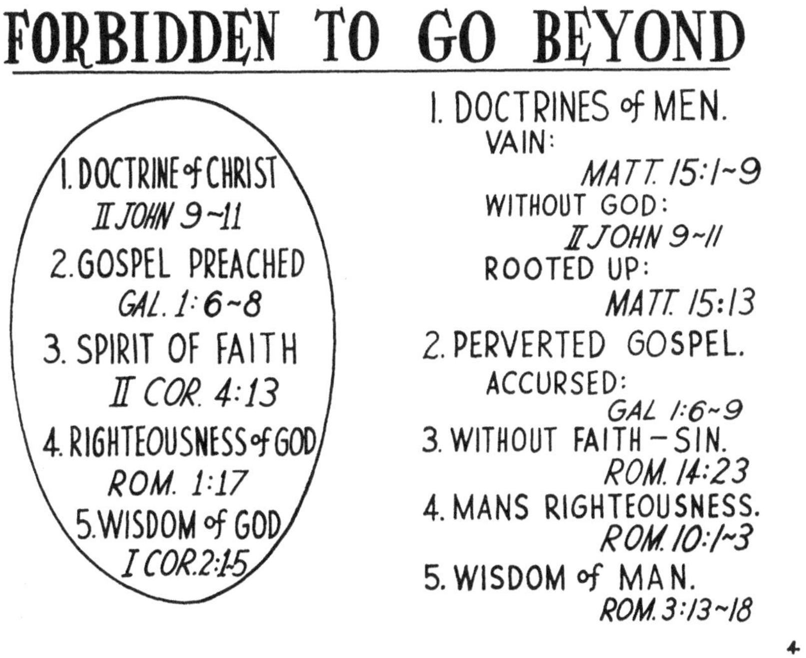

# FORBIDDEN TO GO BEYOND

1. DOCTRINE of CHRIST
 II JOHN 9-11
2. GOSPEL PREACHED
 GAL. 1:6-8
3. SPIRIT OF FAITH
 II COR. 4:13
4. RIGHTEOUSNESS of GOD
 ROM. 1:17
5. WISDOM of GOD
 I COR. 2:15

1. DOCTRINES of MEN.
 VAIN:
  MATT. 15:1-9
 WITHOUT GOD:
  II JOHN 9-11
 ROOTED UP:
  MATT. 15:13
2. PERVERTED GOSPEL.
 ACCURSED:
  GAL 1:6-9
3. WITHOUT FAITH — SIN.
  ROM. 14:23
4. MANS RIGHTEOUSNESS.
  ROM. 10:1-3
5. WISDOM of MAN.
  ROM. 3:13-18

CHART NO. 4. We are not only to be confident that the Scriptures are perfect and entire, but we are to recognize the fact that we are not to go beyond them. God has prohibited going beyond. John said, "He that goeth onward and abideth not in the doctrine of Christ hath not God." (2 John 9-11) The gospel must be preached, and Paul said, "If any man preach unto you, or an angel from heaven, any other gospel than that which we have preached unto you, let him be anathema." (Gal. 1: 6-8) Paul declared again that the spirit of faith is to abide within that which is written, to speak and believe according to that which is written. (2 Cor. 4: 13) The righteousness of God is revealed in the Scriptures. The wisdom of God is made known by the Spirit of God. The mind or will of God can be learned only from that which the Spirit reveals. When you turn away from it or go outside of it, letting the circle represent the completeness of that which God has spoken unto men; when we go beyond, to teach or practice the doctrines of men, we do so in vain and we are without God. All such will be rooted up. They constitute a perverted gospel and are therefore accursed. They are without faith and therefore sinful. (Rom. 14:23) They are therefore man's righteousness, filthy rags, rather than the righteousness of God. They are the wisdom and will of man rather than the will of God.

Acting without divine authority has always borne serious consequences. It is disregard, irreverence, and rebellion against God. It is not the presence of a positive prohibition that makes the sin always, but many times it is the absence of a divine command authorizing the practice. Anything that goes beyond the Law, that has no authority, that is not taught in the word of God, whether doctrine, worship, work, or organization, is transgression, presumptuously invading the realm of God's silence. Apostolic writings are the commandments of the Lord. (I Cor. 14:37) The decrees of the "Apostles and Elders" revealed by the Holy Spirit (Acts 15), were delivered to the churches "for to keep" and so "were the churches established in the faith, and increased in number daily." (Acts 16: 4)

But the question is raised, "How may I know whether the New Testament teaches a thing or not?" This is not too difficult to answer. Brethren have always agreed, I think, that the Scriptures teach by three ways, though I have heard some expressions among Gospel preachers to the contrary in recent years: (1) by express command; (2) by approved example;

(3) by necessary inference. We illustrate these by *Chart No. 5*, on the Lord's Supper. Jesus said, "This do in remembrance of me." That is a *command* (a commanded thing), a thing that

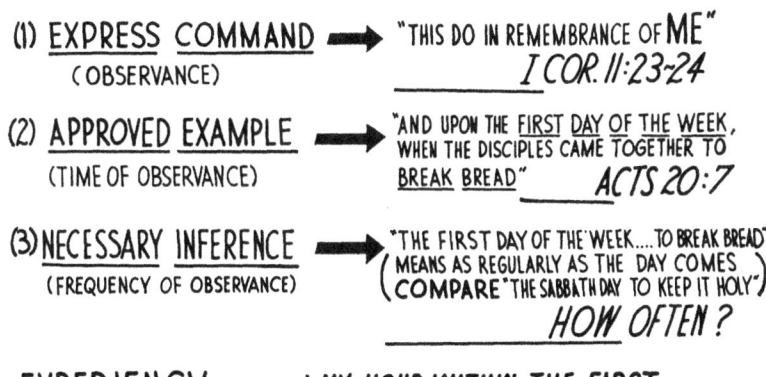

Jesus taught the apostles to teach those whom they baptized (the church) to do. Then we have *approved example*—that is, approved apostolic example. (Acts 20:7) They met on the first day of the week to break bread. In this passage we learn, and it is the only passage in the New Testament that does tell us, that the Lord's Supper was observed and is therefore to be observed on the first day of the week. Under apostolic guidance this is what the church did in the New Testament. There is no other passage in the entire New Testament that I have ever found connecting the Lord's Supper and the first day of the week. If you know of another, tell me about it, and if it is correct, I will correct that statement.

As we have suggested, the force of an apostolic example is seen in the fact that they were to teach the church to do what the Lord had commanded them to do. When they taught a thing or approved a practice engaged in by the church, it was prima facie evidence that Christ had commanded it. Apostolic approval or teaching then established the authority of Christ for the thing approved or taught. Not everything we do by divine authority can be found in express commands or precepts or directly commanded by the Lord. The ambassadors of the Lord, with the authority to bind and loose, spoke and acted officially for the Lord and this is the realm of authority evidenced in apostolically approved examples. Paul commanded the Corinthians to keep the "ordinances as I have delivered them to you." (I Cor. 11:2) He wrote the Philippians, "Those things, which ye have both learned, and received, and heard, and seen in me, do: and the God of peace shall be with you." (Phil. 4:9) Approved apostolic example then, is just as authoritative as if found in the direct commandments of the Lord.

Then we learn the frequency of the observance of the Lord's Supper by *necessary inference*. This means that the plain, undisputed import of the language used necessarily means that they met as often as the first day of the week came to break bread or observe the Lord's Supper. The Jews were commanded to observe the "Sabbath Day to keep it holy." That meant every Sabbath Day, as regularly as it came and they so understood. The first day of the week to break bread likewise means every first day of the week, as regularly as it comes. The only way we can learn that God's will is that the Lord's Supper be observed every week is by these three means of teaching. But where does expediency come in?

In the first chart, we pointed out to you that expediency comes in the realm of faith, that is, within that which is divinely taught or revealed. A thing must first be lawful in order to be expedient. It must be authorized. It must first be taught. Specifically? No! We will discuss that point in a moment. But it must be included in that which is taught so that it plainly and positively can be identified as coming within the scope of that which is authorized. So you have expediency illustrated by the hour within the first day of the week. When an hour is specified by man and it is taught that the Lord's Supper cannot be observed at any other time, this is binding where God has not bound. When men teach that the Lord's Supper can be observed on some other day than the first day of the week or that it does not have to be observed as regularly as the first day of the week comes, they are loosing where God has bound. One is just as serious as the other. Both are sinful. We cannot go beyond the first day of the week nor can we specify any hour within the first day of the week when God did not do so.

## SCRIPTURAL AUTHORITY

| COMMANDED | GENERIC | SPECIFIC |
|---|---|---|
| ARK (GEN 6:14) | WOOD | GOPHER |
| WATER OF CLEANSING (NUMBERS 19:2) | ANIMAL | RED HEIFER WITHOUT SPOT |
| PRAISE (EPH. 5:18, COL. 3:16) | MUSIC | SING |
| EVANGELIZE (I TIM. 3:15, I THESS. 1:7,8) | CHURCH (I THESS. 1:1) | ORGANIZATION (CONGREGATION)(PHIL. 1:1) |
| EDIFY (EPH. 4:16) | CHURCH | ORGANIZATION (CONGRE.) |
| RELIEVE (I TIM. 5:16) | CHURCH | ORGANIZATION (CONGRE.) |
|  |  |  |

CHART NO. 6 illustrates the difference between *generic* and *specific authority*. Sometimes brethren have accused us of demanding specific examples or authority. That is not so! The idea of generic and specific authority is sometimes characterized by two extremes. People sometimes say that when the word of God does not specifically prohibit a thing, that makes it right. Others go to the opposite extreme and say that if the word of God does not specifically authorize a thing, that makes it wrong. There are two extremes represented in this. Neither is true. I never have believed, I never have taught, that specific authority was essential, either in condemning wrong or in establishing right. I do not believe it is so. I readily recognize that sometimes a passage, a precept, or even an example can be general in one respect and specific in another.

When God told Noah to build the ark of wood, if he had left it that way, it would have been generic and he could have used any kind. We have used these illustrations through the years. But when God said "Gopher Wood" the fact that God specified "Gopher" meant that God had made a choice as to the kind of wood, and Noah did not have any choice but to obey or disobey. God did not tell him, as far as we know, how tall the trees had to be, or how big the logs were to be in diameter, or what kind of tools he could use in the construction of it. Many things God did not specify but when He did specify, Noah did not have any choice but to obey or disobey. The same thing is true in the "water of cleansing" (Numbers 19) in the Old Testament. The ashes of a heifer, a red heifer, without spot, was specified and this eliminated any choice. God chose. When God specified a red heifer that eliminated every other animal. I do not know that He said anything about how much she had to weigh, or any other characteristics that were specified, but she had to be a red heifer and without spot. God made this choice and did not leave man any choice in the matter.

In worship God authorized "music." God specified the kind of music by which we are to praise Him. God made the choice and His choice is "sing." That eliminates every other kind of music; hence "playing" is without divine authority. God did not authorize "music" and leave it in the realm of generic authority, giving man a choice as to whether vocal or instrumental or both. "Sing" and "Play" are co-ordinates. Since God made the choice and specified what he wanted and the command is "sing", that limits the music by which we can worship God.

Again in the work of the church God has authorized "evangelism." God has been specific as to the organization through which the church is to carry on the collective activity of evangelizing the world or preaching the gospel in all the world. The specific organization that God has chosen is the "local church." This is God's collectivity, where Christians work together in fellowship one with another in doing the work of evangelizing the world. This is the organization through which the world was evangelized in the New Testament day.

Again, this organization is specific. Philippians 1:, "Unto all the saints that are at Philippi, with the bishops and deacons." We know what organization is to do the evangelizing and we know exactly what that organization is, as to structure. We have no choice but to do our evangelizing as the church of the Lord through this organization. God made the choice and we either do His will or we are disobedient. The church is authorized to carry on the work of "Edifying itself in love." (Eph. 4:16) The organization through which the church is to do this work of edifying is the "local church." It is made up of saints, bishops and deacons, wherever it may be found. God designed it and has given us no other. This "local church" is the only medium that can be found in the New Testament for the collective activity of Christians in accomplishing the work God has authorized the church to do.

Another work that God has given the church to do is the work of relieving the poor saints. Paul instructs the church to relieve "widows that are widows indeed." (I Tim. 5:16) Hence we know that there is some benevolent work that the church is to do, if it is obedient to the will of God. But how is the church to "relieve" those for whom it is responsible in the sight of God? Did God leave the matter generic in authority, and are we permitted to build just any kind of an aid society or organization that we see fit to do this work and take care of those who are the "charge" of the church? Or has God specified an organization through which the church is to discharge its responsibilities in this work? God has specified the organization of the church through which its work—all of it—is to be done. The organization of the church is as specific as the kind of music authorized or the kind of wood Noah was commanded to use. We have no choice but to do the work that God has given the church to do, whether evangelistic, edificational, or benevolent, through the organization that God has specifically authorized (the local church), or disobey God by building another.

When God commanded the church to do its work, he did not leave it without a specific organization through which to function. He gave it one—not a generic organization—but a specific organization plainly set forth on New Testament pages. If "church" means just any kind of an organization, if it is general, then we must swallow the "missionary society" and all of the other human societies that the world has invented right along with those we have fashioned for ourselves. Indeed, every denominational organization on earth would be just as scriptural as the one we would build. But since God made a choice and designed one through which the "church" is to function, we have no choice and every other organization is disobedience.

## ESSENTIALS AND EXPEDIENCIES

| COMMANDMENT | ESSENTIALS | EXPEDIENCIES |
|---|---|---|
| TEACH<br>MATT. 28:18-20 | GOSPEL | CLASS—PRIVATELY<br>PUBLICLY |
| BAPTIZE<br>MATT. 28:18-20 | IMMERSION IN WATER | NATURAL OR<br>ARTIFICIAL POOL |
| LORD'S SUPPER<br>I COR. 11:23-27 | ELEMENTS—BREAD<br>AND FRUIT OF THE VINE | TABLE—CONTAINERS |
| ASSEMBLY<br>HEB. 10:25 | FIRST DAY OF THE WEEK | HOUR—PLACE |
| RELIEVE<br>I TIM. 5:16 | CHURCH<br>(CONGREGATION) | METHOD-MEANS-MODE<br>BUY, RENT, GRATIS |

No. 7

CHART NO. 7 illustrates for us matters of *essentials and expediences*.

Jesus said, "Go into all the world and preach the gospel." He told us what is essential in that teaching—the gospel. If we preach any other gospel, we will be condemned. He did not tell us the manner or method by which it was to be done. The manner or method of going and teaching was not specified. We have a choice in these. God specified the message, but he left the manner or method of teaching generic, whether in a class, whether privately or publicly we do the teaching is a matter of our judgment and therefore in the realm of expediency.

Jesus commanded that those who believed when they were taught were to be baptized. Some things about this command are specific. We know that water is the element. God specified it. Immersion is the action and that is specific. We must not alter or change that. But whether it is in a natural or an artificial pool, no one would have the right to say, for that has not been specified by divine authority. In that matter God made no choice but left it to our choice, and it is therefore a matter of expediency.

In the observance of the Lord's Supper, the elements are unleavened bread and the fruit of the vine. The Lord specified this. He did not specify whether they were to be placed on a table or passed from hand to hand. He did not specify how many containers the fruit of the vine was to be in. We know that it had to have one. A liquid requires a container, so that is an essential thing. How many containers, nobody knows. The elements in the Lord's Supper are the fruit of the vine and unleavened bread. The number of containers for each is a matter of expediency since God has not specified.

Christians are commanded to assemble on the first day of the week and they met on the first day of the week to break bread. The hour and the place we do not know. How it was to be provided, as far as the place was concerned, nobody knows, but a place was essential. The command to assemble could not be carried out without a place. Sometimes people say we do not have any authority for a meeting place in the command to assemble. But the authority for the place is in the command; it cannot be executed without a place. How it is to be provided, no one has the right to say, for God has not made a choice as to that. He has left it in the realm of expediency.

In the work of "relieving" the needy which the church is to do, the method or the means, the mode, whether or not they were to provide the money, or give the food and other necessities out of their own provisions; how they were to provide shelter when it was necessary, whether they were to rent a house, take those to be cared for into their own homes, or furnish them shelter in some other way; whether or not the care that was necessary was to be gratis, or someone was to be hired to take care of those unable to care for themselves, these were not specified. They belong in the realm of expediency. God did not make any choice in such matters and I would freely grant that we have a choice, and no one has a right to bind any certain manner. But the same is not true as to the organization that is to do the work. It is the work of the church. The church is charged with doing this work that God has designated. The organization has been specified and we dare not rebel against God's choice by building another to do the work God designated the church to do. Since God chose the organization through which the church is to do its work, our contention is that it is not in the realm of expediency as to which or what kind of an organization shall perform this function. Rather it is a matter of faith that the church shall perform its work through the specific organization which God designed and Christ has built, and which is revealed on the pages of New Testament teaching.

## AIDS AND ADDITIONS

| COMMANDMENT | AIDS | ADDITIONS |
|---|---|---|
| SING | BOOKS — LIGHTS LEADER — ETC. | INSTRUMENTAL MUSIC ANOTHER KIND OF MUSIC |
| BAPTIZE | BAPISTRY | SPRINKLING ANOTHER KIND OF ACTION |
| ASSEMBLE TO BREAK BREAD | BUILDING, LIGHTS, SEATS, HEAT, ETC. | SATURDAY ANOTHER DAY |
| PREACH GOSPEL | RADIO, LITERATURE, ETC. | MISSIONARY SOCIETY ANOTHER ORGANIZATION |
| RELIEVE THE DESTITUTE | BUILDING, CARE NECESSARIES | BENEVOLENT SOCIETY ANOTHER ORGANIZATION |
| EDIFY ITSELF | PLACE — FACILITIES TEACHERS | SUN. SCHOOL SOCIETY ANOTHER ORGANIZATION [8] |

CHART NO. 8 illustrates the difference between *aids* and *additions*. We have God's commandments and there are aids to carry out the commandments that are permissible. But whenever we employ a co-ordinate to that which God has specified, it is no longer an aid but it becomes an addition. The test is that when the matter is only an aid, the action performed by its use is only that which God has commanded. But when a co-ordinate is employed another element or action is apparent.

For instance, singing: our brethren in the Christian churches, who went out from us many years ago, have always argued that the books and lights and the leader and tuning fork, etc., are on a par with the use of mechanical instruments of music and if we can have any of them, then we can have the instruments too. But instrumental music is a co-ordinate with singing. It is another kind of music. It is not therefore an aid but it is another element or action. It does not *aid* but it *adds*.

So it is with baptism also. God commands "baptize." The baptistry is an aid in carrying out God's command. When you use it you have still just done what God commands and have not engaged in another action. Sprinkling is a co-ordinate with "baptize." It constitutes another kind of action and is therefore an addition and not just an aid. Sprinkling is a violation of what God said do. God said "baptize" and baptizing is a burial, a washing of the body with pure water. Either sprinkling or pouring constitutes an addition or substitution for what God said.

When the church assembles to break bread, the building is provided as a matter of aiding in carrying out the commandment. Someone could furnish it out of his own resources or the church could buy, build, or rent one, and no one has the right to bind any particular method upon us in this matter. The same thing is true in the matter of heating, lights, seats, and other facilities that aid in carrying out this commandment. These are in the realm of aids. But suppose you had the church to meet on another day—Saturday—instead of the first day of the week to break bread. Or on some other day of the week. Where would the authority be for that? We have authority for the aids in the command, but there is no authority for another day. Aids are included within the teaching of the New Testament, and especially when they are essential to carrying out the commandment of the Lord. But additions of co-ordinates to what God has commanded are forbidden.

In preaching the gospel, radio, literature, classes, privately or publicly, are simply means or aids in carrying out the command to preach and teach. But what organization is to do it? God gave the church a local organization, the congregation. Another organization is not an aid but an addition. This is true of the Missionary Society. It is not an aid to God's organization any more than instrumental music is an aid to singing. It is an addition. It is excluded by divine authority for the reason that God's commandments do not include it. We have no more right to set up another organization to help carry out this commandment than we have to meet to break bread on another day than the first day.

In relieving the destitute, whether shelter is necessary, care, or food and the essential things of life, God made these mandatory when our brethren are in need of them and unable to provide for themselves. But he did not give us any choice as to the organization that is to do the supplying of these necessary things to the destitute. Brethren act as though the church had no organization. They talk as if God had not given the church an organization through which to function in this work. They actually affirm sometimes that the church cannot do what God has commanded it to do.

My contention is, and I believe with all of my heart, that God has authorized by specific pattern the organization of the church and it is the local church under its elders. When we

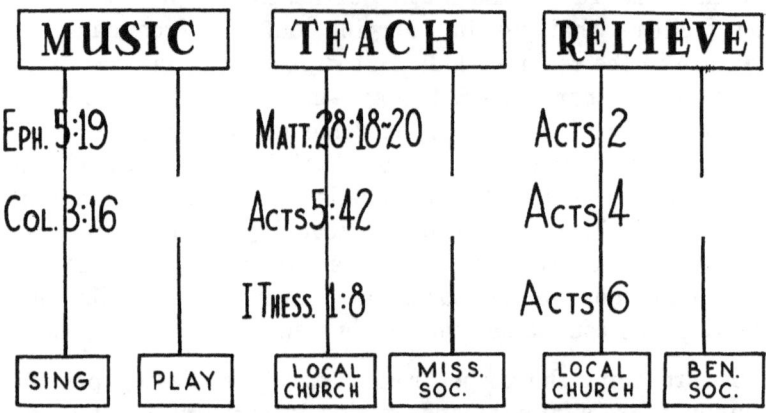

build another one to do anything that God gave His church to do we go beyond the realm of scriptural authority.

Finally, just look at this one chart that I do not have time to talk about CHART NO. 9. We have illustrated here the matter of *coordinates*. God has authorized music in worship. We have specific authority for singing but there is nothing the Bible says that includes "playing." Hence there is no authority for it. It is excluded by the choice that God made and it cannot be done by faith. God has commanded the church to preach and teach the gospel. He has organized and authorized a specific organization to do this work—the church—the local church. But the missionary society is a co-ordinate organization with the local church. It is another organization, not a method or aid. There is authority for the local church, but there is nothing that God has ever said that includes the missionary society. It is therefore excluded by the choice God has made and cannot be employed in preaching by faith.

Exactly the same thing is true in the benevolent work of the church. God has commanded the church to care for its own. The local church is the organization specified to do the work of the church. But the benevolent society is a co-ordinate with the local church. It is another organization. The church through its own organization can function in the accomplishment of this work and did so in the New Testament day. It took care of its own needy under the supervision of its own elders, through the ministration of its own deacons, and out of the resources furnished by its own members (Acts 2: 4-6) We cannot by faith build another organization that is not included in anything the Bible says or teaches to do the work that God built the local church to do. It adds another organization without authority, just as sprinkling adds another action and instrumental music adds another kind of music. They are co-ordinates.

## *How to Establish Bible Authority*

### J. D. Thomas

I'm honored to be invited to meet with this group, and I wish that I could be here all week. I have a previous engagement that causes me to leave tomorrow noon, from which I could not rightly beg off.

I appreciate the fact that brother Cogdill had such a well-prepared and well-presented lesson. It was very fine. I apologize for not having such a well-prepared one myself, inasmuch as I just honestly haven't had the time, in the first place; and secondly, I wouldn't want to do it anyway because I prefer to give you the material with the use of the blackboard from notes, in more or less *ad lib* fashion, as though I were teaching it. I hope that I can make it clearer that way. I know I couldn't work these charts very well if I were using a manuscript. What I really have to say on this has already been said, and some of you, no doubt, are familiar with it—what is in the book, *We Be Brethren*.

---

J. D. THOMAS—*Recently selected to head the Bible Department of Abilene Christian College, Abilene, Texas; author of several well known books; evangelist; much in demand for college lectureship appearances.*

I do feel from the meeting at Buchanan Dam last spring, that some points which I was trying to make in the book were not clearly understood all the way through. However, there is really very much agreement between us, I am confident, on a lot of things. As I heard brother Cogdill speak, for instance, I was amazed at the amount of agreement. Of course, I had no idea what he was going to say, but there is a great deal of agreement. I hope by using this method we can come to pinpoint (and I think he did a good job of this) our differences. When we see these clearly we can truly work on these "pinpointed" areas. This is one of the advantages this meeting will have over the Buchanan Dam meeting; the fact that we didn't even have an agenda when we went down there. We just met and began from "scratch" and spent 18 hours with our heads together—very fine, and very fruitful, I thought. I came away appreciating those brethren, with whom I differ, very much more than I had any idea that I would be able to beforehand, for the simple reason that the lack of communication sometimes causes us to imagine a lot of things that are not really so.

I said one thing in that meeting which I want to say here at the beginning, for the benefit of all who haven't heard me say it. I want you to know, and to hear me say it with my own words, that I believe the Bible is the only authority for us in religion. And the points that brother Cogdill made in this connection, I would agree wholeheartedly with. It is the one and only authority. I personally have been opposed to modernism all my preaching experience; and as a matter of fact, that has been my career, more or less. If I have a hobby in my teaching, it is this. The Bible, rightly understood, is the one and only authority for us, and it is God's revelation. This is what we are anxious to find out—how, in an exact way, and particularly on the points that divide us, to determine God's will in a clear way.

As we learn the teaching of the Bible, we find that we have certain required matters and certain optional matters. If you will bear with me I am going to lead you step by step with the use of the blackboard, in order that you will be fully conversant with the crucial points that I make. Now in God's revealed will, He "requires" certain things of us, and we would illustrate this by the word "go" or "go preach." That's something that we have to do—it's not an option or choice. If we obey God's will, this we have to do.

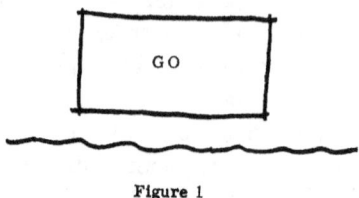

Figure 1

There are some things that we don't have to do—we do have a choice about, which would be "a *way* of doing" something. With a different diagram brother Cogdill pointed out this distinction, but we emphasize that there are "ways" that are optional to us "of doing" commanded things or required things. Now, it so happens that as we contemplate this, we see that in this particular relationship, the optional thing is *a matter of carrying out* the required commandment, and in this particular relationship, the required matter would be a generic, and the optional would be a specific.

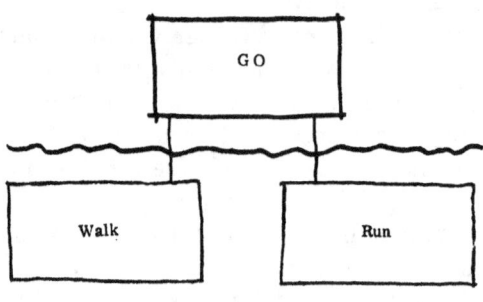

Figure 2

To illustrate with some relationships in the Lord's Supper, let's leave this diagram more or less as a standard one. Let this "box" on our chart represent the requirement to worship God. Now one "way of worshipping" God is to use the Lord's Supper, which itself, however, is also a requirement. In this relationship, however, *worship* is generic; whereas, *the Lord's Supper* is specific.

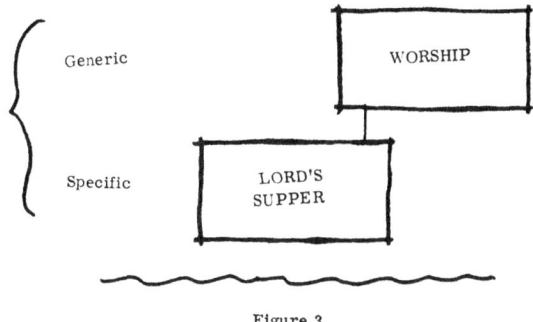

Figure 3

But now, in the Lord's Supper, what do we have? One of the things in this case which is required is the fruit of the vine. This is a requirement, about which we have no choice. Here, then, are three things which we all accept as required things in God's will. In the relationship of worship and the Lord's Supper, worship is generic, the Lord's Supper is specific. In the relation of the Lord's Supper and the fruit of the vine, the first is generic and the latter is specific.

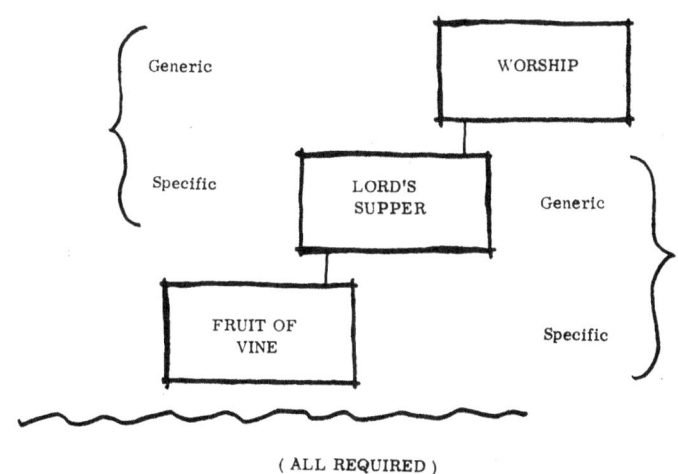

( ALL REQUIRED )

Figure 4

But now, when we consider the fruit of the vine, we come to *one* container, or cup, or *many* containers as optional methods. I am making the "required" item lines heavier. The point of the "wavy" line in the diagram is to draw it whenever we come to *optional* matters.

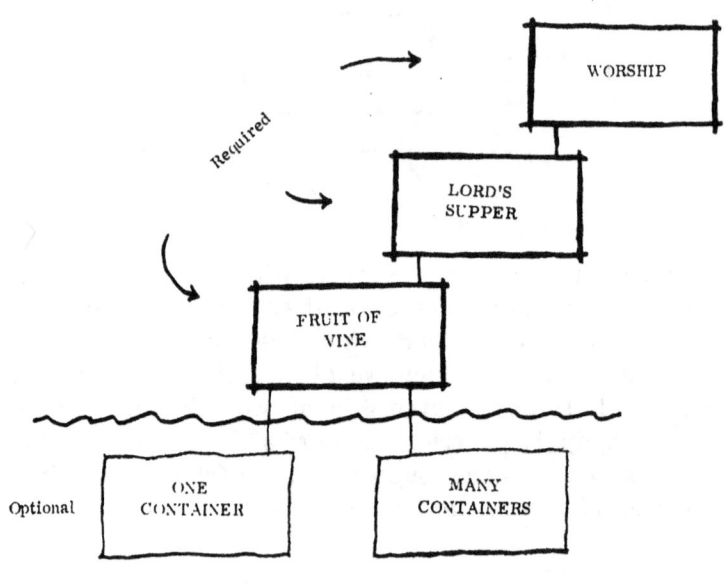

Figure 5

Everything above the wavy line is a required thing, and we have no choice about them. If we please God, we *have to do* these things. When we come down on the chart, though, to the specifics in the particular relationships, when we get down to the wavy line, anything below it will necessarily be an optional matter. In every diagram of authority of a passage of scripture or a particular teaching, there will be some place, below which we will have optional matters only; required matters are above the line. *This is how you know where to draw the wavy line.* Rules of interpretation are employed to know which is which.

We can all see that it would be a violation of God's will to make the fruit of the vine optional and use something else. Again, to draw the wavy line between "Lord's Supper" and "Fruit of the vine," in this particular relationship, would be a sin. It would be missing the requirement. It would be failing to do what God has commanded. On the other hand, if we draw the wavy line below the "one container," and we made "one container" a requirement, and thus thereby made every "way of taking" one container (as sitting down or standing up) to be optional—this would be a sin also. I insist that it is just as great a sin to make a required matter optional as it is to make an optional matter to be required; and by the same token, I say that it is just as great a sin, and as displeasing to God, to take an optional matter and make it to be a required matter. In either case, we are obligated to learn God's revelation exactly and to understand it.

In determining the relationships of His requirements (and the generics and specifics have a part in this) we have to do it just exactly right. The wavy line is used only for purposes of distinguishing them on the diagram from the straight lines, and to mark off the point at which our interpretation shows that God no longer has requirements. Thus we distinguish "ways of doing" the required things, all of which are optional to us. Now then, the matter of whether something is a generic or specific on a given chart, as you see, is really unimportant. In some of the charts that others use, I can see a difference, and distinctions should be made. But here, on this "standard" type chart, whether a matter is in a generic or a specific relationship does not determine whether one is going to sin or not. But whether something is a *required* matter—and all of these above the line are required—whether something is a required matter or an optional one makes all the difference in the world, as far as carrying out God's will is concerned. We have to learn God's exact will and do it.

Now let's study the case of Noah. We have on this chart the matter of *wood*, as the generic requirement, and then certain specifics under that; but the requirement is the specific *gopher wood*. Now, Noah *had to use* gopher wood, on penalty of

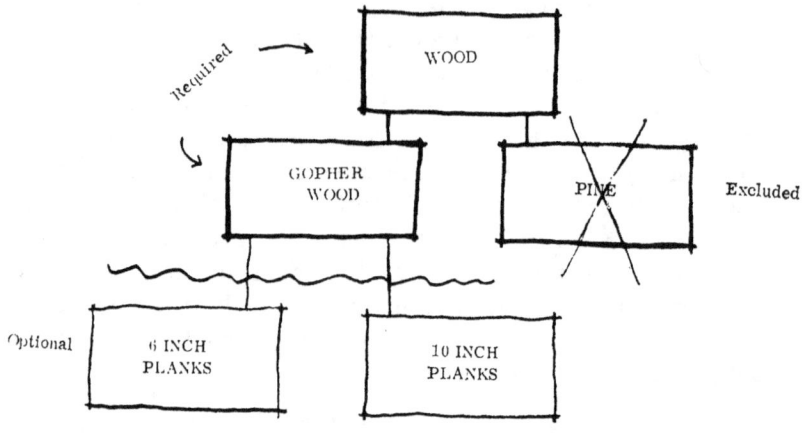

Figure 6

sin; but he couldn't do that without using the generic "wood." In these relationships, every logical generic to required matters is always also a required thing. This is obvious within itself. The specific "gopher wood" could not be required without the generic "wood" being required. Now we draw the wavy line, and we note that it is purely an optional matter as to how wide the boards are, how many nails to the plank, and all that sort of thing. There are optional matters here, but "wood" is required, and "gopher wood" (the specific) is required. Now, when God requires gopher wood, this automatically excludes and makes sinful every other specific to its generic, in this case "wood." You can't use pine. Pine here, is a specific to the generic "wood," all right; but when God required the specific "gopher wood," this excludes, automatically and logically, every other specific to this same generic. No other kind of wood would please God, would meet His revelation's demand, His revealed requirement. Now, if this point isn't true; if, though God said "build it out of gopher wood," I would not be sinning if I used pine, or if I could just do anything I pleased about it, then there would be no way on earth for us to know God's definite will. You just couldn't know it to save your life.

If He makes a requirement but you are privileged to do as you please—I think some of our religious neighbors almost take this sort of a view of the Bible——the whole thing would be irrational. You would have an "unrequired" requirement! The point here is that pine wood is an *excluded* specific, whereas gopher wood is a *required* specific, and "wood," of course, is the required generic on this particular chart with this particular point of teaching. On another chart, by the same token,

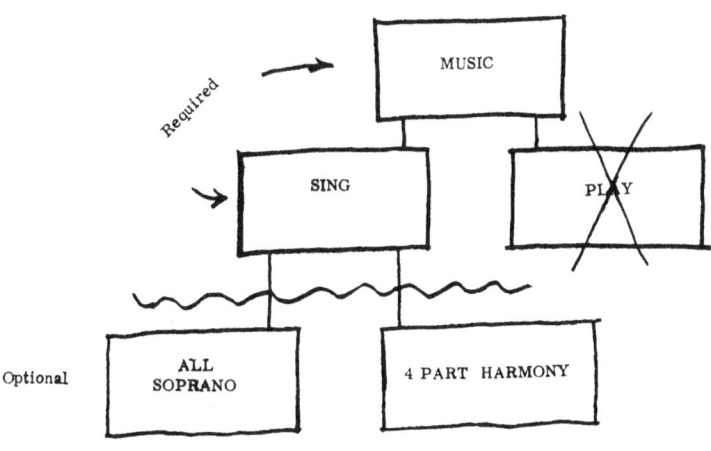

Figure 7

you have music as a generic and singing as the required specific, and then you have the instrument as the "excluded" specific. God has required singing, which excludes instrumental music, and I don't think there is a person who uses the instrument who could stay with us on this point without wincing, because I think it nails him tight. Brethren have made this argument (we've never used this chart, but we've made this argument) as long as I've known of our debating, and I think it certainly holds water. As to "how" we sing, whether all sing soprano or whether we sing four-part harmony or whatever, the optional ways of singing are still obeying God's will!

Now what I am leading to, as we see, is that there are required specifics, or what we might call "pattern revelation"—pattern authority—of God's will. We also have *optional* categories, in which there is no requirement, no demand, and we are free to use our own judgment as to which of them is the most advantageous or the most expedient to follow. Still, on the other hand, there are certain things *excluded*, automatically and necessarily whenever God gives us a specific pattern revelation.

In the matter of worship and the Lord's Supper, we have worship, we have the Lord's Supper, and we have the fruit of the vine all as *required* matters, and then you have the optional ways of partaking of the latter—one container or many. God specified the Lord's Supper as an acceptable and required way of worshipping. Another way, however, of worshipping that we read about in Psalms 150 is that of "dancing." But in the New Testament, which is our authority today, we have the Lord's Supper specified, which automatically *excludes* the dance as an acceptable form of worship. It *logically* excludes it. By the same token, whenever we propose to keep the Lord's Supper, and we have the requirement of the fruit of the vine, this automatically excludes any other liquid that we might choose to substitute which might be pleasing to us. These logically excluded specifics are contrary to God's will.

Now, we have come to a point that is very significant, I think, and this is to say that when you are charting any passage or a point of teaching there is no such thing as a pattern requirement for anything that logically classifies in the relationship as an optional matter. This is because of the very nature of the thing. If the classification is correct, we obviously cannot have a pattern *requirement* concerning something that is optional within itself. The concepts are contradictory. Now, the liberals (the modernists in religion) would laugh at this chart business and everything that we do in seriously trying to get at God's will, for the simple reason that they say that the Bible is not that kind of a book and we are not supposed to pay attention to it that seriously. They accept some things that are traditional, but they do not make it an authoritative book. Our denominational friends who are conservative in theology would say, "Yes! There is such a thing as pattern revelation," but they would also say that there were no really excluded specifics. God says "sing," surely, but you can *play*, too! Playing is *not excluded*, in their view.

Brother Cogdill has pointed out very clearly how this is true—that the instrument is automatically wrong, since singing is specified. Our denominational friends *claim* to follow the word of God, but when they get to something that's merely traditional with them, they do not see its exclusion by Biblical authority. I think if we could lead them to see the logic of all this, they would see that instrumental music in worship is wrong. By the same token, our "one-cup" brethren take the one container, which we say is optional, and they draw the wavy line below it, and thus they say that it's required. Or, the non-Sunday school brethren take the class, which is to us an optional way of carrying out the command to teach, and they classify it above the wavy line as an excluded specific; thus, they say a class is sinful and wrong. So you see, our framework or "pattern of authority" in this chart will help us to keep ourselves in the clear as we contemplate various problems, and it is basically important that we see all these relationships and their implications.

Now, I say that what is called the "sponsoring church" or the orphan home—I say that each of them—as they are "bones of contention" between us—is an optional way of doing the Lord's work. "Visiting the fatherless in their affliction"—that's a requirement, and to do it through the use of the home, as we ordinarily find it—this is optional as I see it; whereas, other brethren would say, no, the home is an excluded specific—well, at least, it is excluded. Now, the orphan home is not a spe-

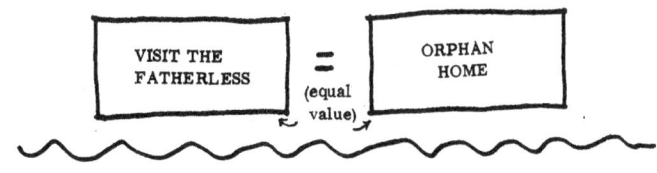

WRONGLY DIAGRAMMED

Figure 8

cific, equal here to the requirement of "visiting the fatherless" in their affliction; it is a *way* of taking care of them—it's one "way." It is not the only way to obey the command, to be sure. In charting the home (a specific to the *generic* "visit the fatherless"), if you draw the wavy line below the "home," as in chart 8, then you're making it an equal specific with "visit," but it is actually a "way" of visiting!

The whole point now is to note that the differences between us can be pinpointed, down to "how we classify" a matter. I argue that the home should be classified in a certain place, here on chart 9 as you see, optional. This helps to pin-

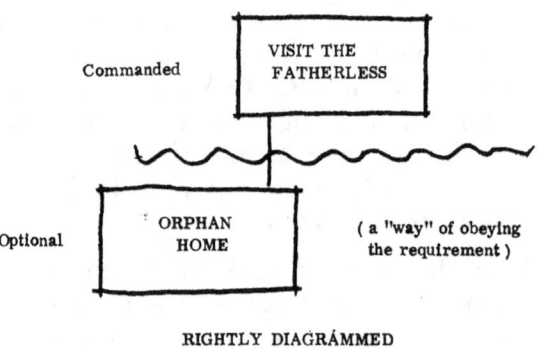

RIGHTLY DIAGRAMMED

Figure 9

point our thinking and our differences. Others argue that it should be classified elsewhere, as an excluded specific, but to do so it would have to be illogically charted.

We now leave this and turn to the matter of examples, which I feel is very crucial here. How do examples teach? What do examples in the Bible have to do with the matter of our carrying out God's will? The example does teach something. I think it teaches whatever it is an example of. I don't think that all "approved apostolic examples" teach pattern, required things. There are many approved apostolic examples that are optional matters. Paul "going in a boat to preach" is one. Not anybody here would say (even though it is an approved apostolic example) that that was a required thing. There are any number of examples which teach nothing, as to what we *have to do*, on pain of sin.

We have, on the other hand, examples that do teach something, and even teach required things. I presume that everybody here believes this, at least to a degree—though I've heard a few people in the brotherhood who have finally concluded that examples teach us nothing whatever. But it is very crucial that we consider this and find out just how an example teaches and how we can be sure about it. As has been pointed out—and this has been pretty common in the brotherhood, so far as I know—we are taught God's revelation by commands, by necessary inferences, and by approved apostolic examples. These are the ways that pattern requirements—this that we *have to do*—are established. Regardless of what may be above or below on this chart—the pattern requirement that I've been discussing—the question is, how is this pattern established—how do we get it? I personally agree that it comes through command, necessary inference, or example. But we brethren do not have problems about commands, nor even necessary inferences (unless it's a very rare case), but we do have differences over examples. Realizing that this is true, let's take a command, and then we'll put a wavy line below it; then we have optional ways of carrying out that command underneath.

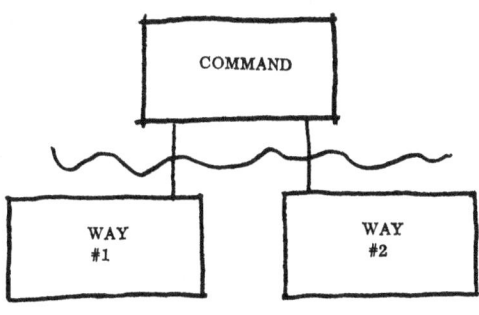

Figure 10

These latter are examples or ways of how the command may be carried out. But now, on another chart, we would say that the example actually is what comes below the wavy line,

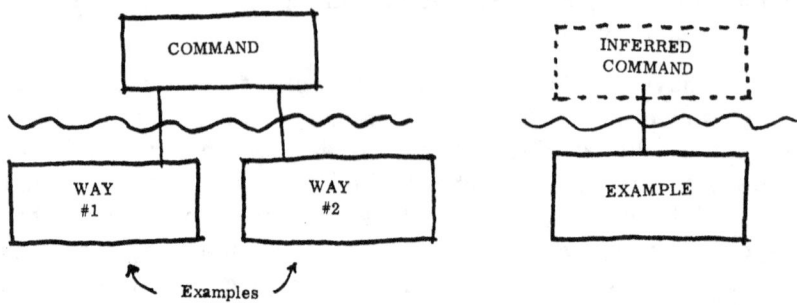

Figure 11

but above it, you would have the required pattern matter, of which it is an example. Here, then, is the authority or pattern of which the example, or illustration, is a "way of doing" it. But the question is, how can we make this objective? I agree with brother Cogdill that our authority has to finally be objective and definite. Brother Roy Deavers wrote me after I published my book—as he was studying this point—and asked, "Aren't you really saying that the example teaches us something which you cannot see in the example, the command authority that is behind it? Aren't you really saying that you learn the pattern, lying behind the example, by necessary inference?" My answer to him was "Yes, but I wouldn't want to say this for general publication because many people would become confused about the 'inference' term, and the sharp distinction."

I truly feel that any example that teaches us authoritatively—that teaches us something which we *have to do* to please God—makes a pattern. And where there is no other teaching in the Bible other than the example itself, it would be what we call "a necessary inference." It must come through sharp and clear. If it doesn't do this, I don't think it teaches us. When an example teaches us—if it teaches a pattern, it is an example of something the New Testament characters *had to do* to please God. But if it is an example of something that they didn't have to do, then it is something we don't have to do either.

The restoration plea, brethren, has been that what the first century Christians had to do, we have to do! And what was not binding on them is not binding on us! In just these few words, that is really what this is all about. This goes right to the heart of our restoration claim—that we restore first century Christianity. Every requirement that God made on Christians after Pentecost day is made of us today. If we see an example of something that they were doing that they understood that they had to do to please God—it was His will, without any question—then this example, logically, necessarily makes us to be required to do the same thing in similar circumstances. It must be contextually clear, it all has to be discernible within the example, and remember, there is no other information—there are no other teachings on it, but the example itself and alone determines it!

Even with commandments—we don't have to have but *one command* to teach anything. And we do not have to have but one example to establish a pattern requirement of God's revelation, if it does it clearly and unequivocally—and, unless it does, it is not significant anyway. An illustration of a binding example which we all accept as such is the teaching of the Lord's Supper on the first day of every week as the only scriptural time for partaking. Some "optional" examples are: Appeals to the civil government—Paul did this a few times—I don't think anybody would say he *had* to so appeal; To preach in a synagogue or to preach till midnight—I know we wouldn't go for these as requirements; To meet in an upper room—we all understand this as optional; just to call attention to several.

Now, concerning examples that do establish a pattern or make a requirement where the example is the only thing we have—one is that it is God's will, within the range of one's judgment and ability, that each Christian "become all things to all men"—that he, "by all means, may save some." But what we have that teaches this is nothing but an example of Paul's doing it, and saying that he had to do so. It was something that Paul had to do to please God. But I think there is enough in Paul's example, as it fits in its context in the Scriptures, to make me feel that that is obligatory upon me, to become "all things to all men" to the extent of my ability.

I think I also have to "buffet my body and bring it into subjection," when it has a tendency to lead me off into sin. But my authority for this is only Paul's *example*. Again, I preach strongly that "God adds to the church day by day those that are being saved." I don't have any command for this—or any authoritative teaching except such necessary inference as I can make out of the example in Acts 2:47. But I preach that. Now, the Bible says only that God did it for the Pentecostian Christians. This is all the information we have—the example of what happened to them! But I preach this confidently as God's clear revelation, and that other people ought to take notice of it and be governed accordingly. But all we have is the example.

I have 17 such binding examples in my book. Some of them may be pretty thin—I would grant that. I read the New Testament through several times looking for those examples—it may be that I stretched a point here and there—I'm just as human as the next person—and maybe I was hoping to find some. But nonetheless—to preach *Jesus* means to preach *baptism*—as we learn from "the example" of the eunuch. There is no particular "command" statement. You can get it clearly out of the example of Philip and the eunuch—if you didn't have any other teachings at all—the fact that when you preach Jesus fully, you have to preach baptism! The example itself teaches it. I think we would agree, that the example does teach something in the case of when to partake of the Lord's Supper—though some of us might word this differently.

I would note here that there are certain commandments in the Scripture that are impossible to obey without more information. Paul says, "Be ye imitators of me." Now that's a commandment. But I don't know whether he means, just from that one passage, to imitate him "as an apostle," which I couldn't do, or to imitate him "as an unmarried man," which I couldn't do. There are ways, you see, of obeying such commands that are not intended, and we need more information before we can obey that type of commandment. Some commands need to be "completed," or need to be *clarified*.

In reference to the Lord's Supper, we have an *example* that completes or clarifies commandments. It is found in Acts 20:7. The total required, pattern revelation of God's will in this calls for several passages to be studied together. But Acts 20:7 only gives us the last bit of information. Hebrews 10:25 gives us a command that gives us *some* information, "not to forsake the assembly, as the custom of some is." There apparently was a customary assembly, well understood in the first century, that Christians are not to forsake. I Corinthians 16:1, 2 next indicates the matter of assembling "on the first day of the week." (We might argue about where they put the money —in the common treasury or not.) Then I Corinthians 11, on the matter of "partaking of the Lord's Supper and remembering His death until He comes." Now you have a customary assembly—you have a first day of the week customary assembly —and each one of these passages is adding something.

In total, we have a definite command to take the Lord's Supper, to do it with some degree of frequency, not specified; but all of these commands together are helpful to indicate to us that the elders at Troas (Acts 20:7) were under obligation to have *some plan* and *some arrangement* for a regular, customary partaking of the Lord's Supper in an assembly. So there is enough information in the Acts 20:7 context—they waited there seven days at Troas—and when they did, this example "fills it all out," to me and shows that this is the *way* they did "what they were required to do." Yes I say anything that the first century Christians were *required* to do, I am required to do today. They waited seven days to partake of the Supper on the first day of the week. This all adds up to giving us our exclusive scriptural information on when to partake of the Supper. And it is the example that extablished the pattern on "when," with adequate background information from elsewhere.

To review now our authority diagram, the box above the wavy line is our requirement, and then we have an excluded specific that is sinful and wrong and which is *also specific* to the same generic as is the pattern. The generic to the pattern is also logically required. Below the wavy line are found optional ways of doing the required thing. Now I think our one-container brethren are wrong in classifying something as required that is not required by any rhyme or reason, either by commandment, necessary inference or example. It is an example, of course, that we have one-container usage in the New Testament; but how I reason that that example is not binding is simply that there is no indication in any passage where the "cup" is mentioned—there is no indication in any context that indicates that anybody thought that it had to be done just that way. So, I say there is no inference in that example or related to it or associated with it in the context on the point. Therefore, it is not binding.

By the same token, there are brethren who say that the class is an excluded specific. Well, specific to what? Here, the command to teach. Class is "a way of teaching"—publicly or privately or however—or other optional ways. And all these are optionals and *there are no commandments concerning optionals*. Now, to say the class is excluded, you've got to have other teaching. You can't make it excluded on this chart because it is not—class teaching is not a specific to the same generic that teaching is. It just cannot logically classify as an excluded specific.

Now, I would say that I feel that in the matter of examples in the Bible, mentioned by several of you in some of your writings, that the only way in which a church can cooperate with another church financially is from a rich church to a poor church, and only in emergency—I would say there is nothing in any of those examples to indicate that that's the only way, on pain of sin, that you can send money from one church to another or that you can have cooperative relations. I believe, brethren, honestly—and I certainly grant that there are a lot of smart people in this room, and I don't think I'm especially brilliant—but I do believe that this is something we ought to really look hard at and consider from every possible angle. We all love the Lord, and we want to do His will. And we all know that if we do, we are going to have to be humble in His sight, and in the sight of the brethren.

## Fifteen Minute Rebuttal Speech

Roy E. Cogdill

I would like to say that I enjoyed listening to brother Thomas. I guess both of us pretty well knew what the other would present. I have read his book pretty carefully several times and I presume that he has read at least some of the things that I write, and he knows the points of difference. It was interesting to me to see how he presented it. I do not have any fuss with him at all about a lot of the things he said. He arrives at his conclusions in a little different manner, through different illustrations, but in many instances, when it is all said and done, it amounts to about the same thing. However, in many applications made and conclusions reached, there are many wide and essential differences.

---

ROY E. COGDILL—*Author of several perennial best sellers in the field of*

*Bible study books; debater; evangelist for the Par Avenue congregation in Orlando, Florida; special lecturer at Florida College, Temple Terrace, Florida; widely used in gospel meetings throughout the nation.*

In the first place, I would like to suggest to you that I think we have used the term "pattern," as far as I am able to understand it, in a different sense. Maybe we have used it a little carelessly and without proper thought or consideration. I may have been guilty of doing that and I think others have. I want to tell you what I mean by "pattern." As far as I am concerned, *the sum total of what God said ABOUT ANYTHING is the pattern of God's will on that thing and it is the exclusive PATTERN.* Let me say it again: The sum total of what we read in the New Testament about anything is the pattern of God's will on that thing. It is an exclusive pattern, or else there is no such thing as authority in the scriptures and there could be no violation and disrespect for divine authority in going beyond the scriptures and invading the realm of God's silence. So, when I talk about a pattern of anything, I mean what I am able to learn from the New Testament about it, including all that I am able to learn from the New Testament about it and excluding all that cannot be found in the New Testament concerning it.

Now, I recognize the fact, of course, that it takes the sum total of testimony to establish a matter. He illustrated that with his circles on the Lord's Supper. From each passage you learn a little more than was learned from the others, and that is easy for us to see—that the circle of our knowledge is enlarged as the different texts are added. It takes all of them: it takes Hebrews 10:25; it takes I Corinthians 11; it takes I Corinthians 16; it takes Acts 20:7; to get the pattern of God's will on the observance of the Lord's Supper on the first day of the week, as well as on every other matter; all the testimony must be heard. Of course, I Corinthians 16 does not mention the Lord's Supper. I Corinthians 11 mentions the Lord's Supper but it does not mention the Lord's Day. Hebrews 10:25 does not mention either the Lord's Supper or the Lord's Day. So none of them would establish the time of its observance and they would not therefore constitute the sum total of the evidence on this matter. It takes Acts 20:7 to learn, and it is the only passage in the New Testament that does say, that the first day of the week was the day for breaking bread. You could not learn when to observe the Lord's Supper without the approved apostolic example recorded in that text. His illustration points out perfectly what I mean by pattern. I want it to be thoroughly understood that I do not believe that every example constitutes a binding pattern. Only an example that demonstrates obedience to that which the Lord has commanded should be regarded as binding and authoritative and then only in matters relevant, material or essential in carrying out the thing commanded. Incidental matters should be separated from divine law as the circumstances of conversions in the New Testament should be distinguished from the law of conversion.

I said a little bit ago that the only authority any apostle had to teach the church anything was because the Lord had commanded it. (Matt. 28:18-20) We do not always have the express commandment of the Lord recorded, but when the apostles taught it or approved it, the commandment and authority of the Lord for it was evidenced by that fact. You cannot find the Lord Jesus Christ saying a word in the world about elders in the church. There is no record of Jesus ever teaching anything about elders recorded in the New Testament. You do not find any commandment from the apostles that elders be appointed. The fact is stated that Paul left Titus in Crete to appoint elders but this is only a statement of fact. We do have examples authorizing the appointment of elders in every church. (Acts 14:23) Jesus Christ must have taught that there were to be elders in every church. He either taught it and the apostles learned it directly from Him, or the Holy Spirit revealed it to them as His will, because all on earth you can learn about elders in the Lord's church is from the examples that the New Testament contains. There is no express command, or precept, from the Lord or the apostles. Yet we know that this government of the church is an authorized matter. There is no such thing as collective action without some kind of government or control. Without government any collectivity would be without form and void like the world was before God brought order out of the chaos. The church has to have organization and God gave it an organization.

Brother Thomas and I differ very fundamentally and essentially on some points and conclusions drawn from this illustration which he has placed on the board.

On the point of where human judgment is allowed, I think he has erred, if he will excuse me for saying so. I am not ugly about it, and when I write, or preach either, I do not mean to be ugly. I do not have a thing in the world against J. D. Thomas.

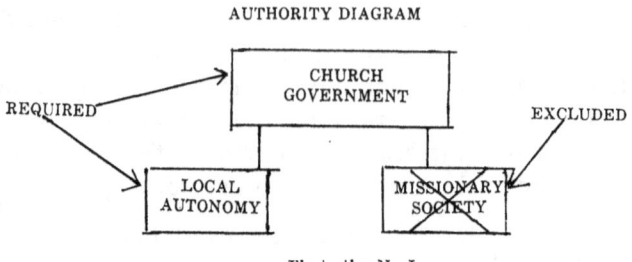

Illustration No. I

I love him and would teach him the truth on these matters, if he will let me. I love his soul and I love the truth and that is my interest in the matter. Any point of disagreement is certainly no indication of bitterness or resentment as far as I am concerned. I cannot discuss what I believe without pressing my point. I sometimes am accused of being mad when I preach. Maybe it is just my disposition or the way I look. I mean every bit of it and I contend for what I believe with all of the earnestness I have, but I am in a good humor.

I think Brother Thomas goes astray in the matter of coordinates. I do not object to his manner of illustrating it, but he misses the point as to what he lists as coordinates. I do not object to his wavy line, but I object to him confusing matters that are not coordinate and listing them below the wavy line as coordinates and therefore making them optional as matters in which men have a choice. The methods are optional expedients but the organizations are not. The organization of the church—the local church—is a required specific and the Sunday School organization is an "excluded specific" in his illustration. The same thing is true of a missionary organization or an organization for edification or the work of relieving or any other work of the church. One could mark out "missionary Society" and put in its stead "edifying society" or "benevolent society" or "Sunday school society." They are all in the same class—they are organizations.

But the church is to edify itself. It is God's teaching agency and it is God's missionary society. It has an organization that God gave to it. It is a specific organization. The New Testament teaches us what it is. It is not an optional matter that you can take or leave. We cannot just do away with the government and organization which God ordained for His church and build one of our own to do His work. You might just as well do away with the Lord's Supper and baptism when you do. The local church and its organization are divinely required matters. Any other organization that men might build—being in the same class or order—an organization—is an excluded specific. What right do we have to put it on a plane as he has done, below the wavy line, with a human organization and make it an optional expedient?

Suppose you put Abilene Christian College out here and make a church institution out of it by the church supporting it. I have nothing against Abilene Christian College. I went to school there. I do not believe it should be a church institution. I do not believe the church has the right to depend upon it to do its edifying or to support it out of the Lord's treasury. It is a coordinate with the local church—both are organizations and when it begins to do the work which God gave the church to do —edifying—then it is an "excluded specific" for it adds to God's arrangement and therefore His Word. A. C. C. is an organization. It uses methods and means of edifying those who attend it. When it does the work of the church it must classify as a coordinate with the organization of the church and as such has no right to exist. It is wrong and must be excluded. It has no right to function in such a capacity or even to exist. I would defend the right of Christian individuals to operate it and teach the word of God in it. But when it is church supported, maintained and built, to do the work of the church, I deny that it has any right to exist. Why? Because it is an addition to the organization that God designed and which is authorized in the scriptures.

Let us go now to the same point on the work of relieving the destitute. God commanded the church to relieve certain persons who were in need of benevolence. Whom did God say should do it? He said for the church to do it. (I Timothy 5) Well, what can we do about it? Can we just do as we please and build us an organization with a board of directors as a substitute for the organization God gave the church? You know, people talk about these "homes" for aged, widows and orphans, as if they were not organizations but just methods. Anyone who stops to look at them should be able to see that they are not methods but organizations that use methods and means to do the work.

Abilene Christian College is an organization that uses methods of edifying those that enroll there. When you build an orphan's home or an old folk's home, as an organization, that organization has to use methods to relieve. It uses the same methods that the local church must use, if it does the work of caring for its own needy. These human organizations, whether benevolent, edificational, or missionary in their nature, are all coordinate with the local church as an organization. If they are not, why aren't they? They are all institutions or organizations that have to use methods. Can we just say, "Well now God gave the church an organization, the local church, but God did not intend for that local church to do anything but meet on the first day of the week and break bread and raise enough money to support these human organizations that we have built to do the work that God built the church to do." If we can do that with God's organization, we can do the same thing with anything else that God says. That is just how much it matters from my point of view and in my conviction.

Where are we going to put the *wavy line?* He drew it in his illustration and he places below it things that are not coordinate at all and which are not "optional expedients" in any sense of the word. This is the main point where he is wrong about the whole matter. He coordinates things which are not coordinate at all for they do not belong to the same class or order. He lists dancing as a coordinate of the Lord's Supper and tells us that the Lord's Supper excludes dancing. Well, now, how on earth did you ever arrive at that conclusion? The Lord's Supper does not have a thing in the world to do with excluding dancing. They are not coordinates. Dancing is excluded for the reason that there is no authority in the scriptures for it—in any way—command, example, or necessary inference. You cannot worship God by dancing for the reason that it is not authorized, but the Lord's Supper being authorized does not exclude it. In order for a specific to exclude another specific, they must be coordinates—of the same kind or class. We need to keep ourselves aware that one thing of a class, when God specifies it, excludes everything else in the same kind or class. Let me show you where he goes astray and this is the same error that characterizes many of you brethren.

In his figure No. 1, and No. 2, he is correct about *run* and *walk* being coordinate and either of them coming within the scope

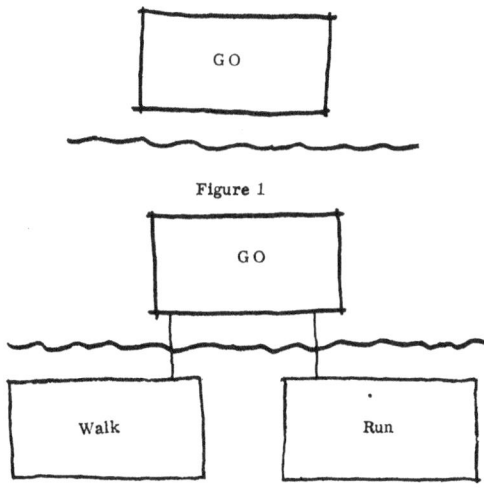

Figure 1

Figure 2

of the commandment to *Go*. In the illustrations that follow he can understand that specific authority and generic authority must be applied to coordinates. Specific authority excludes all of the same kind or class because among those things coordinate God has made a choice and man has none. Like the elements in the Lord's Supper, the unleavened loaf and the fruit of the vine as specifics exclude all of their kind or class such as apple pie and sweet milk. Brother Thomas seems to sense this all clearly in the Lord's Supper. He can also see that SING and PLAY are coordinate terms and because God has chosen SING as the act of worship in the use of music in praise to Him, therefore PLAYING is excluded. It is another kind of music. He understands perfectly that GOPHER WOOD excluded every other kind of wood and nothing else was excluded by God's choice of wood in the building of the ark except *every other kind of wood*. He can understand the principles of coordinates down to this point and illustrate them rightly.

But isn't it peculiar that when he gets down to something that he wants to justify without any authority in the scriptures for it, such as the "orphan home," his concept of coordinates becomes confused? Look at Figure 8 in his speech. He under-

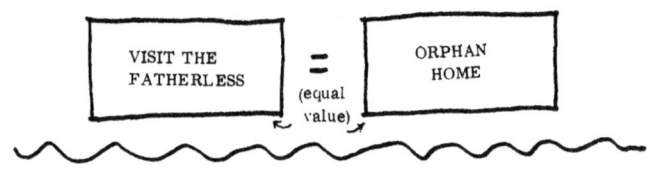

WRONGLY DIAGRAMMED

Figure 8

stands that it would be wrong to claim that the work of "visiting the fatherless" is coordinate with an "orphan home." They are not of the same kind—very obviously. One is a work to be done and the other is an "organization" that does the work. He thinks that an orphan home "organization," a chartered corporate organization under a board of directors, is an optional way of doing the work of "visiting the fatherless." This he illustrates in figure 9. But in figure 10 he illustrates the idea that the command "visit the fatherless" can be carried out in optional ways—No. 1 and No. 2. We simply ask Brother Thomas, "Has God given the church an optional organization authorized in the scriptures in addition to the local church?"

There is no Way No. 1 and Way No. 2 such as indicated by figure No. 10 when it comes to the organization authorized in the scriptures for the church to accomplish its mission whether it is teach or evangelize, or minister to the poor. According to

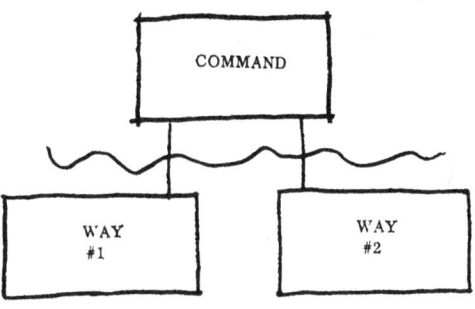

Figure 10

Brother Thomas an organization is a "way" of doing a work. If this is so, then the Missionary Society is just a way of doing evangelism; Abilene Christian College is a way of edifying the church and not an organization. Neither of them is excluded by the local church which God has authorized. According to Brother Thomas a sectarian Sunday School Organization would just be a "way" of doing the work of teaching.

Here is where he goes wrong. He makes an organization coordinate with a "way" when it is only coordinate with another organization. The local church as God organized it with Bishops, Deacons, and Saints, is a coordinate with the Missionary Society, Sunday School Society, Orphan Home Society, and all other organizations that men have built to function instead of and do the work of the local church. They all employ methods, ways and means of doing the work, but the *required specific* is the organization of the local church (Phil. 1:1; Acts 14:23) and the *excluded specifics* are the human organizations men have built. God specified the organization to do the work He has appointed for the church and until the passage can be found showing that some other organization (Way No. 2) has also been given, there is no option for men to exercise but reject God's will when they build some other *organization* to do that work.

Furthermore according to his illustration on the board (Thomas Illustration No. 1) Brother Thomas thinks that local autonomy is coordinate with the missionary society, an organization. With all of his learning, he should be capable of better reasoning than this. Local autonomy is not an organization but only a characteristic of some organizations. It is absolutely essential to a local church of Christ, just as equality and independence are essentials of the same. But in his illustration as a "required specific" he should have the "local Church of Christ." This is God's organization. It is specific both in function and form and it excludes all other organizations just as Gopher wood excludes all other wood of the same (coordinate) kind and "sing" excludes all other kinds (coordinates) of music. The Missionary Society as another organization is excluded by the specification of the local church as God's organization. For the same reason the "local church" organization "specifically required" by God excludes as an "excluded specific" the "Orphan Home," another organization; not just a work, but coordinate as an organization with the local church.

(Three Minutes)

All right, I want to spend those three minutes on Chart No. 10—"Where There Is A Pattern." Let us remember now

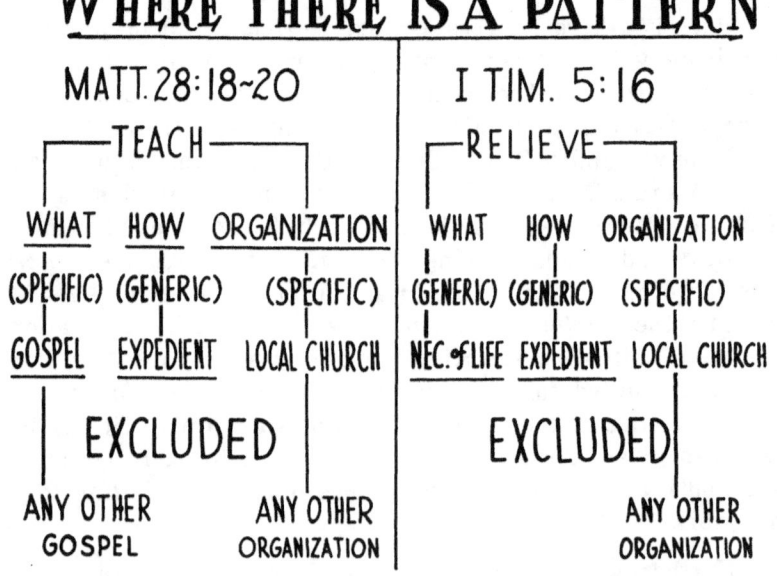

what we mean by a pattern—that is, the sum total of what God teaches about a thing. We have on this chart Matthew 28:

18-20. The Lord said, "Go teach." The method of going is incidental. Here is what might be called an "optional expediency." God made no choice, no method is specified. Therefore any method of going is included and therefore authorized and would be acceptable if some principle of righteousness is not violated in it. The example of how they went in the New Testament day would mean only that it is right to go in that fashion, but it would not mean that you must go that way. I would be just as positive as Brother Thomas that it would be sinful for any man to say that you must go in one particular way, or that you can not have more than one container for the fruit of the vine. No one has the right to so legislate where God has not. I do not believe the Bible says anything about one container. If Brother Thomas can show us where it does, I want to see it. The "cup" we read about in the New Testament is not the container. It is the element—the fruit of the vine—that is in the container, and by figure of speech—metonomy—it refers to it as "the cup." That is what "the cup" is, the fruit of the vine, and there is just one cup. When you add orange juice to it, you have violated the will of the Lord. But it does not say a thing on earth about the container, whether it be a glass or whether it be a cup or whether you can have more than one or just one. You have to have a container for a liquid but how many and whether each shall have his own container is not specified. When a man legislates where God has not, he does wrong, whether he binds something that God has not bound or looses something that God has bound. It would make no difference either way.

Now, here, (back to chart 10) the Lord said, "Teach." He tells us what to teach and that is specific—the Gospel. He does not tell us how to teach, that is generic, and any legitimate and expedient way of teaching is included. The Lord specifies the organization that is to do the teaching and that organization is specific in form. It is the local church. You can draw the wavy line brother Thomas uses anywhere you want to, but any other gospel and any other organization is excluded because God has made the choice and we do not have any therefore. That is why the missionary society is wrong. It is not just the abuse of which it is guilty that is wrong, the domination of the churches, but the thing itself is wrong because it is an *addition to God's Word*. It has no divine authority and therefore has no right to exist.

The same principle exactly is true in the work of relief. God tells us what to do. It is generic in the sense that we furnish anything that is necessary for the destitute as long as it is right and needed to sustain them. The command is generic in the fact that the Lord does not tell us the method to use, as we pointed out in the chart awhile ago. But the command is specific as to the organization that the Lord selects to do it— the church! God gave the church an organization through which to do His work and God's organization excludes *any other organization*. It is the building of a human organization to do the work that God assigned to the organization He built that is the point of our objection. This is where we differ. These human organizations built by churches of Christ to do the work that God built the churches of Christ to do are the things that divide us. Has God given the church an organization? If so, did He specifically set forth the pattern for it? If He did, did He assign this organization any work to do? If He did, then that is what God expects the church to do and he expects it to be done through the organization He gave the church. We do not have the authority and therefore do not have the right to build any other. When we do we have loosed where God has bound and we are guilty of transgressing His law. I thank you.

## "How to Establish Bible Authority"

### J. D. Thomas

Brother Cogdill is, of course, right with respect to "the cup" being the contents and not the container. However, my point is still valid, that if you can get any inference at all about the "number of containers," in one verse or many, out of the Bible the weight of the testimony would lean toward "one" I'm sure, but this is an insignificant matter in comparison with what we are interested in now. The matter of "dancing" not being worship is another small matter, but the 150th Psalm evidences my point. Dancing was done as praise or worship and I was simply using it to illustrate. The other matters here are more crucial and really get at the big differences between us, and I wish to sharpen them as much as I can for the time I have left.

Let's look again at "teach" and "the optional matters" which Bro. Cogdill calls "coordinate." Now, there's something important involved here which I did not get to notice in my

---

J. D. THOMAS—*Recently selected to head the Bible Department of Abilene Christian College, Abilene, Texas; author of several well known books; evangelist; much in demand for college lectureship appearances.*

other speech because of the time limitation, but which is covered in my book. I do not consider the denominational Sunday school as scriptural. I do not consider it an optional way of scriptural teaching. I do not consider Abilene Christian College a way of teaching in "opposition" or competition to the local church. Bro. Cogdill misinterprets me at this point, and I would reject all such matters the same as he.

Let me further explain: I would note here the "required pattern" of *church government*. (It is required that we do have

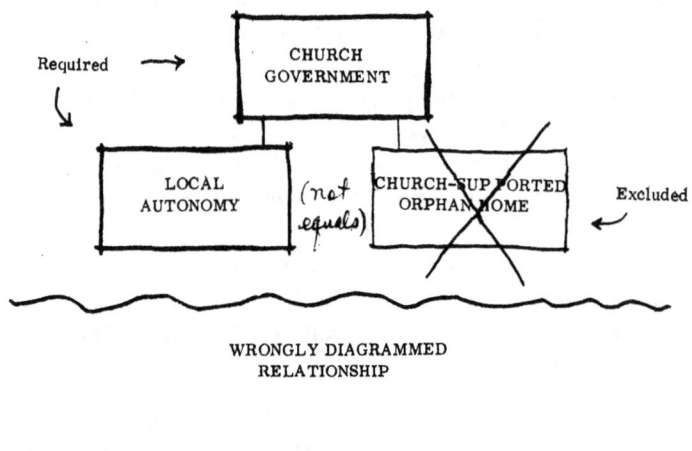

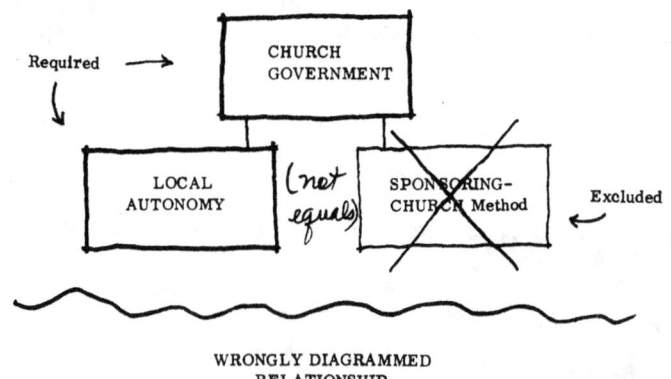

Figure 12

some type of government.) We next note the specific requirement on "local autonomy," which we all accept. I say "the excluded specific" on this diagram is the missionary society, which is a different type of church government from local autonomy. This is the real issue—the missionary society "dominates" the local church through its "delegates" or official representatives voting on matters which are then "binding" on the member churches. We all recognize this, but my argument here has been attacked on the basis that the society claims that it does not "dominate," and certain churches have insisted that they were not dominated. Obviously, their reply to such a leading question would be one of denial.

But now note that here is one method or type (specific) of church government—to have local autonomy, while another is to have any other kind of organization (also specific) that will dominate the local church from the outside, and thus violate its autonomy. But if the autonomy is violated then it is another specific, and the organization is wrong and thus excluded. But you can have an organization, brethren, if it does not violate the autonomy. For instance, you can have a Sunday School, you can have a Board of Trustees to take care of the building and property, you can have a preaching team as we have had, an evangelistic team, and you can even have "a money-carrying team" to take money to the poor saints down in Jerusalem, with even one man appointed by churches (plural) in that organization to do the Lord's work (2 Cor. 8:18, 19).

For a Bible illustration of "organizations" which do not violate autonomy, look at Acts 15:22-16:4 where we find a group (or organization) appointed by the church at Jerusalem to go down and do some missionary work and teach at Antioch. They also went on around to several congregations in Asia Minor and made a few decisions on their own, if we read the story carefully. They were an "organization" (not the church), doing the Lord's work. They were appointed by one church, they were teaching in other churches, but they were a scriptural organization. Of course, one of the things we must do here if we get anywhere this week is to define "organization" in a precise way. Whenever we do, and agree on it, we'll be getting somewhere!

Now, I say that anything—any organization or group—doing the Lord's work that will violate the local autonomy of the church (which is the required pattern that God has given) is sinful and wrong because it is excluded. But I also say that any organization which can be used by the local church—a committee, or a building committee— is not an excluded specific and thus is not wrong. We have many committees in the College church at Abilene that do various phases of the Lord's work. They are all organizations in a real sense, but no one of them violates the autonomy of the church. They are all under subjection to the elders. The whole point is, does the orphan home or the sponsoring church violate the autonomy of the local congregation—the contributing church? This point is the issue. To merely assert doesn't get anywhere. We need proof, clearly shown, that they violate the required pattern of church government. Not assertions, but proof.

To simplify this, let's study a few passages. One chart (one diagram) will fit only one passage or teaching, and must be so limited. (Brother Cogdill brought in other teachings to the one authority diagram.) Here we are concerned with "methods" of teaching. Obviously, we would never be permitted to do anything that is sinful and wrong, from some other passage. If you should "steal an automobile to go preach"—well, that *would* be a "method" of going to preach. That would be one *way* of doing it. You would be having an optional way of teaching, all right, but then you would be violating another teaching about stealing, and we can't do that.

I agree with Brother Cogdill, that we must get all the teaching, get all the revelation, that bears on any point before we have God's will, before we have any pattern. This is the way we determine it. The real question is whether the sponsoring church or the orphan home—in whichever way we may want to structure it for the purposes of debate—whether it involves a violation of autonomy. Just to assert it is so is not adequate. To assert that the church is "all-sufficient"—I'll accept that just the same as anyone. I believe the church is all-sufficient, but that doesn't keep me from having a Sunday School or a Building Committee or a Board of Trustees to own the property legally. Those are all organizations, that are not really the church.

But the point is they do not violate any of God's principles, and I am assuming that you accept this. Whenever we say that "God gave us the organization, the church, to do His work," I'll accept this 100%. But, again, we cannot assume in that statement that everything else is wrong, that "organizations" which do not violate autonomy are wrong. For something to be sinful we must clearly classify it on the authority diagram and show by *"certain,"* positive teachings that it is wrong, and thus is a different type of organization than the Sunday School or the Building Committee are. All I'm contending for here is that I believe that these orphan homes—suppose they're organizations or institutions or whatever word you want (which are the bones of contention among us)—I claim that they are, scripturally, nothing but the church, in the final analysis, doing its own work.

Note now Figure 13. They are good, expedient, advantageous ways of getting the job done. Likewise the sponsoring

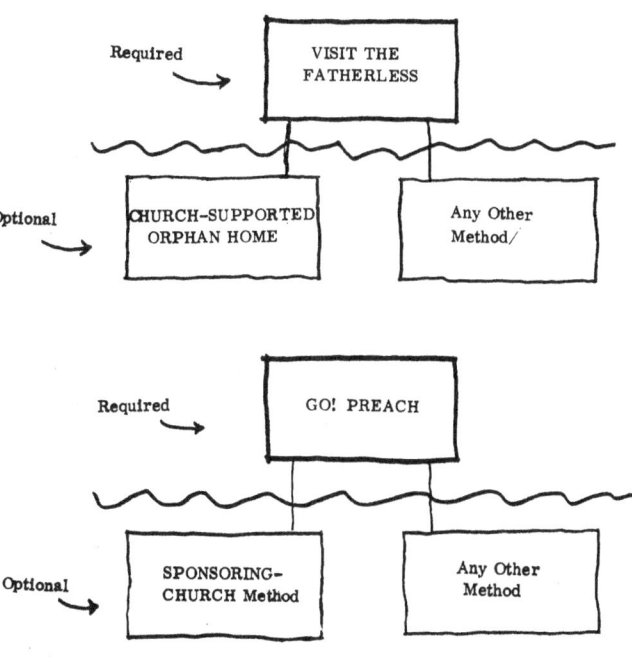

CORRECTLY CLASSIFIED
RELATIONSHIPS

Figure 13

church. You know all the arguments about how "several small churches can send a missionary, and they couldn't possibly do it otherwise," and this should be enough proof on this point. But when we say that "God has given his church as absolutely the only organization to do His work" then we are just going to leave out the FIRM FOUNDATION and the GOSPEL GUARDIAN, and the Sunday School and the Building Committee! Clearly, we *can* have organizations of a sort, and we need to think through *how* we can do God's work, in ways that will not violate the autonomy of the church. I insist that it is possible to have "organizations" that are not the church to do the church's work. I have given illustrations from the Bible and I maintain that we all use all kinds of them all of the time. I have yet to see where the sponsoring church arrangement, as it is commonly used, or the orphan home as it is commonly used (you may know of some contrary instances that I wouldn't in either of these categories), but the point is I have yet to see where they are basically and organically different from the acceptable organizations.

I was amazed to find that I agreed with Brother Cogdill for the first 30 minutes of his speech. I was going to take notes on what I disagreed with but I quit taking notes because I was with him right down the line. One thing that strikes me as significant about our differences here at this time is—and I think this is basically at the heart of our whole endeavor—the one basic issue is how to classify these organizations and how to locate them on the authority diagram. The issue is whether the organization is a violation of God's will (an excluded specific) and, if so, how? Or is it simply a good (optional) way for the church to get its work done and without violating any principle of local autonomy. It pretty well boils down to this.

I know there are a lot of fringe matters and so on that we do and can get involved in but, basically, I think this is what we ought to give ourselves to this week. I honestly am sorry that I am not going to get to be here. I would like to get to know all of you better. I have a great appreciation for brethren Adams and Wharton and Pickup from the previous meeting —I just didn't know you before. This intercommunication is worth a lot and I hope that out of this meeting the determination will come to "keep the fire going." There is great good to be gained by our getting acquainted and coming to appreciate one another personally. I don't think that very many of us "have horns," actually, and I certainly hope that I don't. I hope that out of this we can stay with the issues—stay with the points—and try to grapple with the "pattern," with the total revelation on every point in God's word.

## How to Determine Bible Authority
By James W. Adams

When I make a fifteen minute speech, I prefer a great deal longer time to make preparation for it than I had during the short night which has just passed. However, I do want to mention several things which brother Thomas said last night. I have a number of objections to his analysis of how to determine scriptural authority. In a general way, I can agree with much he said, but I do not agree with his conclusions with regard to where to place his wavy line. As brother Cogdill said last night, I do not object to his wavy line, but I believe he is completely arbitrary in choosing where to put it. After hearing brother Thomas speak here last night, talking with him at *Buchanan Dam* last April, and very carefully reading his book *"We Be Brethren,"* I have not been able to discover any clearcut method or rule set forth in any of this material that would definitely determine in a logical, sensible, and understandable way where to put the wavy line—the line of separation between the *"optional"* and the *"required."*

It also appears to me that brother Thomas depends too heavily on what may be called "common sense" in determining

JAMES W. ADAMS—*Evangelist Mound and Starr congregation, Nacogdoches, Texas. Front page writer for* THE PRECEPTOR.

where to put the wavy line—in determining what is *optional* and what is *required*. I object also to his use of the expression *"required expedient."* I do not believe that anything which may be legitimately classified in the realm of expediency is a *required thing*. I agree that things in the realm of expediency are permissible, but they are optional; they are not required.

Another thing to which I object in the speech made by brother Thomas last night is his analysis of *what is wrong with the missionary society*. This is a matter concerning which much has been said and surrounding which there has been considerable controversy. The result has been widespread confusion. In some of our discussions, it has been argued that, because participation in some of our cooperative arrangements is purely voluntary, it is therefore scriptural. But, participation in the missionary society arrangement is also purely voluntary. Does this make the missionary society scriptural?

Brother Thomas argued last night that the thing wrong with the missionary society is not that it is another organization coordinate in character with the local church, but rather that it is wrong because it infringes on the autonomy of the local church—dominates churches. To illustrate the matter, he drew a diagram on the chalkboard. At the top he wrote, *"Church Government."* Under this he wrote, *"Local Church"* adding the word *"Autonomy."* On the other side of the board he wrote, *"Missionary Society."* He then argued that the missionary society is wrong because it infringes on the autonomy of the local church.

As further justification of his position, brother Thomas said if one were to go to the Christian Church people, they would say that the missionary society does not infringe on the autonomy of local churches. I am not particularly concerned about what "Christian Church people *say"* regarding this matter, but I am concerned about *the fact* of the matter. And it is a fact that until the recent restructuring of Christian Churches, there had existed no *organic* tie between local Christian Churches and the missionary society which permitted the domination of the churches by the society. It is my understanding that in *"restructured"* Christian Churches (which process is yet in progress) there will be an organic tie between the Christian Churches and the society permitting organic domination. Heretofore, however, the domination of local Christian

Churches by the society has been *psychological* in nature, not *organic*. It has been accomplished through influence, pressure, blacklisting, the application of epithets, super-salesmanship, and the infiltration of the congregations by partisan supporters of the societies. Such procedure constitutes an *abuse* of the missionary society arrangement for church cooperation as originally conceived and promoted by the brethren. It has nothing to do with the arrangement itself. It is an abuse of the arrangement.

To oppose the missionary society on the ground of its domination of churches is not to oppose the society itself, but it is to oppose only an abuse of the society. Of course, it is wrong for missionary societies to dominate churches psychologically in the manner previously described, but *this is not the basic thing which is wrong with the missionary society*. May I repeat, *there is no organic connection* between a local Christian Church and the missionary society which, in its very nature, permits domination of that church by the society.

To make this relevant to *our* problems, I could write on the board near "Missionary Society" the expression *"Orphan Homes, Homes for the Aged, or Modern Sponsoring Church."* Having done this, I could show that every one of these institutions *among us* is liable to the same abuses which have characterized the *"Missionary Society."* Not only could I show they are *liable* to the same abuses, but I could also show that many times *they have been guilty of them*. Each one of them has been guilty of dominating churches of Christ psychologically—through influence and pressure. This is the only kind of domination the missionary society has heretofore exercised over local Christian Churches. Our so-called *"Orphan Homes, Homes for the Aged, and Modern Sponsoring Churches"* can and do dominate churches in the same fashion. The psychological domination of churches by the missionary society is not the basic thing wrong with it. As brother Cogdill correctly stated last night, the missionary society is wrong because it is *another organization coordinate in character with the local church*.

I should like to illustrate our contention in this matter by the use of a chalkboard diagram. Let us begin with *Point No. 1* on the drawing. This has to do with the obligation to RELIEVE poor widows ("widows indeed") as commanded in I Timothy 5. Note the term "relieve" with the scripture citation (I Timothy

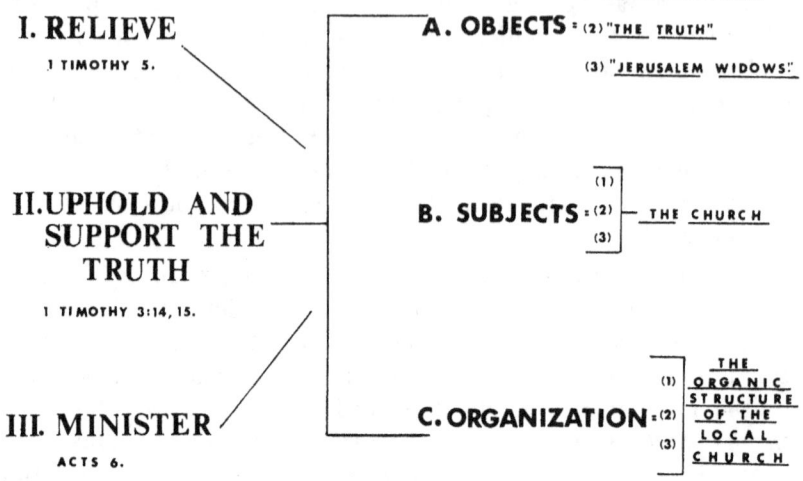

5) on the left side of the drawing. Relieve is the obligation or command. In the bracket to the right of the word *relieve* note three terms: (A) *Objects;* (B) *Subjects;* (C) *Organization.* The *objects* of the relief commanded in our text are "widows indeed." The *subjects* of the command to relieve are "the church" —the local church. The *organization* is the organic structure of the local congregation. The relief of the widows (the objects) is to be done by the church (the subjects) through the organic structure of the local church (the organization). If we presume to set up another organization to take over this responsibility, the organization is wrong because it is coordinate in character with, yet *not* identical with, the specifically required organic situation—the local church. This is what is wrong with such organizations and is the point brother Cogdill made last night.

Note *Point No. 2* on our diagram. Instead of "relieve," we have *"UPHOLD AND SUPPORT THE TRUTH"* or the gospel message. Our text is I Timothy 3:14, 15 in which is contained the obligation of "the church" to be "the pillar and support of the truth." The *obligation* is to uphold and support the truth —the gospel. The *object* in this case would be *the truth.* The *subjects* would be the same as in the previous case; namely, *the church.* The *organization* would also be the same as in the previous case; namely, *the organic structure of the local congregation.* If we establish a missionary society under (C) to "uphold and support the truth," we have created *another organ-*

*ization* coordinate in character, yet not identical with, the local church.

In the realm of organization, there are at least two ways to corrupt the Divine order. The organic structure of the local church can also be corrupted by making of it a "sponsoring church." I believe a sponsoring church arrangement is a corruption of the organic structure of the local church as revealed in the New Testament. It makes the elders of a local church something which God did not make them. Though the arrangement functions under the name of a local church, the functions of the elders of that church have been changed from *local* to *ecumenical*. They have become a *brotherhood eldership*. This perverts the organic structure of the local church. It makes it *another organization* as real as the missionary society. I do not argue that a "sponsoring church" is parallel in every respect to a missionary society. I do contend that in overseeing the work and resources of many churches in the "upholding and supporting of the truth" it performs the same function as does a missionary society. In so doing, it perverts the organic structure of the local church as revealed in the New Testament. This is my objection to the *"sponsoring church,"* and I believe the error lies where brother Cogdill put it last night—in the realm of organization.

In activating a *"sponsoring church,"* there is actually brought into being *another organization* coordinate in character with, yet not identical with, a local church as revealed in the New Testament. This does not mean that it displaces the local church. The missionary society does not displace local Christian Churches. The missionary society is rather an organic agency of the Christian Churches. It is an organization created by them in which they can amalgamate their efforts in the proclamation of the gospel of Christ. *This is exactly what a sponsoring church is.*

Now observe *Point No. III* on our diagram. This time we discuss the obligation to *"MINISTER"* as suggested by our text, Acts 6. In this text, there is an example of ministering, ministration to poor widows in Jerusalem. They were the (A) Objects. The (B) Subjects were the Jerusalem church. Because of complaints concerning the neglect of certain widows, the apostles set up a way for the work to be done. It was done through the (C) *organic structure* of the Jerusalem church. The people who constituted the church selected seven men of their number for the task and the apostles appointed them over the work. These seven men administered the benevolence under the general supervision of the apostles in the Jerusalem church who had appointed them. As stated, the objects were the poor widows. The subjects were the Jerusalem church. The organization was the organic structure of the local congregation in Jerusalem.

If the brethren had started a separate organization and the Jerusalem church had delegated to this organization its resources and responsibilities, there would have been brought into existence an organization coordinate in character with the local church, hence a corruption of the Lord's order. It is on this basis that I object to the missionary society, the so-called "Orphan Homes, Homes for the Aged," and other such institutions.

Brother Thomas confused at great length last night *the systematic way of doing a thing within the organic structure of a local church* and *an organization coordinate in character with the local church.* He mentioned a large number of committees functioning in the College Church of Abilene, Texas. If these committees have a scriptural right to exist (and I presume they do), and if they are doing things they have a scriptural right to do, they *do not* constitute organizations separate from the College Church and coordinate in character with it. They are simply systematic arrangements within the organic structure of the local church.

Brother Thomas himself mentioned the fact that these committees are under the elders. But the organizations to which we object are not in most cases under the elders. Those to which we object which are under elders are engaged in general work and are opposed on a different basis. Brother Turner will deal with this in his speeches on "The Cooperation of Churches." May I repeat, the committees brother Thomas mentioned are within the organic structure of the local church. They are not distinct organizations coordinate in character with the local church. **There is a difference between the systematic way of doing a thing within the organic structure of the local church and an organization distinct from the local church and coordinate in character with it. I think you brethren as well as we have always made this distinction, and I do not see any reason why we should be confused about it now.**

## Minor Speech — Rebuttal

### Lewis Hale

On the matter of organizations within the organization, I think this has been very vital, especially in reference to discussions on the "Herald of Truth." A good many of the things that have been written and a good many of the things that have been said have dealt with the way in which their committees have been set up, the use that has been made of Fidelity Enterprises, and things of this nature. I think that a little bit of reflection would teach each one of us that if Highland had the resources to do exactly what's been done, if that congregation furnished every last dime that's been put into the program, that they could have used Fidelity exactly as they have. They might have had every committee exactly as they have; so, the aspect of other churches contributing to it has nothing to do with the way they've set the committees up or anything of this sort. All of that might have been done by them had they furnished all of the money. I think we'd all agree with that, wouldn't we? That everything they've set up in the conduct of the program would have been true had they completely financed it themselves. If

---

LEWIS G. HALE—*Evangelist for Southwest congregation in Oklahoma*

*City; author; debater; teacher of Bible in Oklahoma Christian College, Oklahoma City, Oklahoma.*

there are abuses, even had they furnished all of the money, they should have corrected that. I believe we'd agree with that. So if we're going to discuss the matter of authority for churches cooperating in it, the way they have organized really has nothing to do with it; it would be the aspect of churches *cooperating* in doing it. Any corruption or any abuses in the manner in which committees are handled, or the agencies they may use in making the film—any abuses in that should be corrected even if they didn't receive any outside help. I think we can see that and agree with that. So I think we really ought to confine ourselves in this discussion as to whether or not we have the right to help, whether or not we have the right to pool some resources, because I believe that's what's vital and I believe that's what's at stake.

In the matter of establishing authority I want to mention a little bit (for my part) about preaching the gospel and co-operating in doing this, and Biblical authority for what we do in preaching the gospel. When we have this general command to teach (I don't know whether I can draw the boxes right or not) . . . if you want to talk about what's "necessary and expedient," if you want to talk about "the optional," then that's fine. Either way you want to say it, I think the principle is still the same. If you want to draw a wavy line, if you want to draw a line straight down the board and put one on one side and one on the other, it is still the same thing and when we get through, our real issue is where we're going to draw that wavy line or the line down the middle. That's really what the issue will be about. But when we operate under this general command to preach or to teach (necessity), we may build a church building and so we may put that here (optional or expedient). If somebody asks you a justification for your building you may say "for preaching" or you may say "for worship"—I don't care which, I think either one would justify it and so we all have our buildings. But when you get the people there, they're going to have to stand or sit or lie, so we usually give them some pews, you know, to sit down on.

You say, that's the way the Christian church argues; they talk about tuning forks, and song books and all. Well, I don't care how *they* talk, let's just look at *this*. We do believe that we justify these things under the command to preach, don't we? I trust we all do that, and then we have our lights and we have our parking lots and we may have nurseries—some of you might not, I don't know how you feel about that. But you *may* have a place to take your crying babies out so those inside can hear, and how do we justify all this? Well, we're supposed to preach the gospel, and we believe this expedites our preaching the gospel. And so after we name all these things—and I could mention a bunch of things that you don't have to have but we believe are allowable in getting the job done . . . an expedient, we get down here and we finally pay the preacher, you know. I think everyone of us in here is in favor of that—we agree that that's scriptural—so we say that that's all right. What are we talking about? Well, we're talking about preaching the gospel at *home.*

Let's say, you're from Arlington, and you say that's allowable. This is our home congregation, let's say, and we preach right here and that's allowable. But, now let me ask you . . . suppose this same congregation decides that they are going to preach the gospel over here in a town that is a hundred miles away. They don't have a church over there so they're going to start a church. This command to preach the gospel—how much does it include *over there?* Can this church that wants to preach the gospel over there go over there and rent a building or else build one? Let's say they're going over there and hold a meeting. What can they do? Go over there and rent a building? Spend the Lord's money in another place and rent a building? Well, if renting a building can be included in the command to preach the gospel *at home,* I'd say it could be included in preaching the gospel *a hundred miles away.* If the command to preach the gospel locally includes the pews, or the lights or heat, I believe it will include that over there a hundred miles away. I don't believe there is any rhyme or reason that would tell us that teaching or preaching the gospel would include all these things here at home, but those that are a hundred miles away you cross them out, and the only thing we'll include over there is paying the preacher's personal support, and if it does rule out everything but the preacher's personal support, I believe we need to show why, Biblically, it is included one place and not the other.

You might say, "What's this got to do with it?" Well, everything because much that I've heard and seen on it would rule out one church's supplying these things anywhere except locally, except the preacher's support. Now, if I'm wrong I'm ready to be corrected. If I have misunderstood, I am willing to be corrected, but I believe that there is not one thing that the Lord's money can be used for locally by the church to preach the gospel that it cannot use anywhere that that church is preaching the gospel. In other words, if it is doing a mission work—I don't care if it is a thousand miles away—I believe it can do everything in that mission point a thousand miles away to preach the gospel that it does locally. You might say, "Well, Paul writing to the Philippians said, 'You sent to *my* necessity once and again.' " I want to tell you that buying communion bread, grape juice, etc. wouldn't be the preacher's necessity. Not Paul's necessity. It might be the congregation's necessity but we're talking about the preacher's necessity. He said when "I was in want . . ." he was talking about Paul. Now, if that is exclusive and means that the only thing that could be sent is for Paul, then it would exclude buildings and it would exclude pews and it would exclude Bibles and it would exclude tracts or anything else. It would exclude buying radio time. If it would really exclude everything but his necessity . . . *his* necessity . . . then it would exclude anything else—*anything* else . . . car expense, *anything* else. I believe this is very vital. Now there is one other point in this matter of our authority for doing something and this involves organization. We talk about the church's being all-sufficient. What do we mean by all-sufficient??? How all-sufficient is the church? I think we have kicked this thing around, misused it and abused it. If the church has to make use of a motel to put up a preacher, does this infringe upon the all-sufficiency of the church? The church didn't have a place to bed him down, they weren't equipped over there at the church building for that, so what did they do? They went out and used a motel, and bedded the preacher down during a gospel meeting. Now does this mean the church wasn't all-sufficient? Why, certainly not. If the church gets ready to do something, we do things in one of two ways, as a rule.

Let's just say for an example the church wants to put out a church bulletin. Where I preach we happen to have an offset press and so we do our bulletins. I have known churches that had theirs done commercially. They sent out copy and a commercial enterprise set up the type and published the bulletin. We have a mailing service in Oklahoma City and if you wanted to, they'd actually fold the thing, address them and mail them for you every week. We don't use them, but they'd do that. I believe we could have our own facilities for doing it or we could go out here and use a human institution to do it. I believe that. I believe that when we get ready to take care of a preacher, that the church may own its property or they may go out and use commercial enterprises to take care of that preacher . . . to house him and take care of him, and I think we all agree with that. And we could expand this and go on and on, showing how that in doing the Lord's work, many times we choose to do it with our own facilities, buy them and own them and operate them, or we may choose to use commercial enterprises to carry that out. That's why I occupy a stand that I know lots of my brethren do not when it comes to the care of homeless children.

I believe that it is entirely possible that a church may own property in which it takes care of its homeless children, that they may immediately employ supervision to take care of those children, may pay the bills for the groceries and actually have its own place for taking care of some children, whether it's five or five hundred. I also believe that it is possible, if they choose to do so, they may use an organization such as Boles Home that is not of a part, or incorporated within the framework of, the local church . . . separate and apart . . . and use their facilities just as much as they would a commercial printer downtown to print their bulletins, or just as much as they'd use a motel to take care of their preacher instead of owning the preacher's home.

And you might say, "Well, there's one difference—in one place you're just going down and paying the bill and in the other place you're just underwriting the thing." I'll say this on that point: That if everyone being cared for by that commercial enterprise is an object of your care and attention, you are, in effect, paying everybody's bills when you underwrite it. It isn't a matter of just giving to it; you are, in effect, just paying everybody's bills. There would be a difference in supporting a hospital which takes care of just any and everybody than in underwriting a hospital which only cares for the poor and helpless. Now, here's a group that's taking care of homeless children and they're *all* objects of your care and they're *all* objects of your attention and, therefore, to give to Boles Home isn't parallel with giving to someone who is taking care of people who are well-to-do as well as people who are poor. Here is a case of just paying everybody's bills. I believe we have the right to do that (if they are needy) and I believe that includes buying services when everybody in there is an object of care; then a gift to them is equal to paying the bills. If I'm wrong, then I'm still willing to study and I'd like to know it, but that's exactly what I stand on.

## Minor Speech — Rebuttal

Melvin Curry

I welcome the opportunity of being here with this group; yet in many ways I feel incompetent to express something on the subject that has not been expressed, something that truly is constructive. Yet I believe one principle should be emphasized over and over again, and we should never lose sight of it. Much has been said about the unity of brethren, and there is nothing that I seek and pray for more, but the principle I mentioned before is set forth in scripture to govern the unity of brethren. When James describes the wisdom that is from above, he says it is *first pure* and then peaceable. The thing that is uppermost in this discussion is the matter of authority. We must establish the purity of an action before we undertake concerted action.

I want to examine for just a moment two concepts that already have been mentioned and that should be kept in mind throughout the discussions. The first of these is called the law of inclusion and exclusion. You have heard this law mentioned many times already. Much has been argued about what is excluded by a specific commandment. I have discovered in discussions with individuals that it is much better to speak about what is included than what is excluded. I do not know if there is such a thing as the law of exclusion. I do know this much. Peter said "If any man speak let him speak as the oracles of God." I do know that when Jesus Christ raised the problem of authority he asked the question, "The baptism of John, whence is it? from God or from men?" I know that when it comes to the matter of worship Jesus also said, "God is a spirit and they that worship him must worship him in spirit and in truth." The emphasis is always on what God says.

---

MELVIN CURRY—*Professor of Bible and Greek in Florida College, Temple Terrace, Florida; evangelist for the University Heights Church, Tampa, Florida.*

When I talk to a person about instrumental music or what is acceptable worship, all I need to do is point to the word of God, which is complete and final in authority (2 Tim. 3:16, 17), and establish what God's will is on the subject, namely, that we are to sing and make melody in our hearts. Now, in response, he might turn to the Old Testament and cite a passage of scripture which he believes authorizes the use of mechanical instruments of music in worship. Thus he has God's authorization for it in worship under the old covenant, but that is not God's authorization for it under the new. Acceptable worship for the Christian is that which God has approved in the new covenant, and when we go beyond his commandments in worship, the result is will worship. When an individual imposes an obligation where God had not revealed His mind, he is guilty of will worship (Col. 2:23) and he is not engaging in divinely authorized worship. We need to examine thoroughly this idea of inclusion and exclusion.

The second concept to be considered is generic and specific authority. We have had charts or boxes drawn for us on several occasions, and when all is said and done, the various illustrations of generic and specific, coordinate and subordinate, come out about the same. Here we have the generic and out of that we must derive the specific.

I would like for you to think about this diagram with me for just a moment. If I have a specific, then I am restricted by the specific. If I start out with a generic and there are no specifics of the generic bound, then it seems true, as we have always said, that I am at liberty to choose whatever specifics are available. If God simply says "Go," there is no room for argument about the expedients that may be used for going. In Noah's case if God (and that is a big if!) had said, "Build an ark," this would have been a generic command and there would have been liberty for specifics. When, however, God became specific, then all I know is what God specified. God told Noah to build an ark, but that is not all that God told Noah. God gave Noah the specific command to build an ark of gopher wood, and I know that both brother Cogdill and brother Thomas agree that the command was specific.

Here then is a command: "Build an ark of gopher wood." I cannot stop and say God gave Noah a generic command to build an ark, because he did not. I do not believe that Noah in any sense could have construed this to be a generic command. God's complete command was, "Build an ark of gopher wood." All I know from that statement is that something possessing the quality of "gopher wood" must be used to build an ark. I might reason on my own now: "If it is gopher wood, then there is such a thing as the abstract generic 'wood.'" I do not know that by what is stated in the command, however. All I know is what God told Noah, "Build an ark of gopher wood." Therefore, I have no right whatever to argue from a specific back to a generic which is not commanded in the specific. A proper regard for this point would eliminate some of our difficulties.

When I begin with a specific and argue back to an abstract generic, and then move in an entirely different direction to produce specific authority that is completely unrelated to the original specific, I have drawn an incorrect inference. If God makes a specific statement, this is his will on the matter. Now, if he reveals another specific, I have the sum total of two specifics for a pattern. If this is all he has specifically said, then this is all that I have for a pattern.

Now back to the violation of the principle. Someone may say, on the basis that we argue from the generic to the specific (and the arrow shows it this way),

that he has the right, all of a sudden, to reason in reverse gear.

He reasons, here is a specific and this specific is gopher wood. Gopher wood involves "wood" as the generic, and, therefore, we can move in the direction of a different specific and justify Noah's use of pine wood.

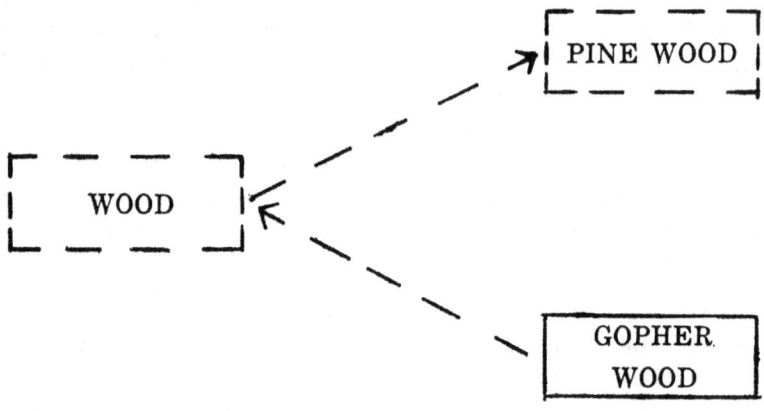

Most brethren would shudder at such reasoning. Some of them, however, will start with an example, what they call an approved apostolic example, which is a specific action. Let us say it involves the matter of cooperation and it is a specific example of cooperation. The argument is as follows:

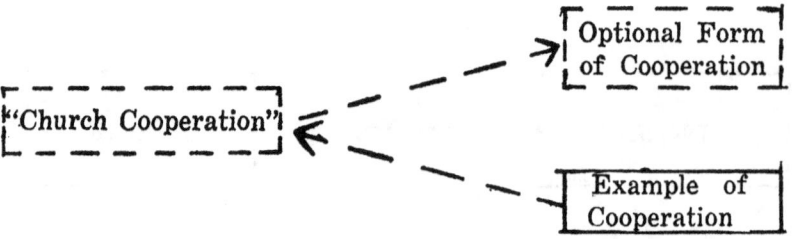

They start with an approved example of cooperation, but from that they go back to the generic and say that the generic involved is "church cooperation." Now that they have generic authority, they contend that they are at liberty not to follow the original specific example but to choose another optional form of cooperation. After all, it is just a matter of choice as to which one you select. One cannot, however, start with this specific over here, (pointing to the diagram) argue back to a generic and go any direction other than back down to the same specific. Somehow we must limit ourselves to the proper use of generic and specific authority.

In conclusion, therefore, I bid us to consider carefully what we mean by the law of inclusion and exclusion. I ask, finally, that we avoid making hasty generalizations about generic and specific authority. If a passage affords specific authority, then it seems to me all we can do is argue from it as if it is a specific, not jump from it to some generalization and then jump from that generalization in a different direction. We say we believe in Bible authority, but somewhere between premise and practice there are grave inconsistencies displayed by some, if not by most of us. I thank you.

## Minor Speech — Rebuttal

### Alan E. Highers

Some things were set out last night on which all of us would generally agree, namely, that we have divine commands, approved examples, and necessary inferences by which Bible authority may be established. Both speakers set this out and both of them agree, as I understand it, that divine authority is set out by divine commands, approved examples, or by necessary inferences. Of commands there are two kinds and this, likewise has been brought out. There are commands that are generic in nature; there are others that are specific in nature.

I would like to deal momentarily with a suggestion made just now by brother Curry that we do not have such a thing as the law of exclusion—that we have only a law of inclusion, that a command includes only what it states and, therefore, there is no such thing as a law of exclusion, that a command does not exclude anything. I believe that is a distinction without a difference because it is agreed that when a command includes only a certain amount, it excludes everything else. Take the gopher wood command as an example. If it includes only gopher wood, it is agreed that it thereby excludes everything else. I have heard this argument made and I do not believe there is any difference in what is being said here and in the use of the expression "excludes." If it includes only what the command itself says, then it necessarily excludes everything else. Therefore, we do have a law of exclusion and the idea that there is not a law of exclusion is a distinction without a difference.

There are two kinds of commands, generic and specific. We would say and have said that the specific command ex-

---

ALAN E. HIGHERS—*Evangelist Getwell congregation, Memphis, Tennessee; debater; soon to become a practicing attorney.*

cludes. Now, in brother Cogdill's address last night he used as an example of this the statement in I Tim. 5:16 in which it is said the church is to relieve. He said this is a specific. He used it on his chart in the same connection with a specific such as gopher wood. That was one of his illustrations. We understand that gopher wood as a specific excludes any other kind of wood. I raise the question whether I Tim. 5:16 is in the same category. Does this exclude any other organization at all, remembering that the home itself is another organization? If this statement is specific in the same sense that gopher wood is, and there is not any other information on it, I believe the argument that was made last night, if it means anything at all, means that it excludes any other organization, and that would exclude the home itself from consideration because that is something other than the church. There would be no other way to consider it. Here is something in addition to the church.

Then, we have the matter of examples and Acts 20:7 comes into special consideration. Just as we have two different kinds of commands, we likewise have two kinds of examples. We have commands that are generic and specific, and we have examples that are permissive and some that are exclusive. Illustrations have been given of this and one of the questions involved is, how do we determine the difference in an example that is a binding example—an exclusive example—and one that is a permissive example? We go to verse 8 of the same chapter and read the example about the upper room and, if I am correct, every time the place is mentioned in connection with the observance of the Lord's supper, it was in an upper room. So, we have uniformity in example, yet we do not believe that is a binding example. I want to come back to that in just a moment and say more about the Lord's supper.

Now, to this matter of necessary inference. We justify a great deal by necessary inference. There are two kinds of inferences just as there are two kinds of commands and two kinds of examples. There are simple inferences and necessary inferences. We sometimes misuse the words "imply" and "infer." We make the inference; the passage may imply, but the inference is drawn. An inference is a logical deduction, a necessary inference is a necessary logical deduction. We have a necessary inference when there is no other possible conclusion from the passage. A good illustration of this is Heb. 10:25 in which we have the command to assemble. From that we necessarily infer a place—we must have a place. That is not a simple inference, that is a *necessary* inference. You cannot assemble without a place; you must have a place. Now then, the question: What kind of place must one have? This gets into expediency and the realm that brother Thomas described as optional. We do not have any kind of place specified. It is not included within the command and, therefore, we may buy a place already existing—many brethren have bought denominational buildings. We may rent a place. We may borrow one—such as we are meeting in at this time. We may build—purchase a lot, hire a contractor, and build. Those are different kinds of structures in which we may meet, different kinds of places that may be provided. We might meet in an arbor, under a tree, outside, or whatever. All of us know that the general kind of a meeting place is a church-owned building, church-owned property, of which we do not have any exact example or specific occurrence, but we believe we are justified.

I appreciate the statement made by brother Cogdill that we should not say, "We have no authority for church buildings." I think I know what brethren mean when they say that, but I do not believe they say it right. We do have authority; what they mean is that there is no specific example. That is not to say there is no authority, but we have it as a necessary inference and from that inference, an expedient in regard to the kind of place involved. We spend hundreds of thousands of dollars per year on that which is an expediency and which grows out of a necessary inference.

I believe the command of I Tim. 5:16, or for that matter James 1:27 or Gal. 6:10 (passages that, no doubt, will be discussed more thoroughly when we come to the topic on the work of the church) indicates that a home is a necessity in the relief or the care of the destitute. That is just as surely a necessary inference from I Tim. 5:16 as a place is from Heb. 10:25. We cannot supply the needs of the destitute who are lacking a home without providing that which they lack. Now, what kind of home is to be involved? We have the same kind of situation that we have in regard to the place. A place is necessarily inferred, the kind of place is not specified. A home where the needs may be supplied is necessarily inferred. We cannot tender the needs of the homeless without providing that which they are "less," that which they are lacking. Thus we have the *home* necessarily inferred, but the *kind* of home is a matter of expediency, provided that it does not violate other scriptural principles. We are concerned about the use of the Lord's money. We are talking about the treasury of the church—how the money that is contributed on the first day of the week may be used. But we will use it to construct a building that is an expediency growing out of a necessary inference, and it is by the same kind of authority and through the same kind of reasoning that we may have various kinds of homes of a legal nature set up through which children may be cared for.

Now, to this matter of example—approved example and especially in regard to Acts 20:7. How do we determine when an example is merely permissive and when it is exclusive? I believe the principle set out by brother Thomas last night is true, that when there is an exclusive example, when there is a binding example, there is some indication of that by background information that suggests, perhaps by a necessary inference that we draw, that there is a command involved. I would like to read a statement, if I may be permitted, not to disagree, but a statement with which I agree and which is a good statement of the principle of the Lord's supper. This is from a tract by brother James Cope. He has discussed divine commands, then he brings in examples and this is under the heading of necessary inference. He says, "We also learn Christ's will by reading or hearing read certain accounts of local church activity in connection with some commands of Christ and, from this, *draw certain necessary conclusions* that other commands, not specifically mentioned, necessarily were given by Christ."

He says we may draw the necessary inference from certain surrounding things that there were commands given by the Lord, even though those commands are not specifically mentioned. He continues: "This is called 'learning from *necessary inference.*' An example of this is observance of the Lord's supper by the disciples assembled at Troas on the first day of the week. (Acts 20:7). Luke makes the statement that it was 'upon the first day of the week' that 'we were gathered together to break bread.' That there was a regular assembly of the saints for the purpose of eating the Lord's supper is clear from Heb. 10:25 and I Cor. 11:20, 33. Putting all the evidence together we conclude that the Lord has *commanded the disciples to assemble on the first day of the week to eat the Lord's supper.*"

That is why Acts 20:7 is an example that is exclusive in nature. As brother Cope has said in his statement, we conclude that there is a *requirement* set down by the Lord which this simply exemplifies.

I have something that I want to present on this if our time will allow, and I would be happy for anyone to examine the reasoning set out. In Luke 22 at the institution of the Lord's supper, in verse 18, the Lord said, "I say unto you that I shall not drink from henceforth of the fruit of the vine until the kingdom of God shall come." We all understand the expression "until." We use Matt. 5:17, 18 to show that the law would continue "till" fulfilled. When it was fulfilled, it ceased. Joseph knew not Mary "till" she had brought forth her firstborn son, indicating that he did know her as a wife after that. Jesus said he would not drink "till," indicating that he would commune with us at the coming of the Kingdom, when the kingdom did come. In a parallel account of this in Mark 14:25 he does not use exactly the same expression, but he says "until that day." He uses that specific expression in the account in Mark. In Luke 22 he says "the kingdom come." In Mark 14 he says "that day." All of us know the kingdom came on Pentecost according to Acts 2, and that Pentecost fell on the first day of the week, according to Leviticus 23. Therefore, I submit that the example was merely carrying out the instruction of the Lord about the Lord's supper and that Acts 20:7 is an example of how that was done. It was to be done "that day" when the kingdom came. The kingdom came on the first day of the week, that was the day. I believe that is the day the Lord himself at the time of the institution of the supper had instructed when it would be observed.

## Minor Speech — Rebuttal

### Clinton D. Hamilton

I, likewise, appreciate the opportunity of participating in such a discussion. I would like to point out that when one begins to set up the basis on which he does what he does in religion that he would have to pay close attention to the concepts we refer to as pattern and faith. The doctrine or the teaching we have, the word of God, is the pattern. It is a pattern of doctrine (2 Tim. 1:13 and other such passages). As was well pointed out last night by both speakers, when one has read all God has said on a particular subject he has the pattern of doctrine on that subject. He has the form by which he is to be governed and in the matter of issues bothering us particularly. In I Corinthians 4:16, 17 the apostle stated that he sent Timothy unto them who knew his ways as he taught everywhere in every church. So whatever the apostle was practicing was that which he did in all the churches. He, likewise, stated in I Corinthians 7:17, "and so ordain I in all the churches." In I Corinthians 11:16 he observed that "we have no such custom, neither the churches of God"; that is, we have no other practice other than that which is pointed out. Then in I Corinthians 14: 33 and 34 "as in all the churches." In Philippians 4:9 he says "the things which ye both learned and received and heard and saw in me, these things do: and the God of peace shall be with you." Now, in the matter of the relation between congregations, and in the performance of the work that is done by congregations, there are passages that tell us what the apostle did.

I think all of us recognize if there is a pattern it must be followed but if there is no pattern (and all of these passages that tell what he did are permissive examples), then there is

---

CLINTON D. HAMILTON—*Dean of Broward County Junior College, Fort Lauderdale, Florida; well known evangelist; for many years Dean of Florida College, Temple Terrace, Florida.*

nothing wrong. On the other hand, if these passages reveal to us what God wanted us to know by virtue of the fact that the Spirit caused these men to pen these words, then we should pay attention to them. If there is a pattern, any violation of what the scripture says is wrong. If there is no pattern with reference to what God said and revealed in these particulars, then there is nothing wrong and we are at complete liberty to do whatever we please in that case. But in Philippians 4:15-18 there is something that Paul practiced; he observed that the Philippian brethren communicated to him more than once, sending directly to him whatever relief they provided, rather, whatever assistance it was that they provided for him. In I Corinthians 9 the apostle pointed out the right of a congregation to support an evangelist and of the evangelist to be supported by a congregation with whom he worked. He also revealed in 2 Corinthians 11 that an evangelist might work in a field removed from a congregation who was giving him support, for he said he robbed other churches taking wages of them. One who reads the Bible will find that in every instance when the apostle was having fellowship in the matter of giving and receiving with others that this is what took place. Now, that either is the pattern, or it is not. If this does not give us the pattern then there is nothing wrong in this area and it may be done howsoever we may please.

In the matter of the relief of poor, there are several passages dealing with the subject. For instance, Acts 6, when a congregation took care of those within its own number. Then in I Corinthians 16:1-4 and 2 Corinthians 8 and 9 there is the instance of a congregation unable to take care of her own and instructions to other congregations to give assistance, together with Acts 24:17 and Romans 15:25, 26 that bear on the same point. One never finds the apostle giving any instruction otherwise and one never finds him practicing otherwise than that which he states. I hold a position of practicing affirmatively that which I find, and affirming that which I practice; the other individual, therefore, who would deviate from that would, of necessity, have to give the scripture for the authority, the basis, on which he says he has the right to do otherwise.

There is a problem also that I want to refer to that has been mentioned this morning that has to do with taking what we practice and, from this assumption, drawing certain inferences. This is a very dangerous procedure; it is a procedure that we ought to hold suspect because what one practices is not necessarily right. One of the big problems with the people in the Lord's day was that they assumed what they practiced was correct and from it drew certain inferences. Thus, over a period of years there built up on top of the word of God, as it were, the dust of tradition and these people fully asserted that they were correct and charged Jesus and His disciples in Matthew 15 and Mark 7, for instance, with violating what was right. Jesus wiped away these traditions and said "Have ye not read"; do not you pay attention to what Moses said? What we ought to be doing, rather than take what we are practicing and from that infer certain things, is to get back and raise the question of what does the Bible say on this particular topic. They practiced error because they forgot the statement of Moses which said "Honor thy father and mother" and "He that speaketh evil of father and mother, let him die the death."

Furthermore, it appears to me that there is a basic difficulty in brother Thomas' position. Last evening he said that Paul gave the instruction "Be ye imitators of me" and said that is command authority. If I understand correctly the way he reasoned in his book on this other topic, this was not a command but was given to somebody else and becomes an example. For instance, why do we have a plurality of elders in every congregation? There is no command to the effect that we shall have a plurality of elders in every congregation. We have instructions to a particular individual that he should appoint elders in every city (Titus 1:5). Furthermore, in brother Thomas' book, and also last evening, he takes the position that I Corinthians 16 is command authority to meet on the first day of the week and takes the same passage and proves from it that cooperation among churches is an optional matter. Here is a basic contradiction that has to be dealt with. All of us who wrestle with this in our own souls (all of us in this room whom I am assuming want to be right—desire to be right), we have to make certain that we are consistent. My inconsistencies or my contradictions may not prove that I am right or wrong except that I cannot be right if there is a contradiction involved. It does not prove what I ought to do if I have shown a contradiction in another man's work, but it does prove that he cannot be right in both instances. If we walk by faith (and we do, all of us admit) and faith comes by hearing the word of Christ, then an individual is obligated with reference to his practice to show that this is in harmony with the teaching of the word of Christ.

I am particularly concerned also with an expression used by brother Highers a while ago with reference to homes. He pointed out that an individual could—or a church rather—could use a home. In fact, it must use a home in the relief of those who are in need. A home had to be provided and he made the statement that it is a necessity; a home is a necessity to relieve. In I Timothy 5:16 I would like to have the word *home* defined with reference to the relief of widows. Does he mean a place of residence? Does he mean a place of domicile? What does he mean? If he means a place of domicile, how, then, can he conclude an organization from this? There has been a great deal of error taught because the meaning of the word *home* has been shifted in arguing. Someone will say, for instance, the home is a divine institution and the church can support the home, and since the home is an institution, then the church can support an institution. What does one really mean, for instance, when he says that the church can provide the preacher a home?

The Bible uses the word *home* in different senses. It may mean a domicile, it may mean one's genealogy (referring to one's house), it may mean those of the household including the domestic servants, or it simply may mean in our language sometime that one marries, and establishes a home. In that instance, we are talking about a marriage relation. If he means by *home* that relationship in which there is a father, a mother, or a husband and wife is a necessity, then in order to relieve a widow he would have to get her a husband. There is a great deal that needs to be done in defining particularly what an individual is talking about. A person can be relieved by providing him with the necessities without there being any such thing that we refer to as an organized home. This would not be a requirement at all. If one is in need of a place to live, to pillow his head, we would say in the relief of that individual that a house might be a necessity but that is a long way from saying what is often meant by the term *home.* An individual, therefore, needs to define his term and stay with the definition of that term in a given argument without shifting the meaning of the expression.

Now, whatever is involved in the term *relieve* with reference to a son or daughter or close relative in I Timothy 5 is that also which is involved with reference to the congregation, when the congregation has the responsibility. If the congregation has the responsibility of setting up an organized home in the sense that some brethren use the term, then a son or daughter has the same obligation with reference to a parent. It is obvious in that passage that this would be the case. But if a son or daughter may relieve a mother or father or some relative without organizing such a home it is shown, therefore, that such a home is not a necessity and, therefore, would not come under what brother Highers referred to as a necessary inference. This would be obvious, I think, in tracing out the obligation of the relatives with reference to that one in need and looking also at that which is the responsibility of the congregation.

# The Distinction Between Church Action and Individual Action

## By Johnny Ramsey

I know better now what Paul meant by "fear and trembling", and I hope that I can say some things that will be helpful. I don't want to presume upon you by writing into this subject assigned me some of the questions and Biblical points that you might suggest. I was assigned to discuss "What Does the Bible Teach on the Distinction Between Church Action and Individual Action or Does It Teach That There Is?" And to that I have addressed myself. In the beginning, God created the individual. Had the Heavenly Father deemed this arrangement sufficient, He would never have ordained marriage as the first divine institution. But the very fact that He set in motion the creation of woman, and subsequently, the home, is proof positive that the individual is not sufficient alone, and that the individual and marriage are not the same thing. This is a matter of distinction between one person and a divine institution.

Centuries later, even though the individual remained as a separate entity, and marriage, or the home, continued as a divine arrangement, God saw fit to establish, through His only begotten Son, another institution or organism. This divinely prescribed arrangement, mentioned by Jesus in Matthew 16:18, was, of course, the church. The individual was made in the image of God, but the church was built upon the foundation of Christ. And in Colossians chapter 1, we learn that Christ is the author of both the physical and spiritual creation, and that they both inhere in Him. Now, it doesn't take deep think-

---

JOHNNY RAMSEY—*Evangelist for the Westside congregation in Corsicana, Texas; frequent cotributor to the FIRM FOUNDATION; spent several years evangelizing in Australia.*

ing to come to the following conclusions: First, if the individual alone had been enough, God would never have established the church; Secondly, if the individual united in marriage could have sufficed in spirituality, God would never have needed to introduce the church of the Lord; Third, since both the individual and the relationship of marriage existed for many centuries prior to the giving of the church, it follows conclusively that there is a distinction between individual action, marital relations, and the activities of the called-out people belonging to Christ.

Let us notice another simple, yet clear-cut argument. For years, gospel preachers have told Sabbatarians that the very existence of the New Testament is indisputable proof that the Old Testament and its arrangement was not enough. We have also stressed that civil government is a divine institution. If the individual Christian can do everything God intended, why did the Eternal One establish the church and why did He ordain civil government? Incidentally, I have never heard it inferred that one individual alone forms our government; but I have read from my brethren the following statement, and I quote, "The individual is the church." We only need one passage of scripture to forever settle the fact that there is a distinction between church action and individual action. It is certainly true that the Bible only needs to state a single fact *once* to forever prove its accuracy.

In Matthew 18, in giving a plan of disciplinary action, the individual who has been wronged is first authorized to go personally to the offending brother and confront him individually. As a final resort, if the erring one has not repented, the matter is to be brought before the church. Surely, everyone can understand from this passage the distinction in church action and individual action; for Jesus was *not* saying, "Just tell it to yourselves." This indeed is the context that brings forth the familiar statement, "Where two or three are gathered together in my name, there am I in the midst of them" (Matthew 18:20).

Let us be very specific about this matter of distinguishing between the action of the individual and the church. Not only does the very existence of the New Testament argue for the abolishment of the Old Covenant as authority in religion (compare Jeremiah 31 and Hebrews 8), it also follows, as the night the day, that the very existence of the church of the Lord argues forcefully that the individual alone could not accomplish God's eternal purpose by himself (Ephesians 3:9-11). To state it Biblically and emphatically at the same time, we only need to quote Ephesians 3:21: "Unto God be glory in the church, by Christ Jesus, throughout all ages, world without end, Amen."

This whole discussion actually resolves itself with this straightforward question: "What does the New Covenant sealed by the blood of Christ (Matthew 26:28), authorize the individual to do?" And then, "What does this everlasting testament of our Lord (Hebrews 13:20) command the church to do?" If, in every single instance, we find the same exact pattern, we shall know that there is no distinction between church action and individual action. However, would it not be exceedingly strange if this were the case? We would naturally ask again, "If the individual functions in exactly the same areas the church operates, why did God establish the church at all?"

It is much like our question to the devotees of Mormonism: "If the Book of Mormon is just like the Bible, why did God endorse something redundant, superfluous, and a waste of money?" Truly, if we are complete in Christ, (Colossians 2:10), and fully endowed with a system of faith once for all time delivered (Jude, verse 3), there could be no valid purpose for these latter-day revelations. In like manner, the economy of God, the economy that knows no waste, would never have permitted the establishment of the church if the individual could have performed and functioned in every way our wise Designer requires. To say that the individual can do everything the church does and that there is no distinction between individual action and church action makes the church redundant, superfluous, unnecessary, and a waste. It does, in fact, impeach God's power and impugn His motives. It would place Him in the category of the latter-day revelation folk, who at the very best, waited eighteen centuries to introduce something totally unnecessary.

There is another passage that shows the distinction between church action and individual responsibility and endeavor. In I Timothy 5, writing to Timothy as he labors with the church of God in Ephesus, Paul was inspired to write that the church be not charged in a matter that was absolutely incumbent upon the individual. This was concerning a matter of caring for the needs of relatives that the church had no responsibility toward. No one can honestly read I Timothy 5:16 and then fail to comprehend the clear-cut distinction of church action and individual response. Note carefully these words: "If any man or woman that believeth hath widows, let them relieve them, and let not the church be charged, that it may relieve them that are widows indeed." When we compare the emphasis of Matthew 18 and I Timothy 5, we find that on one hand, the church could accomplish something the individual could not, and on the other hand, the individual Christian was charged with the responsibility that was not the task of the church. Verily, there is a distinction between individual action and church action.

The very nature of the New Testament church argues loudly for its distinctiveness and contrast to the individual, to business concerns or secular educational societies. The church of Christ is not in the entertaining, educating, body-building business. The church embraced in God's eternal purpose is pre-eminently a soul-saving organism. At times I have thought that some of us are somewhat akin to those who shouted, "Hosanna, save us, we pray," as Jesus triumphantly entered Jerusalem (Mark 11:9). The Savior greatly disappointed them, however, when they realized He had come to save them from sin and not the Romans. Is it not enough for us today, that the blood-bought church of the Lord offers salvation from sin and a closer spiritual walk with our Redeemer? It shall ever be pre-eminently true that the church is the pillar and support of the truth (I Timothy 3:15). The glory of Ephesus, where Timothy labored, was the beautiful marble temple erected to the worship of Diana. This wonder of the world had, as its major attraction, 127 marble pillars that formed a colonnade around the building. These pillars, donated by many earthly rulers, provided the glory of the building. Following this background, Paul tells us that the glory in the church is evinced in the bulwark of righteousness, the pillar and support of truth.

We find another very pertinent passage on our subject of distinction in church and individual actions in I Corinthians 11: 20-34. In this context, the inspired writer speaks of events that take place in the assembly, when the church comes together, and things that can best be done at home or in another sphere.

The very fact that Paul could send greetings to Priscilla and Aquilla and also to the church that is in their house (Romans 16:5) clearly manifests the realm of the individual, the home, and the church. From this passage alone, if language means anything at all, we see a clear distinction in the individual, the family unit, and the church.

The idea that no distinction whatsoever exists between church action and individual action even does violence to the logic of Acts 2:41 and 47. If the individual can function *alone*, in every way the church operates, why did the Lord add the saved individual to the church in the first place? The basic law of supply and demand would be violated if the individual can do everything the church can do.

Now then, let's be very practical. In my home town this past autumn, I coached a grade school football team. It was a golden opportunity for me to have an influence in the community as an individual, serving the Lord and striving to make an impact for good. Football is fun, the environment was wholesome, and the entire community was cordial toward our activities. Incidentally, we also won the city championship, and that made it even better! All of us will agree that, as an individual, I can perform in this capacity. But is there anyone who would affirm that the Lord's church can sponsor and support an athletic program? According to the New Testament, we would search in vain for such authorization. The church distinctively is in another kind of contest—a spiritual battle with Satan. It might be all right for you to purchase a ticket to see the ACC football team play Arlington State, but it would be totally unscriptural for the church of Jesus Christ to expend money for such things. There is a distinction between individual action and church action.

Even the United States government has in the past made a distinction in this regard. The government taxes me as an individual, but it does not tax the church. Jesus made it clear that there is a difference in the spiritual kingdom and civil government in Matthew 22:21 and John 18:36. In Romans 13, we read of another divine institution: civil government. Under the Old Testament economy, Jehovah ruled through a theocracy, a combination of spiritual-civil power. But in the gospel era, He separated these powers. Regardless of one's view of carnal warfare and a Christian's participation therein, we all must agree that there is a vast distinction between individual action and church action in regard to civil government. Even those who ardently believe that members of the church can bear arms and go forth in carnal combat to willfully slay the antagonist do not affirm that the church of Christ ought to train soldiers, buy uniforms, and supply ammunition for the front lines in Vietnam. In fact, brethren have awakened to the fact that where carnal combat wages, there we as the church ought to be with the gospel. Unless we are willing to have a "Church of Christ brigade" on the battlefield and make provisions for such in our church budgets, we must believe, regardless of our position on a Christian's responsibility to government, that there is a distinction between church action and individual action.

There are innumerable things that you can do that the church cannot do. Let us notice a few. First, you can spank your children in an act of discipline (Hebrews 12). But the church cannot inflict *physical* disciplinary action upon anyone (2 Corinthians 10:3, 5). Secondly, you can, as a responsible, able parent, buy ice cream for your children—or a bicycle. But the church has no authority to do so, for a responsible, able parent. Third, you can sell light bulbs in the neighborhood on behalf of some civic club. But this is certainly not permissible as a congregational activity. Fourth, you could raise money for the March of Dimes. But this is clearly out of the realm of church participation. There is a distinction between church action and individual action. Sixth, and I might add, a very important point, individually, you could endorse, support, and vote for a political candidate. But for the church of the Lord to do so would violate New Testament principles. Because of some over-zealous preachers, the church has become known in many areas as a mouthpiece for conservative republicanism. This hinders our ability to reach other precious souls, who are repulsed by that political stance. Let's leave the church in the soul-saving work God ordained. Seventh, you could be a member of the Lion's Club or your wife a leader in the Flower Club. But the church has no mandate from heaven allowing it to be so involved. Eighth, you can lead about a wife, but the church cannot (I Corinthians 9:5). Ninth, you can contribute to the building and maintenance of public highways. But the church paves the way to heaven. Tenth, you can support out of your pocket the

ACC sports program, but the divine church of Christ cannot. Eleventh, you can engage in bodily exercises (I Timothy 4:7). But it would not be Biblical for the assembly of the saints to begin with a calisthenics drill. There is a distinction between church action and individual action.

One of the most enlightening studies concerning the church revealed in the Bible is to discuss from a scriptural viewpoint just what the church is and what it is not. Negatively, according to the New Testament, the church is not a physical building. Christ died not for brick and mortar, wood or stone. The church is a spiritual house made up of living stones (I Peter 2:5f). The church is not a political regime (John 18:36). But it is a divine monarchy with Christ as king and a spiritual reign in the hearts and lives of men. The church is not a denomination where human doctrines find a haven of safety. It is composed of the called-out people that belong to Christ Jesus, with eternal ties of love. The church is an army with the Master as the captain of our salvation (Hebrews 2:10). It is the body of Christ, with the Redeemer as the head of the body (Colossians 1:18). Whoever heard of a body with just one member or an army with just one soldier? All of the figures of speech referring to the church bespeak concerted, united action, and not primarily individual action. These very illustrations of what the church is and what it is not boldly affirm the distinction between church action and individual action.

The individual often sustains relationships toward others that, by the very nature of those arrangements, prohibit the church to be similarly responsible. For instance, the passage in I Peter 3:1-7 informs Christian wives concerning their demeanor and influence before their unbelieving mates. This is such a personal, individual responsibility that the church could not be charged with the very same response. Likewise, in Ephesians 6:1-4, we are made keenly aware of our duties as parents in another divine institution, the home. It is the job of the husband and wife to provide for their offspring, to train them, educate them, entertain them, and provide medical attention when they skin their elbow or break a leg. But this is certainly not the reason Christ shed His blood to purchase the church. There is a distinction between individual responsibility, family duties, governmental allegiance, and church action.

In I Peter 2:13-17, we find a definite statement concerning the Christian's attitude and actions toward those who rule governmentally. First century brethren were taught to submit to the ordinances of the King and to honor the king. The individual member can pay homage to earthly rulers, but the church, especially in lands where the king or queen is also the head of the church, would have to be very careful not to leave the impression of obeisance to religious rule, since Christ is the King of our souls. In view of the emperor worship problem in the First Century, (see Revelation 2:13), there must have been a distinction in individual action and church action in the area of governmental allegiance and responsibility.

In your town or mine, the presence of beautiful, functional parklands can be a blessing to the pleasure of the community. As individuals, in view of our correct responsibilities and civic influence, we can assist in providing these programs or aiding them. But had the Lord intended the church to engage in such social amenities, the New Testament would have so informed us. The church, however, is pre-eminently a soul-saving, spiritually-enlightening organism. Children needed playgrounds in the first century. But Christ died to provide the church as the highway of holiness, so that even those who couldn't find a place to play could one day find a place in heaven. When we divert the energies and monies of the local congregation into welfare programs, we truly prostitute the purpose of the church of the Lord. We search in vain for Biblical authority for several projects brethren are pushing upon the church today. It might be good for individuals to build and maintain a rest station for winos on Skid Row, but the church my Lord died for is not an adjunct of Alcoholics Anonymous. The church, as bulwark of truth, is commanded to preach the only message calculated to convert such sinners. Why should we be diverted from a major thrust, which only God's church can espouse, the actual and absolute cure of all sins, by the perilous schemes of brethren who evidently have never learned the purpose and work of the church in the first place? You, as an individual, might see fit to serve on some committee to curb alcoholism, but the church of the Lord has a far greater, wider scope of service, on behalf of all derelicts and misfits; the salvation of their souls. There is a distinction between church action and individual action.

In Acts 14:27 as Paul and Barnabas returned from the first tour of evangelism to Antioch, the church that had sent them out, we learn that they gathered the church together and rehearsed all that God had done with them. The church had sent them out. Now the church is gathered together to learn of the progress of the work they had supported. The very fact that I Corinthians 16:1 and 2 refers to a collection, and thus a treasury, forever establishes a distinction between church action and individual responsibility. There is, of course, individual giving, to support the one who taught him (Galatians 6:6) and congregational giving to encourage gospel preaching (I Corinthians 9, and Philippians 1:5, and Philippians 4:15f). These passages prove that an individual might have a responsibility personally to a teacher that the church does not. There is a distinction, herein stated, between individual action and church action. Philemon, personally, had a responsibility to Onesimus that no church sustained, and Philemon owed Paul something, also, in a personal way.

In Acts 18:22, as Paul landed at Caesarea, he saluted the church before going to Antioch. Does anyone really think Paul personally greeted every individual member instead of the very apparent meaning of assembling with the church? In the little book of 3 John, we learn that the hospitality of Gaius, an individual member, had been brought before the church. Also, in the same epistle, John states, "I wrote unto the church, but Diotrephes, who loveth to have the pre-eminence among them, received us not. Wherefore if I come, I will remember his deeds which he doeth, prating against us with malicious words, and not content therewith; neither doth he himself receive the brethren, and forbiddeth them that would, and casteth them out of the church." This wording definitely makes a distinction between the individual and the church.

In I Corinthians 14, when the church comes together, verse 23, in assembly worship, Paul stated, "Yet in the church I had rather speak five words with my understanding, that by my voice I might teach others also" (verse 19). So there is even a distinction in the assembly between the whole congregation's actions and the individual response. In Revelation 3:4, we are apprised of the fact that even though a church may be considered corrupt, a few individuals within it may be pure, and thus escape the condemnation of God placed upon the congregation. This is an appropriate illustration Biblically of the distinction between the individuals who composed the church and the church itself.

Does not the language of I Corinthians 16:19 seem appropriate also? "The churches of Asia salute you. Aquila and Priscilla salute you much in the Lord, with the church that is in their house." If there is no distinction in church action and individual action, that verse is highly redundant, to say the least. The same can be said for Romans 16:1, "I commend unto you Phoebe, our sister, which is a servant of the church which is at Cenchrea." In Colossians 4:16, Paul wrote by inspiration, "And when this epistle is read among you, cause that it be read also in the church of the Laodiceans; and that ye likewise read the epistle from Laodicea." Could this verse have been fulfilled by just one member at Laodicea reading the epistle? If the "individual is the church" doctrine be true, who could deny it?

It might be all right for an out-doors-type Christian to engage in Boy Scout work, taking hikes, building fires, and tying knots, but the church of the Lord has no business entering that area of things. There is no scriptural backing for it. There must be a distinction between church action and individual action. Perhaps the real answer to the problem before us in this discussion is for each church, under the oversight of its elders, to be so busily engaged in the Master's work that the full talent of every member is developed, used, and activated. God would thus be glorified in the church (Ephesians 3:21), and we would have that peace that passeth understanding. "A charge to keep I have, a God to glorify, a never-dying soul to save, and fit it for the sky. To serve the present age, my calling to fulfill, oh, may it all my powers engage, to do my Master's will."

## Individual Action vs. Church Action

Floyd Thompson

The failure to recognize that God has assigned certain responsibilities to individuals that have not been assigned to the church is the source of some of our present problems. The loose thinking that is characterized by such statements as, "What the christian individual can do, the church can do," is but evidence that some study should be made on this subject. Although there are some things, I admit, that God has required of the church that are also required of an individual, it shall be my purpose in this lesson to point out certain actions where there is a difference.

God's wisdom made provisions for the person who would obey his law to live and perform in this world as a whole being. The way of life for a child of God embraces every righteous relationship into which he may come. The godliness enjoined upon individuals by the Lord is a godliness governing his life as a citizen of the kingdom of God and as a citizen of his country.

Let us point out a few passages of scripture where it is clearly seen that the church and the individual are separate

WILLIAM FLOYD THOMPSON—*One of the better known preachers on the West Coast; has lived in Santa Ana, California for the past thirty-four years serving only two congregations as evangelist during this period—Birch and Fairview in Santa Ana and Fairview (Berrydale) in Garden Grove; a debater and successful in gospel meeting work over a wide area.*

and distinct. During the personal ministry of the Lord he taught how one should act when a brother trespasses. He said, "Moreover if thy brother shall trespass against thee, go and tell him his fault between thee and him alone: if he shall hear thee, thou hast gained thy brother. But if he will not hear thee, then take with thee one or two more, that in the mouth of two or three witnesses every word may be established. And if he shall neglect to hear them, tell it unto the church; but if he neglect to hear the church, let him be unto thee as an heathen man and a publican" (Matthew 18:15-17). The Bible teaches, and common sense demands, that the body is made up of individual members. The Bible teaches and common sense also demands that they are not the same. "For the body is not one member, but many" (I Cor. 12:14). "Now ye are the body of Christ, and members in particular" (I Cor. 12:27). In perfect harmony with this teaching and that we may further see the distinction made in the church and the individual, Paul said, "In the name of our Lord Jesus Christ, when ye are gathered together, and my spirit, with the power of the Lord Jesus Christ, to deliver such an one unto Satan for the destruction of the flesh, that the spirit may be saved in the day of the Lord Jesus" (I Cor. 5:4-5). There are so many passages that one hardly knows where to stop. Let us look at one more. "But if I tarry long, that thou mayest know how thou oughtest to behave thyself in the house of God, which is the church of the living God, the pillar and ground of the truth" (I Tim. 3:15). In the light of these scriptures, if there are some who cannot see that there is a difference between the individual and the church, they can be described by these words, "For this people's heart is waxed gross, and their ears are dull of hearing, and their eyes they have closed. . . ."

Since the difference between the church and the individual christian has been clearly pointed out, let us continue and see some of the *actions* that God has enjoined upon the individual that are not enjoined upon the church.

In the case of Matt. 18:15-17 there is a distinct *action* prescribed by the Lord. The *action* is that that the Lord told the individual to perform, not the church. Here is a distinction between individual action and church action.

In the case of I Cor. 5, Paul gave instruction to the church to *act* with reference to the brother who was guilty of "having his father's wife." The church was to "deliver such an one to Satan. . . ." Here is a distinction between church action and individual action. In the case of I Tim. 3:15, to emphasize the point of my lesson, namely, the distinction between church action and individual action, can anyone think that Paul was giving instruction to Timothy how to behave himself within himself? Certainly not. So the distinction between church action and individual action is readily seen.

The distinction between church action and individual action can further be seen in the charge that God has given to a christian to work at some gainful occupation. "And that ye study to be quiet, and to do your own business, and to work with your own hands, as we commanded you" (I Thess. 4:11). "For even when we were with you, this we commanded you, that if any would not work, neither should he eat" (2 Thess. 3:10). "But if any provide not his own, and especially for those of his own house, he hath denied the faith and is worse than an infidel" (I Tim. 5:8). Anyone who has any respect for God's word knows that these commandments are to individuals and not to the church as such. This is the distinction between church action and individual action.

The writer of the Hebrew letter said, "Marriage is honorable in all, and the bed undefiled. . . ." Heb. 13:4. Is this a home relationship or a church relationship? To ask the question is to answer it. God has made provision for a man to live with his wife. Has God made provision for the church to live with that man's wife? How thoughtless and foolish it is for someone to say, "What an individual can do, the church can do." You can see the distinction between church action and individual action.

God said, "Let every soul be subject unto the higher powers" (Romans 13:1). Does anyone think that the body of Christ, head and all, is to be subject unto civil government? God enjoins such upon the individuals who make up the church, but not on the church as such.

We should not overlook the obligation enjoined upon an individual by Paul when he said, "If any man or woman that believe have widows, let them relieve them, and let not the church be charged; that it may relieve them that are widows indeed"

(I Tim. 5:16). Here is a case where the Lord told an individual to do a work, and told the church not to do that work. Here is the distinction between church action and individual action!

If it is scriptural for a christian to work with his hands and to provide, (and it is. To this all agree. I Thess. 4:11, I Tim. 5:8) . . . If it is scriptural for a christian to buy and sell, and get gain, (and it is. To this all agree. James 4:13-15) . . . I wonder why someone does not come up with the scripture that authorizes the church to buy and sell and get gain. If it should be suggested that "the scripture just is not there," to this I will agree. I must then ask why some brethren continue to insist that it is scriptural for the church, through elders, to oversee a project that involves growing crops and selling them, raising cattle and selling them, buying farm equipment, hiring farmers, etc., and calling that the work of the church. When a denominational preacher cannot give book, chapter and verse for what the practices, we ask him to cease the practice and join hands with us on a "thus saith the Lord." Is it too much to ask brethren, who cannot give book, chapter and verse for their practice, to cease the practice and join hands with us on the Bible?

I was deeply impressed by a statement made by a brother who wrote concerning " 'Our' Institutions." He said, "Brethren should recognize that in setting up any program, institution, or private enterprise, whether benevolent or missionary, that they are our own private creations. They did not come from heaven and are not going there." (And may I ask, if they are not going to heaven, pray tell, where are they going, and would you suggest going with them?) He continues, "If others do not see fit to support them no one should feel that his sacred cow has been kicked. We keep hearing of reports of congregations being asked why they did not support this or that project." He said further, "All should remember that none of them have any more sacredness than their purely human originators can bestow upon them." This writer surely must see clearly the distinction between church action and individual action, for he wrote again about one of "our" institutions and said, "Two kinds of contributions are needed: (1) the regular contributions of congregations who want to cooperate in this good work, and (2) a few sizeable gifts from individuals. . . ."

The distinction between church action and individual action is seen in Phil. 4:15, 16. "Now ye Philippians know also, that in the beginning of the gospel, when I departed from Macedonia, no church communicated with me as concerning giving and receiving, but ye only. For even in Thessalonica ye sent once and again unto my necessity." One can clearly see that the *action* of the church was to send. The action of the individual was to receive. In this way they had fellowship in the gospel. You can see the distinction between church action and individual action.

Because James 1:26, 27 has so often been used to encourage *church action* we should read and notice it carefully. "If any man among you seem to be religious, and bridleth not his tongue, but deceiveth his own heart, this man's religion is vain. Pure religion and undefiled before God and the Father is this, To visit the fatherless and widows in their affliction, and to keep himself unspotted from the world." Notice. "If *any man* (an individual) among you (the group) seem to be religious, and bridleth not *his* (the individual's) tongue, but deceiveth *his* (the individual's) own heart, *this man's* (the individual's) religion is vain. Pure religion and undefiled before God and the Father is this, To visit the fatherless and the widows in their affliction, and to keep *himself* (the individual) unspotted from the world." Clearly this is *individual action*. To use this passage to encourage church action is a perversion of the text.

A venerable gospel preacher was asked, "Should the church help only the needy saints who have no relatives?" Reply was made in these words. "We easily fall into error when we consider only part of the evidence. If you were to find a man in a ditch, would you wait to see whether or not he had any relatives? If you were to find a man starving and helpless, would you refuse to help him till you found out whether he had relatives, or was even a saint? Paul says: 'So then, as we have opportunity, let us work that which is good toward all men, and especially toward them that are of the household of faith.' (Gal. 6:10). To help the famine sufferers in Judea, the disciples at Antioch, 'every man according to his ability, determined to send relief unto the brethren that dwelt in Judea; which also they did, sending it to the elders by the hand of Barnabas and Saul.' (Acts 11:29, 30). At a later date, when another famine spread over Judea, Paul made a great effort to collect a large amount for the poor saints in Judea (see I Cor. 16:1-4; 2 Cor. 8:1-24; 9:1-5; Rom. 15:25-28). "Let him that stole steal no more: but rather let him labor, working with his hands the thing that is good, that he may have whereof to give to him that hath need." (Eph. 4:28). Emergencies come up in which the most able-bodied men need temporary help. A great storm sweeps through a community, leaving the best of people maimed and destitute of life's necessities. It would be heartless to let them perish while you hunted around to see whether there were any relatives left to help them. In I Tim. 5:1-16, Paul had in mind the rendering of permanent and continued help to certain widows. The widow must be of a certain character, and without relatives to aid her; otherwise the church would not be warranted in assuming her entire support. If she have relatives and they will not help her, they have denied the faith and are worse than infidels. But when an emergency arises in which people need help, whether they be saints or sinners, the Christain will help them." This brother saw the distinction between church action and individual action, as evidenced by the expressions, "If *you* were to find a man starving, and helpless, would *you* refuse to help him....?" "You" are not the church. Now note that the brother uses the expression, "... otherwise the church would not be warranted...." Note again the contrast, "But when an emergency arises in which people need help, whether they be saint or sinner, *the Christian* will help them." "The Christian" is not the church. Therefore, the distinction between church action and individual action is recognized.

Since we are exhorted by the Lord to "... walk by the same rule ..." (Phil. 3:16), and since "the same rule" makes a distinction between church action and individual action, let us all respect "the same rule" and honor its teachings by strict obedience and firm adherence thereto.

Since "all scripture is given by inspiration of God, and is profitable for doctrine, for reproof, for correction, for instruction in righteousness: that the man of God may be perfect, thoroughly furnished unto all good works," let us be careful to perform only such actions, whether they be church actions or individual actions, as are authorized by God's word. On this and this alone can we march as a mighty army, with Jesus Christ as our captain, against the forces of evil.

"Now I beseech you, brethren, by the name of our Lord Jesus Christ, that ye all speak the same thing, and that there be no divisions among you; but that ye be perfectly joined together in the same mind and in the same judgment" (I Cor. 1:10).

## *Individual Action vs. Church Action*

### Jimmy Allen

Brethren Thompson and Ramsey each presented excellent papers concerning the differences between church action and individual action. Personally, I found very little in their speeches with which I differ. It would seem that almost anyone would be able to see the differences between the two. However, I do not believe the questions I raised this morning were answered in either speech. Here are those three questions again: How do you establish authority for congregational practice? How do you establish authority for individual practice? Are there any differences between the two? If differences do exist, please point them out for my benefit.

I do not believe anything an individual may do, the local church may do. Furthermore, I don't recall having ever talked with a brother who took that position without any qualification at all. Yet, all of us seem to have difficulty determining the difference between the two actions insofar as establishment of authority is concerned.

Now please look to the blackboard that I may further illustrate what I had in mind in raising these three questions this morning. First, let us think about the area of teaching. We all know that the Lord expects a New Testament church to teach the word of God. Here is a local church discharging its responsibility to teach the gospel (draws square on board). Here is a college (draws second square on board). [It may be ACC, Harding and Florida College. There are men from all these schools present.] By means of congregational arrangement or organization the word of God is taught. However, in the three

---

JIMMY H. ALLEN—*Professor of Bible, Harding College, Searcy, Arkansas; preacher for one of the congregations in Searcy; widely known as a speaker in cooperating evangelistic campaigns throughout the nation.*

colleges already mentioned the gospel of Christ is also taught. The colleges are not locally organized churches. They are separate organizations but they teach the Bible. Brethren Cogdill and Nichols dealt with this in the same way. Each one said that a Bible teacher in a college is doing that work as an individual. Really, I knew and understood that already. With all due respect to both of these brethren, I feel that they have not answered my question yet. I am asking someone to tell me from a Bible point of view why it is right for a group of individuals to teach God's truth through the college organization and wrong for the church to do the same thing. Where is the command, example or necessary inference for an individual to teach Bible by means of the organization which characterizes ACC, Harding and Florida College? We say a local church cannot support such an arrangement but individuals can. If this is true, obviously we establish authority for individual practice and church practice in two different ways. The individual does not need the same type of authority as does the church. Actually, we are saying the Lord is stricter with the congregation than He is with the individual. Frankly, I do not believe that we have ever really dealt with this most fundamental question in attempting to resolve our differences. At least it has not been dealt with to my satisfaction.

Now, please consider the benevolent responsibility of the church with me. Here is the structure, the local church (draws square on board). For the sake of argument let us momentarily assume that James 1:27 is limited to the individual. As long as we take the view that James 1:27 is an individual obligation, most of us can see the charter, board of directors and superintendent as a part of the arrangement necessary to take care of homeless children. Brethren, why? Because we read James 1:27! Just from that one verse most of us here see all of the organization I have mentioned because we apply the passages to the individual. If one proves that James 1:27 (or a similar passage) can apply to the local church, don't you see that *same* organization would be justified although church supported? Whatever arrangement one gets from the passage in applying it to the individual would also be justified in applying it to the church.

At Harding College we have a Bible department. It is composed of a department head, ten or twelve teachers, a secretary and a curriculum. When our people look at that, they generally justify it by saying it is individually supported. They see the whole organization as long as only the individual is in the picture. However, they go blind when you say church. A similar reaction is produced in some when discussing the structure of Southern Christian Home. Brethren, it is apparent that we have sought one kind of authority for individual endeavor and another kind for church action.

Brother Cogdill said this morning that nine-tenths of the Christian school is secular. I don't share that point of view. How in the name of common sense can a Dallas brother justify giving $200,000 to Abilene Christian College for that which is mostly a secular pursuit? How can I ask a Christian to give $10,000 to Harding College if nine-tenths of it goes into secular work? Surely, he ought to be urged to give it all to the cause of Christ. Brethren, if what I am doing at Harding College is not advancing the cause of Christ, I am ready to get out. Brother Thompson and Brother Ramsey a number of times said in essence, "You can do this as an individual, but the church can't do it." I heard that repeatedly but I did not get the scripture to uphold it. Of course, the Bible was used to show that church action was one thing and individual action another. However, the difference as to how to establish authority for each was never set forth. Johnny Ramsey and I stand identified with the same group. Several times he said you can do this individually, but the church cannot do it. Over and over again I put down a question mark. Why, brethren, why?

I close with this question: To what may I contribute financially in the discharge of my Christian duty that the church may not also contribute? Really, I would like to see that question answered. I believe this is the crux of the whole issue - - - establishing authority for individual practice, establishing authority for church practice, and noticing the differences between the two. As I see it now, I must conclude that the church may support the Bible department at Harding College, or else take the position of Brother Daniel Sommer and say that our Bible department is a sinful organization.

## Church Action vs. Individual Action

### By Harry Pickup, Jr.

I want to join with the other speakers in expressing my appreciation for the opportunity to be here. I think a good part of our present difficulties has to do with definition of terms. The terms that we use do not mean the same to all and are not understood by all.

Much of what has been said here everyone is in agreement with. This was also very true at our first meeting at Buchanan Dam. While we have spoken here of differences, in my judgment, we have not yet come to focus our attention sharply and clearly on distinctions between us. Such would not destroy the spirit of our meeting.

As I sit here and listen to the various speakers "among you" I am conscious of the fact that you feel toward "us" as I feel toward the "non-Bible class brethren." You believe that we are insisting upon detailed and specific patterns for your practices when you have generic authority for them. I do not believe that we have ever insisted upon such from you.

---

HARRY PICKUP JR.—*Evangelist for congregation in St. Petersburg,*

*Florida; associated with the department of publications in Florida College, Temple Terrace, Florida; writer for* **THE PRECEPTOR;** *widely used throughout the nation in gospel meetings.*

On the other hand I feel toward "you" as I do toward Dr. DeGroot of TCU, for example, who claims to believe the Scriptures are our authority but who makes no or poor application of them. And such attitudes involve our definition of terms.

I think either poor or no definition of terms is one of the factors which contributes to brother Allen's confusion in trying to decide why Christians may support a college where the Bible is taught but the "local church" may not.

When you talk about the "work of the church," what do you mean by it? The word "church"—ecclesia—is used in several different ways in the New Testament scriptures. I may not give a perfect category of its uses but I want to try. First, it is used to refer to the results of the deliberate actions of God—the realm of salvation (Eph. 3:10). It is something which God deliberately purposed; that through which His manifold wisdom is made known.

Secondly, it is used to refer to all the people of God without regard to time or place. "The church of the first born ones." "The general assembly" (Heb. 12:23). Thirdly, it is used to refer to God's people in a given locality. "The church throughout all Judea and Galilee and Samaria had peace" (Acts 9:31). Fourth, it is used to refer to people who are physically assembled. "Saul and Barnabas were gathered together for a whole year in the church and taught much people" (Acts 11:26). Fifth, it is used to refer to a body of people in a given locality who work together personally and individually as a body (Phil. 4:15).

When some one of "you" speaks of an organization doing the "work of the church," what does he mean by "church"? Does he simply mean people who are Christians? Or, does he mean a body of Christians other than the "local church" organized to act in the same way for the same purposes as the "local church"?

When some one of "us" speaks about "church action versus individual action" "we" may be misunderstood to view the church as something apart from individual Christians. Are "you" assuming that "we" mean the church is something apart from Christians? Or, when we talk about the individuals doing something, as opposed to the church acting, do you think that we are talking about people doing something who are not at the time in the church? Well, if you do, we are not getting our message over. We are not getting through to you and you are not getting through to us.

Here are a couple of examples of "the church at work." (1) The first is mentioned in I Cor. 5. Paul had received instructions from Christ through the revelation of the Holy Spirit. Paul then delivered them to the church in Corinth. He commanded all the brethren to come to a meeting of minds and to act together in withdrawing from the fornicator.

(2) In Philippians 2 we learn that Epaphroditus was selected by that church to act as their "minister" to Paul. The Greek word for "minister" here means "one who is a representative servant; one who acted on behalf of the public."

When I hear one of "you brethren" talk about the "work of the church" being done by an organization other than the church, I wonder what he means by the term "church"?

When we criticize "you brethren" for teaching and doing things which, in principle, allow the whole church to work collectively, you tell us we misunderstand you and are not justified in our criticism.

I do not see how we are guilty of misunderstanding you when a brother "among you" writes on institutionalism as a basic problem and speaks about organizations doing "the work of the church" but which are neither "the church" nor are they under the eldership of a church. I say if this is right, then this would allow the whole church to be organized so as to act collectively.

By all means let us define the phrase, "work of the church." And, all parts of it. Let us come to grips with it sharply and clearly. Then, we can get somewhere.

When I speak of the "work of the church" I do not mean something done by an organization apart from individual Christians. I don't mean something that is done apart from people acting as Christians. I mean something done by the "local church"—Christians acting as a body, personally and individually.

Christians in their individual capacities are authorized to do some things. There is some over-lapping in these matters.

And, there are some things in which there is a clear distinction. For example: the college which teaches the Bible is something which Christians may support, but which the church is not authorized to support.

That there are other organized relationships authorized to teach the Bible is clear from the instructions given to parents. The home is charged with rearing children—and, doing so "in the nurture and admonition of the Lord." This involves the collective function of teaching the word of God to those who are in the family. The home isn't the college; neither is it the church.

The church—God's people—engage in various matters which are clearly not within the sphere of authorized "action of the church"—the congregation; a body of Christians acting collectively. I Corinthians 7 discusses three of them. Note that this book is addressed to the "church of God which is at Corinth."

Three times in this chapter Paul writes essentially the same thing: in whatsoever relationship one is when he is called to be a Christian (of course, that relationship being right), in that relationship let him "abide with God" (cp. verses 17, 20 and 25). These relationships are: marriage, nationality or governmental and social or economic.

The meaning is clear: if a Christian is married let him live in it as a Christian should. If one is either a Jew or Gentile let him serve his nation as a Christian. If one is either a servant or a freeman, let him so live as a Christian.

This book is addressed to "the church." This part of it is clearly applicable to "individuals" and other parts are clearly applicable to "the church"—Christians acting as a body. A body of people viewed collectively cannot be married. A body has no nationality and is neither a "servant" nor "freeman."

When I distinguish between "church and individual action," I am not suggesting that a Christian does some things as a Christian and some things not as a Christian.

When I hear brethren speak of "one church playing basketball"—or some other action which does not grow out of one's relationship to Christ—I believe them to be either unaware of the above discussed distinctions or, else unconcerned about maintaining it. They sound to me as though they believe this is a "work of the church."

I have read from a brother, whom I believe has an institutional concept of the church, that Paul and Barnabas constitute an evangelistic team, an organization, which is not a congregation. He admits that this "organization" is not a "local church" but that it is in "the church." If Christians may organize to do the "work of the church" and yet not be the "local church", why may not the whole church be organized?

The church is said to be "the pillar and ground of the truth." The Thessalonian church served as such when they "sounded forth the word of the Lord." In so doing the church is charged with teaching everything the Bible teaches on any subject. Whatever the relationship—marital, national or social—the church must teach all that the Bible says on the subject. While it is not charged with improving the relationships as such, it is charged with teaching Christians their obligations "abiding (in them) with God."

Responsibility grows out of relationship. The responsibility of "the local church"—Christians in a given locality who act as a body—grows out of their relationship to God. This involves things inherent in matters spiritual. The same body of people also have responsibility to men because of human relationships. This involves things inherent in matters of the flesh; such as those in the family, in the nation and in society.

How may a church act collectively and act so as to be distinct from individual duty? It acts collectively when the whole body of people personally participates in the action. Thus the whole body of Corinthians were instructed to have no "brotherly associations" with the fornicator. Another example is when the whole church chose the seven men mentioned in Acts 6.

The church acts collectively through its chosen representatives, such as Epaphroditus, who was the agent and representative of the Philippian church in assisting Paul (Phil. 2:25).

"Church work" is distinct from "individual work" in that the former's duties grow out of relationship peculiar to Christ and the latter's duties grow out of relationship peculiar to man.

## Individual Action vs. Church Action

### H. A. "Buster" Dobbs

I join with those who have preceded me in expressing appreciation for the attitude that prevails, and for the opportunity of meeting with you and discussing some things that trouble us. I believe that we have proven we can disagree without being disagreeable. To me that is one of the most satisfactory things about this meeting. I confess to you—and I don't mind this being on the tape and appearing in the book—I have not always been as agreeable as I ought to have been in discussing matters of disagreement. To be here in this atmosphere, with the attitude of Christian love prevailing, and being able to look one another straight in the eye, and say, "We are not agreed on this point, and here is why we do not agree," is to me a marvelous thing. And so I am glad to have an opportunity to make some few comments on the question of individual and church action.

I am not going to undertake, and do not presume that I would have the ability, to answer all of Jimmy Allen's questions. I don't know that all his questions can be answered. There are some questions that are unanswerable. In addressing myself to his questions, I invite your attention to the blackboard. I want to draw a few circles. Now drawing circles is dangerous because sometimes it gets in the way of expressing the very thoughts we are trying to present, and sometimes it implies something we do not intend to say. Nevertheless, I am going to run the risk, and put a few circles on the board. These circles represent various relationships in life. We have our church relationship, our family relationship, our business relationship, our civic and community relationship. There may be

---

H. A. (BUSTER) DOBBS—*Evangelist of Memorial congregation, Houston, Texas; debater; editor of* "THE ANCHOR"—*religious periodical published in Houston.*

some other relationships, but I am going to talk briefly about these four.

Each one of these is an institution. The church is an institution. If you are a member of the church, you are a member of an institution. The family is an institution. If you have business involvements, the business is an institution. Civic undertakings and community projects are institutions. The nation itself is an institution. So, whether you like it or not, you are in many institutions, and we are all institutionally minded. And this business of talking about the "institutional brethren" as if some within the body of Christ are involved in institutional undertakings, and others are not, is a contradiction in terms. Whether you ever contribute a dime to orphan homes, or believe in cooperation between congregations for evangelism, you are involved in institutions and you are institutionally minded.

We participate in these various relationships by varying authority. The authority that controls in the relationship of the church is God's word—we established that on the opening day of this discussion, when brother Cogdill and brother Thomas very effectively discussed how authority is established. When we get over into the relationship of the home, we may have a different authority. Not everything that an individual does in the home is necessarily authorized in the New Testament. The same thing is true of business; the same thing is true of community undertakings.

In some of these relationships, the authority is general, and much of it is nothing more than sanctified common sense. It would be nice if we could stop here. We would have all of these nice, neat divisions, but it doesn't work that way! It's not that easy! Not by a long shot! We have overlapping interests between these various relationships, and that's where the difficulty begins to come in.

The Bible gives certain commands to the husband in the family, and places him under peculiar obligations that are not incumbent upon all other male members of the church. And yet the Bible does not specify everything with regard to the family relationship. The Bible does not specify, for instance, secular education for children. And yet, you and I know that it is necessary to provide our children with secular education. We give them secular education because it is the thing to do. We give them secular education because sanctified common sense demands it, and not because the scriptures require us to do it. The family is also, in the field of education, under pressure from the community. The Mennonites found that out recently when they attempted not to send their children to school. The state stepped in and said, "You must!" So we find the family obliged to do certain things because of the relationship it sustains to the community. And you have overlapping.

The same thing is true of a man's business. Because he is a Christian, he operates his business according to Christian principles. He is honest in his business. He has to represent things as they are. There are many things with regard to the operation of a business that the New Testament doesn't say anything about. There are some things with regard to the operation of a business one must do because of the demands of the community, like filing an income tax report, for instance. That is neither here nor there with reference to Christian teaching, except that he must file the thing as it is—he must not misrepresent.

We have all these relationships, and an individual is involved in many different relationships; and all of them are tugging at him and pulling at him and demanding certain things of him. In the area of his church relationship, the Christian is governed by God's Word—what it explicitly requires. But in the other relationships, he may do those things that the New Testament does not expressly prohibit—like spanking his kids or providing them with secular education.

It is in the family relationship, Jimmy, that the Christian College is established. Regardless of what percentage of the education offered in a Christian College is secular, the purpose is to provide some secular education to fit the student for a place in society. It is not set up to fit him for work in the church exclusively, is it? The Christian College is an adjunct to the home and not an adjunct to the church. That's the reason why the home supports it, and the church does not.

All of these institutions are made up of individuals. The church is made up of individuals. When we talk about the church, we are not talking about bricks and wood and mortar and stone, but we are talking about living souls built up a spiritual house. When we talk about a family, we are not talking about the dwelling place. We are talking about the relationship of individuals in a unit of society. When we talk about a business, we are not necessarily talking about the location or the shop, but the owner and the employees within that business also are a part of the business. And, obviously, the community is made up of individuals. We have individuals involved in all of these relationships.

How much time do I have? (A scanty three minutes.) All right, thank you.

I want to talk about James 1:27 briefly because I believe this is an area where we have been troubled. We have gone to the New Testament, and wherever we have found personal pronouns, we have said that because the personal pronoun is used, the individual is therefore addressed, and not the church. If I understood you, brother Thomas, that's what you said today.

Brethren, the fact of the matter is the New Testament uses personal pronouns in addressing the church. For instance, Revelation chapter two, verses 7, 11, 17 and 29; "He that hath an ear, let him hear . . ." (Those are personal pronouns, "he", "him"); "*He* that hath an ear, let *him* hear what the Spirit saith unto the *church*." The personal pronoun is used, but the church is addressed.

The fact that the personal pronoun "himself" is used in James 1:27 by no means forces the conclusion that it is exclusively individual and the church is not included.

The church is made up of individuals, and the only way you can address the church is to address the individual! The church must sing in worshipping God, but who is commanded to sing? Why, the individual is! Where is the verse commanding the church to sing? Again, the church is commanded to give on the first day of the week. But who is commanded to do the giving? The individual is! Bring a verse of scripture where the church is commanded to give. I Corinthians 16:1, 2—listen to this—"As I gave order unto the churches of Galatia (the command is to churches), so also do ye (individual). Upon the first day of the week let each one of you (individual) lay by him (individual) in store, as he (individual) may prosper, that no collections . . ." All right, Paul was telling the church what to do, but the command was addressed to the individual.

The command must be addressed to the individual. The command in Galatians 6:10 is addressed to the individual but that does not preclude the possibility of the command requiring church action. The command of James 1:27 is addressed to the individual. Yes! Of course, it is, but that fact does not justify the conclusion that the church is excluded from the command. Thank you, brethren.

## Individual Action vs. Church Action

### James W. Adams

I hope I shall have time to discuss the two charts I have planned to present. They were originally presented as a part of three lectures on "Human and Divine Organizations" which I delivered last week at *Florida College*. Their use was preceded by a lengthy lecture on the contrast between human and Divine organizations.

I do not believe there is any organization which is strictly Divine except the Godhead. In this speech, I shall be using the expression "Divine organization", not in the foregoing sense, but in an accomodative sense. I shall be using it to signify an organization *Divinely authorized*. Such organizations as we shall notice are both *human* and *Divine*. They are human in that they are made up of, established by, and sustained by humans.

Please observe *Chart No. I*. At its top, note the title, *"Human Service Organizations Divinely Authorized."* In an earlier speech, *Brother Jimmy Allen* asked how we justify, by the word of God, individual support of colleges (established and

---

JAMES W. ADAMS—*Evangelist Mound and Starr congregation, Nacog-*

*doches, Texas. Front page writer for* THE PRECEPTOR.

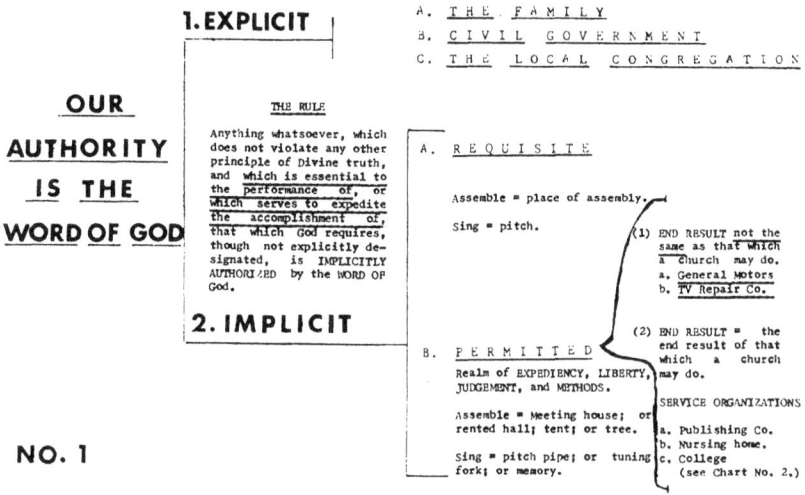

NO. 1

operated by Christians and in which the Bible is taught) while rejecting church support of the same organizations. This speech is intended as an answer to brother Allen's question. I regard colleges (such as those described) as *service organizations*, and I propose to prove they are Divinely authorized. The two charts which I present are to illustrate my argument.

On the far left side of *Chart No. I* can be seen the statement *"Our Authority is The Word of God."* In previous sessions in this discussion, it has developed that all of us here are of one mind in accepting the word of God—the Bible—as our authority, hence this point may be assumed in my speech and not argued. My remarks will have to do with how I find authorization in the Scriptures for such organizations as I defend and support.

There are two kinds of authority indicated on the chart by the terms *"EXPLICIT"* and *"IMPLICIT."* Most brethren employ instead the terms "specific" and "generic," but I prefer the terms on the chart. They may not be preferable to you, but they are more meaningful to me. These terms first came to my attention in a book against the use of mechanical instruments of music in Christian worship written by *Professor John Girardeau*, a learned Presbyterian.

By "explicitly authorized," I mean that the thing under consideration is authorized by the Bible in so many words. Since I am discussing organizations, it should be noted that for them to be explicitly authorized, they must be mentioned specifically. There are only three earthly organizations known to me which are explicitly authorized by the word of God—*the family, civil government,* and *the local congregation.* These I consider to be *Divine* because they are explicitly authorized by the word of God, hence they are placed on the chart opposite the term "explicit."

Next observe on the chart the term "implicit." I mean by this that many things are authorized by the word of God which are not specifically mentioned in the Scriptures either by *command* or in connection with an *approved apostolic example.* They are implicitly authorized because they are clearly implied by something that is said or which may be legitimately inferred therefrom. They are included in that which is explicitly authorized, though they are not mentioned in so many words.

Note *the rule* which is basic to my reasoning in this matter: "Anything whatsoever, which does not violate any other principle of Divine truth, and *which is essential to the performance of,* or *which serves to expedite the accomplishment of,* that which God requires, though not EXPLICITLY designated, is IMPLICITLY AUTHORIZED by the WORD OF GOD." I consider this rule axiomatic. I think all of us accept it as being true. I believe, on the basis of my study of brother Thomas' book, *"We Be Brethren,"* that he accepts it, though he probably states it differently.

Note on the chart to the right of the term "implicit": *A. Requisite,* and B. *Permitted.* The term "requisite" has to do with the first statement of our rule; namely, that which is *essential* to the performance of something which is specifically or *explicitly* authorized. The term "permitted" has to do with the second part of the rule; namely, that which may not be absolutely essential to the performance of the thing explicitly authorized but which *expedites* its accomplishment.

Let us consider *the requisite.* I have noted two examples on the chart: (1) the command to assemble, and (2) the requirement to sing. In order for us to obey the command to assemble, we *m*ust have a *place* of assembly. A place is requisite. We cannot assemble without assembling in some place, not any particular place, but some place. In order for us to fulfill the requirement to sing, we must have pitch. One cannot sing without pitch; it is therefore requisite, absolutely essential.

Now observe Item B. Incidentally, this is where our "service organizations" are to be classified and where I am going to answer brother Allen's question. This has to do with the *"permitted."* It is my contention that service organizations belong in this realm. There are some things which a Christian or a church *may* do (are Divinely authorized), yet they are, at the same time, things which neither the Christian nor a church is *obligated* to do. Relative to the Christian, there are numerous examples of this fact. He may marry, or he may live a celibate life. He may eat meat, or he may not eat meat. He may make tents in order to preach the gospel, or he may be supported by the churches. Paul himself makes these very points. Hence my contention is Scripturally valid. The Christian has the right to do many things which he does not have the obligation to do.

In the apostolic age, the foregoing principle was recognized in the selling of houses and lands and contributing the proceeds for the care of the poor. In the case of Ananias and Sapphira (Acts 5), as long as the house or the money from its sale was in their possession, it was recognized as being theirs to give or not to give as they saw fit. They had the right to give all of the money from the sale of the house, or a part of it. They were not condemned for giving only a part of the money. They were condemned for lying. They desired the name and credit for generosity without having to make the sacrifice to deserve it. In many areas, there are things the Christian has the right to do but not the obligation to do them.

It is my contention that the area of *the permitted* is the realm of "expediency," and it is so noted on the chart. This is the realm of "liberty." This is the realm of "judgment." Brethren are so confused about expediency. Many try to justify their practice by what they call "the law of expediency." But expediency only operates in the realm of *the permitted*, the lawful. It does not determine legality.

Let it be observed that, in the realm of *the requisite*, noted on the chart under A., we have no liberty. We are not permitted to exercise judgment. *The permitted* is the realm of liberty and judgment. Consider again the command to assemble. A place of assembly is requisite. The particular kind of place is in the realm of the permitted. It is a matter of human choice, and is in the realm of liberty. We may have a meeting house purchased with church funds, or we may meet in a rented hall or under a tree. The particular place of assembly is determined by what may be expedient at any given place or time. All of these places are authorized by the word of God. None is authorized to the exclusion of the others.

To obey the command to sing, we must have pitch. This is *requisite*. However, how we obtain the pitch is in the realm of *the permitted*. We may memorize the pitch of each song. We may memorize middle C and work from it. We may use a pitch pipe or a tuning fork. Any of these may be used because this is the realm of choice. It is the realm of liberty, human judgment, expediency, and method.

Now let us move to the far right side of the chart (No. 1.) and within the brace note two different kinds of organizations which exist in the realm of the permitted. May I digress momentarily to point out that the terms "organization," "institution," and "human" as applied to the two former terms are often used by brethren to signify something bad. This is not necessarily correct. A thing is not wrong simply because it is an organization or an institution, nor is it wrong because it is a *human* organization or institution. The thing which determines whether an organization or institution is wrong is the *kind* of organization or institution it is. A human organization can be bad—a thing forbidden by GOD. It is bad if it is in *no sense* authorized by the word of God, either explicitly or implicitly, to the individual or to the church. If it is bad in this sense, there is no way to make it good.

Now, let us return to the chart. Note the two types of organizations, (1) There are organizations the *END RESULTS* of the activities of which are not the same as that which the church of the Lord may do. I have listed two examples on the chart which apply in the matter of a man's duty to provide a living for his family. He may go to work for *General Motors*, thus becoming an integral part of a human organization. On the other hand, he may establish his own *TV Repair Company*, or involve himself in any number of other human organizations. The New Testament requires that he "provide for his own." (I Tim. 5:8.) In obeying this Divine requirement, he may utilize the aforementioned human organizations. It is Scriptural for him to do so. Though human in one sense, they are Divine in another—they are authorized by God in the realm of things permitted. But these are things which a church *does not do*, hence things about which we are not particularly concerned in this discussion.

Brother Jimmy Allen's question, which I am attempting to answer, involves point (2) within the brace on the right side of the chart; namely, organizations the *END RESULTS* of the activities of which are things that *a church may also do*. This brings me in my presentation to the realm of "service organizations." To illustrate my position it will now be necessary for me to introduce *Chart No. 2*.

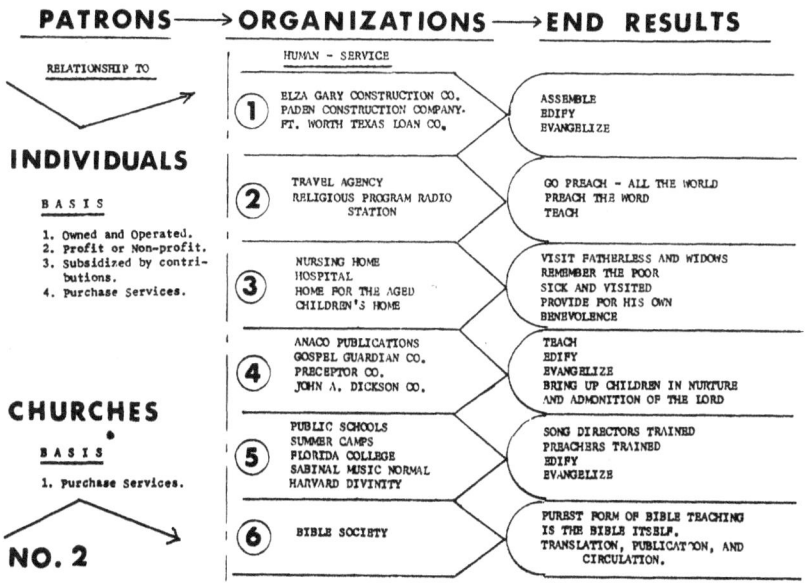

Let it be observed that not all the brethren with whom I stand identified relative to the issues which are the occasion of this meeting will accept my analysis of this proposition. There is some disagreement among us about the matter just as there is among you. This presentation is my personal answer to brother Allen's question. This is how I justify the existence and operation by Christians of a college in which the Bible is taught.

With this in mind, observe the chart. At the top, note three headings: PATRONS; ORGANIZATIONS; AND END RESULTS. I shall be dealing with the patron's relationship to the organizations. The organizations are all of the human service variety operated by Christians (in most cases). By end results, I mean the absolute end. To say "result" is not enough. I am dealing with the *ultimate results of an organization's existence* and function.

Under PATRONS are listed both INDIVIDUALS and CHURCHES. Under ORGANIZATIONS are listed many different human, service organizations. I have tried to divide them into categories as accurately as possible, because they are not all alike. I do not necessarily mean, in listing all these organizations, to imply that both churches and individuals may purchase services from or otherwise utilize all of them. But certainly some of them may be utilized both by churches and individuals, and all of them may be utilized by one or the other or both. *Individuals and churches may utilize human service organizations.*

Now, let us examine the organizations listed on the chart. *The Elza Gary Construction Co.* (Brother Gary has since this speech was made been tragically killed in an automobile accident.) is the first. Some of you brethren are more familiar with a like organization, *The Paden Construction Co.* These organizations build meeting houses for churches of Christ. They were started by brethren Gary and Paden as a means of livelihood but also for the purpose of serving God by helping churches to obtain good meeting houses at very considerable saving of church funds. Churches all over the country have saved hundreds of thousands of dollars—dollars in the Lord's treasury—by employing these organizations. The *end results* of the existence and operation of these organizations is that churches of God have places of *assembly* where *saints gather to be edified and sinners to be evangelized.* I believe that brethren Gary and Paden glorify God in this work in these organizations. I believe that "to him be glory in the church" (Eph. 3: 21.) means to glorify God in *the universal saved relationship* and that it does not refer specifically to the local congregation. In this sense, I glorify God in every relationship of life, and I am in the church (universal) when I do it.

There is, I believe, a loan company in Fort Worth, Texas, operated by brethren, which specializes in loans to churches of Christ for building purposes. If there is not, there could be. These loans are used in the construction of meeting houses, hence the *end results* of the existence and operation of this human organization is the assembling of the saints, edifying, and evangelizing.

Point 2 on the chart calls attention to *Travel Agencies* which could obtain passports and arrange itineraries for people who are evangelizing all over the world. It also suggests a *Religious Program Radio Station*—a station specializing in programs of Bible teaching—established and operated with the idea of providing a service for churches and individuals in teaching the word of God all over the world. Such an organization exists, therefore, to do service to and glorify God.

Point 3 lists *nursing homes, hospitals, homes for the aged,* and *children's homes*. The *end results* of the existence and operation of these organizations are: the "fatherless" are "visited" (Jas. 1:27); the "poor" are "remembered" (Gal. 2:10); the "sick" are "visited" (Mt. 25:36, 40); men "provide for their own" (I Tim. 5:8); hence *benevolence* is accomplished. I contend that such organizations, individually owned, operated, and subsidized, can exist as service organizations providing services which may be utilized both by churches and individuals.

Point 4 notes *Anaco Publications, The Gospel Guardian, The Preceptor Co.,* and *John A. Dickson Co.* in Chicago. These human organizations specialize in the publication and dissemination of Bible teaching. As a consequence of this Bible teaching the saints are edified and sinners evangelized, hence these consequences are the *end results* of the existence and operation of these organizations.

Point 5 calls attention to *public schools, summer camps, Florida College, Sabinal Music Normal,* and *Harvard Divinity School*. The Mound and Starr church which I serve has a program of Bible teaching in *Stephen F. Austin State College,* a public school. Summer camps are conducted by brethren, and in them, the Bible is taught. *Sabinal Music Normal* prepares students to direct singing among churches of Christ. *Florida*

*College* provides a secular educational service, a Bible teaching service, and a spiritual environment in which both may be rendered. Even *Harvard Divinity School* provides preacher training which some of our brethren have no hesitancy in utilizing to obtain theological degrees. Surprisingly, they utilize these sectarian, infidel organizations to obtain Bible instruction while, at the same time, contending it is sinful for brethren to provide the same service. The *end results* of the existence and operation of these human, service organizations are that song directors are trained, preachers are prepared, and others are edified and evangelized.

Point 6 lists *The Bible Society*. Bible Societies translate, publish, and circulate the Scriptures. (We use the term "society" advisedly.) I contend that the translating, publishing and circulating of the Scriptures is *the purest form of Bible teaching*. It unquestionably has more sanctity than my uninspired comments possess. The *end results* of the existence and operation of a Bible Society are edification and evangelization through Bible teaching.

It is my contention that such organizations as I have listed on this chart can exist and function Scripturally as business organizations providing services which may be purchased by churches and individuals. *Florida College* and *Abilene Christian College* are business organizations specializing in education. They propose to provide for the education of young people in a spiritual environment, under the influence of Christians, where truth is taught in all the classes, and where students have the opportunity to study the Bible daily on a college level under the direction of teachers who are Christians. Such schools are permeated with influences that are good for young people and which tend to preserve their faith. Despite these facts, they are still *business organizations with services to sell*.

I believe that an individual, a Christian, may scripturally purchase these services. I would justify this right by the generic command of Ephesians 6:4, "Ye fathers bring up your children in the nurture and admonition of the Lord." I would justify some of the other organizations listed by the generic statement of I Tim. 5:8, "If any provide not for his own, and specially for those of his own house, he hath denied the faith, and is worse than an infidel."

It is my contention that individuals (Christians) may own and operate such service organizations as have been noted. They may be profit or non-profit in character, since such does not change their fundamental character as business enterprises. I further contend that they may be subsidized (by contributions), if necessary, by individuals (Christians), and, may I repeat, such individuals may purchase their services in the discharge of their duties as Christians.

I contend that a church may purchase any service which it is scriptural for her to purchase from these service organizations, but I deny that churches of the Lord may make contributions to them. *I contend there is a fundamental difference between making a contribution and purchasing a service.*

This, brethren, is how I defend the colleges and other organizations of like nature. I justify the existence and operation of a college as a human, service organization. I justify the right of a Christian to purchase its services in "bringing up his children in the nurture and admonition of the Lord" on the same basis that I would justify his right to purchase a book of Homer Hailey's teaching on the Minor Prophets published and circulated by a human organization and edify his child thereby. There is no fundamental difference in purchasing such teaching in the form of a product, a book, made possible by the existence and operation of a human publishing organization and in purchasing the same teaching by the same man in the form of a service performed in a classroom as a result of the existence and operation of a college organization. If a Christian may not do this, why not? There is no violation of Scripture in the existence and operation of a college in which the Bible is taught. It is a thing *permitted*.

One does not *have* to believe in or support a college. He does not *have* to send his children to school there. But, *he may do so*. However, it is possible that one might sin in not doing so if he jeopardizes the faith of his children and destroys their souls by sending them to the wrong place. I do not say such would necessarily occur. I say only that it could happen. The danger is there. *Brother Allen*, I do not know whether this does or does not answer your question to your satisfaction, but this is how I would justify the support of the colleges by individuals (Christians) and deny the Scriptural right of churches of Christ to make contributions to them.

## Individual Action vs. Church Action

### Reuel Lemmons

I know that you men share with me the joy of seeing so many things presented with which you thoroughly agree. On several occasions men have endorsed the speeches which have preceded them from the other side which actually showed that in a lot of instances there wasn't any other side. And I heartily concur with the things which James has put on this chart. I think he has presented the truth all the way through on it. I think he has a partial answer, at least, to some of the questions that brother Allen has asked, and also I think brother Dobbs did a good job answering part of the questions when he showed that a human being has at least a three-fold responsibility—one to his government, one to his family and one to the church if he is a Christian. To the government as a citizen he pays his taxes, as a father of children in a Christian college he contributes to a school, and as a Christian he holds up his obligations to the church.

Bro. Allen has asked the question, "How do you establish congregational authority, how do you establish individual au-

---

REUEL G. LEMMONS—*Editor of the* FIRM FOUNDATION; *evangelist for one of the churches of Austin, Texas; widely known radio speaker on an international hook-up; used extensively as a lecturer and speaker in gospel meetings throughout the nation.*

thority and is there any difference between the two?" I am going to try to briefly answer that. I may not even be satisfied with my own answer by the time I get through with this speech.

All commands are, in the end result, given to individuals. You do not command an institution. In the final analysis God's word is to an individual. So, primarily, commands are to individuals and this is how you establish authority for individuals.

When you have a command given to an individual, to which each individual in the congregation is equally related, you have authority for church action; because when each individual in the congregation discharges his obedience to the command given him you have a "collective command" obeyed by a "congregation" for a *congregation* is a *collection* of individuals. This is what happened when the church prayed for Peter in prison in Acts 12:5, I believe. Each individual prayed and yet it says that prayer of the *church* was made for Peter. You have this same thing in I Cor. 16, the first few verses, where each one of them laid by in store and the collection was sent to the elders of the church in Jerusalem. You have individual action obeyed by those to whom the individual command was given and the result (end result) was congregational action. The individual cannot escape his individual obligation on the grounds that he has made a contribution to the church because commands are given primarily to individuals.

On the other hand, it is just as true that churches cannot escape their obligation by saying that it is an individual affair and none of their business. I think this is one place where some of us get off the track. We try to excuse a congregational obligation by saying it is an individual affair.

A local congregation is just simply a group of individuals banded together to serve the Lord, and the command, given to each individual, to which each is equally related, is a command given to the church.

When an individual cannot carry out the command that is given to him by the Lord, then it becomes the obligation of the church to assist him in carrying out that command. A father is to care for his children and to feed his family. If he reaches the place where he can't obey this individual command, then the church is to take over the obligation. This is made clear in I Tim. 5 where the son is to take care of his widowed mother, but if he is not able to handle this obligation, then she becomes the charge of the church. Thus, the individual need is supplied by the church because the individual is too poor to carry out his obligation or is not able to carry out his obligation. Thus a congregational responsibility actually sprang from an individual command to which each is equally related and which one individual cannot carry out. If I cannot carry out the command given to me, then it becomes the obligation of the church to help me carry out that command.

I think this will help us with James 1:27. I have seen a score or more of different attempts to say that James 1:27 is a command to the individual and not to the church. I do not agree with that at all but for the sake of these thoughts I want to accept that possibility. Let us put beside James 1:27 another passage of scripture—Gal. 6:6. Here is a command to the individual just as thoroughly as James 1:27 is a command to the individual. This command is that a person who is taught must pay his teacher. To this command every taught individual is equally related in Gal. 6:6. We say that everyone has to give into the treasury of the church to pay the preacher—to pay the teacher. The individual member puts into the treasury to pay the teacher, and then the paying of the teacher becomes the congregational responsibility and the church pays the preacher (teacher). The church treasury just simply represents the end result of equally related responsibility for paying the teacher. Now, out of this common fund the preacher's salary is paid.

*No member of the church has a single obligation regarding caring for an orphan.* If he can discharge one of them as individual by James 1:27, he must discharge the other as an individual on the basis of Gal. 6:6. If being equally related to the command to pay the teacher (Gal. 6:6) makes the individuals equally related to the caring for the orphans (James 1:27), then the same treasury that pays the preacher can care for the orphans. The combined efforts of individual action then is pooled in the treasury in Jas. 1:27 and in Gal. 6:6 alike.

And so the preacher draws his salary from the church. This salary goes to provide food and clothing and the other things that he needs. All of these things enter into an individual's primarily carrying out the individual command where he is taught to pay the preacher. Any child-care arrangements (and I like that expression because it gets away from these hard to define "homes")—any child care arrangement requires some expedients too. There has to be food and clothing, recreation and so forth. Just about everything a preacher would need, a child-care arrangement would need and if it is scriptural for the church to act in carrying out the individual responsibility of paying the teacher in Gal. 6:6, then it becomes a church command in Jas 1:27 to care for the orphans.

And when you apply the same sort of reasoning some use on James 1:27 to the 6th chapter of Galatians, we come up with just about the same thing as the "saints only" proposition. That has been introduced into the meeting and many brethren have trouble with this text: "as we therefore have opportunity let us do good to all men and especially unto them which are of the household of faith." I guess we have seen a score or more of attempts to explain away this passage and to rid the church of any responsibility to non-members. Most of these brethren take the position that the church has a responsibility only to help needy saints and no responsibility to help non-saints because they say this is an individual matter. In the first place, Gal. 6:10 is not a command to the individual any more than any other command in the scriptures given to Christians in general is to the individual. Paul addressed the Galatian letter to the churches of Galatia. What he said in that letter was written to those to whom he addressed the letter, the churches of Galatia. Now, naturally, churches cannot read—only individuals can read—and what Paul wrote was to be considered by individuals, but the fact that he addressed it to the church indicates that every individual to which it was addressed was equally related to the responsibility of carrying it out.

Galatians 6:6 shows that the command to the individual to pay the teacher gives authority to the church to carry out the collective commands of the individual, and I think we can prove that this command is to be carried out by the church. In I Cor. 11 we have instructions to individuals on how to act when they meet in the assembly. These commands are given to individuals and among them were commands on how to observe the Lord's supper. The command to take the Lord's supper is an individual command, yet these brethren take money out of the church treasury to buy the elements that make it possible for each one of them individually to take the Lord's supper. The church treasury is tapped in order to make it possible to carry out an individual command. This command is a command to an individual, but every individual in the church is equally related to the carrying out of the command to eat the Lord's supper and, therefore, it becomes scriptural and right that the church, out of its treasury, should supply the elements for the Lord's supper. Why make a law concerning Gal. 6:10 that we will not make concerning I Cor. 11:28? The same principle by which we would prohibit the church from its treasury ministering to non-saints would force each brother to bring his own elements for his own Lord's supper, lest the church be taxed to carry out an obligation that was his individually. We are dealing with individual action versus church action and, in an attempt to answer Jimmy's question and that alone in this 15 minutes, I want to make it clear that I believe that all commands are given to individuals primarily and when a command is given to individuals in which all the individuals which comprise a congregation are equally related, then that command becomes a church command to be carried out (and can be carried out) by the church.

## Individual Action vs. Church Action

### Franklin T. Puckett

One thing that has been demonstrated in this meeting thus far is the fact that brethren of divergent views can come together and act as gentlemen in the presence of each other while discussing frankly and forthrightly their respective views. As long as such a spirit prevails, there is always hope that a meeting of minds may be reached. In many things it is evident we are in agreement. All of us, I think, claim Biblical authority for that which we teach and practice. Every person present seems to feel the need of divine authority in all religious matters. We may differ over what is authorized, but apparently we are agreed that authority is to be established by express command or precise statement, approved example, or necessary inference. So we have an area of agreement that gives us a starting point toward the solution of our problems of disagreement. For this we can be duly thankful.

Understanding that there are areas of agreement, we must also face the fact that there are areas of disagreement. That

---

FRANKLIN T. PUCKETT—*Writer; debater; well known evangelist —*

*presently working with a congregation in Florence, Alabama; formerly special Bible lecturer in Florida College, conducts numerous meetings yearly throughout the nation.*

is why we are engaged in this discussion. As I listened to the various speakers, I found myself both agreeing and disagreeing with some things that were said by almost everybody. Sometimes I even had difficulty agreeing with myself. In our disagreements we should avoid dogmatic arrogance and realize it is possible for everyone of us to be wrong. We are not infallible. It may be that all of us need to do some more studying before we conclude we know all about everything. I agree with brother Nichols that we will never solve any of our problems of disagreement unless we accept the word of God as the sole standard of authority. When we disagree we need to get down to a careful study of that word and learn what it teaches and then do it.

The Bible teaches by words and words are the signs of ideas. They are the means by which the mind of God is communicated unto us. If we understand the will of God, we must understand the meaning and use of the terms in which that will is revealed. I am persuaded that oftentimes our disagreements result from ambiguity of language, a failure to properly define our terms and to apply sound rules of exegesis, or our inability to speak precisely what we mean. In our efforts to teach others, we may use words intended to mean one thing, but because of ambiguity or a lack of proper definition someone else understands them to mean something entirely different. In this way communication between us breaks down and alienation results. To avoid this we must be sure that the word of God comes through to us loud and clear and that we correctly understand exactly what it means. Having come to a right understanding of the divine will ourselves, we must endeavor to present it to others with such clarity that there can be no doubt as to the correctness of what is taught or excuse for the failure of responsible people to understand it. To this end we must clearly define and fully clarify every truth taught, position taken, and proposition affirmed.

The Bible being a revelation of God's will to men through the medium of language, it is subject to all the rules and regulations of language. We should study it just as we would study any other literary document and subject it to the same rules of definition and interpretation that would be used in seeking to discern the meaning of any other piece of writing. If we can come to know the meaning of any writing, we can also come to know the meaning of the Biblical revelation (Eph. 3:3, 4). It can be discerned by using the same laws of language and principles of interpretation employed in comprehending first.

Furthermore, when that will of God is known, it will have the same meaning to all people everywhere. If it does not have the same meaning to all, somebody does not properly understand it. What God's word teaches one, it teaches everyone. It says precisely the same thing to everybody, and what it means to one, it means to all. If there is disagreement over what the Bible teaches, that disagreement arises because someone has failed to correctly understand or properly respect what it teaches. This is true of the disagreements among us. Some of us are failing to understand or failing to respect what it teaches. This failure is our own fault, for we are instructed to be "not unwise, but understanding what the will of the Lord is" (Eph. 5:17).

Since we are divided, it is fitting that we should sit down together and measure the things that divide us by the yardstick of God's infallible word. If we will proceed honestly, fairly, humbly, respectfully, and objectively, I cannot but believe that we can eliminate our differences and come to the unity for which our Lord prayed. I am glad we have some common ground from which to start, but we need to face up to the fact that we are divided and discuss our differences rather than overemphasize our agreements. We need to put our respective positions to the test in the light of what the Bible teaches and sincerely try to come to unity upon the basis of that teaching, rather than simply promote mutual toleration by agreeing to disagree. I have enjoyed the meeting thus far, and I believe a lot of good was done in the first session. Perhaps a better understanding of one of our basic problems was developed. Many things have been said this afternoon which will contribute to a fuller understanding of matters before us.

When we talk about the church, church action, and the work of the church, concerning which brother Thomas has raised some questions, we need to define exactly what we mean. It is evident these terms do not mean the same thing to all people. I want to present some views which have guided me to the conclusions I have reached concerning these matters. Whether I have been logical in my reasonings or correct in my conclusions might in your judgment be open to question. I, like you, can be wrong. I have been wrong in times past and I could be wrong now. I have sometimes had to change my views so that I now believe some things I once did not believe and do not believe some things I once accepted. If you think me to be wrong now, show me by the testimony of the Scriptures where I am wrong and I will change again. For the present, however, I sincerely believe the things I hold to be true, and perhaps you can see by what I am about to say why I hold the views I do.

When we talk about the church, what do we mean by that term? We should give it the same meaning it has in the New Testament and use it in the same way it is used there. The English term *church* is used to translate the Greek noun *ekklesia*, which in its etymological development is derived from a combination of the preposition *ek*, meaning *out*, or *out from*, and the verb *kaleo*, meaning *to call, summon,* or *invite*. The radical meaning of *ekklesia* is the "called out," or "the summoned forth." Among the Greeks *ekklesia* signified the lawful assembly of free citizens who were called out from the non-citizens and slaves and convened together for the transaction of public affairs. In the LXX it was used to denote the assembly or congregation of Israel. According to Trench, in the word *ekklesia* "There lay ever the sense of an assembly coming together for the transaction of business." (TRENCH, *Synonyms of the New Testament*, p. 6.) In the New Testament when *ekklesia* is used to designate the assembly or congregation of God's people, it is rendered "church"— a term which in its early devolpment meant "of or belonging to the Lord." It follows then that the word church as used in the New Testament simply means the assembly or congregation of the Lord's people who have been called out of the world by the gospel of Christ and convened together to transact the business of the King. That is the meaning we should attribute to it.

The term church has two extensions—general and limited. In its general extension it includes all of God's people generally. In this sense it is the equivalent of "kingdom of heaven," "body of Christ," "family of God," or "brotherhood" of God's children. It equates the redeemed of the Lord in the aggregate. In its limited extension the word church signifies a local congregation. We read of "the church of God, which is at Corinth," "the church of Ephesus," "the church in Smyrna," etc. A plurality of such churches was referred to as "the churches of Christ," "the churches of God," or simply "churches." The membership of the local church was composed of members of Christ's spiritual body—the church universal. Their spiritual relation to Christ in His spiritual body gave them the right to belong to and share in the functions of the local church. Membership in the church universal is essential to membership in the church local, but the converse does not necessarily follow. It is a law of logic that the greater extension given a term, the less comprehension it possesses, and as comprehension increases, extension decreases. It follows that when the word church refers to a local congregation, it has less extension and more comprehension than when it refers to the whole body. The local church, therefore, possesses some characteristics and features not found in the universal church. This being true, it also follows that those particular features which distinguish a local church from the universal church cannot be predicated of the "brotherhood" generally. It seems to me this is a logical and an important deduction that should be kept in mind.

Since the word church always denotes an assembly, and since that term is given two extensions, it follows that there are two kinds of assemblies. There is a general assembly and there is a local assembly. The general, or universal, assembly was and is spiritual in nature. It was and is a spiritual assembly of God's spiritual children with their spiritual head, Jesus Christ, in a spiritual relation, and in a spiritual realm (Eph. 2: 4-6; Heb. 12: 22, 23). This general assembly has no worldly character nor earthly place of assembly; it has neither earthly organization nor collective function. It does not and cannot by divine arrangement function as an earthly coordinated collectivity.

On the other hand the local church does have an earthly assembly in an earthly location characterized by an organizational structure and ordained to function as a collectivity in coordinated group action. Though composed of the same people —God's spiritual children, the nature and function of these two assemblies is quite different. That difference must be recognized and respected. I want to emphasize that difference. The general assembly, or universal church, is spiritual in nature, meets in a spiritual location—"in heavenly places," has no earthly organization and no coordinated collective function. The limited assembly, the local church, though possessing spiritual features and functions, meets in an earthly location, has an earthly organization, and is designed to function as a coordinated group in collective action. Let no one say there is no difference in the universal church and the local church, nor that their duties and functions are the same.

As we have two extensions of the word church, and two kinds of assemblies, so we have two kinds of action—distributive and collective. Perhaps these terms need to be defined. Distributive is defined grammatically as "separation among or into individuals or individual groups" (Webster). The word distributive requires separation. Distributive action is performed by separate individuals or separate groups of individuals. A collective is "formed by gathering or collecting; gathered into one mass, sum, or body; united." Grammatically it is said to be "treating of a number of objects as a group, whole, or aggregate" (Webster). Collective action is united group action; it is the action of those who have been gathered into one mass or body and function as a united whole. Collective action is not distributive action, and distributive action is not collective, and he who does not recognize this distinction in action is not thinking logically.

The two kinds of action involve two units of activity—a separate individual person (a Christian) and a separate individual group (a local church). The church universal can only function distributively. In its universal connotation, the church is a spiritual kingdom which knows no physical boundaries, earthly organization, or "brotherhood" programs, and cannot function in the world as a collectivity. The King has distributed the action in His kingdom into separate individuals (Christians) and unto separate groups (local congregations). There are no other units of activity. Whatever is done in the kingdom of heaven under the authority of Christ must be done by individual Christians or by local congregations. Any other arrangement as a unit of church action is without divine authority.

Since all action in the kingdom is either distributive or collective, and since neither the individual Christian nor the church universal can function collectively, and since the only units of activity in the kingdom are the individual and the local congregation, it follows that all collective or group action belongs to the local congregation. Furthermore, according to Trench, the word translated church always denotes "an assembly coming together for the transaction of business," and the only business transacted by such a coming together is that action taken by the local congregation, therefore, only such action as is transacted by the local church can be correctly termed church action." Any other action in the kingdom of heaven is distributive and individual. An individual is not an assembly, and his own individual action is not assembly or church action. All church action is collective or group action. Yet many people will say, "What the individual Christian does as a Christian, the church does. The church is made up of individuals, and when the individual acts, the church acts. The individual is the church!" No greater fallacy could be invented.

There are but two divinely authorized functioning units in the spiritual body of Christ—the individual member and the local congregation. Christ is said to be head over all things to the church which is His body (Eph. 1:23). It follows that He rules as head over both the individual members and the local congregation in all their respective activities. The duties of both functioning units are authorized by the Lord. His is the only voice they are to hear, and that voice is revealed to us through His written word—the New Covenant. There and there only can the duties enjoined by the King upon both individual Christians and local congregations be learned.

The New Testament reveals that the duties of individual Christians embrace many areas of life other than local church responsibilities. A Christian must be subject to the will of his Master in everything. Paul said, "I am crucified with Christ; nevertheless I live; yet not I, but Christ liveth in me: and the life which I now live in the flesh I live by the faith of the Son of God, who loved me and gave himself for me" (Gal. 2:20). To live by the faith is to live by the gospel. When one lives by the gospel, Christ lives in him. The gospel teaches Christians how to properly behave themselves in every relation of life. It teaches how they should conduct themselves in the home. Husbands and wives, and parents and children are taught their respective duties in the home, but the home is not the church and the church is not the home. They were established at different times and for different purposes, and the duties of one are not the duties of the other. The fact that I am a Christian and in the kingdom of God obligates me to fulfill faithfully my duties in the home, but these are not church duties and the acts performed in fulfilling them are not church actions. The gospel teaches Christians how to properly conduct their affairs as citizens in their relation to the civil power, but their duties in this area of life are not church functions. Being a member of the spiritual body of Christ obligates one to be subject to the will of his Master in every relation of life, whether in civil affairs, home relations, business activities, or social and recreational functions, but his duties in these relations are not church duties or fulfilled through church action. Church duty and church action have to do with the function of the local church as we have already seen.

Now, what duties and what actions are required of the local church? These must be established by the authority of Christ and can only be learned by a study of the teaching of Christ as divinely revealed. If something cannot be established by the teaching of Christ, He did not authorize it; and if He did not authorize it, it does not belong to His church. Church duty is that which is required of a church, just as individual duty is that which is required of an individual. We have seen that the only unit in the divine system that is capable of functioning as a church is the local congregation. It follows that only congregational responsibilities are church duties, and that church action is congregational action. Congregational action is joint or collective action by the congregation as a whole, or such action as is accomplished through the duly appointed servants of the congregation.

Actually there are relatively few duties which the word of God assigns local churches to do as churches. Little is said about what is to be done as a collectivity in coordinated group-action. By far the greater portion of the New Testament deals with what the individual is to be and do rather than what the local churches as churches are to do. There are, however, some duties which the Master has assigned local churches and which require collective action on the part of a local church. While these duties require individual participation, the action is to be performed by the individuals as a coordinated group functioning together as a whole. The duty is distributive in its requirement of individual participation, but it is executed collectively in fulfillment of a congregational responsibility. Individual participation is required in the performance of all individual responsibilities and individual participation is required in the performance of all congregational, or church, responsibilities, but the fact that individual participation is required in both cases does not destroy the distinction between the two kinds of action. One is individual and personal while the other is collective and congregational. This distinction must ever be maintained.

Furthermore, as it takes the word of God to establish individual responsibility, it can take no less than the word of God to establish congregational responsibility. Now, what duties are enjoined by the word of God upon the local congregation, or church? May I list those I have been able to find thus far?

1. An assembly of the saints (Heb. 10:24, 25).
2. In such an assembly the saints are to observe the Lord's Supper on the first day of the week (Acts 20:7; 1 Cor. 11:33).
3. They are to sing psalms unto the Lord, and with spiritual songs teach and admonish one another (1 Cor. 14:23, 26; Eph. 5:19; Col. 3:16).
4. They are to pray together for one another and for all men (Acts 12:5; 1 Tim. 2:1).
5. They are to preach and attend to the teaching of God's word (Acts 20:7; 1 Cor. 14:26).
6. They are to lay by in store on the first day of the week as they have been prospered to finance their collective responsibility (1 Cor. 16:2).
7. They are to support the preaching of the gospel (2 Cor. 11:8; Phil. 4:15,16).
8. They are to provide for the fulfillment of the needs of certain destitute saints (Acts 4:34, 35; 2 Cor. 8, 9 chs., Rom. 15:25-31; 1 Tim. 5:16).
9. The local church is to exercise discipline against its ungodly members (1 Cor. 5:1-5; 2 Thess 3:1-15).

Now brethren, I have not been able to find any other duties or responsibilities assigned by the Lord to local churches to be carried out through collective action. Have you? There are many actions which the individual Christian may engage in that are not divinely authorized for the local church. Let individuals perform their duties as individuals and let local churches perform their duties as local churches and do not try to place the responsibilities of individuals upon the church. The functions of the church as a church do not involve it in political action, social reform, or recreational programs. To turn the church into a kind of social club and a recreational gymnasium is a perversion of the divine pattern and for it there is no excuse. May we all think on these things.

# The Work of the Church

## W. L. Wharton, Jr.

INTRODUCTION:

In common with the speakers who have preceded me, I also have been assigned my subject in the form of a question, WHAT IS THE WORK OF THE CHURCH? It would be impossible to develop the answer to this question without a basic understanding of the other subjects that have been before us for discussion and study up until now. So close, in fact, is the relationship of all the subjects that some degree of overlap will inevitably appear in their presentation. Since our material, presented in the papers read here, was prepared in advance of the meeting and without benefit of any knowledge of what would be developed by the other speakers, this is more particularly true.

My subject involves consideration of matters very vital to the spiritual well-being of us all. This is true because (1) we are all members of a local congregation and have our part in whatever programs are carried out, and (2) because as teach-

---

W. L. WHARTON JR.—*Evangelist for Highland Blvd. congregation in San Antonio, Texas; conducts six months of meetings yearly throughout the nation and Canada; staff writer for* THE PRECEPTOR; *formerly served churches in Houston, Odessa, and Wichita Falls, Texas.*

ers we have a special responsibility to accurately know and teach in reference to it (James 3:1).

While conscious of my personal limitations and the gravity of my assignment, I acknowledge the pleasure of meeting with brethren in such moments as these to join in the purposes to which we are mutually committed. The problems associated with my subject are made evident by the many controversies, past and present, that have attended its consideration and, in a special way, to all of us by observation of our present situation. It would be grossly erroneous to deny that there are difficulties associated with, and even inherent in, all the processes by which we approach Bible subjects. We would be wonderfully optimistic, not to say conceited, to suppose that we will settle them all (or perhaps, any). Be that as it may, the good accomplished in each of us will be proportionate to his sincere desire and efforts to know for himself the teaching of Christ (2 Jno. 9), and in respect of this we each shall finally answer to our God (Rom. 14:12).

*DEFINITIONS*

Let us proceed at once to some definitions of terms. By the term "church" I refer to the particular New Testament use of it in reference to a local or limited collectivity of saints, banded or joined together in connection with Christ to collectively provide for those things which peculiarly relate to their being Christians. While readily granting the use of the term in other senses in the scriptures, we shall, unless otherwise noted, use the word church throughout our presentation to refer to the church local.

That a local church is a collectivity is seen in the fact that both the English word church and the Greek "ekklesia", from which it is translated, are collective nouns.

That the units of the collectivity (church) are saints is readily seen in such passages as *1 Corinthians 1:2* "Unto the church of God which is at Corinth, even them that are sanctified in Christ Jesus . . ." and *Philippians 1:1* "Paul and Timothy, servants of Christ Jesus, to all the saints in Christ Jesus that are at Philippi, with the bishops and deacons: . . . ."

That they are joined together in Christ is seen in the modifying prepositional phrase "in Christ" as it is used to explain their sanctification or being saints.

That they are joined together for the purpose of joint action (collective action) is seen from *1 Corinthians 1:10* "Now I beseech you, brethren, through the name of our Lord Jesus Christ, that ye all speak the same thing, and that there be no divisions among you; but that ye perfected together in the same mind and in the same judgment." While individual and independent action on the part of each saint in Corinth could obtain in the absence of mutual mind and judgment, collective action would be impossible. This being true, we regard this injunction as necessarily involving collective action of the members.

That their collective action was in reference to those things peculiar to the state of their being Christians can be seen from the above passage in *1 Cor. 1:10* in the light of the fact that the injunction itself was "through the name of our Lord Jesus Christ" and for that very reason related particularly to the Lordship of Jesus Christ over those addressed. The Lordship of Jesus extends only over those who are his; those who are saints. His Lordship is a point of distinction between the saint and the non-saint. Therefore, the sameness of mind and judgment commanded must relate to things common and peculiar to the grounds of faith in Christ and acceptance of his Lordship. Or, to express it differently, the command must have related to such practice as was established by Christ and such as would only be practiced by persons separated to his service. We shall say more of this presently.

From these definitions we can make application to our immediate subject and say we are proposing to examine the work (collective action) of the church (local collective of saints).

## SOME DISTINCTIONS OBSERVED IN COLLECTIVE NOUNS

Having pointed out that the term church itself is a collective noun we necessarily encounter the need for understanding what is involved in that fact. At the risk of being burdensome, I read a definition of a collective noun.

"A noun that under the singular form expresses a grouping of individual objects or persons, as *herd, jury* and *clergy*. The singular verb is used when the noun is thought of as naming a single unit, acting as one, as *family* in *my family is related to Washington*. The plural verb is used when the noun is thought of as composed of individuals who retain their separateness, as *My family are all at home."*—The American College Dictionary.

It is absolutely essential, in obtaining a right answer to our present question, to clearly understand that collective nouns may be used either collectively or distributively. The writer or speaker will indicate the choice made by the modification given in the choice of verbs or explanation. We may well pause a moment to consider simple distinctions between singular, plural and collective. I like to illustrate it by first pointing out that one may use the term "link" (singular). Advancing in thought one may use the plural "links." While continuing with the same thought he may advance to the collective, "chain." Now, one could not have a chain without having links, but he could certainly have links and not have a chain. By the same token one could not have links without having a link, but he could have a link without having links. No one would say that a link is a chain. Now take the terms Christian, Christians, and church. Each represents an advance in thought. No thinking person would say that whatever a Christian does that the church is therefore doing it. Nor will it be true that whatever Christians do that the church is therefore doing it. While it is most certainly true that if the church is doing something Christians are *collectively engaged* in the doing of it.

Is this a strained or fanciful play upon words? That it is not will be seen in the injunction of our Lord respecting the settlement of differences between brethren as it is set out in *Matthew 18: 15-17.* "And if thy brother sin against thee, go. show him his fault between thee and him alone: if he hear thee, thou hast gained thy brother. But if he hear thee not take with thee one or two more that at the mouth of two witnesses or three every word may be established. And if he refuse to hear them, tell it unto the church: and if he refuse to hear the church also, let him be unto thee as the Gentile and the publican."

We have in this account a clear distinction between singular ("thee"), plural ("them") and collective ("church"). It is abundantly clear that, when the brother went to his brother alone, the church did not go. Equally true that when a plurality of witnesses went, the church was not involved. While collective nouns involve plurality of units they involve more. Unless we distinguish between *plurality* and *collective* we confuse ourselves as well as those we try to teach.

*OBSERVATIONS CONCERNING COLLECTIVE ACTION*

We are confronted with the need to lay out a clear ground or foundation upon which to procede from this point: Most certainly it will involve us in explaining collective action. Since "church" is a collective noun then it must follow that the work of the church is collective work or action. Recall that our question is "What is the work of the church?" This is asking about the work of the church as a collective, whereas if our question had been "What is the work of all of the church?" we would have been regarding the church distributive. It is sometimes an easy way, if not completely in keeping with good grammar, to make these distinctions between collective and distributive use of the word church by saying, when we refer to the church as doing something in a collective capacity, that the church, as such, is doing it. One cannot write long on the subject of the work of the church without seeing the need of this distinction.

Since the work of the church lies in the field of collective action let us seek to define it as best we can. It is a simplification to say that "collective action is that of many acting as one." It is not that action is performed or that many are acting but that (1) the many (2) are acting (3) as one. What is necessary for this to be true or what is essential to collective action?

1. There must be unity or agreement between those acting together in reference to what is to be done. While this is rather self-evident it is in keeping with our purposes to notice that Amos asks, "Can two walk together EXCEPT THEY BE AGREED?" (Amos 3:3, and also I Cor. 1:10)

2. Mere agreement does not, in itself perform anything. Before many can act as one their efforts must be co-ordinated. This involves an element of oversight or supervision. As this concerns a local church, we observe that in the fully developed congregation the Lord has set out the qualifications of bishops or overseers (I Tim. 3; Titus I). This is not to conclude that the element of supervision or oversight is lacking in congregations where there are no bishops but that such function is essentially present in the work of a local church. The men

of such fellowship, meeting together in what we commonly call "business meeting" would, in the absence of bishops, constitute the element of oversight or supervision by their mutual deliberations and decisions. While a congregation can have being without bishops, bishops cannot exist without a "flock" or church over which to superintend. This is why, presently, we will find evidence for the existence of a local church and action in reference to its members when gifts were made from one congregation to the "elders" of another.

3. There must be a pooling of resources and/or abilities of the units of collective.
4. The uses of things pooled constitute the collective action of the units, whereas the preceding three items are the essential pre-requisites of it.

## SCRIPTURAL ILLUSTRATION OF OUR VIEW OF COLLECTIVE ACTION

In the fourth chapter of Acts and beginning with vr. 32 we have this account:

"And the multitude of them that believed were of one heart and soul: and not one of them said that aught of the things which he possessed was his own; but they had all things common . . . for neither was there among them any that lacked: for as many as were posssessors of land or houses sold them, and brought the prices of the things that were sold, and laid them at the apostles feet: and distribution was made unto each, according as any one had need."

In this we easily trace the element of agreement on the part of the disciples. Also, it is clear that this particular instance of collective action involved a treasury of material things viz., . . . the prices of the things sold. The element of oversight is seen in the fact that the apostles had charge of this treasury . . . attested to by the statement that the prices were laid at the "apostles feet" i.e., under their power. But if we stop here we miss the whole point toward which these things were directed. The fact that out of these funds "distribution was made unto each, according as anyone had need" sums up the action made possible by the many and which truly is seen to be an action as if by one person. The act of collectively providing for something is the essence of collective action. Hence, in Acts 6 when, in response to the need for a fair distribution of funds to the needy, seven men were selected by the multitude and set forth by the apostles to look after the matter. They were truly deacons or servants of the church in that particular. In this way the church distributed its goods to its needy. This does not mean that something besides saints functioned to relieve their needy, but it affirms that by this means (collective action) they did it. The local church is not an organization but the local church has organization. When the units of the local church function by means of their arrangement or organization they necessarily act collectively. Hence the church is said to do what people, by means of collective action do.

*A DISTINCTION BETWEEN DOING SOMETHING PERSONALLY AND CAUSING IT TO BE DONE*

An individual may act in either of two ways or both. He may actually do a thing by his own resources and/or strength . . . do it individually and personally, independent of any other person. Or, he may employ the services of others to do his wishes. In either event he is truly credited with the action.

Consider the story of the Good Samaritan in Luke 10 as an illustration of the point. This good man personally "came to him, and bound up his wounds, pouring on them oil and wine; and set him on his beast, and brought him to an inn, and took care of him" (vr. 34) I speak of such as individual, independent action. Whereas, "on the morrow he took out two shillings, and gave them to the host, and said, take care of him; and whatsoever thou spendest more, I, when I come back again, will repay thee." (vr. 35). While this action is also the action of the individual it differs from the first in that, while not actually himself performing the service, he caused it to be done and was morally responsible for it as much as if he had done it personally. On this point it is of interest to recall that in John's gospel he records: "When therefore the Lord knew that the Pharisees had heard that Jesus was making and baptizing more disciples than John (although Jesus himself baptized not, but his disciples) . . ." (Jno. 4 vr. 1-2). Here is something the Lord is said to have done (baptized more disciples than John) which is explained by the fact that he caused it to be done rather than by personally doing it. Since we have no problem of understanding, in this connection, how the Lord did something in one frame of reference that in another he did not do by understanding the principle of agency, then we can appreciate the fact that collectively a people provide for something to be done rather than, or in contrast with, personal performance. The only way a church can act is by causing something to be done. In causing something to be done agents are involved and the act of the agent is regarded as the act of the church. It was in this frame of reference that Paul wrote "But I counted it necessary to send to you Epaphroditus, my brother and fellow-soldier, and your messenger and minister to my need;" (Phil. 2:25). He further states: ". . . because for the work of Christ he came nigh unto death hazarding his life to supply that which was lacking in your service toward me" (vr. 30). You will observe that the work under consideration was "the work of Christ" (something relating to Christ in contrast with things not related to Christ . . . something special or peculiar to the grounds of the Christian calling). Now it turns out that Paul is speaking of a gift from the church to him that was brought from them to him by Epaphroditus. My conclusion is that the work of the church here was in the collective provision, involving both the gift and the selection and sending of the messenger by which each who had part personally had "fellowship" with Paul's affliction (vr. 14 of ch. 4). Each person, by contribution toward Paul's support and by the combined efforts of all through means of the organization and talents common to them, enjoyed this fellowship. Hence to say that the church sent to Paul is expressive of HOW the disciples acted. We would conclude that COLLECTIVE ACTION is a matter of HOW people are acting, not a *something* acting apart from people.

*HOW ALL OF THIS BEARS ON OUR PRESENT QUESTION*

In order to arrive at some standard by which it can be determined that collective action is present and at the same time relate this to what is peculiar or special to the grounds of the Lordship of Jesus, so that it may be seen that it is "of Christ", I submit the following proposition:

All duties of a Christian, which rest upon grounds peculiar to his being a Christian, and which are authorized for performance together with other Christians, are also duties for which a local congregation is authorized to make provision.

It will be observed from this that I regard the Christian as the unit of the local church and that for the collective to act there must be authority for the individual (unit) to act. It would be impossible to address a local church without addressing the units which constitute it! "He that hath an ear to hear what the Spirit sayeth to the Churches" (Rev. 2:7). But one could address either a local church or an individual on matters that did not involve collective action. I trust this will serve to explain why I begin by saying "all duties of a Christian"...

Next, there is the qualification that must attach even to the consideration of Christian duties because many of them relate to duties which one has before he becomes a Christian and which are only more emphatic to the Christian. I refer to such duties as a husband's love for his wife and a citizen's duties to the government and humanitarian activities. Such duties are comprehended in the apostle's injunction: "Was any man called being circumcised? Let him not be uncircumcised. Hath any man been called in uncircumcision? Let him not be circumcised" ... (1 Cor. 7:18). If I mistake not this refers not simply to the act of circumcision but is put for all the things distinctive and characterized by the act. Hence, Jewish citizens (circumcision), having the obligations of the customs of the Jews and Jewish government, were not relieved of these duties by the fact that they had obeyed the gospel of Christ. By the same token, Gentiles, who never had these Jewish customs, were not to assume them or think the performance of them vital to their salvation. But we are told "that he might create in himself of the two one new man" (Eph. 2:15) so that we understand that both Jew and Gentile, while having human relationships and obligations before becoming Christians, and continuing to have them afterwards, (as per 1 Cor. 7:18 above) nonetheless are, in connection with Christ "a new man" ... possessing new and special relationship and duties peculiar to the grounds of the Lordship of Jesus. We do not believe that a local church exists in reference to these prior things (hence denying the contention of the advocates of the "social gospel") but rather to those things which are peculiar to Christ. If we are persuaded that the Christian sustains peculiar and special obligations to Jesus by virtue of his calling, then we must believe that the local church, a collective of such Christians, must relate to their collective action in such things. In Eph. 2:10, Paul expresses the point quite well . . ."for we are his workmanship, created in Christ Jesus for good works, which God afore prepared that we should walk in them." As certainly as the units (Christians) are "in connection with Christ" and their work as Christians (all of it) "afore prepared" by God, then their collective action (the work of the local church) would also be peculiar to this qualifying affirmation.

Again, authority for a Christian to act, in a matter peculiar to the grounds that he is a Christian, would not, in itself, authorize him to act collectively with others to accomplish it. Therefore we insert the phrase "and which are authorized for performance, together with other Christians." It is here that we believe the essence of distinction between individual and collectively performed duties lies. Be that as it may, we pass on to then conclude the proposition by pointing out that "such duties are also duties for which a local church is authorized to make provision." We are trying to point out that while the individual Christian is active in such duties that there is more than his action . . . his action alone cannot be the action of all . . . but in the same manner he and others are authorized to act together, then authority is expressed for the need and utilization of the means by which these things can be done. We have frequently said that when God commands a thing to be done the command authorizes everything essential to its execution even though the things essential be not stated. I believe this to be a true principle. No "together" action of saints would be possible if the means for its accomplishment were not allowed. But there is more here than I have said. It is true that saints might work concurrently at the same task, and in that sense work "together," without working jointly or collectively. But the facts we have previously pointed out, in which it is indicated that the Lord provided that saints work "collectively" (many acting as one), (I Cor. 1:10) will allow authority for collective action to be drawn from together action. What is equally the duty of all, and which is authorized for performance together, cannot fail of authority for collective action.

We have previously stated that even in past times brethren have found it necessary to discuss the work of the church. While their differences have been many, they have been almost altogether agreed on the three basic fields into which that work falls. Representative of this general area of agreement is the following from the pen of Brother R. L. Whiteside. "What is the work of the church? I believe it is comprehended in the three following divisions: First, edifying, or building up, itself; second, relieving the wants of the poor and needy; third, preaching the gospel to people who are not Christians" *(Doctrinal Discourses . . . pg. II)*.

## DEMONSTRATION OF THE THREE DIVISIONS

The manner in which various ones have set about to establish authority for these three divisions of the work of the church affords an interesting insight into their personal understanding of authority. While the Lord has not spelled out the processes of thought and reason one must use to arrive at a conclusion, we are none the less responsible to make decisions and reach conclusions agreeable to all the great principles by which He makes his will known. While truth is inspired of God our individual methods of apprehending it are not. Recognizing this to be true, I am happy to proceed with showing you my own method of study.

In the matter of edification we deal unmistakedly with an obligation that rests upon grounds peculiar to the calling that is in the Lord. None but saints are so related "in" Christ that it is their duty, rising out of that relationship, to edify one another in the Lord: "In love of the brethren be tenderly affectioned one to another; in honor preferring one another" (Rom. 12:10); "From whom all the body fitly framed and knit together through that which every joint supplieth, according to the due measure of each several part, make the increase of the body unto the building up of itself in love" (Eph. 4:16).

Again, consider the fact that the Christian work of edification is authorized for performance together with other Christians. "So also ye, since ye are zealous of spiritual gifts, seek that ye may abound unto the edifying of the church" (I Cor. 14:12); (v. 26) "What is it then, brethren? When ye come together, each one hath a psalm, hath a teaching, hath a revelation, hath a tongue. Let all things be done unto edifying." From this I conclude that brethren are authorized to collectively provide for edification of saints. This is done when, through the organizational arrangement peculiar to a local church, brethren select teachers, make appointments, buy and distribute suitable study materials etc. When one so appointed edifies the assembly, the church does it; when one is rebuked by means of the collective instrumentalities, he is rebuked by the church.

## HOW THIS MATTER OF EDIFICATION IS SEEN IN THE PUBLIC WORSHIP

To abbreviate my presentation as much as possible and yet develop what is here a basic part of edification, consider with me what are commonly called the items of public worship; singing, prayer, the Lord's Supper and the contribution.

*Singing*, as a general matter, does not rest upon grounds peculiar to a Christian nor involve him in Christian duty. But such singing as that in Eph. 5:19 that resulted from being "filled with the Spirit" (v. 18) most certainly is. Christians are commanded: "Let the word of Christ dwell in you richly; in all wisdom teaching and admonishing one another with psalms, hymns, and spiritual songs, singing with grace in your hearts unto God" (Col. 3:16). Here is a singing that is the duty of a Christian and which rests upon grounds peculiar to his being a Christian and which is also authorized for performance together with other Christians. Therefore, the church is authorized to collectively provide for such by selecting ones to lead, arrangement of the singing in the service, procuring song books out of congregational funds etc.

Prayer is not, as a general matter, peculiar to the Christian. But such prayer as that produced by the Spirit of God (1 Cor. 14:15) "I will pray with the spirit, and I will pray with the understanding also" most certainly is. While this refers to inspired prayer we advance to praying in the name of Jesus by any man, past or present, and point out that this is special to the grounds of one being a Christian. Further, the example of disciples praying together in the house of Mary (Acts 12:12); the command to pray without ceasing (1 Thes. 5:17), and the expressed desire of Christ through the Spirit given to Paul: "I exhort therefore, first of all, that supplications, prayers, intercessions, thanksgivings, be made for all men . . . for this is good and acceptable in the sight of God our Saviour . . . I desire therefore that men pray in every place, lifting up holy hands . . . (I Tim. 2:1, 3, 8). From this I would say that it is the work of the church to collectively provide for these things to be carried out in the assembly by appointing men to lead in prayer, appoint intervals and place for prayer and to cause teaching to be done concerning it.

*THE LORD'S SUPPER* immediately identifies as both the duty of a Christian and as also resting upon grounds peculiar to this calling. It is shown to be such by it's declaration of his death and the memory invoked (I Cor. 11:25-26). Apart from Christ there would be no Lord's Supper.

That it is a duty authorized to be performed together with other Christians is made clear by the fact that disciples came together to eat it (Acts 20:7; I Cor. 11:20).

Therefore, the work of the church is to collectively provide for the eating of the Lord's Supper. This is done by supplying from common funds or resources the bread and cup; by appointing a time for it's observance and selecting men to serve at the table etc.

*THERE IS A CONTRIBUTION THAT IS* "in connection with Christ" and a duty in which a Christian has responsibility; (I Cor. 16:2) "Let each one of you."

That is a contribution resting upon grounds peculiar to his being a Christian (Acts 4; I Cor. 16:1-2; I Cor. 8:7).

Christians are authorized to act together in the matter of making a contribution (I Cor. 16:2).

Therefore the church is authorized to provide for a contribution to be taken; treasury provided and means by which such funds may be expended etc.

## *EXAMINATION OF THE MATTER OF EVANGELIZATION*

The gospel itself, along with it's proclamation to the lost, is peculiar to the grounds of one's being a Christian. "And ye became imitators of us, and of the Lord, having received the word in much affliction, with joy of the Holy Spirit; so that ye became an ensample to all that believe in Macedonia and Achaia. For from you hath sounded forth the word of the Lord, not only in Macedonia and Achaia, but in every place your faith to God-ward is gone forth; so that we need not speak anything" (I Thess. 1:6-8). This could only be true of saints.

That saints are authorized to act together in teaching unbelievers can be seen from 1 Cor. 14:23: "If therefore the whole church be assembled together and all speak with tongues, and there come in men unlearned or unbelieving, will they not say that you are mad? (v 24) But if all prophesy, and there come in one unbelieving or unlearned, he is reproved by all, he is judged by all; (25) and the secrets of his heart are made manifest; and so he will fall down on his face and worship God, declaring that God is among you indeed." While the ability to edify was, in this instance under consideration, supplied by supernatural gifts of the spirit, the fact and purposes of evangelization remain the same. Therefore we conclude that saints may act collectively to preach the gospel. They do this by collectively selecting teachers, providing appointment and places, arranging gospel meeting etc. Of course we can also produce examples from the scripture to illustrate that they did have authority to preach the gospel by means of the collective action of saints, but just now we are illustrating the accuracy of a rule which, though not essential in this immediate instance, is helpful in other places. If we can see clearly its operation in instances that we otherwise know to be correct, then we can have confidence in it where the matter is clouded or questioned.

We come now to speak of the work of the church as it concerns benevolence. First, we must all be aware of the fact that benevolence, in general, is the work of a Christian in common with all other men. It does not rest upon grounds peculiar to his being a Christian. Gentiles were condemned for being "unbenevolent" (unmerciful) (Romans 1:31) and the Good Samaritan practiced benevolence, as did Cornelius, before Christianity was commenced. It is a God given responsibility to all men because of their common humanitarian relationships and could never be shown to be peculiar to the teaching of Jesus or practice of his disciples. But, while Christians have, in common with other men the responsibilities of what might be called "general benevolence" (for sake of a distinction we need to make) they also have a very special relation to "Communicating to the necessities of saints" (Rom. 12:13). Perhaps the most prominent case of benevolence in the New Testament was that accorded the poor saints in Jerusalem by Gentile Christians. In this case the benevolence is urged on the basis of relationship and debt: ". . . but now, I say, I go unto Jerusalem, ministering unto saints. For it hath been the good pleasure of Macedonia and Achaia to make a certain contribution for the poor among the saints that are at Jerusalem. Yea, it hath been their good pleasure; and their debtors they are. For if the Gentiles have been made partakers of their things, they owe it to them also to minister to them in carnal things." (Romans 15:25-27). This will also serve to explain why the over-riding tone of this contribution was that of unity and peace between Gentiles and Jews in Christ. While the immediate effect was to supply necessities to the poor saints, it's higher and overall purpose was to cement Jew-Gentiles relations in the gospel. This affords the light in which one must view Paul's great expectations and hope in reference to it: "For the ministration of this service not only filleth up the measure of the wants of the saints, but aboundeth also through many thanksgivings unto God; seeing that through the proving of you by the ministration they glorify God for the obedience of your confession unto the gospel of Christ, and for the liberality of your contribution unto them and unto all; while they themselves also, with supplication on your behalf, long after you by reason of the exceeding grace of God in you" (2 Cor. 9:12-14). You will observe that this expresses a hope which Paul entertained in reference to the gift that, as yet, was not even made. He hoped it would reach beyond relieving the needs of the poor saints and cause all Jewish Christians to think well of their Gentile brethren in Christ. Whether it accomplished this worthy object we are never informed. This explains why the contribution was said to be unto "them" (the poor Jewish saints who actually received the funds) and "unto all" Jewish Christians in that the gift to the poor among them was also a gesture of good-will towards all of the Jewish saints.

Every instance of benevolence in the New Testament that can remotely be argued as authority for church benevolence carries in its text the modifications that show it was to saints. Keep in mind that we are speaking in reference to the subjects *toward whom* the congregational benevolence is directed. We propose no limitation as to who may have received a benefit from that provision. In Acts chapters 4 and 6 the fact that the needs of saints were met through the collective action of saints in no wise implies that the dependents of such needy saints (if indeed there were any) could not share in the provision. On this the scriptures are silent. But the action of the church was to the saints. When the church provides for the Lord's supper to be eaten it makes that provision for the saints but in so doing it does not say that a non-saint cannot partake. While no man can establish authority for a church to provide the Lord's supper for a non-saint, few would be so bold as to say that a non-saint cannot eat. While the New Testament affirms the class of persons provided benevolence by the church to be saints it does not seek, in any way, to restrict the benefits derived from it, to them alone. We are all recipients of benefits that were never a contribution to us personally. There is a vast difference in restricting the contribution and restricting the benefit. Any contribution to a saint would not meet his need until it made possible his meeting responsibilities toward those dependent upon him. A man's paycheck is to him, and not to his dependents, and the employer sustains relation with his employee, not his employee's dependents. But this is not to say that the dependents of the employee may not, on that account, receive any benefit from the pay check!

In this connection, it is proper to point out that current issues between brethren over the scriptural subjects of congregational benevolence *did not* arise, as some would imply, from a dictatorial criticism of congregations acting in some border-line cases of benevolence. We all will to be pleasing to God, I trust, but are not always possessed of the good sense to see clearly in every instance the application of our principles.

Current issues *did* grow out of a concerted effort to make brethren accept brotherhood programs of work such as Herald of Truth, colleges, camps etc., supported out of the treasury of the churches on the basis of appeal to the general practice of their support of orphan homes. Out of that controversy came a focal interest in the orphan home and in turn, because it was contended that churches sustained a charge to care for orphans and that the building and maintaining of institutional orphan homes was simply a means by which this was accomplished, a controversy over the subjects of congregational benevolence. There is no way that the problem of institutional homes for orphans, as supported out of church treasuries, can be discussed or settled without dealing with the scriptural subjects of congregational benevolence.

But, to return to our point. Since the benevolence performed to fellow saints is peculiar to the grounds of one's Christian calling, and seeing that such benevolence is authorized for performance, together with other Christians, we conclude that it is a benevolence for which the church may collectively provide. This is done by causing such a collection of funds as may be necessary to be made and/or by use of such funds to either give directly to needy saints or to provide for services or needs in their behalf, etc.

## WHEN CAN IT BE DETERMINED THAT THE CHURCH HAS DONE SOMETHING?

To make a practical analysis of what we have affirmed in reference to the work of the church, let us observe how we can determine, from bible evidence, that the church has acted. The previously mentioned incident of Acts 4:32-35 is one that we believe to involve "church" work. While it is no where stated that the church did what is here said to have been done, we none the less know that it did . . . not on the basis of mere assumption but by analysis of evidence. What was provided for out of a common treasury in connection with Christ, brought about by individuals in Christ with common conviction, generosity and devotion toward their own needy people in Christ, cannot miss being action of a church of Christ.

In Acts 11:29 when the disciples, every man according to his ability, determined to send relief to the brethren that dwelt in Judea: and did so by sending through the "hand" of Paul and Barnabas, they afford us an example of what, if not church action, was by the very circumstance authority for such. Their action may have been distributive rather than collective but, by what I have set out, the facts would authorize it to have been done by a church.

When it can be shown that brethren either acted or were authorized to act on some matter that is peculiar to the grounds of their being a Christian and, in addition, that such action was authorized to be performed together with other Christians, then I would conclude you have authority for the church to do it. Even though a letter is addressed to a church it may not, on that account, be regarded as authority for brethren to collectively perform what is contained in the letter. Whatever is said to the church is said to the member (Rev. 2:7) "He that hath an ear to hear, let him hear what the Spirit saith to the churches." To whom it is addressed is not important, as regards whether it be the work of the church or an individual; it is *what* is authorized to be done and how, that counts.

## CONCLUSION

If there are categories or divisions of fields of work other than edification, evangelization and benevolence to saints that are authorized for collective action of saints as we have herein qualified them, I am not aware of them.

Again, accepting the church as it is set forth in the New Testament as sufficient to do everything that God wants brethren to collectively do in Christ, I stand opposed to the formation of any other collective to provide for these things, either a collective of churches or Christians. By the same token I stand opposed to placing upon the church responsibilities to provide for matters that are not properly identifiable with the above three categories. Hence I stand opposed to institutionalism on the one hand and the "fun and frolic" social gospel on the other.

To accept either another collective or other fields of work is presumptive; without divine authority; and therefore displeasing to Him who called us in Christ.

May all of us "give diligence to present ourselves approved unto God" both in our individual and personal duties as well as in those we seek to discharge by joining with other saints so as to collectively provide for them.

## The Work of the Church

Gus Nichols

Mr. Chairman and the distinguished brethren. I want to thank those who invited me to be one of a group of twenty-four brethren gathered here to spend three and one-half days together in intensive study of the causes of divisions among us, and the way of peace and unity for which our Lord prayed in the shadow of the cross.

Of course, we are not here as delegates to some sort of a convention. We were not sent here by our home congregations to represent them in all their foibles and follies, faith and triumphs. We are not here to foolishly try to make laws for Almighty God, nor to nullify laws of God in his word. But we are here to hear all things commanded of God. We are here because somebody thought we are good men, mature men, big enough to scripturally and fairly deal with a big problem, honestly, and in the fear of God and eternal judgment.

We ought not to be here to defend some good preacher of the brotherhood, some religious school, or some good paper, or some fine church somewhere. We are not here to represent anybody, even ourselves, but we are here, or at least ought to be, for the purpose of representing and defending the truth of the Bible, the only basis of lasting peace and unity among believers. The challenge of a torn and bleeding brotherhood of the finest people on earth is crying out for strong men, good men, men who yearn for that unity which we have so eloquently preached and so poorly practiced in a world religiously divided.

If Christ who so earnestly prayed for unity among us, that the world might believe God sent him, were in our midst in per-

---

GUS NICHOLS—*Evangelist for the original congregation in Jasper, Alabama since 1932; author; prominent debater; widely used on college lectureships—regular lecturer at Freed-Hardeman College, Henderson, Tennessee; staff writer for the* GOSPEL ADVOCATE, *Nashville, Tennessee.*

son, what would he say more than that which he has said. And would he not shame us, rather than commend? And what will that Christ say, and do, at the judgment?

## WHAT IS THE WORK OF THE CHURCH?

The divisions among us are found in the work of the church. Of course, those following the truth, and the principles of peace in the scriptures are not to be censured for our divisions and factions. Paul only condemned those who "cause" divisions and offenses contrary to the "doctrine" of Christ. (Rom. 16:17-18)

The apostle did not say this "doctrine" is so complex and mysterious that we would have no way of ever knowing who is guilty, and who to mark and avoid, and who is not guilty. But the Bible is so plain that we can know and reject those in error and false doctrine. (Titus 3:10)

For the purpose of topical arrangement we may say the work of the church is, in its nature, (1) EVANGELISM, (2) WORSHIP, (3) EDIFICATION, and (4) BENEVOLENCE.

## THE CHURCH AND WORLD EVANGELISM

Of course, I need not argue at length to this group, that the church is to evangelize the whole world in our day. Neither do I need to prove that, with the proper faith, wisdom, and the love Jesus had, we could, by use of world media of communication, as well as by other congregational and individual effort, reach the world with the gospel in our day (Mk. 16:15-16; Mt. 28:18-20).

The apostles and early Christians reached their small world in their day with the gospel. (Col. 1:23; Rom. 10:18) The apostles first orally committed that gospel unto the churches, later giving it unto them in letters and written form, and made the church the pillar and ground of the truth. (I Tim. 3:15) They taught that the church is God's missionary society, and that through it His manifold wisdom is to be made known. (Eph. 3:8-10) The apostles were set in the church and functioned through the church. (I Cor. 12:28). They had no organization larger than the local congregations, nor smaller than the whole body of Christ; they had no ecclesiasticism, through which to preach the gospel. The elders or bishops exercised no authority over anything but the local congregations over which they were to take the oversight, and had no authority anywhere in matters of religion, except in the congregation where each held his membership as an elder. (Acts 20:28; I Pet. 5:1-4)

## THE CHURCH WAS GOD'S MISSIONARY SOCIETY

As we have shown, the church was the "pillar and the ground of the truth," (I Tim. 3:15) and was so organized as to function in the fullest capacity, and to do its most effective work, just as a congregation. Neither were the congregations to be tied together into any sort of ecclesiasticism. The autonomy of each congregation was demanded. (Acts 20:28; I Pet. 5:1-2) And this specific divine law excluded everything contrary thereto.

## MODERN MISSIONARY SOCIETIES

Modern missionary societies are excluded by God's specific divine law. And they are in competition with the church, as Christ's kingdom would have been in competition with Caesar's kingdom if it had been a literal kingdom of this world, in its nature. (Jn. 18:36) But since Christ's kingdom was spiritual, it did not clash with Caesar's, and therefore, had a right to exist. The missionary societies gotten up by men are in the spiritual realm, as is the church, and are human additions to the church, and are thus additions to the doctrine of Christ.

Their introduction was not under any sort of Bible authority. There is no specific authority for them, and they do not function under any generic authority. There is no command, approved example, nor necessary inference for their existence. Therefore, those who contend for them, and support them, cause the division over them in the church, and are to be marked and avoided. (Rom. 16:17-18) They are wedges driven by those of a liberal attitude toward the Bible.

The New Testament congregations, under divine background command, simply as churches, sent out men to preach the gospel. (Acts 13:1-4) Later the missionaries returned to the sending church and reported concerning their work unto the church. (Acts 14:26-28) And let us remember this was done by a specific command in the background. (Acts 13:1-4) Their example is, therefore, a binding example, and excludes the modern missionary societies.

In the commission given by Christ unto his apostles, and in principle applied unto the church, all nations were to be taught, or to have the gospel preached unto them, and those baptized further taught to obey all things commanded by Christ. (Matt. 28:18-20)

### THE COMMAND TO "GO" SPECIFIC AND GENERIC

The command to "Go" and teach is specific, as to the THING to be done, but it is generic as to the how to do the THING commanded. They had no liberty as to whether or not they would go. But they had liberty as to how to go. All the various ways of travel were alike authorized by the generic command to "go." If Jesus had been specific and said "Walk into all the world and preach the gospel," the church would have long ago perished off the face of the earth. Such a specific command as to method would not have fitted into our modern age of speed and travel. Walk, ride, swim and fly in a plane are all alike authorized, and we are to choose what is expedient in that realm. Obedience in the realm of generic law does not mean uniformity of action. Here we are to have unity in diversity. Let those who may have been denying this come forward and try to defend this ground. Fortunately, no one has made a law against obeying the command to "go" by use of the automobile, or airplane. No one argues for the apostolic method of travel under such generic commands. Such would be as sinful a move, and as radical as liberalism in those who trifle with specific law.

### DIVISION OVER TEACHING

But the word "Teach", in the commission is just as specific as the command to go, as far as the THING to be done is concerned. But "TEACH" is generic as to the method. And here should be liberty. As the old pioneers said, "In faith unity, in opinions liberty." "TEACH" is a matter of faith, but as by what method this may be done, there is room for opinion. Here we should have liberty. No one should make any law that the teaching must be done by any one exclusive method, nor that it may not be done in some other expedient way. But our "Anti-classes" brethren have caused division here—in the realm of generics, where there could and should have been unity, by all being silent where God was silent, under generic authority. Here we could have unity, by each respecting the liberty of others. Classes are a matter of liberty, and this being the truth of the matter, all should teach this, and then let each church decide for itself whether or not to use the class method.

I had a debate with these brethren at Piedmont, Alabama, on these issues, and now one congregation prefers to use classes, and the other does not, but both are in unity and work together. This is the way truth makes for unity. There must be unity and uniformity in doing *the thing commanded*. But there can be unity and diversity under generic law, if all want unity, as did Jesus who died for it. (Eph. 2:14-16) I have no right to make a law that all churches must have classes, and no one else has any divine right to make a law against classes. The authority for classes is abundant, but everything that is authorized is not bound. Classes are authorized but not bound. Teach is bound, but not any certain method. All of us can see this; or can we?

You can apply this same principle of interpretation to the use of a baptistry, which is authorized, but not bound. Baptism is bound, but no certain place is bound. Therefore, any expedient place is authorized, one the same as another, provided it is also expedient. There can be unity in this, with diversity in practice. Just let all preach the truth about its being a matter of generics, and then let all exercise their God-given liberty as to the place of baptism. Make no laws, either positive or negative, in the realm of generics. In matters of expediency like eating meat, neither one is to despise or judge the other. (Rom. 14:3) But if one makes a law "commanding to abstain from meats" he is teaching a doctrine of devils, and is sure to cause division. (I Tim. 4:1-5; Col. 2:14-16)

Yes, we can fully fellowship brethren who choose to use only one class, if they teach and practice the truth that it is in the realm of generics, and is a matter of liberty, which Paul defended. (Gal. 2:1-5; 5:1; Acts 16:1-4)

And let us not forget that a method or way of doing something under a generic command may be authorized without being binding. An approved example is authority for doing a thing, but if the example is under generic law, it is only optional with us, as it was with those who left the example.

Our Anti-classes brethren, have a way of saying in reference to the method of teaching used by the apostles and early Christians, under generic authority: "You see? This is the way they did it." After awhile they will change it and say: "This is the way the Bible *says do it*." No, if it is under generic authority, it is not the way God said *to do it*—he did not give any certain way *to do it*, or it would not be under generics, but would be under specifics.

## EVANGELISM AND COOPERATION

It is usually admitted that churches can cooperate with each other in evangelism, but by some sort of interpretation, they claim a *certain* and *exclusive kind* of cooperation is authorized in the New Testament which would exclude *one church* from sending funds to another church in evangelism. They teach that this can be done in benevolence, but not in evangelism. They say evangelism and benevolence are two distinct and separate patterns. And when they present their so-called proof, it is not under specific authority, but they depend upon examples which are in fact under generic authority, and that without showing the example of such was under specific authority. Remember, any example under generic authority *is not an exclusive example, but is optional,* and what they need is an exclusive example. The Lord has not told the churches how to cooperate, so long as autonomy prevails. (Acts 20:28; I Pet. 5:1-4) In fact, the New Testament churches did not themselves follow an *unchangeable pattern* in cooperation, and in giving and receiving.

## JERUSALEM CHURCH SENT BARNABAS

The Jerusalem church sent Barnabas, a preacher, unto the Antioch church. (Acts 11:22-26) If the sending church did not support him, it could have done so scripturally. It is implied in the record that Antioch was a rich church, and needed no money, but needed the gospel preacher and could support him itself. Then the New Testament was not written, and the gospel was being orally transmitted by the few who knew the truth, and could teach it. We may be sure the preacher did not steal for a living the year which he spent at Antioch. This is an approved example of one church sending to another in evangelism, and is under no revealed specific background command, and is, therefore, optional with us. In Acts 15:22-35 the Jerusalem church again sent help to Antioch church in evangelism —sent four preachers and teachers.

## MUST WE SEND ONLY WHAT THEY SENT?

To say we must give unto another church in evangelism only what they gave back there, is to make a human law. Where did a church then send to another church its discarded pews? Pulpit? Old, but good, used song books? A tent? Bibles?

When I was in Jerusalem in 1962 Brother Hendley needed Bibles in Hebrew for the Jews to read, but suggested that we send the money and let them buy them from England at about half what we would have to pay here for them, and save on transportation, an additional sum. Yet some say it would be unscriptural to send money to the Jerusalem church with which to buy such Bibles. Brethren, do we really want unity, as Jesus did?

Money was handled in connection with evangelism under generic authority in the days of the apostles. Paul says to the Corinthian church, "I robbed other churches, taking wages of them, to do you service." (2 Cor. 11:8) Here were churches cooperating to do another church service. Hence a church can do service to another church and aid it in evangelism.

But some say this money, or wages, was sent *directly* unto Paul, the preacher. There is no proof of this. The Bible does not say *how* it was sent, nor *to whom*. It may have been sent to the church for Paul. In Acts 11:29-30 some "relief" was sent unto "the brethren" in Judea, but it was *not sent directly* to the "Brethren" but they *"sent it to the elders"* for the *"Brethren."* If it had made any difference as far as divine law is concerned, God would have told us to whom the money was sent in 2 Cor. 11:8. It seems that God intentionally left this point out of the record so we might know that it was a matter of no importance, as far as God's plan is concerned.

It all reminds us of the anti-classes brother who argues that there is a fixed pattern in I Cor. 14 against our Bible classes. The one cupper also argues that Jesus used *"only one"* container, and thinks we have a fixed pattern against the use of individual cups. They all build their theories on the argument that *"This is the way they did it* in the days of the apostles," as though everything they did was a bound pattern for us, and without any regard as to whether or not it was under generic authority making it optional for us, as it was for them.

Money was sent unto elders of the church. (Acts 11:29-30) This shows the elders could be trusted with money, the same as a preacher. This whole theory by-passes the elders of the church who handles *both the money* for evangelism and *for benevolence* as contributed by their own members, and *who are over all the work* of both evangelism and benevolence done by the local congregation (Acts 20:28; I Pet. 5:1-4; I Cor. 16:1-3; 2 Cor. 11:8).

## CHURCHES COOPERATED IN EDIFICATION

One church may cooperate with another church in edification. Paul said unto the church at Colosse: "And when this epistle is read among you, cause that it be read also in the church of the Laodiceans; and that ye likewise read the epistle from Laodicea." (Col. 4:16) Here one church could "cause" or sponsor a work to be done in another church, and still respect autonomy. Hence, churches can aid each other in edification, which is a work of the church. (Eph. 4:8-16) Stronger churches can aid each other in edification, which is a work of the church. (Eph. 4:8-16) Stronger churches may often help weak congregations to put on a radio program in their communities, or publish articles in their local secular papers, help them build meeting houses, help support preachers, etc. And all of this can be done without violating the autonomy of the churches, and without any ecclesiasticism.

## CHURCH WORK AND WORSHIP

We may say our worship is a work of the church. The church is commanded to assemble. (Heb. 10:25) This specified service is to be on the first day of the week. (I Cor. 16:2) And this service was for worship. (I Cor. 11:17-34; Acts 20:7) Singing, praying, teaching, the Lord's supper and giving as we are prospered, are the items of the regular Lord's day worship (Eph. 5:19; Acts 11:26; Acts 2:42; I Cor. 11:17-22; Acts 20:7).

However, some with a liberal attitude toward specific authority have caused division over the music of the church. God selected the kind and specified and commanded singing. (Eph. 5:19; Col. 3:16) But they have added playing, and trifled with the specific command and changed the word of God and made it to merely say "make music" in worship, so as to get to play.

The church is plagued with liberalism as well as with radicalism. If the background command had simply said, "Make music in worship," then the command would have been generic and we could both sing and play, or do either. We would have had a choice in the matter, and the whole thing would have been a matter of liberty.

But God specified *"singing,"* and "making melody *in the heart."* (Eph. 5:19) This *specific command* excludes playing, just as gopher wood excluded pine in building the ark.

Some brethren today are liberal with the word of God. Some would put the church into the entertainment business, into profit-making businesses, etc. Some would put it into politics, into the secular education business, into a social club, etc. Whatever is not involved in evangelism, worship, edification, and benevolence is not a work of the church.

All of us realize that the church has its own business affairs to look after, and that it may build a meeting house as an aid to evangelism, edification and worship, and build a parking lot, have a drinking fountain, and do whatever may be expedient which is authorized in generic authority, such as the command to assemble, and to worship, etc.

## DIVISION OVER CONTAINERS

Some have caused a division over the use of individual containers in the communion service. They argue that such is equal to the use of instrumental music in worship. But the cases are not at all alike, in that the instruments *are not authorized*, either by specific command, approved example, or by necessary inference, while Jesus used a generic term in saying, "Divide it among yourselves." (Lk. 22:17) He did *not tell us how* to divide the cup, but he did tell us what kind of music to make. He said he wanted "singing." (Col. 3:16)

It is argued that the early disciples *"did it this way"* — "used only one vessel." They may or may not have so done. But they did not have to use only one; for they were under the background command which said, *"Divide it,"* and did *not tell them how,* leaving the matter as a thing of liberty. Therefore, their example, though approved, would not be binding on us; though it would be optional, and shows their method was one of the authorized ways of doing the thing commanded, when He said, "Take this and divide it among yourselves." (Lk. 22:17)

It is just as sinful to make a "one cup law" under our *generic* authority for individual cups, as it would be to add instrumental music to the worship. For to add an *anti-cups* law is adding to the word of God, the *same as adding instrumental music*. The same is true of an *anti-classes law*, an *anti-baptistry law*, etc. Neither side is permitted to make any laws for God, *either to use the cups, or not to use them*. We can be united by teaching the truth *that it is a matter of liberty*, and then *let each church decide* for itself how it will handle the matter, and all be united, even in brotherly love, and in liberty under generic authority in such matters.

## CARE OF THE POOR AND NEEDY

Another work of the church is to care for the poor and needy. Benevolence is a work of the church. The Old Testament required God's people to be merciful to the poor and needy. (Psa. 68:5-7; Ex. 22:22-24; Deut. 10:18; 24:17; Job 22:16-22; 29:1-13) The poor stranger was also to be aided by God's people, as well as the Israelite, and even to be fed out of the treasury supported by the tithe. (Deut. 14:22-27, 28-29; 15:11) Hence, we should expect to find the church a benevolent institution, unless Judaism was better then than Christianity (Mt. 19:21; Mk. 10:21; Lk. 6:30; Lk. 19:8; Lk. 10:25-37).

## JERUSALEM CHURCH AND BENEVOLENCE

Following the establishment of the church on Pentecost, Acts 2, there was a new religion, but no written record containing it, and it was needful for Christians to tarry for awhile in Jerusalem and be taught by the inspired apostles. (Acts 2:42) They needed to be indoctrinated so as to take the gospel back home to various nations. When the regular "fellowship" of Acts 2:42 in worship was not enough to care for those whose funds had given out, the disciples sold their possessions and goods and parted them to all men, as every man had need, and had all things in common, *and all this to aid the gospel meeting in progress daily in the temple*. (Acts 2:44-46, 47) Later they all did this, and the apostles were the treasurers of the funds. We do not know the details of this distribution, but it was *"at home"* that the food provided was eaten. The church was the giving institution, and the home was a receiving institution. (Am. Std. Ver. Acts 2:46) Later, widows were cared for, who were thought neglected. (Acts 6:1-7)

## ARE THESE THREE EXAMPLES ALIKE?

In Acts 2:44-47 it seems that the disciples sold and gave directly to the poor among them and in order to help evangelism to continue. In Acts 4:34-37 the money was placed in care of the apostles as treasurers. But in Chapter 6:1-7 the distribution was in the hands of seven men chosen by divine direction. How could these differing examples be unchangeable and bound?

Again, in all three cases the money was raised by the disciples selling all their possessions and goods and even lands, to have all things common. But Peter argues that this was voluntary on their part, and that God had not commanded them to thus sell all and give it (Acts 5:4) Since this selling, etc., was not demanded of them, their examples of voluntarily doing this made their example in the matter *only an approved* and *optional* example with us, and *not a bound example.*

But if their example and all approved examples are bound upon us, brethren, why did not other churches later follow this example? Talk a lifetime about it and you can't prove that all approved examples are bound upon us. How about someone trying to prove we should sell all and give it away by saying, *"This is the way they did it?"* And also to argue, *"It is safe to do as they did it."* Yes, and it is also safe to do things under such *generic law* differently from the way they did them, if we wish to do so, such as to have classes, church-owned meeting houses, Sunday morning Lord's supper, instead of at night, individual cups, baptistry, etc.

Yes, and *"This is the way they did it,"* when it comes to their benevolence; the record says they had *"daily ministrations."* (Acts 6:1) In this latter reference, they had *"seven men"* over the work. Is this number of men bound upon us? What other church then ever followed that part of the example, or raised money like they did? Is an *unalterable* example changeable as you want it? "They had all things in common." Is this bound on us? How do you brethren know when an approved example is bound, and when it is not? When it is optional and when it is bound? Until you get out of confusion on this point, you will be making laws for God.

## WAS THE ANTIOCH EXAMPLE BINDING?

*To the extent* that God *specified* that certain details should be carried out, an example was a bound one. But *to the extent* that details were a matter of *liberty* and choice on the part of the disciples they were loosed, and their example in that point a matter of liberty with them, and with us as well. No detail could be bound upon us in an example *which was not first of all bound* upon them in the performance of the things in the example.

It seems that some prophets came from Jerusalem to Antioch to solicit funds for Judaea in a famine that was prophecied to come later. "Then the disciples, every man according to his ability, determined to send relief unto the brethren which dwelt in Judea; which also they did, and sent it to the elders by the hands of Barnabas and Saul." (Acts 11:27-30) Some brethren tell us that this is another *"unalterable"* example, and the details are bound upon us "to do as they did it." But let us examine the case more carefully.

1. They did not raise the money here by selling all things and having all things common, as in Acts 2 and 4.

2. Not the apostles, nor the elders, but *"the disciples,"* "every man according to his ability, DETERMINED to send this relief." Therefore, there is here no positive proof that this was church action.

3. They sent this contribution for foreign relief, and not for local relief, as in Acts 2, 4 and 6.

4. They sent it *"by the hands of Barnabas and Saul."* (Acts 11:29-30) Must we always send by the hands of two gospel preachers? Is this an "unalterable example," and all its details bound on us? It is *"an approved"* example, and is *"optional"* with us in all optional details. But all the details are "approved." Are they all binding? Must we send by two men only, *or may we send by a bank check, and send it by mail?*

Some brethren argue that we must send as they did. They argue that because on one or two occasions money in evangelism was sent to the preacher that *we must always* send money in evangelism to the preacher, and not to the elders of the church —not to the church. Don't you see? They are contending that we must send as they did. Again, they argue that *money* in

Acts 11:29 was sent to elders, and so they claim that *money* in benevolence must go to the elders—that we must give and send as they did. You say we can send *"a man"* to a church to aid it in evangelism, but *"not money"* to pay a preacher or put on a radio program. Hence, *you are arguing that we must do it as they did,* and *send as they sent it.* They sent by two men. *"This is the way they did it."*

And must we send what they sent? You make a distinction here when it is *"money,"* and when it is *"a man"* that is sent. According to you, we must only send what they sent. As far as we know, they only sent money in benevolence. *May we send food? Clothing? Medicine? A load of coal? A check? Yes, a check?* And may we send a *hundred dollars* to a church, *fifty* to be used in *benevolence,* and the other *fifty* to apply on a *radio program?* According to your doctrine, brethren, the church would have to return the *fifty* sent for a *radio program* and have you send it back—not to the church but to the preacher, or radio station. Is this true, or is it not? If you are making these things a test of fellowship, *you ought to be able to make out a strong case in favor of every point, or give up your demands for unity upon such errors. Must we do all things as they did* then? Do you do this? If you are going to teach this doctrine, why do you not practice it in regard to the classes, baptistry, cups, etc.? *Why not?*

After arguing that the church now must send *as they did,* and *only what they sent,* and *to whom it was sent then,* do you admit that a church can send things they did not send? *Bibles? Old church pews? Old song books? Tracts? Communion table which has been discarded? A used tent?*

## MUST WE KEEP THEM SEPARATE?

It is argued that we must keep evangelism and benevolence separate. Well, as we have seen, benevolence at Jerusalem by the church was to care for people during a meeting in progress, *was to aid evangelism,* and *for the spreading of the gospel.* The *two were mixed then.* Acts 2, 4, 6.

The church is to be like a city set on a hill so its light may shine and others see its good works and glorify God. Here are good works, including *"benevolence,"* for the purpose of getting an *"evangelistic"* result—glorifying God. (Mt. 5:14-16.) Jesus did his signs of *"benevolence,"* and feeding the thousands in a miraculous way, that John might write these good works and the result be faith in Him as the son of God—an evangelistic result of His "benevolence"—(Jn. 20:30-31; Mt. 15; Jn. 6.) *There is a teaching element in good examples,* even converting power in them when accompanied by the gospel. (I Pet. 3:1-4) Paul *"taught"* by *"example."* (Acts 20:35.) The *church* can teach by example, and who will deny it? Oh, yes, and you brethren believe that the examples of the church in benevolence recorded in the Bible teach us *that we must do as they did.* Don't you? Then, why do you make it a test of fellowship that one method of cooperation of churches must be, *in evangelism,* to send to some one other than the elders, *"while in benevolence"* to send to the elders?

## CHURCHES COOPERATED IN BENEVOLENCE

There is a background command for churches to cooperate in benevolence. (I Cor 16:1-3). Then there is the approved example of doing it. (2 Cor. 8:1-5; Rom. 15:25-31.) The approved example alone would be optional authority; but in view of the command in the background, the example was a binding one under the same conditions, and to a church with means and opportunity. (Phil. 4:14-18; Acts 11:29-30) No congregation can ignore the needs of destitute congregations around it and treat them as if they were of Satan, and please God. "Love the brotherhood." (I Pet. 2:17)

But it is argued by some that if a church sends to another church in evangelism, it loses its autonomy. This was not true in benevolence, and why think it true in evangelism? (I Cor. 16:1-3) But it is argued again, that the giving church in turning any funds over to another congregation loses autonomy, in that it loses control of its funds. Well, churches by approved example did send to other churches and did not lose autonomy.

Again, some contend that the receiving church is exercising authority over the giving church. Again, we say that was not true then, when they were giving and receiving churches.

*Again it is contended that the church becomes tied to whatever it contributes to, and if it gives to an orphan home it becomes tied to an orphan home,* and is an ecclesiasticism. What about *a church* giving to *another church? Are the two then tied toghether?* They gave to each other back then, and this did not happen. And if the church gives to a family of its own members, *does it become tied to that family?*

It is argued also that since *orphan homes are incorporated* it would be a sin for the church to give to an incorporated home. Well, many of the churches among you good brethren are also incorporated. If one such church were destitute and in great need, could a church contribute to it despite the fact that it is incorporated?

It is argued that the church is all sufficient for its work, and there is no place for an orphan home. However, the work of the church is not to be a home, but to contribute to those in need, *even in their own home.* The elders don't have to take over the homes of needy people and oversee the homes. God put elders over the church, and put men over homes. (I Tim. 3:4-5; Gal. 4:1-2) Though elders may be over a bank, a school, and the like, but not as elders, so they may be trustees over a home.

The issue is not the home, but the doctrine that the church has no obligation to any but saints in benevolence. Could the church contribute to two or three destitute children, even in Grandmother's home? Such would be an orphan home, the same as a home with a hundred children. But they sometimes say the church can't give to another institution, another organization. Well, you admit that churches did give to other churches in the New Testament, and can you deny that churches then also gave to individual homes in need? Such homes were institutions the same as a legal orphan home.

But you often argue that the orphan home is like the missionary society—both against the church. No, the missionary society is in the same realm with the church—both are in the spiritual realm—and clash as Jesus' kingdom would have with Caesar's kingdom if Jesus' kingdom had been material and literal in nature. But Jesus' kingdom was spiritual. (Jn. 18:36) Hence no clash between it and Caesar's kingdom—no competition between them. So of the orphan home, it is a literal and fleshly institution for the primary benefit of the fleshly man, while the church is spiritual in nature, and the two are in no way in conflict with each other, no more than the church and your home.

# CHURCH MAY CONTRIBUTE TO SAINTS AND OTHERS IN BENEVOLENCE

Another point which must be ironed out before there can be unity among us is that our brethren have debated: *"That it is a sin to take money out of the church treasury to buy food for hungry destitute children, and they which do such things will go to hell."* They teach that when the church is giving to saints, it means saints only, as denominational preachers think salvation by faith is faith only. (Rom. 5: 1-2; Jas. 2: 14-26) Our brethren are inconsistent in their interpretations, for when individuals are giving to "saints" in the scriptures, it is admitted that they gave also to others not saints. I Cor. 16: 1 says that contribution was for the saints, while 2 Cor. 9: 12-13 says it was "Unto them and unto all men." But our brethren say this just means some more saints. But in Galatians 6: 10 it is admitted that the same words include more than the saints. But they say, the word "men" is in italics in 2 Cor. 9: 12-13. Well, it is the same in Gal. 6: 10. The Greek word "Pantas" when used apart from some other word meaning man, is translated "All men" eleven times in the New Testament, and does not mean *saints only* a single time. (See John 2: 24; Jn. 12: 32; Acts 21: 28; Rom. 16: 19; 2 Cor. 9: 13; Gal. 6: 10; I Thes. 3: 12; 5: 14, 15; 2 Tim. 2: 24; I Pet. 2: 17)

If church contributions to saints, means saints only, then individuals in giving to saints (I Cor. 16: 15) means saints only. Then what becomes of their admission that individuals can give to "all men," and *especially* to the household of faith? (Gal. 6: 10) Paul says individuals are to distribute to the necessity of saints. (Rom. 12: 13) Does this exclude individuals from helping the "all men"? (Gal. 6: 10) Some have two rules of interpretation, in the same chapter. In I Cor. 16: 1 they say "saints" means saints only, but when individuals are addicted to the ministry of "saints" (vs. 15), they say this does not mean "saints only," but individuals can help all. Does I Tim. 5: 10 mean "saints only"? Why say it means that when the church is helping saints? Individuals were ministering to saints, in Heb. 6: 10. Does this mean saints only? If so, it contradicts your doctrine that individuals must help all men in need, as they are able.

In Psa. 37:28 the Lord does not forsake saints—does this exclude babies? Does assembly of saints exclude all others? (Psa. 89:5,7; 49:1.) The Lord *preserveth* the souls of saints—is this "saints only"—to exclude little children? Does Psa. 116:15 exclude little children? Will the Lord not bring souls of children with him? (I Thess 3:13, 14; Jude 14) Saints are to praise God—is this to exclude children from singing? (Psa. 148:14; Psa. 30:4) Saints are to fear the Lord—does it exclude children? (Psa. 34:9) We are to love saints—does it mean hate others—little children? (Eph. 1:15; Col. 1:4) Does pray for saints exclude praying for children? (Eph. 6:18) Is it wrong to sow discord among "brethren" only? (Prov. 6:19) Does relief of "brethren" mean to exclude children? (Acts 11:29-30) Does salute "saints" exclude saluting all others? (Phil. 4:21; Acts 21:7) Does the command to read the scriptures to *"holy brethren"* exclude reading them to all others? (I Thess. 5:26; Col. 4:16) Paul mentions a contribution to the "saints" and then says it was "unto them, and unto all men." (2 Cor. 9:12-13) Why say "all men" here means saints only, then admit it means the needy outside of the household of faith in Gal. 6:10?

Should we put the sign on the drinking fountain, that it is for saints only, since it costs the church money? Or, what about making it read "FOR POOR SAINTS ONLY"? Is the church a selfish and devilish institution which can receive contributions from the outside world, but if one of such contributors becomes destitute, it must say, *"We can receive from you; but we can't give you a dime?"* What of the doctrine that a little child can give to the church out of its savings from its infancy, but if destitute the church couldn't help it?

## The Work of the Church

### By W. L. Wharton, Jr.

Brother Nichols has said a number of things with which I am in complete agreement. But there are also some things, particularly in the closing half of his speech, which occasion response and clarification.

To take the last of his remarks for first consideration, he made a lengthy series of statements and repeatedly asked of each, "Does this exclude?" "Does this exclude?" Well, to me, brother Nichols, none of these statements exclude anything. However, I ask you, "Do they include" what you are affirming? It is your duty to establish them as being in the scope of what the Bible teaches . . . not mine to merely say "they are excluded."

He argued that "eis pantas" (UNTO ALL — ASV) (2 Cor. 9:13) means both saints and non-saints. But this is not the case at all. "All" is a substantive and takes the place of a noun. The identity of the noun it stands for must always be determined by context. If we say that "Jim, Don and Bill went to town," and then say: "All had a good time," does anyone sup-

---

W. L. WHARTON JR.—*Evangelist for Highland Blvd. congregation in San Antonio, Texas; conducts six months of meetings yearly throughout the nation and Canada; staff writer for* **THE PRECEPTOR**; *formerly served churches in Houston, Odessa, and Wichita Falls, Texas.*

pose that we are talking about any others than Jim, Don and Bill? Whoever is included in the "all" of 2 Cor. 9:13 will be in the context and not because "eis pantas" inherently means "everybody, whether saint or sinner."

He says the work of the church is not that of the home, and, therefore, the church must contribute to the home so the home can do that particular work. But he says the work of the church and that of a missionary society are coordinate; that the missionary society is doing the same work as that of the church. This concept of the missionary society is in complete harmony with my personal thinking. Since I believe that the work of the local church in evangelization falls in the realm of brethren acting collectively to provide for the preaching of the gospel, I can see that this is exactly what a missionary society is doing, i.e. many acting together as one (collective action) so as to provide for preaching the gospel. This not only says that the missionary society and the church are doing the same work, but says what the work is.

He says that the work of the church is to collectively provide for the orphan. If he is right, then his institutional home is wrong on the same grounds that the missionary society is wrong because it is also doing the work of the church! The work of an institutional home is to "collectively" provide for the support and care of its subjects. There is not an orphans' home in the country that ever burped a baby or fed it a meal. The home *provides* for such services to be performed. The "home" is a collective (exactly like a local church) and acts collectively to provide for something to be done. If God placed the responsibility for collective action on the local church (local collective), by what right do you form another collective for doing this very action (collectively providing for . . .) and tax the local church to support it on the basis that it is not the same work? How do you shift it off the church to the orphans' home and then back on to the church for support, brother Nichols?

He next asks about evangelization and benevolence, as to the matter of the examples of each found in the New Testament, and then in citing his evidence runs his examples together. And, what is more confusing to me, having confused his examples in the first place, he makes the second blunder of failing to identify his example as to whether it is illustrating generic or specific authority. Examples may illustrate either generic or specific authority. But when he takes an example of benevolence and argues that it falls in the scope of some generic of authority for cooperation, and that without the slightest pretext of proof but by assertion only, I want that matter dealt with and if he can show that there is a general authority for "churches to cooperate" under which his example of churches sending to "poor among the saints" falls as an illustration, then I will cease my opposition on this point. I want proof that there is *generic authority* allowing churches to cooperate. If he gives us the case of churches "cooperating" in the particular above, I observe that this example is *specific* (one could not have a general example . . . it would have to be a particular example, though it might be an example of a general matter). No one can prove the nature of authority (as to generic or specific) by analysis of an example only. One must have more information. We frequently refer to it as "background authority" and with it complement our knowledge of whatever example we are studying. Brother Nichols assumes his example to be of a generic matter . . we insist on proof.

He said that Jesus practiced benevolence in order to get people to believe. Amen! But to believe what, brother Nichols? That he was the Christ, the Son of God. He did that by many kinds of miracles. This is the point made by John: "These truly and many other wonders did Jesus in the presence of his disciples . . . etc., etc." (Jno. 20:30-31) and this reference is not limited to simply feeding people by miracle. Without Jesus having done what he did, men could not have believed that he was the Christ. Can a man believe today that Jesus is the Christ without stuffing him with a loaf of bread? Does feeding him today augment his faith in Jesus Christ? Your point needs some clarification.

I believe that brother Nichols shares a common fallacy that it is incumbent upon those with whom he differs to prove to him that something is excluded or else accept his idea that it is included. "Show me where it is excluded. Show me that it doesn't include it." "Show me that when the widow washed the disciples' feet, she didn't wash somebody else's feet." Brother Nichols, that is your problem, not mine. You show me that when the widow washed the disciples' feet, she also washed somebody else's feet. It is not my proposition; it's yours! You have the practice and, therefore, the obligation to prove it. The example we have is in what she did. Make your case on what she did . . . that's all we know about it.

Examples do not bind! Authority binds. Examples merely illustrate authority. That's all examples are . . . illustration of authority. If we can find out whether the authority being illustrated is general or specific we will then be able to make progress. But we are going to establish this first before we argue our case. Certainly examples illustrate something and we must all accept what they illustrate because they are divinely given. I am happy to accept the matter of the I Corinthian 16 example of benevolence as authoritative, but I take the background to be specific rather than generic. Consider the background of the case of the benevolence carried down to the poor saints: "As I gave order to the churches of Galatia, even so do you . . . etc., etc." This is a statement of fact that is recorded. It is specific as to who raised the money, when it was raised, and what it was for. How can we take that as simply a general matter of raising money for any purpose and sending in any manner to whom or what we choose?

The problem we are having over "anti-ism" and "liberalism" is an outgrowth of our difference over authority. Brother Nichols went into a lot of this in his references to Bible school and the matter of the communion cup, concerning which there are no differences among brethren present. When a man takes generic authority, which allows liberty in choice of specifics within that generic, and shrinks it down to the choice (specific), he chooses and allows no one the right to make his own authorized choice; he is what I would call an "anti" . . . one who denies liberty where God has granted it. On the other hand, one who takes specific authority (that which allows him the thing specified) and expands that specific back up into a generic field and than takes his choice of action from the general authority (?), that man is a "liberal." Either the "anti" or the "liberal" changes the nature of God's authority . . . both are guilty of the same sin, only in different form. I claim no kinship in this to either of them. I am not an "anti" (as per above) nor a "liberal", and I am not a "middle-of-the-roader"' either. When the road itself is faith, God's revelation, it is inconceivable how there could be either a middle or a side to it! If that faith is expressed in generic authority which allows you a choice of lawful specifics of it, then any lawful choice by any man amounts to being the road itself to him. Men, taking such scriptural options, though they be not the same options, travel the same road, neither to the right or left of the other nor the middle in reference to others. There is no middle of faith! We either have authority or we do not.

He wants to know if in Acts 6 (the matter of the seven chosen to serve) the number of seven is bound. Well, since it is illustrated, we will both agree it is authorized. But he keeps speaking of something bound, "Is it binding?" I am not interested in binding or loosing as if I am in authority myself. We must have authority for all we do. I can demonstrate authority for what I do religiously. I want him to illustrate or demonstrate some of his. He assumes that a matter is proved by something neither of us knows anything about. I want him to prove his practice by what we both know. He asks me, "Can a church do this or that?" He wants to prove it by what I say . . . that is, if I should say that it can do this, then from that he would conclude that it can do something else. This is Bible proof of nothing. It is "proof" (?) only out of the consent of our own mind (rationalism).

In these closing moments, I wish to point out that all mankind are under law to God. They were all under law to God before Jesus came to this earth and they still are. The coming of Christ did not change anything in this respect. In Acts 17, Paul points out that the idolaters of Athens (in common with all humanity) are "the offspring of God." Because we are descended from Adam who was created by God and given power to reproduce after his kind, and because God gives to each person his very life and being, we are under God's care and direction. This accounts for why men can sin before they hear the gospel, because they are under law to God whether they ever hear the gospel or not. All men are sinners (Rom. 3:22).

Because we are the Sons of God by creation, we have certain humanitarian obligation laid on us by God. These duties touch family, government, and society in general whether we ever become Christians or not. We are answerable to God for our responses to these obligations and the first chapter of Romans will bear this out, as it depicts the responsibility of Gentiles who had neither the Law of Moses nor the Gospel (during the time referred to), but who did sin against God and, therefore, had law. When a man becomes a Christian he enters into a phase of life that rests on grounds peculiar to his being a Christian. These prior duties to family, government and society are not transferred into some different realm; one's obligations here are not exempt from his Christian calling . . . neither are they peculiar to it. A Christian continues to have every divine obligation he had before he became a Christian and as a Christian he has some duties that he has, simply because he is a Christian. Some of the duties peculiar to his Christian calling are performed by him alone, in his own right and without anyone else doing anything.

There are also some divinely assigned duties wherein the Christian is authorized to work together with other Christians, to act as part of a collective of saints to collectively provide for certain things to be done. If a Christian can act in any other way than (1) personally, individually and independently or (2) as a part of a collective, I would like to have it pointed out to me. To put it simply, he can either do it himself or work with others so it can be done. The very fact that God authorizes Christians to work together in certain matters proves the divine wisdom and foresight for "togetherness" of Christians (a local church if you please!). If there were lack of authority for Christians working together, there would be lack of authority for "organizing" a local church. Ask yourself, what authority is there for having a local church? Let us not start our processes with a local church already in existence, let's start at the beginning and find out authority to even form one. This will explain why I start out with the unit (an individual) to build my case for determining what the church can do.

I was a human being before becoming a Christian and had obligation to God; having become a Christian I still have those prior obligations and some additional ones besides. This is why I could contribute personally to a merely humanitarian institution as a humanitarian work . . . work to which all human beings are obligated by relationship to Adam. But as a Christian I sustain a relationship to some matters that rise much above mere humanitarianism and rest upon grounds peculiar to my calling in Christ. If I have authority to form a collectivity of saints, it must rest in the proposition that Christ has authorized his disciples to work together. Further, such authority must express itself in giving direction to what is to be done collectively . . . that is, if God gives the church its work. If God has granted his people the right to form themselves into other collectives than a local church to do the things (collectively provide for) he has charged his people with doing, I am not aware of it. As a citizen of the world there are many organizations in which I may hold membership and function, but as a Christian I know of no organization peculiar to his people other than a local church. This is why, as either an individual or member of some human humanitarian institution, I can find authority for benevolence in general. This will account for the civil, city government of Israel providing for a feast, paid for out of tithes, in which both Jews and non-Jews ate. The government of Israel was theocratic; church and state; civil and religious combined.

Brother Nichols has asked: "Is Judaism better than Christianity?" Do we, who are Christians, hold citizenship in a civil government? Indeed we do! We are citizens of two separate kingdoms while the Jews had their two in one. Is it his point that the church of our Lord must also do the work of a civil government?

A Christian contributes to a human benevolent society because he is also a human being and has humanitarian obligations. But what about a missionary society? On the grounds of one being a Christian he cannot organize or support some other collective to provide for the preaching of the gospel. On the grounds of his being a citizen and having humanitarian obligations he cannot find authority for supporting the gospel . . . this rests upon grounds peculiar to the Christian calling. A missionary society can neither be justified as a collective of Christians doing the work of the Lord nor a collective of citizens doing their duty as citizens. There is no authority in the realm of humanity or Christianity for a missionary society. A missionary society has no commission in humanity and no authority in Christianity. But there is a realm for a benevolent society . . . the realm is humanitarianism and there it must rest. But there is no authority for placing upon the local church the obligations that God has placed on humanity as a result of humanities' relationship to one another and to God. While the individual, who is also a Christian, is bound to discharge those responsibilities, they are not to be a burden of the church.

There was something suggested about the city on a hill letting its light shine, with the implication that we are to let the light of the church shine through its benevolent programs. The verse is not speaking of a collective or church light, but the light of an individual, like that of a city, is to be seen, etc. Certainly, all that we do in every phase of our life, whether it be individual or collective with others, ought to be done in the name of the Lord (Col. 3:17). Certain it is that such conduct will come under the observation of men, and its proper influence will be to cause men to glorify our Father.

James 1:27 and Gal. 6:10 have been introduced with the question as to whether they "exclude" the church. We insist, that the question is not whether these passages "exclude" the local congregation but rather, by what process of thought can it be shown that they are "included." I do not believe that "specific" authority excludes anything! I believe that specific authority is specific and shows what God wants done or not done (depending on whether it be positive or negative in character). Specific, positive authority is not a negative of any kind; it is positive and positive authority does not inherently express a negative. Thank you.

## The Work of the Church

### Harold Fite

I appreciate the invitation extended me to participate in this program. It has been stimulating and most profitable for me, as I'm sure it has for you. Without these lines of communication we can never realize unity, but by re-establishing them (which we are doing this week), we are taking a step toward resolving our differences. I for one, trust and pray these lines will continue to be open and would like to see more gatherings such as we have engaged in this week.

Last night I was impressed by a statement made by brother Nichols. In the course of his speech he said, "there is nothing larger and nothing smaller than a local congregation and the elders can only oversee the local congregation and its work."

I concur in this statement; I believe it's a good one. However, at the close of his speech last evening, while pleading for unity, he said in essence, you do the work the way you like to do it and we'll do it the way we like to do it. It is evident by these two statements that this particular problem is not a theoretical one, but rather one in application and practice.

---

HAROLD FITE—*Evangelist for Castleberry congregation, Fort Worth, Texas; associate editor of* "THE GOSPEL TEACHER," *published in Dallas, Texas; soon to move to 62nd and Indiana congregation in Lubbock, Texas.*

In stating there is nothing larger or smaller than a local congregation, and that elders can only oversee the local congregation, he cited I Pet. 5:2 and Acts 20:28. I think it would be good for us this morning to refresh our minds upon this particular point, since in most cases we agree, yet recognize in application and practice we are apart. I do not want to infringe upon brother Turner's speech which will be presented later, and I think I can assure him that what I say will not take anything away from what he may present even though it is related to his subject.

In Acts 20:28 the apostle Paul said to the elders at Ephesus, "Take heed unto thyself and to the flock over which the Holy Spirit hath made you overseers to feed the church of the Lord which he hath purchased with his own blood." In 1 Peter 5 and verse 2 the apostle Peter said, "Tend the flock (shepherd the flock), which is among you exercising the oversight thereof." Thus we have the work of elders stated—they are to oversee. Now, what are they to oversee? Peter tells us they are to oversee the flock. Which flock? Peter tells us it is the flock which is among them. Therefore, we have the limitation of elders' oversight.

Based upon this truth, I advance the following principle: When elders oversee more than the flock among them, they are overseeing more than the Lord allows. When arrangement is made whereby various churches operate through a single agency, you have the wrong kind of arrangement. When other churches (flocks) contribute into a local treasury, under a local eldership, to do a general work of preaching or teaching or benevolence, then you have a brotherhood work which is a violation of 1 Pet. 5:2, and violates principles brother Nichols mentioned last evening that "there is nothing larger or smaller than local churches," and that, "elders are limited to oversight of the local church and its work."

To illustrate this truth I use the example of Herald of Truth. (Diagraming on blackboard) This has been a bone of contention for a number of years and we all recognize it. It is an arrangement whereby one congregation or sponsoring church receives monies from various congregations to do a general work of preaching the gospel. Thus, you have a number of congregations (over a thousand) sending a portion of their contribution into the treasury of a local church, overseen by elders, to do the work of preaching the gospel to the world. In this arrangement (pointing to blackboard) you have something larger than a local congregation. You have a number of churches being involved in a general work of preaching through a sponsoring church.

As we think of the Herald of Truth, all of us by now should recognize that it is more than a local congregation or just the name of some particular program. It has an administrator; a follow-up man and at least five fully supported men in the field. There are approximately 286 key workers in various parts of the country who get together from time to time in their state meetings and report back to Abilene. In this arrangement there is a separate treasury, and the Herald of Truth is spoken of by a number of men who are affiliated with it, as their employer.

This is a violation of the principle that elders cannot oversee anything but the local church—nothing greater or nothing smaller. In this arrangement (pointing to blackboard), you have something greater than the local church. In fact, when you add these things it ceases to be just a local church. It is a perversion of the organization of the church. It is a violation of 1 Peter 5 and verse 2, and what we find in Acts 20 and verse 28.

The last brochure I received from Herald of Truth stated that support is solicited from every congregation in the world. I don't think I misread that; I might limit that to the United States but I believe this is so. Solicitation from every congregation. Thus, we have a multiplicity of churches sending money to be placed under the oversight of one eldership to do a general work. Is this not a brotherhood work? Does it not violate the principle of 1 Peter 5 and verse 2 which was stated by brother Nichols?

When a number of churches are involved in such an arrangement you have more than simply the work of a local congregation. The scope is much greater than that. Thus you have a local eldership overseeing a brotherhood work. You have local elders over too much.

This is one point we all know has been a bone of contention. This gets right down to the "meat of the cocoanut" concerning those things we must remove in order to have unity. We mention such cliches as "there is nothing greater or smaller than the local church, and that elders can only oversee the local church," but do these things mean anything? We are united on a number of things as far as theory is concerned, but what about application? What about the practice? If this arrangement (Herald of Truth) is not a violation of 1 Peter 5 and verse 2, then pray tell what would be? I thank you.

# The Work of the Church

## H. A. "Buster" Dobbs

Good morning, brethren. We are blessed with another good day and an opportunity to be together and discuss the teaching of God's word. I want to pay my respects to some of the things that brother Fite just presented. Brother Fite is laboring under the impression that when a congregation sends money to another congregation that, by the very act of transmitting funds, autonomy is lost. Brother Fite, as a matter of fact, this is precisely what was done in the first century. The apostle Paul took up a contribution from many congregations and by his own hand, being attended by other messengers appointed by the church, he carried that money to the elders in Judea. Therefore, I know that you are mistaken in your contention that such an arrangement constitutes violation of the autonomy of a congregation.

This is what they did in the first century, brethren. This was the practice. Many congregations did send money to another congregation. The apostle Paul being inspired certainly did not participate in an arrangement that would violate I Pet. chapter 5 and verse 2. Now, brother Fite, you're concerned about autonomy; so am I. You seem to think that somehow the Herald of Truth arrangement is a violation of the autonomy of the local congregation. Let me put this question to you. How much money do you brethren at Castleberry send to Fifth and Highland for the support of the Herald of Truth program? How much money did you send last month? Last year? Not anything? Well, then brethren, it seems to me that you have your autonomy.

---

H. A. (BUSTER) DOBBS—*Evangelist of Memorial congregation, Houston, Texas; debater; editor of* "THE ANCHOR"—*religious periodical published in Houston.*

I want to pay some attention to some things that were said by brother W. L. Wharton last night. An apostle requires that we maintain a simplicity towards the gospel. That is, we ought to maintain an honest attitude toward God's revelation. I believe, however, that also inherent in this and elsewhere taught in the New Testament is the idea that the gospel itself is a message that is easy to be understood; that it is not complex and difficult. In listening to brother Wharton last night I got the feeling that what he was presenting was so complicated that it would take four or five Philadelphia lawyers to figure it out. I tried to listen to brother Wharton very carefully and I tried to proceed with him from point to point, but after awhile we got so lost in all of these rules and regulations coming at us from almost every direction until it became such a maze that no man could find his way through it. I contend, brethren, just on the face of the thing, that anything that difficult and that complicated doesn't have anything to do with the salvation of my soul.

Brother Wharton in presenting his thought last night began to lay down certain rules in order to establish the activity of what he called the collective. He defines that for us over in a parenthesis and says this is the church. (I wish, brethren, that we'd just say church). Here are the rules: First of all, there has to be agreement among all the people who are a part of this collective. I presume that if there is a single dissenting member of the church, it is impossible for the church to act. Anybody in a congregation that is born in the objective mood can keep the church from ever doing anything by virtue of just being opposed to everything. He says, secondly, there must be oversight involved. Third, he says, there must be pooling involved. And then he went on to say "Brethren, these are my rules. If you don't like them, make your own rules." "Aye," brethren, "there's the rub." You're trying to bind your own personal rules on us. This is the issue. This is the point. This is exactly the thing separating us and causing difficulty. Jesus said, "In vain do you worship me, teaching for doctrine the precepts of men." (Matt. 15:9) It is vain worship for anybody to lay down rules that hedge up and bind God's people that are not found in the word of revelation. That's one of the things that has alienated us. This is what has put the strain on our fellowship, the making of rules that God's word has not made, binding the precepts of men as doctrine, and it is vain worship and I am not going to have it bound on me. When somebody tries to pin his own rule on me, that is where we put the strain on our ability to work together. Stating it is germane and to the point and critical to this discussion. I think that this pinpoints an attitude that I see on this question that is responsible for much of the difficulty that is in the brotherhood today.

On the first night of this discussion it was pointed out to us in a most capable and effective way as to how authority is established with regard to religion and I concurred in most of the sentiments expressed. I think all of you believe in the all-sufficiency of the scriptures. I believe that the Bible does not contain the word of God, but that it is the word of God and to it we must pay our allegiance. I believe, therefore, that we must turn to the Word and not human rules if we are ever to discover what the collective (or the church) can do. I believe that it is far better for us to just say what God's Word says on the point and then stay with that. And I believe that it is presented to us in such a way that we will have no difficulty whatever in understanding it.

And I think finally in the speech last night that there was a recognition of what is the basic work of the church. I think it comes under two categories. The one is evangelism and the other is benevolence. In evangelism we include edification. The benevolent program of the church is authorized on the basis of Gal. 6:10, "as we have opportunity let us work that which is good toward all men, especially toward them that are of the household of faith." We are told that this is personal and individual and doesn't involve the church, but I insist that this is a synthetic argument. The book of Galatians (Galatians 1:2) was written to the "churches of Galatia." Anything in the epistle that it is possible for the church to obey becomes a command to the church. We've been told that Gal. 6:10 is not a church obligation but an individual obligation because personal pronouns are used in the context and in the verse. You and I know that the fact personal pronouns are used by no means forces the conclusion that individuals only are addressed and that the church is not included. Galatians 6:10 on the very face of it in the passage, in the context, and in the larger context does apply to the congregation. It also demands benevolence on the part of God's people directed not only to the saints, but to those who are outside the pale of the church, as an expression of the compassionate mercy of God and a sympathetic spirit on the part of those who profess to be followers of Jesus Christ.

# The Work of the Church

### Dudley R. Spears

In reference to what was said about brother Fite's illustration of the sponsoring church, showing no loss of autonomy, the statement was made that in New Testament times they took up money and sent it to the church and did not lose their autonomy—but that was in the field of benevolence. Brother Fite was dealing with the general work of evangelism and benevolence being limited. Benevolence is a local matter; this other is a general matter.

The question was asked, "How much money do you send to Highland?" We don't send any. The observation was made, "It seems to me that you have your autonomy." That's what we feel like would be the results if everybody would observe that.

I think brother Wharton's speech was a very fine one. There were some things I feel were complicated in it, but because a speech is complicated or seems a bit dense, maybe we have the density in the wrong place. The Hebrew writer said that Jesus was called to be a high priest after the order of Melchisedec. In Heb. 5:11 he says, "seeing there are many

---

DUDLEY ROSS SPEARS—*Evangelist for the Tenth and Francis congregation in Oklahoma City, Oklahoma; editor of a four page weekly,* THE GOSPEL VISITOR, *which is widely circulated.*

things hard to be uttered, seeing ye are dull of hearing." Because a man's speech appears to be complicated does not mean such is a denial of it.

As to whether Gal. 6:10 is to the individual or to the church, I believe the context bears out that the passage primarily has to do with individual duty. I cannot see that there would be anything gained if you grant that it was collective action, for there certainly is no orphan home, no old folk's home, no do-gooder society "in doing good unto all men" in the passage. If you say it is to the church, then let the church do it.

In reference to some things said last evening, the anti-class people and the one-cup people were mentioned time and time again. Our difference with the anti-class brethren and the one-container brethren is not over application but over interpretation. We are divided with our anti-class brethren over the interpretation of I Cor. 14 with reference to tongue speakers and prophets. They do not have the truth on that passage and do not teach the truth. As far as fellowship or recognition is concerned, we are divided over a doctrinal matter with them.

There are some areas of application where we differ with them, but the primary views that they have involve the "assembly rule" supposedly in I Cor. 14. The one-cup people believe the word "cup" in the Bible always refers to a literal container. They say you cannot have the cup without a literal container and only one. He doesn't mean the literal container that Jesus had. He doesn't believe in the holy chalice or grail. He believes that the word "cup" itself always means one literal container.

He misunderstands what the Bible teaches, and our difference with him is not a matter of application. It is over interpretation. I can quote brother Nichols on the local congregation being the only organization and belief in the authority of the Bible, and everyone of us has to be impressed with the fact that we have talked about principles on which we agree. We are not disagreed on what the Bible says except in a few places, and those don't amount to much. We are divided over where you put the "wavy line." We are divided over application, and so I reject the idea that your relationship to us is as our relationship is to the anti-class and one-cup brethren.

The anti-class people tell you that Bible teaching is a work of the home, and that the local church, when it begins to engage in Bible teaching in classes, is usurping the function of the home. They say that ought to be left to parents in the home. If I understood the speeches made on the benevolent question in the work of the church, the argument has been made that you cannot do it without a home. Of course, that's been left undefined. The only definition I can find for the home as it applies to the orphan home or old folk's home would be an "asylum." I don't say that in a disrespectful manner. An "asylum" is a place where people are put under supervision of others, such as an institution.

The argument has been made that you can't do it without a home. The conclusion always comes out that the home is an organization. It has its own entity; its own government; its own head and so on. If there is an *essential* requirement that the home provides for the needy and the church provides the home with money, who is making laws where God has made none? Who binds the church down to one method? What else could the church do, if in the care of the needy, the home is an absolute requirement?

The argument is that the church does the providing of money, and the home provides the care. What else can the church do, in benevolence, but provide money? And so, actually, there could be quite a discussion over who is making laws and limiting the church. This idea of the church only providing money reminds me of how brother A. O. Rainey said it, "the church has the choice of 'how'—cash, check or money order."

In a speech last evening concerning Bible examples, reference was made to several of the examples. Do you have to have seven men? What about sending it with two men? What about the fact that it was in foreign work? I used to hear my father preach a sermon concerning examples of conversion. One point he made was called, "law and circumstances." He usually illustrated it with reference to different circumstances involved in each case of conversion. The circumstances attending the conversion of Saul of Tarsus, for example, were no part of the plan of salvation. They were just attendant circumstances. The fact that it was mid-day, that there was a vision and various other things, does not mean that they were part of the pattern. But, our sectarian friends include them as part of the plan of salvation. Basically, that is what has been done in reference to the examples of congregational action in the work of the church, particularly in church cooperation. Circumstances vary and are no part of the pattern.

Just as in the pattern of conversion, there are things uniform, which are the pattern, also in church cooperation examples. What are the uniform things in these examples? (Acts 11:22; 27-30; Rom. 15:25-27; 2 Cor. 11:8; Phil. 4:14-17). (1) There was no organization but the local church, (2) Each church acted independently and autonomously. No one here would deny that each local church is to act independently and autonomously. These examples show that uniformity in action.

In the operation of churches there is concurrent action, i.e., simultaneous action—each church doing its own work together with others. Brother H. Leo Boles made a statement that when each church *operates* they *cooperate*, and that is the only cooperation taught in the Bible.

When you find the example of churches in Macedonia sending to Paul in Corinth, they sent directly. When you find the church in Antioch sending benevolence to Judea, they sent it to the elders. In these you find nothing other than the local church. That's the law. The messengers were circumstantial.

The statement has been made with reference to cooperation and work of the church—that there is no pattern, and since there is no pattern it really makes no difference how you do it, and we have this business of the "wavy line." I am going to draw the "wavy line" first.

We all recognize that examples of cooperation are specifics. They describe specific action. This has, in the minds of some, an assumed generic command for cooperation. I know the church is a preaching agency; that the Great Commission says, "go into all the world and preach the gospel," but you can preach and teach without ever having any kind of amalgamation of churches. This is a pre-supposed and an assumed command with no Bible basis for it. Just suppose somebody could find the command for churches to cooperate, leaving the method below "the wavy line." According to the rules of generic and specific commands, you could not bind any one particular method of church cooperation. The Missionary Society is a method of churches cooperating. The Missionary Society is an arrangement of churches. So is the Baptist Association; so is the Baptist Convention; the sponsoring church; the committees for Campaigns for Christ. They are all arrangements, ways, methods and means of combining and amalgamating the funds and work of local congregations. If one of them is wrong, then all of them are wrong. If one of them is right, how in the world could you reject the arrangement of churches characteristic of the Missionary Society? How could you reject the arrangement of churches characteristic of the Baptist Convention? There was a Baptist Convention in Oklahoma City not long ago, and their theme was "Go into all the world and preach the gospel." That's the reason they brought all the churches together through their representatives into the assembly. It was an arrangement of churches, and that's exactly the objection I offer to the type of cooperation characteristic of the Herald of Truth or the Campaigns for Christ.

Concerning the type of cooperation found in the Bible, if all churches want to follow New Testament patterns and all of them operate in accordance with what the Bible plainly teaches, we wouldn't be sitting here today talking about "brethren with whom I am identified and brethren with whom you are identified." Instead of building anything other than the local church, just build churches and put the church to work following the New Testament.

In benevolence, when churches fall victim to circumstances beyond their control and need help, churches with ability should help them. In evangelism, when a preacher needs to go into a field, either send the preacher or let several churches send to the preacher. There would be no problem along that line, because we are not divided over what the Bible teaches; we are divided over our application of where to put the "wavy line."

# The Work of the Church

Alan E. Highers

I am indebted to brother Adams for supplying me with some transparent plates and for showing me how to use them, and I think it is only fair to say that he did not help me to prepare this chart. I would like to express my sincere gratitude to brother Lemmons and brother Starling for the invitation to participate in this meeting. I have enjoyed it and profited from it and I appreciate the spirit of congeniality that existed throughout.

I want to address myself to some remarks that brother Wharton made about the objects of church benevolence and in doing so, I make reference also to one statement made by brother Spears a few moments ago regarding Gal. 6:10. He said he did not believe that anything would be gained even if it were admitted that Gal. 6:10 applied to the church. That may be true in regard to some of the issues we have discussed, but that certainly is not true regarding the position that brother Wharton took on the *objects* of church benevolence. It would make a vast difference regarding that particular position, which was also set out by brother Thompson.

I would like to have the chart now to refer to some things relating to Gal. 6:10 and James 1:27.

I raise the question on the chart: Is this individual only? I do not deny that it is individual. I believe that the statement made the other day by brother Lemmons is true, that commands are primarily addressed to individuals—individual saints —but there is a collective responsibility. We give in the church, but it is a collective responsibility carried out by individuals. Commands may be addressed to individuals, but that does not

---

ALAN E. HIGHERS—*Evangelist Getwell congregation, Memphis, Tennessee; debater; soon to become a practicing attorney.*

necessarily say that they may not be collectively discharged. I do not believe we have answered the question when we merely say that this is to individuals. The question is: Is this command purely to individuals and one that cannot be collectively discharged? That is what I am asking about James 1:27 and Gal. 6:10.

## INDIVIDUAL ONLY?

| James 1:27 | Galatians 6:10. |
|---|---|
| "Pure religion and undefiled before God and the Father is this, to visit the fatherless and widows in their affliction, and to keep himself (HEAUTON) unspotted from the world." | "As *we* have therefore opportunity, let *us* do good unto *all men,* especially unto them who are of the household of faith." |
| 1. To twelve tribes (church) —(1:1) | 1. To churches of Galatia — (1:2) |
| 2. Any man among you (HUMIN)—(1:26) | 2. Brethren, ye—(6:1) |
| 3. My brethren (2:1) | 3. Let us—(6:9) |
| 4. Your assembly (church)— (2:2) | 4. Written unto you (HUMIN) — 6:11) 2nd person plural — churches of Galatia (1:2) |

LORD'S SUPPER: "Let a man examine himself (HEAUTON) and so let him eat." (1 Cor. 11:28)—Individual duty, but collectively discharged.

CONTRIBUTION: "Let every one of you (HUMON) lay by him (HEAUTON) in store."
(1 Cor. 16:2)—"Unto the church of God." (1 Cor. 1:2).

PAY PREACHER: (Gal. 6:6) — How? Through treasury of church!

INDIVIDUAL DUTIES FULFILLED THROUGH THE CHURCH

Your attention is called to James 1:27 (pointing to the chart), "Pure religion and undefiled before God and the Father is this, to visit the fatherless and widows in their affliction, and to keep himself (or oneself) unspotted from the world." In one of the addresses it was pointed out that in verse 26 it says "any man," and the emphasis was placed on "man." But in the same passage where it says "any man," it also says "among you," and the "you" there is a plural pronoun. Who is the "you" under consideration in that passage? "If any man *among you*"—a plural pronoun—"thinketh himself to be religious and bridleth not his tongue . . ." Then, "Pure religion and undefiled before God and the Father is this . . . to keep himself." Here we have a personal reference—himself—but in James 2:1, "My brethren"—a plural reference is given. In James 2:2 it says "If a man come into your assembly . . ." I believe here is an undoubted reference to the church—"if a man come into your assembly."

So, he speaks in James 1:26 by saying, "If any man among you . . ." That is an individual that has been denoted in this collectivity, then he speaks to the collectivity when he says "brethren." He speaks regarding the church when he says, "If a man come into your assembly . . ." You have the pronoun again "your," as you do up here "among you," referring to the church.

Then, in Gal. 6:10 we have the address made to the churches of Galatia. (Gal. 1:2). Personal pronouns in Gal. 6:10 and other places in the chapter are plural in number. "As *we* have opportunity, let *us* do good unto all men, especially unto them who are of the household of faith." This is the brethren. In Gal. 6:11, "unto you"—and again we have the plural pronoun when Paul says, "See what a large letter I have written unto you." We have the plural pronoun exactly as we do over here in James 1:27, addressed to the church or the collectivity. Notice in that second person plural in Gal. 6:11 that he addresses the letter unto *you*—the plural pronoun. Find to whom he addressed the letter and we will know who the "you" was. In the first chapter, the second verse, he addressed it to "the churches of Galatia." Therefore, the "you" of Gal. 6:11, the very next verse after verse 10, comprehends the church or what has been described as the collectivity.

Now, to the application of these in the collective manner.

In I Cor. 1:2, "Unto the church of God at Corinth." I Cor. 11:28, "Let *a man* . . ." There is your "man" of James 1:26; yet, every one of us believes that is collectively discharged. "If *a man* thinketh himself to be religious . . ." That is, a man "among you." Let a man examine "himself." Identically the same pronoun that is found in James 1:27. So, you have *a man among you* in James 1:26 (plural pronoun), then you have *himself* in verse 27. You have *himself* in I Cor. 11:28 and, yet, while that is an individual duty to partake of the Lord's supper, every one of us believes and accepts that it is collectively discharged, even though it is an individual responsibility.

In regard to the contribution in I Cor. 16:2, "Let each one of you . . ." There is a plural pronoun again. What do we have? One of the collectivity. Here is an individual duty that is emphasized, but when that individual duty is emphasized it is *one* of the *group*. We have an example of the same idea in James 1:26. "If any man among you . . ."—the plural. Here we have "let each one of you . . ."—the plural. The one of the group. Here we have one of the group. If this means that it is individual only (pointing to James 1:27 on the chart), we would be forced to the same conclusion with the same kind of construction that fits down here. I am not denying that this is individual; I am not denying that Gal. 6:10 is individual, neither am I denying that the Lord's supper is individual or the contribution is individual. But I do not believe that it is individual *only* and that the collective action is thereby excluded. "Let each one of you"—a plural pronoun—"lay by him . . ." A form of the same word that is found in James 1:27 and also in I Cor. 11:28. Here we have the individual application, but these are individual duties discharged collectively just as is true with the Lord's supper. Each individual has the responsibility, but when we come together that responsibility is discharged. It is done in a collective manner even though it is an individual responsibility. It is true with the Lord's supper, it is true with the contribution, and I believe it is true with James 1:27. We have the same kind of terminology here that we have in the other, and it is also true in Gal. 6:10.

Somebody pointed out in James 2:2 that this is the word "synagogue" in the American Standard Version. But it is a form of the same word that is translated "assembling" in Heb. 10:25. In the King James Version it is "your assembly," thus it is a reference to the church. We have one individual among many. An individual responsibility charged upon the individual, but which may be discharged in a collective fashion.

I raise the question before leaving this particular chart: Why, if it does not make a difference as to the issues, has so much been said about this being individual only and that it cannot be applied to the church? I have, of course, writings going back a number of years among brethren on the other side of this question which say James 1:27 does apply to the church. It was not called a matter of wrong-doing. Why has Gal. 6:10 also been argued so stoutly as not applying to the church? I believe it is crucial because it deals with whether the church can help anyone who is not a member of the church.

Another question. Brother Thompson did not deal with it specifically, nor did brother Wharton. When we say that the church cannot help anyone but saints, does that exclude children not old enough to be members of the church? I would like to have that clarified because some brethren have taken the position that children are saints and, therefore, that children can be helped. I would like for brother Wharton or brother Thompson especially, to state whether children are excluded from the relief of the church if it is limited to the saints. These passages do include more than saints and they do have an application to the church.

## UNTO ALL MEN

1. "And great fear came upon all the church, and *upon as many* (EPI PANTAS) as heard these things." (Acts 5:11).

2. "Abound in love one toward another, and *toward all men* (EIS PANTAS)." (I Thess. 3:12).

3. "But ever follow that which is good, both among yourselves, and *to all men* (EIS PANTAS)." (I Thess. 5:15).

4. "Let us do good *unto all men* (PROS PANTAS), especially unto them who are of the household of faith." (Gal. 6:10).

5. "For your liberal distribution unto them (saints), and *unto all men* (EIS PANTAS)." (II Cor. 9:13).

Now, brother Adams, if I may have the other chart, this relates to the other passage introduced last night on 2 Cor. 9.

I have five passages to which reference is made, not merely because they have the word PANTAS in them because we can find multiplied instances of that word in the New Testament. That is the word translated in 2 Cor. 9:13 as "unto all" "or unto all men." As brother Wharton himself said last night, whether the word "men" is present does not alter the case. But the reason that I set these passages before you is this: The meaning of "all" must be determined by the context. I believe that to be true; however, I do not believe the illustrations that have been given are parallel to the passages under consideration. These are the passages that I have been able to find where PANTAS is used *in addition to* the church, and that is true in every one of these.

(1) The first one is Acts 5:1 in which it is said, "And great fear came upon the church . . ." There is the one class, then your coordinating conjunction which has the significance of a plus sign, "Great fear came upon all the church, and (or *plus*) upon as many . . ." Now, the preposition may be different, but the construction is the same in every case. It is the preposition used with PANTAS. "Great fear came upon all the church, and *upon as many*"—that expression is from EPI PANTAS—"as heard these things."

In our discussions the question is always raised, "Is that unlimited? Is it to all men without restriction?" I submit that so far as this discussion is concerned, that is not relevant. The question is: Does it include more than saints? If it does, then you do not have "saints only." Regardless of how we might restrict that otherwise, I am suggesting that it always includes more than the first class named. You have here great fear upon the church *and* upon this many. That is someone *in addition to* the church in Acts 5:11.

(2) "Abound in love one toward another"—there is one class—"and toward all men" (I Thess. 3:12). That certainly extends further than to one another. It includes more than the first class named.

(3) "Ever follow that which is good, both among yourselves, and to all men." (I Thess. 5:15). Here again we have one class named—yourselves—then we have the preposition

with PANTAS. That is an additional class that includes more than the first class. That is the point I am making.

(4) Then we have the same thing in Gal. 6:10. "Let us do good *unto all men*"—PROS PANTAS—"especially unto them who are of the household of faith." Household of faith and the all men in Gal. 6:10—one class extending beyond the other, including more than the other. I have never met a brother of the opposite persuasion who does not agree that Gal. 6:10 extends to others besides saints or members of the church. That is why it is made individual only by some of my brethren. It is acknowledged that it includes more, but it is the same kind of construction that is in all of these other passages. That is the preposition used with PANTAS, naming another class in addition to the first class. That is true in every one of these cases. It is acknowledged that this includes more and that is the reason why it is so stoutly argued, brother Spears, that it does not apply to the church. So far as the *objects* of benevolence are concerned, it is an important question and I am not charging you with believing that, but some do and it has been stated here.

(5) We come now to 2 Cor. 9:13, "For your liberal distribution unto them"—saints, every one will agree, is the antecedent of the pronoun, them—"*and* unto all men." Again we have a stated class *and* another class in addition, and the same construction—the preposition with the word PANTAS. It is the same in every case that we have here.

Briefly, in the moment that remains, let us notice brother Wharton's illustration: Bob, Bill, and John went to town; *all* had a good time. He said "all" is limited by the context to those three. Well, I do not believe the illustration is parallel to the case here. We would have to say: Bob, Bill, and John went to town; they had a good time *and* all others. That would mean there were some others there. But you have to have a stated class in order to make a parallel, *plus* an additional class, and when you have that, the additional class of necessity includes more than those stated in the first class.

FROM THE AUDIENCE: Mr. Moderator, I do not aim to argue, I just want to ask a question. From what text did you get that?

HIGHERS: Among you?

VOICE: James 1:26, it is not in there.

HIGHERS: The expression in James 1:26. This is found in some of the texts. It is not in Nestle's text, I have observed that.

VOICE: What texts do you mean?

HIGHERS: It is in George Ricker Berry's *Interlinear*, and he gives a footnote in which he tells which texts it appears in. You may check it in Berry's.

## *The Work of the Church*

### Stanley J. Lovett

Well, I certainly want to express my own personal satisfaction and appreciation for being at this meeting. It has been an unusual treat, I think, as far as I personally am concerned to see some whom I have not seen for a good many years and to meet some others of whom I had heard but had not had the privilege of meeting. I think is has been fine. I think it has been and is productive of a great deal of good. Certainly, I think we all are interested in doing everything we can that will promote true unity among one another. It seems to me this is certainly a step in this direction. I understand, and you do too, that any efforts toward union—I shouldn't say "union" but "unity"—must be as a result of the individual; what the individual does. That's the only way in the world it can happen. So it is as we individually will occupy positions that are common to all, that are based upon the Bible, that we can have the unity of which the Bible speaks.

I want to mention a few things—not in any particular logical order but just as I have noted them down and these are just passing references.

---

STANLEY J. LOVETT—*Evangelist for the Highlands Blvd. congregation San Antonio, Texas; conducts six months of gospel meetings yearly throughout the nation; editor of* THE PRECEPTOR, *a nationally circulated religious monthly.*

I have known brother Nichols for over 30 years and have held him in high esteem and his family. It has been a real pleasure for me to renew acquaintance with brother Nichols again. In connection with some of the things Brother Nichols said last night, if I did not misunderstand him, he simply mentioned the fact that the position some of those with whom I am identified occupy, would mean there are two patterns with reference to cooperation. That is, one in evangelism and one in benevolence. Well, unhesitatingly I would say that such is so; that it does make a duality of patterns so far as cooperation is concerned. I wouldn't question, in fact I would affirm, that such is so. The pattern, if I understand what patterns are, would be the sum total of everything that is found in the New Testament that is germane to the subject.

Certainly, there is a difference in the New Testament with reference to the patterns. With reference to benevolence we have the information that a church would send directly to another church that was in need. In evangelism we have the information that a church should send a man to a church. It also sent funds to a man; and, also that churches (in a plurality) sent money to a preacher; so I would say certainly there are two patterns with reference to these matters.

With reference to the matter of cooperation I had an experience a good many years ago that I think illustrates this matter of cooperation. We, I think, are disposed to say that churches can cooperate. Well, that's true as far as the general statement is concerned, but to cooperate according to Bible principles is quite a different thing. I don't know—it must have been a dozen years ago—and there are some of the men here in this meeting today that were in that meeting. Brother Nichols and brother Williford came to Dallas, Texas when I was preaching for the Shamrock Shores congregation. They called all of the preachers in Dallas down to a luncheon at the YMCA to resolve some of the objections that some of the brethren had to the Herald of Truth radio program early in its first years.

Now, some criticisms were made with reference to some things that I thought were rather incidental; for instance, someone said that the camera was on the face of the preacher too long and they thought that ought to be changed. Someone else thought they ought not to focus the camera on the front of the Highland meeting house. They thought they were giving them too much credit for the thing; and other things of that nature. Well, I did not think we were getting very far with reference to that, so I raised the question of the right of the program to exist as it then was. Whereupon brother Nichols began discussing the matter in an animated way. Finally he ran around and pulled a blackboard around and wrote something on it and he said, "Now, do you believe that?" What he wrote on it was "Churches can cooperate." I said, "Certainly, I believe that," and he said, "Then you believe in the Herald of Truth because that's all it is." I said, "Now, wait a minute. When I said that churches can cooperate, and I believe they can, of course I meant according to Bible principles—according to what the New Testament teaches." And so it is. It isn't enough just to say that churches can cooperate, but they must cooperate according to such information as we have in the New Testament. I think you would all agree with that. Perhaps our division would be with reference to how we view what the Bible says with reference to these ways in which churches can cooperate.

Brother Gus Nichols also made the observation, which I would say is true, that the modern missionary society is not by Bible authority. Well, I think there would be universal agreement in this group on that, but also I would like to say that neither is a cooperative benevolent society, such as we see in some places today, by Bible authority. Also, as far as the cooperative evangelistic societies among us are concerned, neither are they by Bible authority.

And he made the statement that teaching is generic. Well, that's certainly true. However, teaching is generic with reference to the means by which communication may be presented; but teaching, or the word teach, is not broad enough to include within it the sponsoring church arrangement, in order to say that the sponsoring church is a method of teaching. It isn't a method of teaching, it is an arrangement that selects a method of teaching, and we ought to keep that in mind.

Also, brother Nichols mentioned Col. 4:16 about the matter of the brethren at Colosse causing the epistle to be read in the church at Laodicea. Well, that would certainly be a communication as far as brethren and churches are concerned, but I have never heard of anyone objecting to the fact that churches might communicate with reference to certain matters and certainly that expression "cause it to be read," I think, simply means to make it available to them for their information and I think that's all in the world it is. It certainly is a far cry from any such thing as the Herald of Truth arrangement for evangelism and other matters when it simply says cause the epistle to be read in another congregation.

Now, with reference to Galatians the sixth chapter that brother Highers has mentioned and in a very fine way has pressed his point, as far as that's concerned. There is a question in my mind with reference to Galatians 6, certainly from the first verse on down through the end of that paragraph as in the American Standard Version (that's past the 10th verse) as to whether it has reference to material matters or not. In fact, the whole context beginning with the latter part of the fifth chapter (the works of the flesh and the fruit of the spirit) refers to matters that are spiritual in their nature: works of the flesh and the fruit of the spirit. In Gal. 6:1 he is talking about "Brethren if any man be overtaken in any trespass you who are spiritual restore such a one in a spirit of gentleness looking to thyself . . .," then in the sixth verse let him that is taught in the word communicate unto him that teacheth in all good things." There was a time when I thought that meant pay the preacher but now I don't think it does. I don't think it has anything to do with the paying of the preacher. It's the same word in the original that is used in 2 Cor. 8:4, "fellowship."

In other words, let him that is taught in the word communicate (have fellowship with, participation in) the things of his teacher. The teacher communicates the word, the teacher teaches the word; the recipient (him that is taught in the word) not only listens but he also receives and applies to his life the things that are found herein. And when we get down to the 9th verse, certainly that is individual because he is talking about sowing and reaping and I do not know of anything that can be more personal than sowing and reaping—the church does not sow and reap as a collectivity. Individuals sow and reap, and the whole thing, it seems to me, is referring to spiritual matters. Now, that is not a "way out" view, certainly.

I think Lenski in his commentary on the book of Galatians makes a very strong case as far as that's concerned, and I think he is exactly right with reference to his comments on Galatians, the sixth chapter. I think that this part in Galatians

6:1-10 is taken out of the discussion actually when we understand just exactly the true nature of that part.

VOICE FROM AUDIENCE: Brother Lovett, would you state again for my benefit what you said about Galatians 6:6?

All right, I said, in Gal. 6:6 where it says "let him that is taught in the word communicate unto him that teacheth in all good things," it means, let him share with and enter into the things that the teacher is teaching. The teacher communicates truth to him; he listens to the teacher, he receives the teaching of the teacher, he applies it to his life and, thus, he participates in the things of his spiritual teacher. Here is the teacher, there is the taught; it is a fellowship together with reference to the matter.

VOICE: Do I now begin to teach what you have taught me or do I begin to live what I have been taught?

S.J.L.: This is just illustrating with reference to the matter of the term "communicate." I would say it might include both as far as that's concerned.

ANOTHER VOICE: I would suggest this to you men who want to study this point further: H. A. W. Meyer in his critical commentary takes this position at great length and discusses it with great learning.

## The Work of the Church

### Hardeman Nichols

I appreciate the privilege of being here and having the opportunity to hear these fine discussions and also to engage in the matter of seeking a basis of unity in our understanding of the Word of God. I think it is important that we understand fully and completely the fact that there are many points of agreement among us. Yet there are some basic disagreements and it is to those disagreements that we want to mainly address ourselves in these few minutes here.

First of all, there ought to be an understanding by all of us that Jesus did not require an application of a "social gospel" that would seek as its goal to eliminate poverty from the world. Sometimes brethren have falsely accused those of us who believe that the church can help those who are not saints of thinking that it is the duty of the church to eliminate poverty from the world. What a tremendous and impossible job that would be! Jesus said in Mark 14: 7, 8: "Ye have the poor with you always." Jesus understood that poverty would never be eliminated from the world. It would continue to exist always and

---

HARDEMAN NICHOLS—*Evangelist for the Sunset congregation in Dallas, Texas; on the editorial council of* POWER FOR TODAY; *well known for his work at Sunset congregation in Lubbock, Texas and at "A" and Tennessee church in Midland, Texas.*

therefore a social gospel is certainly not the gospel that we preach. What Jesus did say was that although you cannot eliminate poverty, you can do good whensoever you would.

God has always required those who serve him to be benevolent. The benevolence must extend beyond those of their own people, or His own people. For instance, under the Old Testament law, God required in helping "the poor" (using the same term Jesus used in Mark 14:7, 8) that they include aid to "the stranger." In Deut. 14:28, 29 we read concerning the third year tithe: "Thou shalt bring forth all the tithe of thine increase the same year, and shalt lay it up within thy gates: and the Levite, (because he hath no part nor inheritance with thee,) and the stranger," (they were to use the tithe for the stranger—the foreigner) "and the fatherless, and the widow, which are within thy gates, shall come, and shall eat and be satisfied."

Keep in mind that this was the use God commanded to be made of part of the treasury of Israel in the Old Testament. It is extended beyond the saints and included the stranger—those not saints. In the next chapter it is written concerning the same tithe every third year (cf. Duet. 15:9. This is the statement Jesus alluded to in Mark 14:7): "For the poor shall never cease out of the land: therefore I command thee, saying, Thou shalt open thine hand wide unto thy brother, to thy poor, and to thy needy, in thy land." Keep in mind that in the previous chapter, He declared the "poor" to include the "stranger." Therefore, the benevolence of Israel extended beyond "saints only" in the Old Testament.

Brother Wharton pointed out last night that he doesn't believe there is any law that excludes. There is disagreement among these brethren on many points and this is one of them. Some of these have written books where they make the argument of exclusion. They are divided on application on some of these points. Some believe in exclusive authority; that is, that a law providing certain things excludes other things. In fact, we all do when it comes to prescriptions and many other matters. We understand that the law that demands the inclusion of certain specific things in filling a perscription excludes everything not prescribed. The doctor doesn't have to say in the prescription, "Thou shalt not put in poison, etc." Things are excuded simply by the specifics included. But he says that it would be our duty to find the including of those not saints in the benevolence of the New Testament church. "Where is the scripture that allows the church to help those not saints?" That is what we are going to deal with.

Here is the proof in an argument that I think is very simple; yet one not used too widely in our discussions. I believe it deserves attention. In the 14th chapter of Mark there is an occasion where a woman comes and anoints Jesus. According to John's account (John 12:4-6), Judas raised an objection to this. John adds that Judas had the bag. There was a treasury of the disciples during the personal ministry of Jesus. This was before the cross. They used this treasury, according to John, both for evangelistic and benevolent purposes, for we read in John 13:29 that when Judas left the group that night, they thought (and how trusting they must have been of their brethren then) instead of his going out to betray Jesus, that he was either going to "buy those things that we have need of against the feast; or, that he should give something to the poor." There is the expression "the poor" again. Jesus used that same statement and alludes to the 14th and 15th chapters of Deuteronomy where they helped their brethren and also strangers as well. Jesus said, "The poor ye have with you always."

Then he goes on to say, "But me you have not always" (Mark 14:7). There is a sense in which He would not be with them always. That is, he would not be with them bodily always. He is with us always in another sense, for Matthew 28:19, 20 says, "to the end of the world." That is what "always" means. After Christ goes back to God, the poor will still be here; they will "never cease out of the land" (Deut. 15:11). "The poor you have with you always." Jesus anticipated the fact that after he goes up to Heaven and he is not with his disciples bodily, they will still have the poor with them down to the end of the world. And he says, "Whensoever ye will"—using the plural "ye." This has every requirement that brother Wharton says you must have for collectivity in action. You have agreement, you have oversight and you have legal resources. They had a bag, a treasury. You have all those things existing and Jesus said, "Whensoever ye will" (and He means after He is not with them, as they would grow and increase in numbers, of course, and teach others)—"Whensoever"—from there on down to the end of time—"Whensoever ye will ye may do them good." Jesus said you can help the poor always and his rebuke to these disciples was when they said, "Why this waste?" Jesus says whensoever his disciples want to help the poor (which includes as we have shown from the Bible in Deut. 14: 28, 29 "the stranger"—the foreigner—the poor in general) out of the bag—the treasury—you may. Now brethren, that needs to be observed along with all other things Jesus has commanded. That is a statement Jesus made concerning helping the poor and I believe in following Jesus.

We are not obligated to eliminate poverty from the world. We'll never do that. Jesus said you will always have it. What governs the giving? What does Jesus say? "Whensoever you want to." Who is considered in the context? The disciples of our Lord giving out of the bag—the treasury. As we have therefore opportunity, "let us do good unto all men" (that includes "the stranger").

Now then, in these closing minutes, I would like to discuss some things that have been brought up by other speakers There were several things stated in the major speech last night. Our beloved brother Wharton in most of his epistle "spoke things hard to be understood" by me, so I went to him after the speech and asked for a little more definition. I wonder if there is agreement among you brethren on his definition of his major thesis. His definition is that the church collectively cannot help any family—no family—only the individual. I am not misrepresenting him on this; I asked him and we talked at length about it. He believes the church can help no family, not even its own members' families. It can help only the individuals. You brethren surely are not agreed on that. I know some of you do not believe that. Others of you are not agreed on the "saints only" proposition.

Here is my point: If you can disagree upon such matters, yet you can have fellowship in your diversity, surely our disagreements can be worked out. You can also disagree on what appears to be the position of some similar to that of Daniel Sommer in his opposition to Christian colleges and their right to exist. I wonder, brethren, if that speech last night is not going to demand that as the logical conclusion to his arguments and rules. Does he think a Christian college has a right to exist at all? We need clarification upon some of these implications that were brought up last night.

Then, there is disagreement over "exclude and include" arguments. I know there is. And I know there is disagreement over brother Lovett's "communication" argument. For I know some of you who have used Gal. 6:6 and have applied it to the matter of the contribution. Brother Lovett in his argument applied the communicating to the communication of these teachings to one's heart. He said the pupil receives from the teacher the truths and applies them to his life, thereby communicating these things of Gal. 6:6. But the text says, "Communicate unto him that teacheth," not to your life or heart; but to him that teacheth. The communicating is from the pupil back to the teacher.

And there is disagreement among these brethren on that. Brethren, if you can disagree so vastly and widely and yet fellowship each other without attempting to sow discord in the various congregations where you preach and hold meetings, why, in the name of Christ and His plea for unity, why cannot we have unity in diversity under matters of generic authority?

Brother Spears in his speech made an argument about when you can tell that a thing is binding. He mentioned law and circumstances. He said there are circumstances connected with all examples that are no part of law—they are simply circumstances. Of course, this is true. However, his rule of interpretation in finding out whether the circumstances are circumstances or law is, if they are uniform, then it is not a circumstance, but a part of the law. Evidently then, he believes if a thing is uniform it is binding. He said if we would treat this—the matter of cooperation—and the uniformity of example like the plan of salvation we could see this. I would like to ask him about some other uniform matters. What about the Lord's supper in an upper room? Those are uniform examples. What about the Lord's supper at night? That is also uniform in the examples of the New Testament? Are these circumstances or law? I believe your rule is wrong.

## Co-operation Among Churches

By Roy H. Lanier, Sr.

That churches of Christ in the days of the apostles co-operated with one another, and that such co-operation was endorsed and encouraged by apostles is admitted by all present. But that the manner in which they co-operated and what details of that manner are binding upon churches of Christ today is an area in which there is disagreement. Some have picked out three, others more, points which they think are essential and have declared that churches which operate contrary to this pattern are committing sin. It is difficult for some of us to see why these particular points have been selected as binding upon us today when other points of equal importance have been overlooked. Furthermore, it is not clear to us who gave these brethren authority to include these certain items and exclude other certain items from their pattern. Neither are they agreed among themselves as to the number of essential items in their pattern of co-operation.

For instance, one brother does not include the messengers of the churches as an essential item in his pattern, but an-

ROY H. LANIER—*Evangelist for Bear Valley congregation, Denver, Colorado; teacher in the Bear Valley School of Preachers; author; debater; former staff writer for the* GOSPEL ADVOCATE; *frequent contributor to the* FIRM FOUNDATION *and other periodicals; conducts many gospel meetings throughout the nation.*

other brother makes the messengers of the churches a very important part of the pattern. According to him, the messengers of the churches must be individuals. This would exclude corporations and human organizations of every kind, even Uncle Sam. He further says the service of these messengers "consisted of being entrusted with the funds of the church appointing them until it was delivered to the preacher or the elders where it was to be used." This means that if the church in Denver wishes to help a little church in a disaster area in Florida, we must select an individual, a brother in the Lord, and entrust him with the funds until delivered to the church in Florida. We believe there are broad fundamental principles to be learned and observed from these examples of co-operation in the New Testament, but we do not believe that individuals are at liberty to select certain items acceptable to them and bind them upon others while they leave out certain other items of equal importance. This we believe to be responsible for much of the differences and division of sentiment among us today.

If we are going to study co-operation, we must have an authoritative definition of the word. Webster says co-operate means "to act or work together with another or others for a common purpose; to combine in producing an effect." So co-operation would be the act of doing such.

First, are we taught that churches must co-operate? Is there a command, example, or necessary inference that all churches of all time must co-operate with other churches? If so, as soon as a new church is established it must find another church to co-operate with it and a work on which both can agree. No one believes that such is true.

If the scriptures teach us anything about co-operation, it must be with reference to the manner in which it is done. Is there a plain positive command as to how churches are to co-operate? I know of none. Is there any one single example of church co-operation in the New Testament which serves as a pattern from which we may not deviate without sin? Again, I know of none. Neither do I know of any scripture which necessarily infers just how churches must co-operate. If there is such, it will be the duty and privilege of these brethren who oppose our manner of church co-operation to produce it.

But I am told by some that there is a binding pattern of

church co-operation set forth in Acts 11:27-30. (1) From this passage we learn there was to be a famine. (2) We learn the disciples determined to send relief. It is not clear whether this was an individual response and that the disciples gave their money to the messengers, or if they contributed on the Lord's day and the elders of the Antioch church gave the money to the messengers to take to the elders in Judaea. Some of these brethren have differed in the past as to whether this was individual or church action. How can this be a binding pattern when this important matter is not made clear? (3) This was one church sending to several churches. Is this part of a binding pattern? (4) The money was carried by two brethren to the churches in need. Is this part of the binding pattern? Must there be two messengers for one church? Can we now use Uncle Sam to do this work for us? Though we may learn some principles about benevolence from this passage, I deny that we have a pattern binding upon us today.

Another brother thinks he has found a pattern in 2 Cor. 8 and 9 from which we cannot deviate without throwing churches into apostasy and losing our own souls. (1) In this passage we have many churches sending to one church in need. This is directly opposite to the example in Acts 11. (2) We have quite an organization, a group of men, working under the oversight and direction of Paul in stirring up the churches in Asia and Europe to take part in this co-operative effort. Paul sent Titus and with him "the brother" whose praise was wide-spread . . . and "with them our brother whom we have many times proved earnest" to Corinth to be sure the church had "its aforepromised bounty" ready when he arrived (2 Cor. 8:16-22; 9:3-5). Is this a part of the binding pattern? If not, why not? (3) Since the zeal of the church at Corinth had stirred up very many brethren to give liberally and Paul wanted their "aforepromised bounty" ready, I conclude that they had promised a definite amount. This I find to be true from 2 Cor. 8:12, where I learn that they made a beginning a year before by willing. They made a pledge, promise, to give a certain amount one year in advance of the time Paul was to arrive, and they were told to contribute on the first day of the week to liquidate that pledge. Is this pledging a part of the pattern? If not, why not? (4) The churches which sent aid to the "poor among the saints" at Jerusalem were in debt, they owed carnal things, to the Jerusalem church in return for the spiritual things they had received from them (Rom. 15:27). If Corinth, a Gentile church, owed this to Jerusalem, a Jewish church, is not the same true of Antioch, another Gentile church? So in both cases of church co-operation recorded in the New Testament this matter of paying carnal things in return for spiritual things received by the giving churches plays an important part. Is this a part of the pattern binding upon us today? If not, why not? (5) Churches chose messengers to carry their contributions to Jerusalem. Paul was not sure he would go to Jerusalem, so it was not essential for the one who sparked the campaign for raising the funds to accompany the funds to the destination. But it was necessary for the messengers to do so.

Brethren are on record as saying these messengers must be individuals, that they must be brethren, and that their "service consisted of being entrusted with the funds of the church appointing them until it was delivered to the preacher or elders where it was to be used." (*Walking By Faith*, Roy E. Cogdill, p. 51). As proof that I am not taking this out of context this is taken from items Nos. 5 and 6 under "CONCLUSION: Thus New Testament scriptures furnish us a complete pattern for congregation cooperation." This rules out Uncle Sam as the carrier of funds from one church to another. I frankly admit that these messengers carried the funds to the church in need in this example of co-operation, but I deny that such example is binding on us today. But if this item of the example is not binding on us, who has the right to say that other particular items in the example make a binding pattern from which we must not deviate? Sure, this is the way Paul conducted this co-operative effort among the churches, but did he intend this example to be of binding authority on all churches for all time regardless of greater distances and faster means of transferring money? I deny that he did. This I believe to be sufficient to prove that there is neither command nor example binding us to any certain manner of co-operation.

I now raise the question, Is it scriptural for a church to undertake a nation-wide or a world-wide evangelistic effort? I freely admit that we have no example of a church in the New Testament doing such a thing in exactly the manner in which it is being done by more than one church today. Must we refrain from doing it simply because we cannot cite one single verse, or passage, of scripture which gives all the details of such a co-operative effort? This was the position of brethren who opposed our Sunday school program. They challenged us to show one example of a church with apostolic sanction that conducted a Sunday school and used women as teachers. They demanded an impossible task, but it was no more impossible than it was unnecessary. Good brethren are now challenging us to show a New Testament passage which describes such co-operative efforts as we are conducting. The task is both impossible and unnecessary. And it is no more necessary for us to show a passage that describes our co-operative efforts in detail than it was necessary for us to describe our Sunday school program in detail. We simply showed,

1. The thing done is scriptural—teaching God's word.
2. The thing doing it is scriptural—the church.
3. The purpose is scriptural—edify the saints and teach others.
4. Source of finance is scriptural—the treasury of the church.

The time, place, methods, equipment, arrangement of students, literature, use of women to teach children, etc. are incidentals which are left to human judgment. Some of you brethren present rendered valuable service through writing and debating to defend the right of churches to conduct Sunday schools in spite of no New Testament example of such.

Now let us apply this same method of reasoning to our co-operative efforts at nation and world-wide evangelism. We have abundant scripture to prove,

1. The thing done is scriptural—preaching the gospel to all.
2. The thing doing it is scriptural—the church of our Lord.
3. The purpose is scriptural—save the lost and glorify God.
4. Assistance is scriptural—many churches aiding one church (2 Cor. 8, 9).
5. Source of finance is scriptural—treasuries of the churches (I Cor. 16:1, 2).

If these five things are true, and I see not how a single one of them can be disproved, why oppose such a worthy scriptural effort? Some of you are on record as saying that the size of the effort is enough to condemn it; that you still see nothing wrong in one church allowing others to help it do a work in its own city too big for it to do alone, but you are opposed to a world-wide effort. This reminds me of poor old Bro. John F. Rowe who, during the controversy over instrumental music in worship during the last half of last century, said, "a small organ . . . was permissible, just so it was not a large one" (*Search for the Ancient Order,* by West, Vol. 2, p. 163).

There will likely be argument over the great number of churches co-operating in these national and world-wide co-operative efforts because it is thought that this is activating the universal church. But if Paul could enlist many churches in his day in a great co-operative effort to aid the poor, why cannot we today enlist many churches in such an effort? We do not know how many churches in Asia and Europe co-operated in that effort, but when compared with the small number of churches in existence the percentage was probably as great as the percentage of churches co-operating in any single effort now. But if every church on earth had assisted Paul and the church at Jerusalem, that would not have meant that the universal church had been activated. It would simply mean that there was one hundred per cent co-operation of the churches in the world. The fact that Paul worked diligently for a period of about four years to bring a sizeable amount of money from as many churches as possible to aid Jerusalem is sufficient proof that we may enlist any number of churches in a co-operative effort.

The matter of how money may be transferred from the giving church to the receiving church may come up for discussion. We have already seen that New Testament churches had no well defined practice at this point. The Antioch church used two brethren, but it is implied that two or more churches might use the same messenger in the Jerusalem contribution. And some of you brethren are on record as saying that is true. And I dare say that some of you use Uncle Sam to carry your money from one church to another now. This being true, how can you make this matter an issue that threatens the peace of the church?

Now let us apply this same method of reasoning in the field of benevolence. We say,

    1. The thing done is scriptural—remember the poor (Gal. 2:20).

2. The thing doing it is scriptural—the church (I Tim. 5: 16).
3. The purpose is scriptural—fill the measure of wants of saints and others (2 Cor. 9:12, 13).
4. Assistance is scriptural—many churches aiding one church (2 Cor. 8, 9).
5. Source of money is scriptural—treasuries of the churches (1 Cor. 16:1, 2).

Again discussion is anticipated on the subject of objects of the charity of the churches. May churches aid "saints only", or may non-saints be included? Let it be understood that I believe that benevolence, regardless of how deserving people may be, is not the primary purpose of the church. But if reasonable financial assistance to a family of non-saints will open their hearts to receive the word of God and we fail to help them we may have to answer for their souls in judgment. But Paul's statement to the church at Corinth that their liberality to them (Jerusalem saints) and unto all (men) is sufficient evidence to prove that Corinth assisted others than saints. I am aware that the word "men" is not in the text, though added in the A.V. But the fact that the word "all" is in masculine gender demands that we supply the word "men." Similar and identical constructions occur eleven times in the New Testament and no one objects to supplying the word "man." In a letter addressed to a church Paul said he wanted them to abound in love toward one another and toward all (men). Here the word "men" has to be supplied (I Thess. 3:12). The same is true in I Thess. 5:14 and 15.

I also anticipate discussion on whether churches may care for orphans who are not saints. I may be told that this is individual obligation and not the obligation of the church. But I ask, May Christians discharge individual obligations through the church? Individual Christians are told to sing. Do they do this as individual action only? They pool their voices in harmonious praise and adoration. Next, are individual Christians obligated to "communicate unto their teachers in all good things" (Gal. 6:6)? Are we to do this as individual action only? Or may we pool our money and communicate to him through the church treasury? All admit and practice this. Next, may individual Christians pool their money in the church treasury to care for widows and the fatherless? According to I Tim. 5: 16, widows may be cared for in this way. If the individual is obligated to care for the widow and the fatherless (Jas. 1: 27), and Paul teaches that he may care for the widows through the church, who has the authority to say that the individual sins when he cares for the fatherless through the church treasury? And who will say the church sins when it uses the contribution of individuals in this way?

Now let us come to another area of the study of church co-operation. I affirm that co-operation is necessary and authorized when one church has a greater work *of its own* than it is able to do. If I were to stop here I would anticipate no opposition to this statement. But there will likely be a difference of opinion over what constitutes the church's *own work.* We raise the question: Can a work outside of its own community be a church's own work? I believe it can. If this is not true, churches can never do mission work; they can never send a preacher into another state or nation to preach the gospel. It is true that when a church is established that church is not to be ruled by the sending church, but the work of establishing the church in the mission field is the sending church's own work.

Next, a church is related to its own work in a way that no other church is, so that if a church has a work in another state or nation which is its own work, no other church has the same relation to that work as the sending church.

Next, if several churchs can aid this church to do its own work in its home community, they can help this same church do its own work in another state or nation. Several churches aided the Jerusalem church to do its own work in its home community (2 Cor. 8, 9), therefore these same churches could have assisted the Jerusalem church to do its own work in another nation if the need required.

But I am gravely told that such co-operation will eventually rob churches of their autonomy. I have two things to say to this. First the churches in Asia and Europe did not lose their autonomy by sending money to the Jerusalem church. Would Paul encourage churches to set an example which if followed would rob churches of their autonomy? We are told that it was this kind of co-operation that led to the establishment of the Missionary Society. I deny that this is true. The second thing I have to say about this is that I have been circulating among churches for more than fifty years and I do not know of one, just one, church that has lost its autonomy by such co-operation, and they have been practicing such co-operation all through these fifty years. Can you brethren cite one church that has lost its autonomy? If not, why continue to make the argument?

Next, I anticipate that we shall hear statements to the effect that it is not right for churches to create jobs larger than they are able to do alone, but if God allows a famine, flood, tornado, etc. to come, a church may call on others for assistance. All needy situations are created either by churches or by God. There are not other situations. Now, if a church cannot plan a work larger than it can do alone, there can never be any co-operation between churches except in God-made situations, which would be what we call natural calamities. If this be true, it follows that no little church may ever ask affluent churches to assist in the building of a house for work and worship. If a church is not obligated to do more than it is able, and if it is not able to build a house, it is not obligated to do so. It must wait until it grows big enough to build it alone. If it cannot build until it grows, and it cannot grow until it builds a place of worship, it is in a difficult position. If that little church is obligated to do all it is able, and if it is able to solicit and gain the assistance of other churches, is it not obligated to do so? I fear some of us wish to measure the ability of a church by its money alone.

Would the breaking of a home by divorce be a God-made situation? If two homes in a little church are thus broken and eight or ten little helpless children are left, deserted by both parents and the little church is over-taxed, may it call on other churches to aid it?

If a little church in a mission area may not plan anything larger than it can do alone, it can never plan and ask for help to preach the gospel over the radio. The question will not be answered by saying churches can send to the preacher, for in this case there is no preacher. They plan to use tapes sent by a preacher in another state. But if they cannot do a work bigger than they can do alone, that preacher in another state has no business sending them the tapes, since he serves a church there and in reality that would be received aid from another church to do what they cannot do alone.

The Jerusalem church is often used as an example of a church unable to do its own work and receiving assistance from other churches to do its work. Was this a God-made situation? Was this situation brought on by some natural calamity? What caused so many "poor among the saints" in Jerusalem that the church was unable to care for them? Was this situation created by long-time residents of Jerusalem being impoverished by natural calamities? I deny that it was so created. The fact that people came to Jerusalem from every nation under heaven, thousands of them were converted, stayed in Jerusalem until it was necessary for those who had property to sell it and live out of a common fund with those who moved in are the things that created a situation too large for the church to handle properly alone. Yet some of my brethren say it is sinful for a church to gather widows and fatherless children from many communities to feed and teach them the word of God. The only example we have in the New Testament of many churches helping one church is a case where people from all over the world were brought together in one community and created a situation which the church was unable to care for alone. Whether the indigent move into a community of their own accord, or whether brethren move them in for the sake of convenience and economy in caring for them seems to me to be a matter of judgment. I know of no legislation in the New Testament on the point. "One only is the lawgiver and judge, even he who is able to save and to destroy" (Jas. 4:12). Until we are appointed of God to save and to destroy people we would do well to refrain from acting as their lawgiver and judge.

Just as this point it may be well for us to give some consideration to the difference between creating a need and recognizing one. If I kill the husband and father, the provider, in a home, I certainly have created a need. Someone must be found to provide for the widow and fatherless who have become such by my act. If a man deserts his wife and children, he has created a need and some person or church must step into the gap he has made. But for the church to gather the fatherless, the helpless, from a small area, or from a large area, into one place where they can be reared most conveniently and economically is not to create a need. This is simply recognizing a need which already exists. Who has the authority to set a limit on the area from which a church may gather these helpless children? In a city like Dallas, shall the area be zoned? And shall each church be forbidden to cross those zone lines in doing its benevolent and evangelistic work? If we do not zone cities and states, shall we make a law against crossing state lines and forbid churches to transport helpless children across state lines in order to care for them? There *are* helpless children who need homes. No church has created their need; no church can create this need. Churches everywhere ought to recognize this need. And if there are one hundred helpless children in need, what scripture is there that tells us that fifty churches have to care for two children each, or if all may be gathered into one place and cared for by one church?

This reminds me of our anti-Sunday school brethren who used to tell us that a woman might teach twenty other women if she taught them one by one, but that she must not assemble them in one room and teach them all at once, especially on Sunday morning. So some other good brethren say that churches may care for a hundred helpless children provided they are scattered among a lot of churches, but we sin if we gather them into one place and care for them. And surely no one is going to quote, "Tend the flock of God which is among you" (I Pet. 5:2) to prove that helpless children cannot be transported from one community to another to be given a home.

We come now to consider what is called the "sponsoring church arrangement." I do not like the word "sponsor." According to Webster that word does not describe what our churches do when they agree to send a man to a work and see that he is supported. The only one of four definitions given remotely resembles what is done. The third definition is, "A person or agency that gives endorsement to or vouches for some person or thing." The word "promote" describes a part of the work done. The third definition of this word is, "to work actively and stir up interest for the accomplishment of something." So I prefer to say that churches promote and support a man in a certain work; they promote and support a radio program.

Paul promoted a contribution for the poor among the saints in Jerusalem. No one contends that it was wrong for Paul to promote this work. Would it be wrong for a church to do exactly what Paul did? Is there something in the nature of the work which made it right for an individual to do it, but wrong for a church to do it? Could the Antioch church have taken the responsibility for doing it and used Paul as its agent? Until some one brings forward a scriptural reason why an individual can promote such work but a church cannot, and since such brotherhood co-operative efforts do not spring up of themselves but must have a promoter, there seems to be no good reason to oppose such activity on the part of churches.

Let us put the matter in this form.
1. Brotherhood-wide co-operative efforts are scriptural and sometimes necessary (2 Cor. 8, 9).
2. Promoters of such efforts are both necessary and scriptural (Paul's work).
3. There is nothing in the nature of this work to make it wrong for a church to do it.

Since the activities of churches are determined and carried out by the elders, a plurality of men, and since there is safety and wisdom in numbers, it seems wise for churches to do such works rather than leave them to individuals. We have been plagued enough by one-man-missionary societies in the past to convince us that it is better for churches to promote these brotherhood-wide co-operative efforts than to have one man promote them and be responsible to no one for his activities.

I anticipate that the opposition will say that no one church has the right to determine how the money of many churches shall be spent. I agree with them. But the sending church determines that its money shall be used to care for orphans, or for preaching the gospel over the radio. If the promoting and receiving church uses the money for any other purpose, it is guilty of criminal action. I know of no example of such among us.

But the opposition may say that the pooling of great sums of money by many churches in the hands of one church is unscriptural. Paul did not think so, for he gathered a great sum from many churches and placed it in the hands of the Jerusalem church. But it may be argued that the money Paul promoted was spent by the Jerusalem church in its home community while the money promoted by churches today is spent outside their home communities. I grant the truth of this statement, but ask if a church is obligated to spend all monies received in its home community. Where is the scripture that teaches such? We have before shown that a church may have a work of its own outside its home community. All mission work is outside the home community. Radio and television programs are usually classed as missionary work. And it is a little difficult for a church to use a powerful radio station without getting outside its home community and into the area of other churches, especially in metropolitan areas. So if a need exists, I think a church can promote a radio and television program which costs more than it is able to finance; that this is its own work; and that its programs may reach beyond the limits of its home community without violating any principle taught in the scriptures.

I suggest that there are a number of principles to be observed in this connection:

1. The promoting church is not to exert any undue pressure on churches to obtain their co-operation.
2. There must be no inter-congregational organization formed.
3. Congregation should not curtail their local work, fail to meet their local obligations in order to co-operate with other churches.
4. There should be no shirking of individual obligations by writing checks because it is the easiest way out. People need to be involved in benevolent work in order to develop Christlikeness. The fact that co-operative efforts present churches the opportunity to slip into the practice of these abuses is no argument against these efforts as scriptural. The co-operative effort promoted by Paul could have given Corinth the opportunity to be guilty of every one of them.

We come now to the last area of my assignment which I am told involves "human institutions operated by a board of directors." I will cover this area by laying down three principles which I think should be accepted by all who respect the authority of the New Testament:

1. The Lord established his church for the purpose of doing his work in three areas: evangelization of the world,

edification of the saints, and benevolence. The Lord did not activate the universal church; he does all his corporate work through congregations.

2. Churches, local congregations, are authorized to perfect any organization (arrangement of its own forces) necessary to do what the Lord demands of them. First, in the area of evangelism there is a special arrangement of resident forces. A committee for advertising, one for house-to-house solicitation, another for greeting visitors and seating them, etc. This is accepted by all.

Next, there is a special arrangement of resident forces to carry on the work of edification. In large congregations this organization becomes rather complicated. The elders have the oversight and usually one has a special responsibility for the area of edification, including Sunday school, classes for special groups, etc. In large Sunday schools there is the superintendent, usually an elder, department heads, teachers, assistant teachers, nursery attendants, etc. Our anti-Sunday-school brethren oppose this on the ground that it is a separate corporate body, but since it is all kept within the framework of the local church and under the oversight of the elders none of us present will object to it. Such organization could be carried to such extremes that it would be unwise, but such organization as is necessary to do the work most effectively and efficiently is authorized in the command to do the work.

Such is true in the area of benevolence. The church, local congregation, is authorized to perfect whatever organization, arrangement of its resident forces, as is necessary to do its benevolent work most effectively and efficiently. If a section of town is visited by fire or tornado, the church needs people to collect clothing, household goods, food and any other items necessary to supply the need. Another committee is needed to determine who is most worthy to receive the goods. Others are needed to distribute the goods where they will do the most good. All of this needs direction, oversight. The elders will furnish this oversight while the deacons will head committees to carry out the direction of the elders.

If permanent assistance is needed for widows indeed, the most efficient and economical way might be to provide them with a permanent place to live. If this is the decision of the elders as the manner in which the church should do what it is commanded to do (I Tim. 5:16), there is plenty of scriptural authority for doing it. And I believe I have shown that if a church may do that for widows indeed it may also do it for orphans. The manner in which churches must care for indigent people has not been specified by the Lord, so we are left to our best judgment so long as we do not violate some plain principle of scripture. But remember that the commandment has been given to the church and when it is taken out of the hands of the church a principle has been violated.

3. Human institutions which have been established for the sole purpose of doing what and only what the church has been authorized to do are themselves unauthorized and tend to minimize the importance of the church. First, if a group of Sunday school teachers were to organize a separate corporate body for the purpose of doing the work of edification, choose their own officers, select their own teachers, and order their own literature, I think we would all agree that this is an unauthorized movement.

Next, suppose that a group of good brethren organize a separate corporate body for the purpose of evangelizing a certain state, or a nation abroad. I think every man in this assembly would oppose it on the ground that it is unauthorized in scripture and that it tends to make the church unnecessary. That body exists for the sole purpose of doing what and only what the Lord intended to be done by his churches.

So in the area of benevolence I not only believe that churches are authorized to perfect whatever organization is necessary to do all the Lord expects of churches, but I believe that forming a human organization, corporate body, to do what and only what churches are authorized to do is taking a step for which we have no scriptural authority and that it tends to make the church unnecessary. The fact that I have used this comparison does not mean that I believe missionary and benevolent societies are parallel. To be parallel two things must, according to Webster, be alike in all essential points. These two are not parallel, but they are identical in one point—both are unauthorized by scripture in that they are doing a work the Lord authorized churches to do. No one can deny that Paul said churches are burdened with the care of widows indeed (I Tim. 5:16). No one can affirm that the Lord ever told any church just how it is to care for these widows. If one church wishes to pay a family to take one or more into its home, it is authorized to do so. If another church wishes to gather two or more such widows into a house and pay all the bills, it is authorized to do so. And since this is a work of the church the elders of said church are obligated to oversee the operation.

For several years I have had a syllogism in circulation on this point which no one has taken the trouble to answer. In my first printing of it I carelessly inverted the major and minor premises, which was criticized, but since this correction has been made no one has attempted to answer it. I include it here for your inspection.

1. All corporate activities of a church are to be under the oversight of the elders of that church.
2. Care of widows indeed (I Tim. 5:16) and care of widows and fatherless (Jas. 1:27) are corporate activities of a church.
3. Therefore, care of widows indeed (I Tim. 5:16) and care of widows and fatherless (Jas. 1:27) are to be under the oversight of the elders of that church.

Homes for widows and orphans under self-appointed and self-perpetuating boards are not under the oversight of elders of any church. The work is not being done by any church. I begged prominent and capable brethren, who objected to my *Middle of the Road* series, to tell me what church is caring for the orphans in Spring Hill, Tennessee. The best they could do was to tell me that the church is not a home. Well, I knew that before they told me. But I also know that the Lord authorized the churches to provide a home for widows and fatherless for which they are responsible. That is a point which many of my brethren have been unable to see. And when churches are authorized to do anything we have no authority to build a human organization to do the same work. If you take the position that the home under a board is a divine institution, a family unit, I deny it. But even if it were a divine institution, whom has the Lord authorized to build it and govern it? If it is the work of the church to care for these helpless people, it is the business of the church to furnish the organization, arrangement of resident forces, to do the work and oversee it. But I am told that this puts elders in the business of preparing and serving formulas and doing laundry work for babies. I can't see why brethren object to elders overseeing this work when they don't object to elders furnishing practically this same service in the nurseries maintained in churches all over the country. If their objection is valid, they must remove and cease to maintain all nurseries and rest-rooms in church houses. I am not saying elders have to do the work personally, but they provide and oversee the work.

I believe this covers the areas allotted to me. And I pray God we may have the ability to weigh these matters impartially; that we may love truth so much that we will be incapable of prejudice; and that all of us will have the courage to stand for truth regardless of what our associates think or do. And may the Lord use what we say and do here for his glory, for our edification, and for the peace and harmony of his church.

# Co-operation of Churches

Robert F. Turner

## HISTORICAL BACKGROUND FOR OUR SUBJECT

When the above subject was assigned for this paper, something "rang a bell." It took some doing to recall, but now I know that this was David Lipscomb's subject for a paper which he wrote and presented at the first meeting of the Tennessee Christian Missionary Society, in Chattanooga, Tenn., October, 1890. (The paper, with comments, is to be found in the *Gospel Advocate* of Oct. 22, 1890.) Lipscomb was present at the convention as an observer only—we might even say as a "hostile witness"—and I do not know if he or the liberal brethren worded the subject; but I do know that then, and now, it needs clarification. The word "cooperate" means different things to different people; even different things to the same people under different circumstances; hence it must be clearly defined in this or any paper, if we are to avoid ambiguities. And for our particular use in these special studies, this subject should be put in focus with its place and use in church history, where it has had a long and colorful career.

ROBERT F. TURNER—*Engaged in full time meeting work throughout the nation; lives in Burnet, Texas where he formerly preached for the Oaks West congregation; editor of a widely read and quoted eight page monthly,* **PLAIN TALK**; *formerly served congregations in San Antonio and Gladewater, Texas and Phoenix and Prescott, Arizona.*

During the past year I began to collect and collate material concerning the "free church" movements in church history. Hundreds of religious movements have adopted, through convictions concerning the scriptures, or as alternative to some despised domineering hierarchy, some form of independent congregational government. They have declared each congregation "autonomous" or "self-ruled;" and many have devised various safe-guards, seeking to protect this independence. My research along this line is still too limited to warrant truly scientific conclusions; but at this point it seems evident that when this independence is lost—as almost invariably it is—its destruction comes from inside the movement, and via some "cooperative" effort. Of course in these developments "cooperation" almost always means some form of collective action on the part of churches; and further, it is rarely recognized as the true culprit, even by many who decry the loss of independence. (See "End of Independence of Southern Baptist Convention Churches" by Noel Smith; and *Bogard-Penic Debate* on "Mission Methods", of 1910.)

It is certainly no secret that congregational independence in our own restoration history floundered on "Missionary Societies" which grew out of "cooperation meetings." In the *Millennial Harbinger,* April, 1835, Alexander Campbell reported a General Meeting of Messengers, held in Wellsburg, Va., in which "cooperation among congregations" (actually, collective action) was discussed. In the lengthy report Campbell opened the doors for his many articles which were to follow, urging collective action (he called it "organized cooperation") upon the churches. These articles had a tremendous influence in shaping the thinking of brethren, and bringing about the establishment of the American Christian Missionary Society in 1849. I believe it is germane to our present study to understand the line of reasoning that brought our digressive brethren of the last century to their conclusions.

Almost from the beginning of the restoration movement in this country there existed in the minds of many a misconception regarding the universal church. The great commission—with its "go" "teach" "baptize"—was thought to have been assigned to "the church" *as though there existed some universal functional entity* which could carry out such obligations. Then, thinking of local churches as the *units* of this universal institution, various methods of organization (from the sponsoring church, the "Louisville Plan", to United Christian Missionary Society) were suggested whereby the resources of these units could be harnessed to various projects, and these units could function as one. This was called "cooperation" when, more specifically, it was "collective action"—a distinction we must honestly face if we are to deal fairly with the problems before us.

Campbell said we must consider *"the relations in which the congregations stand to each other"* (emphasis mine, rft) "for all duties spring from the relations in which we stand to God and one another." He then contended:

> "The kingdom of Jesus Christ consists of numerous *communities* (emph., rt) separate and distinct from each other; and all these communities owe as much to each other as the individual members of any one of them owe to all the individual members of that single community of which they are members. Every individual disciple is a particular member of that body (or congregation) with which he is united in Christian communion; and *the whole of that community to which he belongs is but a member of that great body which is figuratively called 'the body of Christ.'* He is the head of the whole body, or Christian congregation; not merely or specially of one community, *but of all the separate communities as constituting one kingdom.*" (all emph. mine, rft) *Millennial Harbinger*, Vol. 6, pp. 168.

Campbell conceived of each individual Christian as *a member of a member* of that great body of Christ; and of each congregation as a unit of the great universal church. THIS WAS A BASIC MISCONCEPTION, AND FROM IT SPRANG MANY OF HIS ERRORS CONCERNING COOPERATION. He reasoned from this misconceived "relation" to "duties"—and from "duties" to "devising ways and means" for the whole kingdom to "cooperate." But the kingdom of Jesus Christ DOES NOT consist of communities, or congregations; it consists of individual citizens. The members of the body of Christ are individuals (John Doe, an eye; Mary Smith, an ear; 1 Cor. 12:) and the branches on the vine, Christ, are individuals (Jn. 15:6). Under the heading "Cooperation" Campbell was actually pleading for *collective action* of churches—a harness that would eventually denominationalize those churches that submitted to it. The same misconceptions are alive today, with the same inevitable results.

It is this misconception that leads many to think of the universal church as a "brotherhood" (?) made up of churches —a misnomer if I have ever heard one. "Adulthood" is a "hood" of "adults"—all adults, or the state, condition, quality, or character of adults. "Childhood" is a "hood" of "children." There are no adults in childhood—well, maybe not many. The word "brotherhood" should signify to our minds exactly what it says— a "hood" of "brethren." If we allow ouselves to think "churches" when we say "brethren" we are inviting a denominational concept of the universal church that will plague and confuse our reasoning.

Over seven years ago I wrote a series of articles on this subject for a prominent religious paper, and its editor made light of the matter, saying: "So far as we know brethren have always understood that the individual Christian is the unit of the 'church universal' . . . We were unaware that any thought or taught that congregations were units of the body of Christ, in the sense that individuals are." (I had not said, "in the sense that individuals are.") But the concept thrives—often among people who would never put it in so many words. There were multiple examples of this sort of thinking then, and today the examples increase.

The January '68 issue of a widely read west-coast paper carries this opening sentence by its editor: "For more than 30 years I have held to and vigorously taught that as members work together to build a congregation, congregations should work together to build the church—the whole framework of Christianity should function as does a human body— 1 Cor. 12." Significantly, this paper is a leading proponent of what its editor calls "all-church" action. He decries the attitudes of his own generation, saying, "The church to most of us was limited to the local level. . ." We admire the editor's zeal, but this is Campbell's misconception repeated.

The fruit of such attitudes is all about us. The huge 1964 inter-congregational "Campaign" in Dallas, called forth these three reports in one paper. One preacher: "We have been allowed to rise above personal loyalties and congregational lines and see the church as it really is—One Body and One Spirit."

Another: "For one thing, it gives the congregations a sense of oneness and of strength in the universal sense rather than in a small congregational sense." And another: "The key to success either collectively as in this cooperative effort or on a congregational basis is PLANNING and WORK!!" This is not the time nor place to argue with these men. I only seek to project my subject upon the actual current scene.

In 1960 one preacher wrote me, "To my way of thinking, there should be as much unity and harmony (and, may I be permitted to add, "cooperation") among different congregations as there is among individual Christians of a single congregation." Then, clearly indicating that in this preacher's mind "cooperation" means "collective action", he proposed some kind of "organization among churches" but said, "By now you are probably asking what kind of organization among churches that I would propose. At the present time I have not come to any conclusion upon the matter. But, should I suggest something that in any way would resemble a 'missionary society' of any type, the whole brotherhood would look upon me as a fanatic." This preacher was not only saying that all brethren should love one another ("Love the brotherhood") and that we should feel a close fellowship with each other in the work of the Lord ("every one members one of another"); but he called for a type of inter-congregational "organized" cooperation which I believe is wholly unwarranted by the scriptures; and destructive of the congregational independence and non-sectarian characteristics of the church, which I believe the scriptures do teach. It is upon this background that the sermons and articles of so-called "anti-cooperation" brethren are presented; and to ignore this setting is to do your brethren a grave injustice.

Make no mistake about it; the "issues" that divide brethren of our generation (Herald of Truth, Orphan Homes, and any other "churchhood" projects) are essentially related to basic differences in our conceptions of the *organizational structure of the church*. Every new "churchhood" project—binding churches together in collective action, every move to strengthen and increase "organized cooperation," is a dividing wedge, driven deeper, between those who believe in *actual* congregational independence, and those who do not, or who are satisfied with the name only. Meantime, back at the ranch, the great bulk of the brotherhood moves blindly along, following one or the other concept of polity through prejudice or apathy, with too little understanding of the choice they are asked to make.

DEFINITION OF TERMS

But now we need to clearly define the terms of our subject, and of other words indispensable to the discussion of this matter. I direct your attention to "cooperation" and "collective action."

Webster's unabridged dictionary says of "cooperate": "1. To act or operate jointly with another or others; to concur in action, effort, *or effect.*" *The New English Dictionary*, a 12 volume set, puts it this way: "Cooperate. 1. To work together, act in conjunction, *with* another person or thing, *to* an end or purpose, or *in* a work." Of "cooperation" N. E. D. says, "The action of cooperating, i.e., of working together toward the same end, purpose, *or effect.*" (all emph., rft) Numerous other standard dictionaries were consulted, and all recognized multiple types of cooperation. Note that these definitions include both joint operation *and concurrence in effect:* the first being collective action, while the second may be accomplished by two or more units working independently, but having a common goal —producing the same effect. In fact, the example given in Webster's, (viz., "Whate'er cooperates to the common mirth.") more readily fits this later type of cooperation. There is nothing new or novel in this use of the word.

Periodically our little town of Burnet, Texas promotes a "clean up" week. The mayor publishes a proclamation in the town's weekly paper, and announcements are made over all 300 watts of our local radio station. I am proud to say that my neighbors and I *cooperate* in this matter. I shift my rocks about, cut the weeds, trim the cactus. One neighbor paints his fence, another trims his trees, and each cuts his grass, and hauls off accummulated trash and trivia. This IS "cooperation", and no reputable dictionary or philologist would deny it. Yet, there is no collective action involved, or as Campbell might put it, no "organized cooperation." Each neighbor plans his own work, uses his own resources, and maintains complete responsibility and independence throughout.

But while we have this illustration before us, let us make it an example of *another kind* of cooperation. Suppose we neighbors all meet to discuss "clean up" week, and someone suggests we pool our resources, select and recognize some sort of coordinating leadership, and *work as one* to beautify the area. One man has a paint-spray outfit, and so is assigned to paint all curbs and fences. Another is appointed to mow all lawns, and another will haul off trash. To meet the expenses of this operation we establish a neighborhood treasury, into which each neighbor places a portion of his money. This fund now becomes the property of the group—not of any one neighbor—and is administered by a selected treasurer or executive board. Now this is cooperation—the collective-action variety. It should be inserted here that "neighborhood" is "collective" in both cases (all neighbors *considered* as one), but "collective action" occurs only when the neighbors *act as one*.

The essential elements of collective *action* are: (1) agreement on the part of a plurality to act as one; (2) the *pooling* of means and/or abilities in order that the plurality may act as one (money usually being the medium of exchange by which plans are executed); and (3) the acceptance of a common mind; some common direction or guidance so that the plurality may act as one. In this type of cooperation each participant becomes dependent upon the whole, which in turn exists and functions through that which its parts supply. There is a vast difference in this type of cooperation (especially as it affects the individual units) and that of totally independent units working toward the same goal. Can you not see that one might disapprove of one *type* of cooperation, without being *against all* cooperation—without being "anti-cooperation"??

The word "cooperation" is not found in our standard versions of the Bible, but that does not rule against its use. The generic nature of the word does, however, place upon us this responsibility. In declaring "cooperation of churches" to be scriptural—and I do so declare—I am obligated to clearly define the specific type of cooperation I have in mind; AND, I am obligated to produce scriptures FOR THAT TYPE OF CO-OPERATION. Finding "wood" in God's authorization did not allow Noah the use of any specific wood he might choose, for God specified one wood—gopher. There was no authority for any other kind of wood. Finding vocal music in the N.T. scriptures does not justify the use of mechanical instruments of music in N.T. church worship. God specified "sing," and there is no authority for any kind of music other than vocal. By exactly the same process of reasoning—in the absence of generic authority, we urge brethren to be satisfied with the *specific type* of cooperation authorized in the scriptures. We do not find the phrase, "cooperation of churches" in God's word. Therefore, *in whatever sense we use that expression,* and declare the *idea* scriptural, *we must find THAT sense or idea* approved by the divine will, and conduct ourselves accordingly.

But we are not yet finished with our definitions. Webster's unabridged says of "collective": "1. Formed by collecting; gathered into a mass, sum, or body; aggregated." Then, with respect to collective *action* Webster's says: "3. Characteristic of the experience in common or the united action of the members of an aggregation or group,—*distinct from that of individuals.*" *The Shorter Oxford English Dictionary* defines "collective" thus: "1. Formed by collection; constituting a collection; aggregate, collected. *(Opposite to individual, and to distributive; so in sense 2.)* Sense two has to do with collective action: Of, pertaining to, or derived from, a number of individuals taken or acting together." (emph., rft)

Please note that collective action is OPPOSITE or OPPOSED to individual and distributive action. A "collective" (such as "church") may be considered distributively, its units act independently; or the units may act collectively. BUT WHEN THEY ARE ACTING INDEPENDENTLY, THEY ARE NOT, IN THAT MATTER, ACTING COLLECTIVELY; AND WHEN THEY ARE ACTING COLLECTIVELY, INDEPENDENCE HAS BEEN SACRIFICED IN THINGS PERTAINING TO, AND TO THE EXTENT OF, THAT COLLECTIVE ACTION. Here is a vital point, and a source of much misunderstanding and ambiguity of arguments among brethren.

We are in agreement that God authorizes *saints* to *act collectively;* and we seem to agree that this gives saints in a local church some organizational structure. Now, if God authorizes *churches* to act collectively, let us cease to write and preach that "the organizational structure of the church begins and ends with the local congregation." Let us either produce some specific form of inter-church organization authorized in the scriptures; or, with Campbell, admit that the specific form of such organization is not given, and that we are therefore at liberty to "devise ways and means" for the "whole kingdom" to cooperate. Let us cease to argue about opinions and expediencies, and get on with the job of *restructuring* the churchhood—for that is exactly what collective action of churches demands and produces. BUT IF THE LOCAL CHURCH IS THE EXTENT OF DIVINELY AUTHORIZED ORGANIZATION among God's people, then let us cease this double-talk about "independent" and "autonomous" churches acting collectively, and let us act accordingly.

At times, particularly when the early "church fathers" were seeking justification for organic union in the universal church, the scriptures which teach love, concern, and a *general working together* of all brethren, were used to promote collective action. (Example: 3 Jn. 5-8, re. hospitality for traveling teachers.) It is true that the universal church is one brotherhood—a "body" whose parts (individual saints) should recognize need for one another, give honor to one another, have sympathy for one another, and share both joy and suffering (1 Cor. 12:). This passage teaches cooperation among all members of the body of Christ—*as cooperation exists in an organism*. This cooperation is the result of common purpose, and does not establish the universal church as a single functional organization. Rom. 12:5 carries the idea of oneness further, saying, "So we, being many, are one body in Christ, and every one members one of another." Thus we "rejoice with them that rejoice, and weep with them that weep"—the empathy and sympathy of all members in a single organism. Other illustrations or figures are used to teach this common purpose—in fruit bearing (Jn. 15:1-6), fighting the good fight (Eph. 6:10-f), working in the Master's vineyard (Matt. 21:33-f), etc.

This commonness of purpose encourages Christians to "visit" with one another, attend and encourage gospel meetings conducted by neighboring congregations, sing praises to God together, and in many other ways be of one spirit in our efforts to further the cause of Christ. Because this often brings members of various local churches together it is sometimes called "fellowship of churches"; but it is, in reality, a fellowship of brethren. At the risk of being considered "picky," we suggest that more accurate terminology might avoid the acceptance of a relationship of churches which the scriptures do not teach. Saints may mingle together, consult with and worship with those of another congregation, without becoming a part of their company, and without blending two or more congregations into some larger functional unit. (Consider Antioch brethren in Jerusalem, Acts 15:22; the Cenchrean woman-servant Phebe, in Rome, Rom. 16:1-2; and the Philippian messenger Epaphroditus, in Rome with Paul, Phil. 2:25-30.)

I find nothing in the cooperation of members in an organism, which would justify what Campbell called "organized" co-operation of congregations. I find no scriptures which teach that the universal church has organic entity—exists as a catholic functional institution. In the past, gospel preachers frequently said, "The church of Christ has no earthly headquarters, no organization larger or smaller than the local church." I sometimes wonder if we have realized and truly understood what we were saying.

## THE "INDEPENDENT, AUTONOMOUS" LOCAL CHURCH

Which brings us to that great Fourth-of-July word, "Independence." To my knowledge, without exception, our brethren preach that each local church is "independent and autonomous." So did Alexander Campbell, first president of the American Christian Missionary Society. So do dozens—perhaps hundreds—of various religious groups whose organizational structures (as regards a plurality of churches) range from episcopacy to monarchy.

*Handbook of Denominations in the U.S.* by Frank S. Mead, (edition of 1951) lists 237 different religious groups in our country. A surprising number of these denominations claim to believe in "congregational independence;" but a wide-eyed look at their practices reveals some startling contradictions. Here are a few samples: *"Congregational in government, each local church is completely independent.* The churches are grouped in five districts and five annual conferences; over them is a national general conference, which meets biennially." Another: *"Local churches are left quite independent in polity and in the conduct of local affairs.* District officers have a pastoral ministry to all the churches and are responsible for the promotion of home missions. Work is divided into forty districts in the U.S., most of which follow state lines, each with a district Presbytery, which examines, licenses, and ordains pastors." (p.

18, 23.) There are many other like examples. In each case, if we read only that portion I have emphasized we might think this was written about the Lord's church. But those first lines do not tell the whole story. Is this the kind of "independent and autonomous" congregations we believe the scriptures authorize? Surely not!!

We must do more than just SAY we believe in congregational independence and autonomy. The "framework of the local church" is not some scheme for district, churchhood, or universal collective action. It is God's limitation of collective action—*the extent to which God authorizes organized church functions*. If this is not the case, our use of the words "local church government" is exactly as meaningless and ambiguous as that of denominationalism. If we use the "framework of county government" to run the nation—say, let the Tarrant county sheriff serve as Commander-in-Chief of the nation's armed forces, receiving operating funds from all over the country, and functioning in the national interest—(continue to call him "Sheriff" of course) would this mean we *had no armed force on a national scale?* To ask is to answer. And yet, many seem to think no brotherhood (churchhood) action is being taken as long as the elders of some local church have control of the project.

We must come to a more accurate understanding of such matters; agreeing on a use (a *scriptural* use) of the idea of "independent" church government, and giving particular attention to those things which violate this independence. It is here that congregational independence becomes a part of my subject; for not only in our own history, but in the history of many other religious groups, independence has been *given away*, yes *given away*, in "cooperation." Bear with me for one more quotation from Mead's *Handbook of Denominations*. "In 1814 the Baptists organized their own separate General Missionary Convention of the Baptist Denomination in the United States of America. This convention, representing a national Baptist fellowship, marked the first real denominational consciousness of American Baptists." This has a familiar ring to those who know our own history well.

How do we *prove* this congregational independence we so freely claim? Suppose you were pressed to *give the scriptures which prove* each church independent and autonomous; or "organizational structure begins and ends with the local congregation." Most knowledgeable saint would cite Acts 14:23, "elders in every church"; or 1 Pet. 5:2, "Feed (shepherd, rft) the flock of God which is among you." And what is the point? HOW do these scriptures prove local church independence? They indicate (1) *each congregation is on an equality* with reference to oversight; and (2) *oversight is on a local basis*, not on a district, churchhood, or universal scale. And does this limit organizational structure to the local church level? We usually agree that it does. Our reasoning, if we stop to analyze it, is that since oversight is on a local basis, and each congregation is on an equality in this respect, and since God provides no oversight on a district, "brotherhood" or other basis, God must intend that each congregation be independent and autonomous (self-ruled). I believe this is sound scriptural reasoning, and preach it this way. Of course we understand that we speak of "rule" from the viewpoint of coordinating oversight in matters of judgment, necessary for collective action of saints. We understand that Christ is sole Ruler of His citizens in all matters of faith (as Legislator, Executor, and Judge) and in this sense the church has but ONE overseer.

Another proof of congregational independence has to do with the church treasury. We have already shown that collective action requires not only the acceptance of a common oversight, but also the pooling of means and abilities, money being the usual medium through which a plurality act as one. As the *scale* or *extent* of *oversight* indicates the level of operation which God approves, so also does the *scope of the pooled fund* by which the joint operation is powered. 1 Cor. 16:1-3 reads: "Now concerning the collection for the saints, as I have given order to the churches of Galatia, even so do ye. Upon the first day of the week let every one of you lay by him in store, as God hath prospered him, that there be no gatherings when I come. And when I come, whomsoever ye shall approve by your letters, them will I send to bring your liberality unto Jerusalem." The funds were *accumulated* on a local scale—each church being instructed alike, each providing its own fund—and they were *controlled* on a local basis. "Whomsoever *ye* shall approve by your letters—" etc.)

An "independent" church is "not dependent" for direction and guidance (over-sight) nor for support. It "has a competency" to function in all things essential to its existence. (See Webster's, or other standard dictionary.) Such information as we have on the subjects suggest that elders are selected from among the flock to be served, and that the funds of a particular church come from the contributions of its members. This means that *each* church has a capacity to act commensurate with its own resources, and functions according to its own ability. (See 2 Cor. 8:11-12) A single independent local church may fulfill its purpose before God, if there were not another church in existence.

Within a single congregation the individual members own and control their private funds, and make their own decisions as to how much they will place in the pooled fund of the group to be used in "acting as one." (1 Cor. 16:2; 2 Cor. 9:7) The gift is made in view of a pre-determined purpose, and it is here that the individual's responsibility for its use is based. But once that fund is placed in the common treasury it then belongs to the collective, held in trust, to be used in carrying out those purposes. (See Acts 4:32-37; 5:1-4) All of this is authorized —on a local basis—and this puts collective action of saints on a local basis, making the local church a thing divinely authorized. But where is the authority for a *district* treasury, an *area-wide* or *"brotherhood"* treasury?? Can we not see that if *churches* have a pooled fund, as do individuals, that the *contributing churches* must relinquish control in favor of the larger operation? This is the very nature of collective action, as we have seen in our definition of terms.

Independent distributive action and collective action (even though, in one sense, they may both be called "cooperation") are not compatible terms; the two types of action are opposites. No matter how well intentioned are those churches which join in collective action; no matter how freely they enter such a compact; THE ARRANGEMENT ITSELF demands something *less* than independent autonomous churches, equal with respect to oversight and function; and something *more* than organizational structure that ends with the local church.

Please note that I have not said that collective action in one work destroys independence in *all* works. The contradiction of terms noted in Mead's *Handbook of Denominations* is explained on this ground. Various denominations claim independence in certain internal functions (their worship, Bible school, etc.) which do not claim, and certainly can not prove, independence in churchhood affairs. It is my contention, sustained by church histories in general, that such "churchhood level" collective action as they do espouse, "marks the first real denominational consciousness" of the various sects. It *can* happen to us.

On this course the paths of history are too deeply marked to be easily ignored. Our digressive brethren of the past century are even now engaged in a re-structuring movement—the outgrowth of their early collective action ventures—and seem bent on establishing a denominational status for themselves. We must either maintain strict congregational independence in *all* fields of endeavor, or, holding to our non-denominational plea, eventually accept organic entity for the universal church. Brotherhood that is less than the whole of God's people, is the very essence of denominationalism.

## COOPERATION AMONG INDEPENDENT CHURCHES

Now if our conviction that N.T. congregations were "independent and autonomous" is correct—and we know but few who will deny it; and if those churches *did* "cooperate"—and all seem to agree they did; we may expect to find a *type* of cooperation in the scriptures that respects independence and autonomy. Should we find something different—evidence of collective action among churches, or any form of organized interchurch activities—it would be necessary to revise this premise. We are aware that some may question our approach to this subject—the establishment of an "independent church" foundation, from which to launch an investigation of cooperation—but we believe this approach is justified. (1) Evidence for independent churches greatly exceeds the few examples that offer even moot arguments for collective action. We believe we are reasoning from the known to the doubtful or unknown. (2) We wish to emphasize what is at stake in this matter. We believe thousands of brethren are being swept along with the ballyhoo of popular interchurch activities, who have not recognized its threat to a principle they have long believed, but failed to apply.

We have seen that "cooperation" takes place when two or more units "concur in effect;" and in this sense all faithful churches of Christ cooperate constantly to influence the world and one another with the "flavor" of Christianity. The church at Corinth was a public monument to the work of Paul, as well as testimony in the apostles' hearts. (2 Cor. 3:1-2) All faithful churches today fill a like function. Together, each in its several way, they tell the world of Christ, and demonstrate the manifold wisdom of God. The Thessalonians were involved in this type of cooperation. Paul said they were examples to all that believed (1 Thes. 1:7-8), imitators of other churches in their acceptance of persecution for Christ's sake (1 Thes. 2:14); and Paul boasted of them, to increase the zeal of other churches (2 Thes. 1:4). This is cooperation, but it gives no hint of organized inter-church activities.

A second class of cooperation involves a more direct contact between churches and/or their members. The Romans were asked to assist Phebe, servant of the church in Cenchrea, in a manner unrevealed. (Rom. 16:1-2) But it was Phebe they assisted, "as becometh saints;" with no hint of collective action of churches. The letter from Jerusalem to "the brethren in Antioch and Syria and Cilicia" (Acts 15:22-f) was no doubt read before churches (vs. 30). The Colossians were told: "When this epistle is read among you, cause that it be read also in the church of the Laodiceans; and that ye likewise read the epistle from Laodicea." (Col. 4:16) This likely involved some "messenger" work, although we are given no details; but we do agree that a certain type of "cooperation" took place: brethren and churches did their several tasks toward the common goal of spreading the truth. When the Jerusalem church heard about the new converts in Antioch (Acts 11:22-f) they sent Barnabas; who, with Paul, exhorted the brethren and turned others to the Lord. One church showed concern, and a willingness to send a preacher to a place where he was needed. If we can be content with what is revealed in the text, this example also falls neatly into place with well established principles of congregational independence, and there is no evidence of collective action of churches.

There is a vast difference in giving assistance to one in need (giving "alms"), or even in furnishing a portion of one's wages; and in working collectively through a pooled fund. An individual is "in need" when he lacks the means of *self-maintenance;* NOT when he lacks the means of meeting world obligations beyond his ability. The same may be said of a family, or a church. In such circumstances (lacking the means for self-maintenance) the unit is no longer self-sufficient (in that field where the "want" exists) but is dependent. Alms given in such a case become the sole property of the needy unit. When alms restore that which was lacking the unit again becomes *independent*, alms are no longer needed, and each unit goes its independent way. There is no "pooling" of funds, for at no time are funds involved "common" to both parties, either in reality or in principle. There is no agreement to "work as one," no "acceptance of common direction or guidance to work as one."

Where two or more donors send support to a single worker, the funds become the sole property of the receiver to be used at his discretion. If the funds are "wages" in the usual sense of the term, the extent of obligation is the rendering of service in keeping with agreement. There is "value received" by each employer, to the extent of each one's involvement—but no collective action. The same is true where two or more customers buy products or services at the same store. These are ordinary affairs, readily recognized in every day life, but so often forgotten when we have some cause to "prove by the scriptures."

In class three of our "cooperation" study, are cases where a plurality of churches concur in meeting the same specific need. While Paul was in Thessalonica, and at the time of his leaving Macedonia, ("the aorist marking the simple date," says Alford) the Philippian church alone supported him (Phil. 4: 15-16). But later, in Corinth, he recounts: "I robbed other churches, taking wages of them, to do you service." (2 Cor. 11: 8) Name the other churches? I can't do that, nor can you. How did they get the sustenance to him? I do not know, nor do you. But it was "churches" he "robbed"—*not a pooled fund where the plurality of the donors had been lost in collective action.* When Paul's funds were depleted (vs. 9) he said brethren which came from Macedonia supplied his want. It is reasonable to *suppose* that the Philippians continued to help Paul, and their example *may* have encouraged other Macedonian churches to send aid—*perhaps* even using the same messengers—*but conjectures must not be allowed to destroy Paul's clear statement of the matter.* If Philippi was a "sponsoring church" it was unrevealed in the inspired scriptures. Paul did not say he was supplied by a special missionary fund under the control of *one* church; he said, "I robbed other *churches*, taking wages of them—." This is an obvious case of cooperation, but contains nothing to alter the concept of equal autonomous churches engaged in concurrent independent action.

Of course the classic case of cooperation is that of the Gentile churches sending alms to Jerusalem. Like instructions were given to a plurality of churches concerning the need of the "poor among the saints in Jerusalem" as is seen in 1 Cor. 16:1 and Rom. 15:25-26. Several years elapsed as these gifts were being collected (2 Cor. 9:2); first, as each church "makes up beforehand their bounty" (2 Cor. 9:5), and then messengers were chosen and conveyed the gifts to Jerusalem. (1 Cor. 16: 3-4; 2 Cor. 8:19, 23) There are many interesting and profitable facets to this account but we must limit ourselves to the task at hand. Did these churches act collectively in providing or distributing these gifts? Is there anything here to justify "organized cooperation" among churches? As in the case of churches supporting Paul, the fact that a plurality of churches work to meet a single specific need, does not endanger nor violate their individual independence. There, Paul was the one in need of support—the *end;* and each sending church addressed itself, according to desire and ability, to this end. Church "A" *assisted Paul;* church "B" *assisted Paul*, etc. In this case, "the poor saints which are at Jerusalem" constitute the target. (Sometimes "saints" are mentioned alone, and sometimes simply "Jerusalem.") Churches were individually informed, each exercised its own "will" to help (2 Cor. 8:10-11), each gathered a contribution (1 Cor. 16:2), and each controlled the sending of its own gift to the target.

I have said "each" because 1 Cor. 16:1 shows that Paul instructed the churches alike. *Corinth's control* over the sending of its *own fund* is seen in vs. 3: "Whomsoever ye shall approve, them will I send with letters to carry *your* bounty unto Jerusalem."(ARV) (emph., rft) Paul does not use his apostleship to "push" himself on these churches. In vs. 4 he says, "And if it be meet (worthwhile, fitting, rft) for me to go also, they shall go with me." He stresses that the messengers were "chosen of the churches," to avoid any suspicion that they were simply *his* choice. (2 Cor. 8:18-f) In fact, it seems that Paul "leans over backwards" in this last passage, to impress the fact that individual church interests are guarded.

But right in the middle of this is an expression upon which many have pounced, to prove (?) collective action. The messengers were "chosen of the churches." At this some immediately lose sight of all else, and see a convention of churches, voting upon various "candidates" by a show of hands, so that finally certain men are elected to represent the whole. So far as I have been able to determine, the language used would allow either a number of churches, independent of one another, selecting the same man, or, collective action. The phrase "chosen of the churches" is not conclusive. However, those few words of the text are not alone. They are surrounded by all else we have seen concerning this operation, including Paul's pointed statement to one church, "whomsoever ye shall approve—etc." The immediate context is, "And we have sent with him the brother, whose praise is in the gospel throughout all the churches;"—(the churches could *praise* the brother independently)—"And not that only, but who was also chosen of the churches to travel with us with this grace,—." (2 Cor. 8:18-19) I believe the fair and logical conclusion must be that he was also *chosen* independently.

There remain but scraps of arguments to be cleared up—most of which would never have been made by our brethren except in the heat of conflict. One brother thinks "The churches of Christ salute you" (Rom. 16:16) is a N.T. example of collective action. But the verb "salute" (aspazontai) is plural. Another thinks Paul was the Chairman of a "company" comparable to a benevolent "board," which received and disbursed alms on behalf of the churches. Some of this idea comes from a misunderstanding of "administered" (2 Cor. 8:19, K.J.) But the greek is "diakoneo" and carries no official connotation whatsoever. It refers simply to the task of conveying the gifts; R.V. translates "ministered." A few brethren would like to believe that Jerusalem was a "sponsoring church," the media for a program of general benevolence. All such arguments call for *much* supposition, unique uses of greek grammer, and a brand of interpretation which makes the wish mother of the conclusion. There is no footing in the divine text for such arguments —not even enough to justify further treatment here.

## APPLICATION AND SUMMARY

But honest, forthright application of truth to our daily life is always justified. Without it, our studies become sterile exercises and we become hypocrites. There are very real, concrete reasons for my believing the points of this study are needed today among members of the church of Christ; and I shall try to set them before you in understandable language.

### 1. WE ARE ADOPTING THE "ALL-CHURCH" FALLACY.

A common argument of the day is this: (a) The "church" must go to all the world. (b) No one congregation can do this. (c) So we "devise ways and means" for the whole kingdom to "cooperate" in World Radio, Inc., and many like projects. "Brotherhood" has almost unanimously become "churchhood" in our thinking; with multiple interchurch projects in progress, and more to come.

### 2. OUR PRACTICE HAS OUT-RUN OUR THEORY OF LOCAL CHURCH INDEPENDENCE.

In theory we still acknowledge that God provides no oversight or treasury beyond the local church level; but in practice "churchhood" treasuries and "boards" are common stuff. Some still name the elders of one church as that "board," and we salve our conscience by calling this "the framework of the local church," but we know better than that. As one brother put it: "If a little 'board' is scriptural, why is not a big 'board' scriptural? If it can control or direct the actions of ten congregations, could it not control and direct the actions of ten thousand congregations?" The truth is, of course, that neither "elders" nor "boards" have the right to function over a collective larger than the single local church.

### 3. WE HAVE CORRUPTED THE SCRIPTURAL USE OF "ALMS."

To justify sponsoring church machinery (as Herald of Truth) we evoke passages that sanction *alms* to a *dependent* church or people. Of course we know that Highland in Abilene is not dependent. It is the inter-church missionary or benevolent projects that are hungry, and churches are sending "ante," not "alms."

4. WE ALLOW "VOLUNTARY" TO BLIND US TO STRUCTURAL CHANGES.

Churches entered the 1849 Missionary Society arrangement "voluntarily." Exercise of free-will is not what keeps the local church scriptural: the church must "will" to operate according to God's plan, *and do it*. It is the inter-church *arrangement itself* that is unscriptural, and free-will participation makes the error worse, not better.

5. WE ARE BUILDING "PARTIES" BY PREJUDICIAL TREATMENT OF BRETHREN.

The party spirit has run rampant in our discussions of "co-operation," with "party practices" the standard for "fellowship." "Anti" and "Liberal" branding has taken the place of objective Bible study. My disappointment that my brethren could drift so far into doctrinal error, is far over-shadowed by my abject shame at the spirit they (must I say, "we"!) have manifested in the ensuing struggle.

In the final analysis, I am pleading now for a re-evaluation of our faith and practice, before it is everlastingly too late. I do not plead to save "our" party, or "our" church; but I plead to save "our" souls, and the souls of thousands yet to come. May God strengthen our hearts!!

## Co-operation of Churches

### Roy Lanier

I was interested in brother Turner's use of Acts 11:27-30 and wondered if he believed that was church action or individual action. During the intermission, I asked him and he says he doesn't know. He didn't think there was any way of determining positively whether it was one or the other. I think that is significant, especially in view of the fact that so many of you have taken the position that it positively is church action. If this is true, this takes it out of the realm of any certain example for us. If you can't tell whether it is church action or individual action, it follows that you can't use it as an example of church or collective activity; neither can you use it as positive proof of individual action. Since we don't have enough information on it we won't use it for either one.

Another matter—if every church is to do no more than it is able to do by itself (cannot depend upon help from other churches) in the matter of preaching the gospel, why would Paul rob other churches to help him preach to Corinth when he said he had a right to be supported by the brethren at Cor-

---

ROY H. LANIER—*Evangelist for Bear Valley congregation, Denver, Colorado; teacher in the Bear Valley School of Preachers; author; debater; former staff writer for the GOSPEL ADVOCATE; frequent contributor to the FIRM FOUNDATION and other periodicals; conducts many gospel meetings throughout the nation.*

inth? Now, if he had the right to be supported by them, they were able to support him. But he said he'd rather die than use that right, so he robbed other churches to work for them while they were able to give him support. Consequently, when the churches sent to Paul, if they sent to him individually which I think can be proved from this reference—but if they did send to him directly it was the same as sending it to the church and allowing them to use it for him or some other work.

Another thing—a good deal was said about collective action as opposed to individual action. Now, if each church operating in its own community is the only cooperation the Lord allows, it follows that cooperation is demanded of all churches. This illustration was used: the city is going to have a clean-up and they're going to do it by every man cleaning up his own property. That is one way. Another way is to pool their money and resources and pay for it to be done. Or they will assign all the painting to one man, all the hauling off of trash to another and so on around. Now it was implied—if I understood it right and if I didn't some of you may correct me—it was implied that that was the kind of cooperation, and the only kind of cooperation, that is allowed in the New Testament. So every church is to do its own work and that is cooperation.

Brethren, there simply isn't any cooperation about that. According to your own definition of cooperation, that's independent, simultaneous action and there is no cooperation where there is nothing but operation. And now, suppose that I have a property here and I clean up my own property, paint my own fence, etc., but here's a widow over here with two or three little children and they have a big accumulation of trash out here that they just simply can't handle. But I can't go help her because we are following this individual cooperation and then we have that situation exactly.

Here's an affluent church—it's able to take care of its own back yard and front yard, etc., but here's a little church over here that cannot do its work. It needs a building, it needs wide representation in the community, it needs a radio program, but this affluent church can't go over there and help it. Why? Because that's outside the pattern of New Testament cooperation. You simply cannot have one church helping another and Paul violated his own rule when he asked the churches of Asia and Macedonia to help Jerusalem. There's Jerusalem, the little widow, over there with more children than she can take care of and here's your affluent Corinth and some more poor folks up here at Macedonia. Paul said you folks ought to help this widow down here. Oh no, Paul, we can't do that. We can't do it because cooperation means everybody doing his own work and so Paul violated his principle of New Testament cooperation if your position is true.

But again, I'm told that there is one pattern for evangelism and another pattern for benevolence and that we ought not to mix the two. Now brethren, you're going to get yourselves into a lot of trouble. You're going to be some of the worthy destitutes that need money because the only place you get your check on Sunday night or Monday morning is from the contribution on the first day of the week. But the contribution on the first day of the week is in the benevolent pattern and nowhere else.

Oh, don't come to me and say that I Cor. 9 authorizes the church to pay the preacher. I know it does, but I Cor. 9 does not authorize the church to take that money out of the benevolent contribution on Sunday. The contribution on the first day of the week is in connection with benevolence and not evangelization and if you make one pattern for benevolence and another for evangelism, you forever cut yourself off from the right to take your check from the Lord's day contribution. Now, that's a problem you brethren have got to deal with or you're going to be in the destitute area. But again, as a conclusion to this argument since there are not two patterns—and this argment I've just made destroys the idea of two separate patterns—if there is only one pattern it follows that money may be sent to a church for benevolence or evangelization. Now, if you're going to continue to take your check—your salary check—out of the Lord's day contribution you are, by consistency, obligated to say that a church (an affluent church) may send a contribution to a poor church for evangelism.

Let me add one more thought to this, Paul said "as I gave order to the churches in Galatia, so also do ye at Corinth." Upon the first day of the week let every one of you lay by in store and I'll pick up the contribution and take it down to Jerusalem. Now, there Paul gave an order for a church to help another church. This is contrary to brother Turner's idea of each one cleaning up his own back yard. He said cooperation consists in this church doing its work, this church over here doing its work, every church in the world doing its own work in its home community, but Paul gave order to the churches in Galatia and Macedonia to send money to Jerusalem. That was not doing its own work in its home community when it sent money down to Jerusalem. So if Paul demanded that this church at Corinth send money to Jerusalem (outside its home community), your illustration of cooperation breaks down completely, unless you're going to take the position that Corinth was not cooperating with Jerusalem and I think that would not do you very much good.

Well, the matter of autonomy. It has been claimed when one church gives to another that it loses its autonomy, but the Corinthian church was ordered—Paul gave orders—that they send money to Jerusalem. Did Paul say to the church at Corinth, "You must lose your autonomy to Jerusalem"? I think, as a necessary consequence of the argument, you are saying that Paul would demand that Corinth allow Jerusalem to rob her of her autonomy. Another thing, it's said no one church has the authority to oversee the work of all churches. Well, of course, brethren, I believe that as much as you do. All the rest of these brethren out here believe it.

And when Corinth sent money to Jerusalem, Jerusalem was not overseeing the work of the church at Corinth. And if Corinth can send money to Jerusalem without the Jerusalem church overseeing the work of the Corinthian church, then a church today may send to another church for a radio program or a benevolent program without the receiving church taking over and running the affairs, overseeing the affairs, of the sending church. Now, it's absolutely ridiculous to say that when one church sends to another church that the receiving church oversees all the work of the sending church. Surely you brethren won't go that far. You can only sensibly say that this receiving church is overseeing that portion of the work of the church that this money represents. That's all you could sensibly say, but when you do that you're saying that the Jerusalem church oversaw that portion of the work at Corinth and if the Jerusalem church could oversee that portion of Corinth's work, why can't the receiving church today oversee that portion of the work of the sending church? What's wrong about it? Paul encouraged it, Paul demanded it—gave order that they do it—and anything that Paul gave order to do certainly ought to be acceptable to all of us, and I'm sure you would say that it is.

Now, I'd like to talk about the purpose of benevolence. Do I have as much as three minutes yet? Well, in Luke 4: 22-24, and following Jesus was being criticized for not doing the great works he did in other places and he said "Elijah did not feed all the widows in his day and Elisha did not cleanse all the lepers in his day" and by implication Jesus was not out to feed all the hungry people of his day and heal all the sick people of his day. These three simply fed and healed those who gave them opportunity to do the main part of their work. The primary work of the church is to convert people and the primary work of Jesus was to convert people to the idea that he was the Son of God and he fed people and he healed people when it gave him an opportunity to prove to them that he was the Son of God and, thus, caused them to believe Him.

Now, the church today is not obligated to feed all the hungry people in the world or to take care of all the orphans, but they can feed and take care of those people who afford them an opportunity to do their primary work—and that's to convert them. I take the position that no church has any right to feed anybody outside of the church other than those whom it expects to reach through that act of charity with the gospel and that this limits the obligation of the church to feed nonsaints. When, through feeding them, I can reach their hearts with the word of God I am obligated to feed them.

I met a man in California a few years ago who asked if I remembered him. A great big heavy fellow, red-faced, and I said "No, I don't know you from Adam's off-ox." Well, he reminded me that a few years before back in Waxahachie, Texas, he was a poor barber and he was sick, his children were sick, he was unable to work and got in arrears with his rent and grocery bills. He was a Baptist but his wife was a member of the church. He was prejudiced against her, but I went down with a check to pay the rent and I took in groceries and he gave consideration to my preaching and I had baptized him in the year of 1923. I'd never have reached that man had I not taken advantage of that opportunity for the church to help him. Then I reached him, converted him and he's been a faithful Christian ever since so far as I know. Thank you.

## Co-operation of Churches

Robert Turner

I would like to take the statements that were made in the order in which they were given. I. *Acts 11: 27-30.* He said I told him that I didn't know whether aid went from the church or whether it went from the saints distributively, and that's correct. He concluded that *I couldn't use this as an example of cooperation of churches.* Well, I can *where* I use 'it. I used three classifications of cooperation. (1) General cooperation, everyone working toward a common purpose and they don't even have to know that anybody else is doing anything that goes on all the time. (2) One church doing something to help a dependent church; and I used as one example, Jerusalem sending a man down to Antioch. I didn't try to make any sort of collective action of churches out of it but, rather, contributing to the general purpose of strengthening the cause of Christ. That's exactly where Acts 11: 27-30 fits—Class 2.

II. *Paul said that he had the right to be supported by the Corinthian church, therefore, the Corinthian church was able.* Well, I wouldn't argue that they weren't able. Paul criticized

---

ROBERT F. TURNER—*Engaged in full time meeting work throughout the nation; lives in Burnet, Texas where he formerly preached for the Oaks West congregation; editor of a widely read and quoted eight page monthly,* **PLAIN TALK;** *formerly served congregations in San Antonio and Gladewater, Texas and Phoenix and Prescott Arizona.*

himself to a very strong extent. He even said he may have done them a wrong because he took support from somewhere else. *So when they sent to Paul, one church was sending to a neighbor church.* The point is they sent it to *Paul.* We don't have an example of somebody sending to a neighbor church there. We don't have an example of that. They sent it to Paul. You really haven't gotten my point there at all.

III. *Cooperation demanded by all churches; He said, on my definition all churches have to be cooperating.* Exactly right. That's type one. Of course, *he said independent concurrent action is not cooperation.* But the definition said it was, and I quoted from three standard dictionaries and gave a long run-down on it that said such was cooperation. That's one of the definitions of cooperation for people to work, even independently, but toward a common effect, and that's exactly what I put in Type I.

IV. *Can't help the widows who are not able (like in the clean-up business) and, therefore, you couldn't help a small church who is not able.* No, I objected only to assisting—(now, watch it)—in doing evangelistic work or anything that goes beyond that church. But I would not say you could not help that poor widow who couldn't clean up her own lawn. You'd be supplying what is needed by a dependent unit. I said you could supply a dependent unit to make it independent. Oh, I'd help the poor widow. I'd help a small church that couldn't help itself —a dependent church. I would send alms to help it, but its alms. I made a distinction between alms and "ante." I made a difference in sending where the end itself is the church and sending where the church is simply the means for going on somewhere else.

V. *The only place you get your check, he said, is from the contribution on the first day of the week, but this is for benevolence.* I Cor. 16 tells us when the collection was made but, as you know and all the rest of you know, there are plenty of other passages showing that churches can support preachers. *But you can't take preaching funds from a benevolent fund.* Why, of course not. Absolutely not. These is purpose, intent and purpose, back of contribution. When I make a contribution on the first day of the week to support the collective action of saints, I give with specific purposes in mind.

In fact, if the church where I'm preaching was doing something I thought was wrong, I wouldn't make a contribution there because I would be putting into a fund whose purpose is wrongly committed. They tell me beforehand that this fund is going to be used to do so and so, and I can't do that, so I wouldn't give to that fund. But as long as the church is operating scripturally and doing what it has a right to do, including paying preachers, alms work, etc., then the purpose is established before I put my money in there. It's true that I Cor. 16 speaks particularly of benevolence; but what about Phil. 4:15-16 where a church sent to Paul. Also, I Cor. 9. In other words, we don't argue about that. No, that's no point.

VI. *"One pattern,"* he says, *"benevolence and evangelism are all the same."* Well, actually, in the way I presented this thing this morning I didn't make any distinction in patterns. Now, there are ways in which that could be done, but I didn't do so. My arguments are strictly on this business of sending to one unit funds, that go from there somewhere else, making collective action; a *pool* of funds that is common to two churches or more. I made a clear distinction between that and sending alms to a dependent church so it could become independent.

And besides all that, if it is true that there is no distinction, then Paul's company—which he set forth this morning as an evangelistic company and as a separate company—Paul's company can become an evangelistic company supported by churches. Don't you miss that point. In fact, I don't know how he could rule out a board-operated home on that basis. Now I appreciate what he said about the board-operated home, but I don't know how he's going to rule it out if Paul and company were a separate organization that received funds from churches to do alms work. I don't know how in the world he's going to take the board out. And if there is no difference in the patterns he can't take evangelistic work out of it, so he's got a missionary board. I don't say that to prejudice. He's got an evangelistic board, if that sounds better.

VII. *Autonomy.* A lot about autonomy. *When one gives to another it loses autonomy.* I didn't say that. No, I said when you pool funds that autonomy suffers, independence suffers. I didn't say that giving to another church destroyed autonomy. You don't lose any autonomy sending alms. *Oh, but we've got examples of churches sending to another church.* Of course we have. Sending alms. I came to bring alms to my nation (Acts 24:17). I came to bring alms to my nation. They were dependent and the dependency existed in this case with respect to physical needs. Those needs were supplied, and there is not a thing in the world wrong with that. Doesn't have a thing to do with the cooperation of churches upon which we differ, like the sponsoring church, for that is not a dependent unit. The only way you can make anything out of that point is to make Jerusalem a unit that received funds from all over the country and then went somewhere else—by that I mean went to another needy place—and took care of them. That's the only way you could make a point out of that.

VIII. *Sponsoring church oversees a "portion" of the contributing church's work.* Of course, that's what I said. I even had a paragraph about that long in my text that I was not saying that if they lost autonomy in one thing that that meant in everything, or that if they went into some sort of collective action that that meant that it destroyed their *whole* independence. In fact, I can give you multiple examples of where that wasn't so, even going back into Mead's denominational history and pointing out that that was the distinction. Without that distinction being true the whole book's statements about "independent" churches is just one big mess. But mainly what he was talking about (and I'm not using him as an authority) but the point is, that distinction was clear in his mind. They were independent with respect to *some* work but not independent in others. Well, that's *my* point. So we say we lose autonomy to the extent of the portion of the work done collectively. Exactly so. Exactly so.

IX. *The purposes of benevolent work—not to feed all of the world.* That's not the subject; not on the subject so I won't discuss it. (May I have the chart please.) I appreciate what you said. I don't say that to belittle what you said but its just not our subject. Here's the thing that we seem to be missing along. Here's a local church, here's a sponsoring church in which funds are pooled from other churches. That's all I mean here. Now, here's a missionary society. Now, the word "go" is generic but "go" can only authorize things that are under "go." I'm willing to make any big word out of it I can and I'm not

# A "FUSS ABOUT METHODS"?

| ORGANIZATION | "GO" | "TEACH" | "CARE" |
|---|---|---|---|
| Independent local church | Drive car / Fly / Walk | Private Tracts Class ~~PREACH~~ | House Clothe Medicate ~~FEED~~ |

ALL "GO" ON THE SAME TRAIN --- ETC.

"Sponsor" church plan

"Board"/plan, Evangl. or Benev.

ISSUE DOES NOT ENVOLVE METHOD OF "GO" "TEACH" "CARE"; BUT— SCOPE OF ORGANIZATION.

much on big words, but it's "locomotion." *Means of locomotion* and that's all that "go" can authorize. "Go" authorizes means of locomotion. "Go" doesn't authorize writing tracts. That's a method of teaching. "Go" authorizes means of locomotion, walk, fly, swim or go on a train.

Now then suppose the church up here sends a preacher. He gets on this train. The sponsoring church sends a preacher and he gets on the same train—(of course, they won't sit in the same car). The missionary society sends a preacher and he gets on the train (They'd put him out on the caboose). But they're all going the same way—that's a method of travel right there.

Now, here's a method of teaching. "Teach" only authorizes methods of pedagogy or instruction. One method of instruction is questions and answers or pulpit preaching (didactic teaching) or writing or something like that. Well, I'm not going to object to anything like that. These are methods of teaching. Those are methods of going. The *issue* is what is God's *plan of organization.* We're not talking about methods of "going" or "teaching." We're right back here. Here's where our objection lies. Did God plan that local churches, independently and autonomously, should send according to their ability, or that sponsoring churches should take funds from many churches, pooling them, and then some out of their own funds and put into that fund? That in itself sets it up as a separate fund. Or some other "company" . . . I think you brethren are really leaving the gate open when you say Paul did this, for you're just letting the whole fence down for a separate organization when you say Paul did. The question is what are the methods of organization that God gave us. That's the issue.

X. *The manner of cooperation binding.* (Now, I'm back on the first speech.) Is the manner of cooperation binding? No, the type of cooperation. The type, that's the distinction I made. The type. I'm not concerned about how the check is written or whether somebody takes the cash and puts it in their pocket. That's not what I'm interested in. I'm concerned about the type of cooperation.

XI. *Organization under Paul. Paul and his company.* If we accept this under alms and say no distinction should be made: 1. How do you object to a Board-operated home? 2. How in the world can you outlaw missionary societies? You just could not do it to save your life.

XII. Then he had a real good line-up here on the thing done (that was preacher care), *the ones doing it (the church),* the purpose (to save the lost and fill the needs), the source (the collection). I agree with it. That's a good line-up. What church? *The church can do it.* What church? Are you talking about the church universal? Devising ways and means for it to operate? Or will he go back to the local, independent, autonomous church within the limits of its ability doing what God told it to do?

XIII. *Its own work. How do you define what its own work is?* Well, I certainly don't do it by geography. I go back to the ability. Let me give you an example, Suppose I made up my mind now I'm going to give $5000 every Sunday, the first day of the week, the time for the collection. I'm in a good little church, they need the money. I'll give $5000 every Sunday. Of course, I'm $4,596 short but I call on all you brethren now to give me some of your contribution (and we'll have to go outside this bunch to get that much money), but I call on you to give me money so that I can make that contribution. Nothing wrong with making the contribution. I make it on the first day of the week, I make it in a church that's doing good scriptural work. Nothing wrong in that. But you say, wait a minute, Turner, you give your contribution according to your ability and we'll give out contribution according to our ability. That's exactly right. That's all I'm asking the church to do. I'm saying the church ought to work according to its ability. That's just exactly what I'm saying. We are failing to get the distinction in alms, and this evangelistic work through another church; and *the difference is not simply that one takes care of some physical need and one preaches.* Of course, that is a difference, all right, but that's not the difference that I'm talking about. That's not the issue between us. The difference I'm talking about is that in sending alms, there is a unit that has become dependent in some way or another, here is a unit that can supply that, and so they send to supply. The gift goes from here to there and that's it. It becomes the property—not pooled, but the property—of that church. That fund at no time is common to two churches. It's *this* church's fund, then it's *that* church's fund. It never becomes common, therefore, it's not a pooled fund; therefore, that point doesn't fit.

*XIV. According to ability to raise funds.* If I were debating somebody that I really wanted to say something ugly about, this would be a good place to say it, but I'm not going to say it. I'm just not going to say it because I know Roy too well for that. Think about that, Roy. Think about that. How in the world would you measure a person's ability and really make any kind of point about ability if it had to do with whether or not they could raise funds from somebody else or not?—like that $5000 illustration.

*XV. One-man missionary society has plagued us.* Well, that's right. So has one-church missionary society. Now, just stop and let that sink in. So has the one-church missionary society. The issue is collective action of churches. I no more favor sending the funds from a group of churches, pooling them under one man, to go on and do something out here than I favor pooling funds in one church. No, the man is not dependent. You're not supplying his meat, you're not even supporting him. Such has gone beyond support. I'd no more agree with that than I would with taking funds from a bunch of churches and sending that over here to the elders of one church and then letting them take it on to do something else. The issue is collective action of churches.

XVI. *It's not wrong to pool in one church because the Corinthian church and the Macedonian church did at Jerusalem.* No, they didn't pool it. You're missing the point on pooling it. The fund never became common. It wasn't common in the hands of Paul and the messengers any more than when 4 or 5 denominations each send a check somewhere. The Methodist church may be sending money to a Methodist missionary, the Baptist church sending to a Baptist missionary and the Catholic church sending to Rome and all that money goes in the same mail bag.

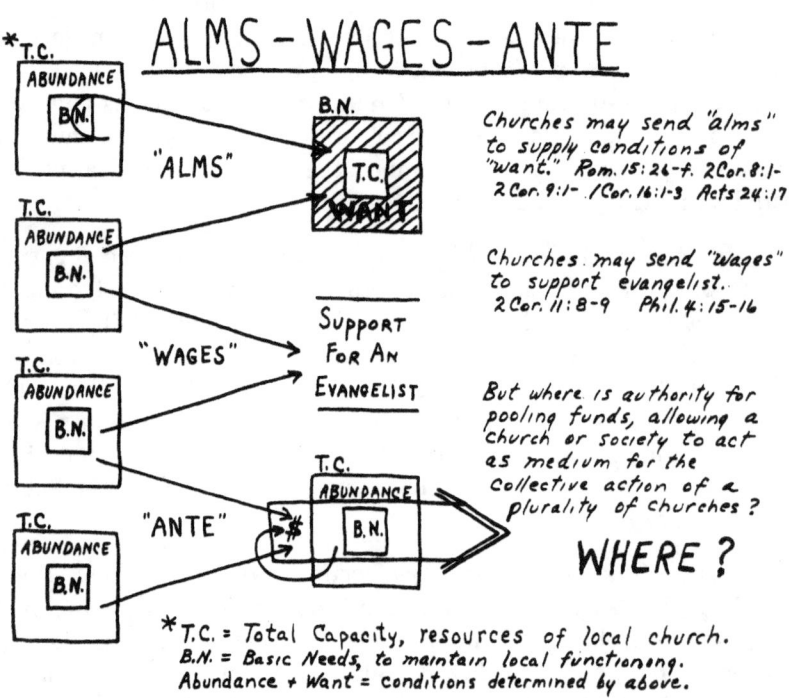

## Co-operation of Churches

Hulen L. Jackson

Brethren, one of the refreshing experiences down at Buchanan last year was the realization by both groups that our brethren who disagree with us are not nearly as bad, perhaps, as we had permitted ourselves to think. We truly learned to think more of each other—the eight of us who were there—and repeatedly, during those days the statement was heard: "I'm glad to know that. I'm glad to learn that." And, I'm hoping that our meeting this week here at Arlington will result in the same. We are brethren, we all love each other as brethren, and we sincerely are striving toward the same objective—salvation of souls through the building up of God's kingdom. May we respect each other's sincerity and honesty and may this association this week draw us a little closer together making us realize though we do have differences, all are sincere in those differences. Maybe we ought to admit to each other that we've misrepresented each other. We did just that at Buchanan last year concerning the non-cooperative brethren and as I recall they admitted they had at least thought some things about us

HULEN L. JACKSON— *Evangelist for churches in Dallas, Texas for twenty-seven years—Preston Road and Trinity Heights. Presently laboring at Trinity Heights. Regular contributor to the* FIRM FOUNDATION, GOSPEL ADVOCATE, *and* POWER FOR TODAY; *conducts numerous gospel meetings throughout the nation.*

that were not true. By way of illustration, we pointed out to them that often one of their number will read in some church's bulletin about a pet project of theirs and conclude from that report that we all endorse such a project when this is not true at all. No one of us could be expected to endorse all such projects being carried on out on the "fringes" of the brotherhood. In fact the vast majority of our brethren would as conscientiously oppose these matters as the non-cooperative brethren. You should not judge all of us by what some brother or some church here and there might be undertaking. And, last year we discussed several such projects and it seemed refreshing news to all that we opposed these digressive endeavors as did they. Maybe our continued fellowship this week here will continue to clear the air among us and between us. We pray to that end.

I think Bro. Roy Lanier entered into fully the subject of the scripturalness of congregational cooperation and I much prefer not to reiterate or even re-emphasize these arguments, but I should like to set forth this proposition in question form. Will what we've said really work? Will our position toward congregations work? Will your position? Can we relate these views and these positions to the growth and progress of the Lord's church? Will our views permit us to seize the opportunities that arise to spread the kingdom of God and reach souls with the Gospel of Christ? I'm going to say some things about your work and about our work but not in a critical tone at all. Let's deal for a while not with principles but with the application of those principles to our work for the Lord.

Privately to some of you a few minutes ago I said that to me behind and beyond this question of congregational cooperation is another question that must be answered and I plead with you non-cooperative brethren for an answer. Frankly, if this question is answered it will greatly simplify the matter of cooperation among churches.

Are the responsibilities and opportunities of a church limited by the financial capabilities of that church?

Or in other words, can a church plan a work—one project or a dozen—bigger than that local church can pay for themselves by themselves? Can they receive any aid from anybody in any way, individually or congregationally, outside that local membership?

Now, I think if we could determine the answer it would settle to a large extent the question of congregational cooperation. I'm not saying that your answer would be yes or no, but are you really teaching, brethren, that no church can ever plan any work for which they cannot pay by themselves? If they cannot pay the bill, the whole bill by themselves, must they turn down the opportunity? It is evident that we don't believe that a church's work is limited by its own financial resources, and to be perfectly honest with you I don't believe that you either believe or practice that. You may laugh this matter off by saying it is irrelevant but it is vital to our discussion and somehow must be settled before we can be one again in the realm of church cooperation. What if I visited your place some Sunday and listened to a report of some appealing project you were about to undertake as a congregation, would I be willing while there to give you a check to assist on it though I'm not a member there? That check would be outside the financial capabilities of that local church. If I gave you the check voluntarily, would sin be involved? Or, would sin begin only when you asked me for help as one outside the local group?

Could a local church plan a work and ask the Akin Foundation for financial assistance on that project? I frankly feel that they can and do not violate any scriptural principle in doing so. No church autonomy has been violated in the least. Your Akin Foundation for years has done a great work in this very way and I heartily endorse it. As maybe you know I'm connected with the Bell Trust, a similar financial arrangement by which we assist churches to carry on various works for which they cannot fully pay all alone. Brethren, are you contending that individuals or Trusts can assist churches but one church cannot assist another church under any circumstance? When the Bell Trust or the Akin Foundation sends money to a church for any purpose, that is money outside the financial capabilities of that local church in the same way that money sent from a sister congregation would be. If not, why not? I don't believe our opportunities, and I don't believe our responsibilities—and I don't believe you do either seriously—are limited geographically. I can't believe it. To me some of our fuzzy thinking is based really on a misconception of the church. Maybe we're institutionalizing the church too much or we're congregationalizing the church too much, instead of realizing we're all members of the body of Christ.

With these thoughts as background, may I now raise or point out several illustrations? I can't conceive of the Lord establishing the church and giving the great commission to go into all the world and preach the Gospel, and yet, in doing so precluding our taking advantage of golden opportunities to do the very thing, in the ultimate end, that He had in mind. Our mission in the world is to save souls and preaching the Gospel is but the means to that end. Don't say, now, that I'm arguing the end justifies the means for that is another question entirely and I'm not indicating that in the least. Follow me closely all the way. Let me show you what I mean. The *Reader's Digest* I can imagine has 50 million readers and by the time a copy is destroyed millions more will have read it where on a one page ad the Gospel in print is being taught. Say that ad would cost $40,000, far beyond the financial reach of any one congregation. We could place an ad teaching conceivably 150 million people the simple New Testament truth. But, brethren, how can that be done scripturally? One church alone simply cannot financially. Could others assist and the Gospel be preached around the world by the printed page? Are we to conclude that the Lord's plan for church autonomy and congregational relationship altogether prohibits such a great step? I cannot in all honesty believe such. Either there is some scriptural method by which it can be accomplished or else the New Testament church must never undertake an effort to preach the Gospel of our Lord on a scale of such magnitude.

May we forget, for the moment, our prejudices for or against the Herald of Truth and consider another pointed illustration? Imagine the officials of N.B.C. called offering some church of Christ somewhere a choice 30 minute spot on Sunday at which time we could around the nation and likely around the world present the plea for New Testament principles. They wouldn't permit a thousand churches to sign a contract for the time you know full well. No one church would be able to pay the bill for such a golden opportunity to do His will. Brethren, if the way we're doing such preaching is sinful, in violation of Bible principles of church independence, then I pray tell us how we can take advantage of this great challenge in preaching the Gospel to millions. Either present a scriptural plan or admit that such a project is just too big for the church of Christ. Are you willing?

Or, take another step in the same direction. In Dallas we have an auditorium seating 12,000 people. In our eagerness to preach the Gospel we want to rent it—$500 nightly—for 15 days. Advertising to fill it with 12,000 each night will cost thousands. Tracts to give away to the many outsiders who will attend and other expenses will run the total bill to around $50,000. Brethren, can we scripturally preach to 12,000 nightly for 15 days and as a result baptize into Christ more than 200 people? If so, how can that be done and Bible principles not be violated? Must one church and one church alone do it? If so, it will never be done. Are you claiming, my brethren, that such an endeavor is unscriptural if conducted in any way? It's too big for churches of Christ——doesn't sound plausible or sensible.

These same thoughts could be raised concerning a teacher training school in any city of more than one congregation. We've been having them annually for more than 25 years in Dallas and no church has to any extent lost its autonomy. Could we carry it out in our building, invite other churches to attend and to voluntarily assist us with the expenses of such a school without destroying their autonomy or violating the Lord's will concerning the church? I do believe we can and that we have all these years. You are going to have to either say these projects or methods are entirely too big for churches of Christ or come forth with a scriptural plan of procedure. These fundamental truths are basic to a solution of the question of congregational cooperation and must be faced before we can have peace in the House of God again.

I don't believe that any of us believe that a congregation's work is limited by its financial capabilities for at least none of us are practicing it. I believe that some way, somehow, we ought to find some plan by which we can take advantage of these and other great and golden opportunities and challenges in this modern age.

## Co-operation of Churches

### Melvin Curry

I want to say again that I appreciate very much this opportunity of being with you and of having the privilege of speaking to the group. Tuesday morning I had something to say about inclusion and exclusion. I would like to refer to those thoughts again as a preface to my remarks today. I was not consciously attempting to alter a human rule of interpretation, and yet I believe very often we find ourselves guilty—all of us—of looking for what a passage excludes rather than what a passage includes. Therefore, I want to direct your attention to a passage of scripture and try to find out what it means, because I take a different view of the passage than some of the other brethren.

I want you to realize that when one seeks the meaning of a passage and its included meaning, that that meaning has to correspond to the immediate context, and on the principle of what we call the analogy of the scriptures (simply interpreting the scriptures by the scriptures) the passage must also be in harmony with all that God's word teaches on that subject, and once he has all that God says on every subject—or on any one subject—then all else becomes "will worship" or a matter of mere human opinion rather than divine revelation.

The passage that I have in mind is 2 Cor. 9:13. Brother Highers brought it up and gave a rather elaborate discussion of the word "all" in that context. It has been mentioned since that time by brother Lanier and perhaps by others as well. In order for us to see the point of argument clearly I want to read this passage from the King James Version. The verse says, "Whiles by the experiment of this ministration they glori-

---

MELVIN CURRY—*Professor of Bible and Greek in Florida College, Temple Terrace, Florida; evangelist for the University Heights Church, Tampa, Florida.*

fy God for your professed subjection unto the gospel of Christ, and for your liberal distribution unto them, and unto all *men*" (the word "men" is italicized in order to show that the translators supplied it).

I want us to look at this particular passage in the light of its context. I do not believe that we are looking simply for the meaning of "all"; we are also looking for the meaning of several terms that are used in connection with it. Now I would like to show a transparency of some expressions that are used in the context. The transparency is based on readings from Nestle's *Interlinear Greek-English New Testament* edited by A. Marshall but is made to conform as nearly as possible to the King James Version.

## II COR. 9:13

8:4 — "the fellowship of the ministry to the saints" (Τὴν κοινωνίαν τῆς διακονίας τῆς εἰς τοὺς ἁγίους)

9:1 — "the ministry to the saints"

9:13 — "through the proof of this ministry they glorify God for" (ἐπὶ)

| | | |
|---|---|---|
| (1) "the submission of your confession | PURPOSE | "unto them" (εἰς αὐτοὺς) |
| and | END | and (καὶ) |
| (2) "the liberality of the fellowship | OBJECT | "unto all" [MEN] εἰς πάντας [SAINTS] (See Matt. 3:5) |

First of all, we recognize the fact that the background for the discussion of 2 Cor. 8 and 9 is found in I Cor. 16. There Paul said, "As I have given order unto the churches of Galatia, even so do ye." And the "order" pertained to the matter of "the collection for the saints" which was to be sent to Jerusalem.

Now, just here I want you to look with me at 2 Cor. 8:4 (and by the way, please indicate when I have about five minutes left). In the verse [pointing to 2 Cor. 8:4 on the chart] is this particular expression found (and I believe it is the key to understanding this verse in its context), ". . . the fellowship of the ministry to the saints." Look at the expression very carefully, "the fellowship of the ministry to the saints." We need to determine what this "fellowship" is because in 9:13 this same word occurs again. You notice [looking at the chart] that "through the proof of this ministry they glorify God for the submission of your confession and the liberality of the fellowship unto them and unto all." Some versions supply there "all men." The word "fellowship"—what does it mean? What does it include in the expression "the fellowship of the ministry to the saints?"

Look at the genitive that is used here (2 Cor. 8:4), *tēs diakonias,* translated "the ministry" (or in the KJV "ministering, ministration"). There are at least two ways, as far as I can see from the standpoint of Greek grammar, logically to construe this genitive. One way would be to take it as a genitive of apposition. If you did that it would read something like this: "the fellowship, namely, the ministry to the saints," and that would equate the fellowship with the ministry to the saints— as identical, the same thing. Or you might take it as the objective genitive and that would give the rendering: "the fellowship, having as its object (or some similar expression) the ministry to the saints." But in either case the term "fellowship" is given its meaning by its context. That is, it has reference to the ministry of the saints.

Now, this being the case, follow through the rest of the context carefully. In 9:1 again you have the expression, "the ministry to the saints." There is a quotation from Psa. 112:9 in verse 9 in which the phrase "he gave to the poor" becomes an incentive to contribute to the cause under consideration. Again, we find in verse 12 the expression, "the administration (*diakonia*) of this service . . . supplieth the want of the saints" (KJV). So whether you consider the term "fellowship" or the term "ministry" in the context, the reference is to the relief of the needs of the saints.

Next, |turning to the chart| look at verse 13, "Through the proof of this ministry they glorified God for (*epi*, expressing the basis on which they glorified God) . . ." There are two reasons stated. First, "The submission of your confession to the gospel." The saints are glorifying God for this reason, namely, that the Corinthians love the Lord enough and have submitted themselves to the principles of the gospel to the extent that they are willing to make this contribution. Second, "They glorify God for the liberality of the fellowship." Now, I have said all of that to say this. I might take the term fellowship out of this context and conceive of its having at least two meanings. I could say that a contribution is a fellowship simply because when brethren take their money and put it into the local treasury, then whenever or however this money is spent, it is a fellowship by virtue of the fact that brethren have contributed together for a common cause. I think that is a possibility of the meaning of the word. When I take it, however, in its signification here in 2 Cor. 9:13, the Jewish brethren are glorifying God for a gift, a gift of grace, a ministry to the saints, to their needs, and they call it a liberality of the Corinthians' fellowship. So I am constrained by the context to believe that it is a fellowship expressive of the relationship of the Gentile Christians to their Jewish brethren in the Lord, that not only eliminates the physical needs of these Jewish brethren but also welds this relationship as brethren.

I believe that this is demonstrated in the purpose, object, or end of the submission of their confession and the liberality of their fellowship, because it is a liberality of the fellowship unto them and in this respect would take care of, or supply, their physical needs in Jerusalem. But also they glorify God for the liberality of the fellowship "unto all." Now, a point was made by one of the brethren (I do not remember the one) that the expression "unto all" (*eis pantas*) is masculine and, therefore, implies "all men." Well, it is masculine but you can suply a whole group of masculine nouns here—unto all *men*, unto all *saints*, unto all *the brethren*—any noun in the Greek that is masculine could be supplied with "unto all" (*eis pantas*). However, by implication of the context the ministry to the saints is the fellowship that is involved. So to what does the liberality of the fellowship perceived by Paul and these brethren refer? It refers to a ministering to the saints!

Then someone else made this point (I believe it was brother Highers). He suggested you have "unto them"—this is one class. (I do not want to misquote or misrepresent him; he and I have talked about this.) Following this first class, the saints, there is a conjunction ("and," *kai*) and then "unto all," a separate class other than the saints. He contended that the "all" must be an entirely different group from the "them."

I believe I can point to a parallel in Matt. 3:5 that destroys this concept and I bid you consider it because from the standpoint of Greek construction it is identically parallel.* There you remember that people came out to hear John the baptist preach and it is suggested in verse 5, "Then went out to him Jerusalem and all Judaea, and all the region round about the Jordan." Jerusalem is in Judaea! "There went out unto him Jerusalem *and* all Judea." When one argues that here (pointing to the chart again) the two classes "them" and "all" are mutually exclusive, he is affirming something that does not necessarily follow, and, in fact, Matt. 3:5 is an instance where the argument does not hold.

What bearing does the context of 2 Cor. 9:13, therefore, have on the meaning of "all"? Well, it shows what is said so many times, the saints are the recipients of the contribution; thus pointing out the dual purpose of this gift or this contribution: that is, to supply or fill the needs (the physical needs) in Jerusalem, and at the same time, to weld saints everywhere in their relationship one to another. Therefore, the passage is properly understood in the light of its context.

What I have said is not primarily in defense of any particular position but, rather, to demonstrate that when we interpret a passage of scripture, we ought to study that passage, look at it in its own context, and look at it in the light of a multiplicity of other passages that are parallel. So I bid you to give attention to what I have said about 2 Cor. 9:13, for I believe this is what the passage is teaching.

J. W. Roberts is quoted in Lewis Hale's book *How Churches Can Cooperate* and he takes the position (though I must say I disagree with him on his particular application) that "unto all" means, and I quote, "for all the Christians in the region who are in need." Now, despite our disagreement on the interpretation of 2 Cor. 9:13, the point is he recognizes the fact that saints are involved in both groups, "unto them" and "unto all." Thank you very much.

*The difference between *Pantas* (2 Cor. 9:13) and *pasa* (Matt. 3:5) pointed out by someone later in the discussion in order to destroy the parallelism is a difference of case only and does not materially affect the argument.

# Co-operation of Churches

### Hardeman Nichols

Mr. Chairman and brethren, we want to discuss some matters which I think are coming more and more into the focal point as major differences between us. If we can make progress in our study of these, and that has been indicated by some of the statements that have already been made, we'll be able to accomplish a big step toward reaching the goal that we have set out for these meetings.

Let us go back and gather some statements that have been made thus far concerning "Examples." It was suggested last evening that examples do not bind; authority binds. Similarly, it has been admitted over and over again that not all examples are binding examples. All of us have recognized and it has been repeated again today that there are found in examples some matters that are *permitted,* yet which are not *binding* upon us. Those things that have to do with permissive authority have even been brought out in some of the charts presented this afternoon. By way of illustration, we may "go" (Matt. 28:19), using the identical methods of "going" found in the examples

---

HARDEMAN NICHOLS—*Evangelist for the Sunset congregation in Dallas, Texas; on the editorial council of* POWER FOR TODAY; *well known for his work at Sunset congregation in Lubbock, Texas and at "A" and Tennessee church in Midland, Texas.*

in the New Testament. That is permitted and it is scriptural to "go" as they went. However, permissive examples are not binding; for they were performed under generic authority where the method was not bound. Therefore, we may go as they did not go— as they never thought of going—by airplane, for example. In this we would be as scriptural in going by plane (though there is no example of it in the Bible) as in the apostles' walking, riding or sailing.

Each of us agrees, I'm sure, with this principle. Now the application of it to the study at hand becomes somewhat forgotten, for some have suggested that an example is binding if you find uniformity of action upon the subject in the New Testament. In other words, if you always find a uniform practice of a thing in each case in the New Testament, then, they say, that practice is binding. Uniformity of action does not necessarily mean that a practice is binding, however. If their action was under generic authority, the method was not bound on them and certainly could not be considered as bound on us! A uniform practice doesn't prove in itself that specific authority was the reason for their uniformity. Now, when they did things under specific authority, their practice in the New Testament was uniform, to be sure. But sometimes they did things under generic authority and their methods selected were uniform; but these were matters of choice to them and were not binding on them and are not binding on us. For example, in the New Testament in observing the Lord's supper, the disciples met in an upper room. The examples found in the New Testament are uniform when stating the place of observance.

In Abilene, there is a group who formed what is known as The Church of the Upper Room. Their church building is erected on telephone poles. They have it up in the air because they believe one must follow the New Testament in meeting in an upper room when observing the Lord's supper. But they even failed in their purpose after all their effort; because they do not have a room underneath. How can there be an "upper room" without a lower room? They have their room up on stilts and are not even meeting their pattern! Well, we understand that even though an upstairs room was used in the examples of the New Testament where the place of meeting is cited, it isn't binding. Why? Because a place of meeting is under generic authority and not under specific authority. Hebrews 10:25 commanded the assembly; but not the place.

Now, specific authority assuredly makes uniform practice; but uniform practice doesn't mean specific authority in each case. For instance, the only example in the New Testament that we have of the confession being made at the baptism of one, it was made in sight of the water. "See, here is water" (Acts 8:36). Must we have the water in sight before we can make the confession? Can the curtains be closed? Can one confess Christ in one place and be baptized at a different place? There is the uniform example (the only instance in the New Testament, in fact); but it isn't a binding example.

Those methods that fell under generic authority in the New Testament examples were matters of choice to them as they are to us. The Lord's supper at night is another matter that we have uniform examples of in the Scriptures. Jesus instituted it "the same night in which he was betrayed" (1 Cor. 11:23). Acts 20 was a night meeting at Troas: "There were lights in the upper chamber, where they were gathered together" (Acts 20:8). Yet the Lord's supper at night isn't a binding example upon us, though uniform. The Lord's supper upon "the first day of the week" is binding (Acts 20:7); but whether we commune in the night of the first day or in the daylight part isn't binding. The day is specific; the time of day is left to our choice.

We may use post offices and those not brethren in sending a contribution. We understand that, I'm sure, with reference to the matters of cooperation. Now we are getting down to some of the important applications in this discussion. We can have and use things that first century brethren never gave us examples of in the New Testament *if the things which we have and use fall under generic authority rather than specific authority.* Illustrations have already been given: Bible classes before worship (or even after worship), church houses owned by the congregation, song books with notes, individual cups, baptistries—these all fall under generic authority.

Now, brethren, if we will abide by the fact that there are some uniform examples under generic authority, we will go a long way toward solving our differences; because we won't try to bind those upon others. If you say that all uniform examples are binding, then you have to start doing these additional things that we have suggested which are uniform also.

Some mentioned that there are two patterns that are unchangeable in their nature: one in benevolence, one in evangelism. But we have pointed out some differences in these patterns that some of you do not agree to. For instance, in the second chapter of Acts in benevolence, they sold their houses and lands. We don't follow that example. We may, but we don't have to; because they did it under generic authority. They were not commanded to sell their possessions; for in the case of Ananias and Sapphira, the apostle Peter states in Acts 5:4, "Whiles it remained, was it not thine own? and after it was sold, was it not in thine own power?" In the fourth chapter of Acts, again they sold houses and lands. That is not bound on us, for it was not even bound upon them. Brethren, for you to find an unchangeable pattern you've got to find things that are the same in each case and you've been hard-pressed to find these things and are found wanting.

It was argued from 2 Cor. 11:8 that in evangelism, money was sent directly to the evangelist, declaring "This is the way they did it." Then some of you later admitted, "We don't know how they did it." I think that is the truth in the matter. I believe it was brother Turner who said you have Church A and church B sending and assisting Paul (2 Cor. 11:8). He said that was the end; but the rest of the verse says that wasn't the end. It says: "To do you service." It was to assist Corinth church; not just Paul, but to do service to Corinth church. You see the point of the example and that is the very thing that he says you can't do—you have to stop right there with Paul; it can't go on to the church. It did in that case. They sent it to Paul; but it was for the church's benefit, to do service to the church at Corinth. "I robbed other churches, taking wages of them, to do you service." Service done to Corinth, paid by other churches. Cooperation! The end wasn't where brother Turner suggested it was.

It was also stated that a dependent church may receive aid from other congregations to become independent; but 2 Cor. 11 doesn't deal altogether with a dependent church. Corinth may have been dependent in the past; but no longer, for in I Cor. 9:12 Paul says at this time Corinth is supporting other preachers. In 2 Cor. 8:7, the church in Corinth abounds in everything and can abound in the grace of giving liberally. So they are an abundant church, supporting at least a plurality of preachers. Not only that, but they are making a generous contribution out of their abundance to aid in benevolent work in Judea, as "ordered" in I Cor. 16:1-3. Yet Paul says that he under these circumstances is coming to them at Corinth again. He says that what he has been doing while preaching at Corinth in the past, he will do again while at Corinth this time. He says in 2 Cor. 11:10, "No man shall stop me of this boasting" (of never having received support at Corinth from the church at Corinth). He intends to do again this time when he comes what he had done before—take "wages" of other churches to do service to the church at Corinth. Corinth is now rich. Brethren, this idea that a church can only help another church to become independent cannot be upheld in the light of the Scriptures.

Brother Turner also suggested that when congregations pool funds, then independence suffers. I want to suggest to you that there can be a scriptural pooling of funds without setting up either a benevolent or a missionary society and without violating autonomy. There was a pooling of the funds from congregations in Macedonia and Achaia in sending relief to the poor among the saints at Jerusalem. Roman 15:25, 26 tells us about this collection. It is the same collection taken in I Cor. 16:1-3 and it included "the churches of Galatia." Paul says, "It hath pleased them of Macedonia and Achaia to make . . ." (if he had said simply "a contribution," that would have eliminated the idea that the funds were not pooled; but he said) ". . . to make a *certain contribution*" (Romans 15:26). He also refers to this combined contribution from a number of churches not as "fruits" but "fruit" (Romans 15:28). They pooled the funds there; but they didn't violate autonomy in doing it.

Brethren, we ought to be able to see these truths. And when giving according to ability, it doesn't mean that you're limited to what you can do alone. In 2 Cor. 11:8, when Paul previously came to Corinth these "churches" helped Corinth then to do a work they couldn't otherwise accomplish at that time. These funds from other churches were ear-marked and accepted as ear-marked funds.

Now I want to refer briefly to the idea of whether a church is limited geographically. Paul in 2 Cor. 11:8 recognized that these churches who were giving to him to do service to Corinth were not limited to their own geographical locations. In Acts 11:22-24 the Jerusalem church was sending Barnabas from Jerusalem to Antioch—miles away. They were not limited in their evangelistic work to their own geographical locality.

In closing, I want to pay some attention to brother Curry's chart. He did not put the Greek, oddly enough, on the chart from the one passage that he said is the parallel to Gal. 6:10 and 2 Cor. 9:12, 13. The parallel, he says, is Matt. 3:5. He didn't put the Greek on there because it is not "pantas" at all in Matt. 3:5 as it is in Gal. 6:10 and 2 Cor. 9:12, 13. Now, if you want to find a parallel passage on the use of the phrase "all men" in these passages, see John 12:32: "And I, if I be lifted up from the earth, will draw all men ("pantas") unto me." Was it Jesus' will to draw saints only, or all mankind unto himself? What was his will in that matter? "Pantas" in this passage means all men. His death is "for our sins and not for ours only but also for the sins of the whole world" (I John 2:2). Likewise, the scriptures say the church may do good to all men (Gal. 6:10). This was true of the contribution from churches delivered by Paul to the poor among the saints. He declares it was "unto them, and unto all men" (Greek "pantas") (2 Cor. 9:12, 13). Therefore the church is not limited to the aid of "saints only" in benevolence.

I thank you.

## Co-operation of Churches

### Clinton D. Hamilton

Whenever brethren have the opportunity to sit down together to reflect upon the truth of God—the mind of God—it is indeed an exalted occasion. The consequences of one's response to what the word of God says are fearful. Consequently, all of us ought to enter into such discussions, as we have, with all gravity and with all mental faculties working as well as possible.

The word of God is our pattern and it takes all the testimony in the word of God for a person to have the truth. The word of God is the truth. It is not a part of the truth with reference to redemption; it is the truth. One never knows the truth until he knows what God says. Whenever we try to ascertain what it is that a man must do in order to be saved, we have to take all that God has said on that point. If a man wants to know what God has taught relative to a matter such as the cooperation of churches now under discussion, he must listen to all that God says. When one studies the passages that show what churches did in the matter of cooperation, he has the truth of God on that point. Whenever he reads all the passages that deal with this point, he has all that God says on it. If he is to be limited in his convictions to that which God teaches, this is all that he can teach and this is all he should teach.

In evangelism, according to Philippians 4:15-18, on more than one occasion the Philippian church sent to the apostle Paul, the evangelist. In Philippians 2:25, Paul stated that on one occasion Epaphroditus was Philippi's messenger to him. A messenger is subject and subservient to the one who does the

---

CLINTON D. HAMILTON—*Dean of Broward County Junior College, Fort Lauderdale, Florida; well known evangelist; for many years Dean of Florida College, Temple Terrace, Florida.*

sending. A congregation cannot become the messenger of another congregation because the relation between them, which the Lord sets out, would be destroyed. Messengers operating under churches, subservient to those churches' will, do not violate the relation between congregations.

According to I Corinthians 16:3, churches had the liberty of choosing their own messengers. Consequently, since they had that choice they could select whomsoever they would of whatever nature they desired. In 2 Corinthians 11:8, more than one congregation sent to the apostle Paul, the evangelist in the field. In Acts 11:22, the brethren in Jerusalem (the Jerusalem church) sent Barnabas to exhort those who were at Antioch. In this instance the preacher, the evangelist, was sent by the church. When one studies these cases, he knows what the Bible reveals on the matter of churches in relation to the support of an evangelist in another field, in the proclamation of the truth. Whatever it is that these passages reveal on cooperation, with the same logic, they would reveal whatever else is there. If one takes these passages as the authority for cooperation (i.e. an evangelist's being sent to minister in the preaching of the gospel to others) he, likewise, by the same logic, would have to accept what these passages say about who did the sending and in what relation these two stood one to another. Furthermore, what the passages say on this is all that God says on it and when an individual sustains a practice that is exactly that which he finds revealed, he is walking, without doubt, in the truth of God. There is no question about what he is doing.

On the matter of benevolence in I Corinthians 16:1-4, 2 Corinthians 8 and 9, Romans 15:25-26, and Acts 24:17, there is the case of more than one congregation sending to the same congregation for the relief of the poor within that congregation. In Acts 11:27-30, there is the sending from brethren at Antioch to the brethren which dwelt in Judea. They sent it to the brethren that dwelt in Judea by sending it to the elders by the hands of Barnabas and Saul. If one takes the expression "in Judea" to mean that the brethren were dispersed in Judea, then whatever the prepositional phrase "in Judea" means with reference to the brethren it means exactly and precisely the same with reference to the elders. If, therefore, one takes the position that the contribution went to the church in

Jerusalem, that is where the elders were. If one takes the position that the contribution went to the congregations dispersed throughout Judea, that is where the elders were.

When one reads these passages, he understands what God says about the matter of relief going from one congregation, or one group of brethren, to another congregation. When, therefore, one's practice is that which this reveals, he is absolutely safe and is walking within the truth of God. There is no question about it. There is no doubt. In 2 Corinthians 5:7, Paul says "we walk by faith, not by sight." Romans 10:17: "So belief cometh of hearing, and hearing by the word of Christ." This, therefore, says beyond any doubt that when one does that which is revealed in these passages he is walking by faith.

There is nothing in the truth of God that says that any church ever sent to another church to preach the gospel. No church in the truth ever sent to another congregation to preach the gospel. That is not in the word of God. Second, no church ever sent to another church unless it was to relieve a need. No church ever sent to another church except to relieve a need. No church ever sent anything by another church. That is not in the word of God. Now, if an individual wants to do this, he owes it to all of us whom he teaches and whom he seeks to influence to produce the passage that says a church could, should, or did do these things.

If the generic *relieve* permits a benevolent society to be built, then would not the generic *teach* permit the building of an evangelistic society to teach? Now if *teach* is a generic and if *relieve* is a generic and if brethren defend a benevolent society, a separate organization, to relieve the poor on the basis of the fact that the expression *relieve* is generic and brethren are free to do what they would in that matter, then would not the same logic and the scriptures say that if *teach* is generic this would permit the church to form an evangelistic society for the purpose of teaching? If Acts 11:27-30 is a pattern for benevolent work being done under elders and not under a separate organization, such as some brethren believe, then why not respect other scriptural examples dealing with evangelism about what was done? If one takes the case of benevolence in Acts 11 to show that that work should be kept under the elders and, therefore, any way of taking care of those in need should be in the local church under the local elders (and Acts 11 example is the authority for it), why not take the same position with reference to the passages on evangelism and show that one must follow what those passages say in the sending of money, or whatever it was, to support the evangelist? Now, if that case is authority in the matter of benevolence (that example), by what logic or by what system of reasoning would one say that these other cases on evangelism are not the authority for doing evangelism as those passages say?

Sometimes I have talked with Mormon elders and, invariably—the first thing they do when we sit down to talk—they begin to talk to me about contradictions in the word of God. They do this in order later to get around contradictions in the Book of Mormon. Sometimes brethren will sit down and talk about what we are doing and ask the question, "Can't we do this?" Now if we can do this, and if we have done this, and if we cannot do this, then look what you do to us. The issue is what does God's word say! Now, once one has determined what God's word says, if he is going to walk by faith and respect the truth of God and maintain action that is in harmony with the will of God and walk according to a "thus saith the Lord," he must do what men did in the New Testament in order to be saved, and I take the cases of conversion in the New Testament —they are different in many respects but when I get all of them I learn what it is that an individual should do in order to be saved—and ask him to do that. Could he not ask me likewise once I am saved and I am about doing God's will that I follow the same logic, the same reasoning, and have the same respect for the word of God? That is the real issue and all of us, in our hearts, ought to seek to do that which we can find in the word of God and on that none of us would disagree. Every one of us would say, "Yes, we are united." And that is the way for us to be united in Christ: it is to walk according to that which God says, a "thus saith the Lord."

## Co-operation of Churches

### Bill Humble

In 1809 Alexander Campbell arrived in America, and one of the first things that he did after his arrival was to read the galley proof of Thomas Campbell's *Declaration and Address*. One of the key statements of the *Declaration and Address* said that nothing ought to be bound upon the church of God in the matter of faith or practice except that which is taught in the New Testament by direct command or by approved precedent. After Alexander Campbell read this, he said, "I think there is some ambiguity in the approved precedent." I do not think Campbell ever solved that ambiguity, and I believe there has been a great deal of ambiguity ever since in dealing with the approved precedent of the New Testament. And, somehow, I feel that in the discussions we have been carrying on we have not resolved all of the ambiguity that lies there. We have not finally and fully solved the question when is a New Testament example mandatory and, therefore, binding upon us, and when is it an optional matter.

---

BILL J. HUMBLE—*Recently selected Dean of Abilene Christian College; Abilene, Texas; formerly professor of Bible in Florida College; well known evangelist.*

We have just heard, for example, from my long time friend, brother Hamilton, that churches sent to the preacher in evangelism and to the church in benevolence. He believes there are two specific patterns that must be followed this way. Yet, there are so many other specifics in New Testament patterns that somehow are not binding upon us in the same way. Attention has already been called to the example of the early Christians meeting in the upper room for the observance of the Lord's supper. This is what the New Testament says. But must we do it? Attention has been called to the fact that the early Christians met at night for the observance of the Lord's supper. This is a specific New Testament example. But is it absolutely necessary for us to do it in this way? It seems to me that there is some ambiguity when we have selected certain examples dealing with cooperation and say these are two specific patterns and must be done in exactly this way, and yet there are so many other examples which are not similarly bound. We hear that I Cor. 16:1, 2 is a pattern for taking up a collection for the relief of poor saints elsewhere. Brother Hamilton just said emphatically that no church ever sent to another church to preach the gospel. He said, "It isn't in the scriptures. No church ever sent funds to another church to preach the gospel." I would say similarly that no church ever took up a contribution on the first day of the week to pay the preacher or build a church building or do a hundred other things. Why do we bind one and not bind the other? Is there not some ambiguity in our minds in deciding when an example is absolutely mandatory and binding and when it is optional?

I think that half the speakers who have preceded me have paid some respect to Noah and his ark of gopher wood. I mention this because I want to comment on the same point also. Brother Turner, in his major address, using the example of gopher wood as a specific, said that one specific, gopher wood, does not allow another specific such as pine. But in the case of congregational cooperation we have, at least, two specifics. Let me assume for just a moment that there was no direct statement in the Bible that God commanded Noah to build the ark of gopher wood. Suppose it simply wasn't there. All we have is a description of Noah's building the ark and in this description it explains that he built the bow of gopher wood and the stern of pine and the decking of hickory and the ceiling over the whole thing of redwood. Now, would we assume that there is an absolute binding pattern and that each part of the ark had to be built in that specific way? Or might we assume that God said build an ark and use wood in it and left it to the discretion of Noah what kind of wood would work in what place? I am simply saying that after 150 years of restoration history there is still some ambiguity as to when we bind apostolic examples as absolutely mandatory and when they are left in the realm of the optional.

Another thing that has impressed me is the fact that when we are discussing congregational cooperation, we ought to be able to use the same method of argumentation that we use on other issues that have involved the welfare of the brotherhood. Yet, somehow, it seems to me that we are not allowed that liberty—to use the same method of argumentation here that we have used on other issues. I will give you just one illustration of it. I am not a debater by any stretch of the imagination. I have had only one public debate and that may be the only one I will ever have. That debate was with brother Leroy Garrett and involved the located preacher question. I can recall that when I was making my preparations for that debate, I knew that brother Garrett would say again and again, "Where is your authority in the New Testament for the located preacher such as you have?" And I knew that he would actually mean, "Where is there a specific example in the New Testament of a preacher locating with a church that has elders, being supported for his work, etc."

I had to admit to myself quite frankly that there is no one example in the New Testament that involves every single part of our practice. But here is the way I tried to build a case to justify our practice in having what we call located preachers (and this is the way that I would *still* attempt to build a case for this parctice). I took all of the things that are involved in our practice, one by one, and in each case inquired whether it was scriptural. Is it right for a preacher to stay for a period of time with a congregation? The Bible answer is yes. Is it right for a preacher to be paid for his work? Again, the answer is yes. Is there any Biblical authority for a preacher to work with a congregation having elders? And again the answer is yes (the epistles to Timothy). Is it scriptural to preach the gospel to the church? This was one of the key issues, and I found scriptures to justify preaching to the church. Thus, I took each one of these points and studied each individually. Can a preacher stay? Can he be paid? Can he work for a congregation that has elders? Can he preach the gospel to the church? When I had proved that each one of them was scriptural I believe that I had justified my practice.

Later, I began to wonder whether the same method of reasoning would not apply to the issue of congregational cooperation. I believe that we can take each part of the practice that is involved in one congregation's embarking on a program of evangelistic work and receiving support from other congregations, and by taking these one by one I believe we can prove that it is scriptural. May a congregation preach the gospel of Christ? Of course, all of us admit that. May a church preach the gospel away from its own locality? I think that all of us would admit that. May a congregation receive funds from another congregation? Again, the answer is yes. If I understood brother Lanier's first major speech, this was one of the emphatic arguments that he made. By taking each part of the practice and putting them all together we have shown that the total practice is scriptural. You would, perhaps, object that we've jumped the track when we assume that one congregation may receive funds from another congregation for doing evangelistic work. Let's suppose that when I put my argument together with brother Garrett, he had said, "Yes, a preacher may stay, and yes, a preacher may be paid. But how can you show that a preacher may stay and be paid at the same time that he is working with a congregation that has elders? Where can you put all parts of it together?" I am simply saying that on this issue of congregational cooperation we ought to be able to use the very same methods of argumentation that we use on other issues that we have studied.

When brother Turner delivered his opening address on this topic (and I think that both he and brother Lanier delivered unusually fine addresses), he began with an eight or ten minute resume of certain salient facts from restoration history which serve as background for the problems that we have today. This was one part of his discussion that I especially appreciated. I have loved the story of the restoration movement for so long that it delights me to find someone who has read widely in the literature of the movement. He spoke, for example of the Wellsburg Cooperation Meeting of 1834. The cooperation meetings that developed in the 1830's lead ultimately to the American Christian Missionary Society in 1849, and brother Turner surveyed all of the material extremely well.

I too have spent some time reading the literature of the movement during the same period, and there is one thing that has impressed me again and again. This is the fact that the Missionary Society and even these cooperation meetings that preceded the missionary society (and they were actually the embryo out of which the missionary society sprang) were never without opposition. The society never received the support of a united brotherhood. From the day of its establishment, the missionary society always had its opponents. But the thing that impresses me is that again and again in the writings of these opponents as they stated their oppositions to the missionary society, they proposed what they believed to be a scriptural alternative. They described the way they believed the same work could be accomplished, and again and again I find that what they proposed was for the work of evangelism to be done through a congregation under the oversight of the elders of that church and supported by other congregations.

Brother Turner mentioned the Wellsburg Cooperation Meeting. It was a very significant event but it had its opponent. T. M. Henley, who was a very prominent gospel preacher in Virginia, wrote to Alexander Campbell shortly after the meeting. Henley said that he was opposed to anything like a cooperation meeting with its presidents and secretaries, its representatives and delegates. He pointed out that Baptist associations had begun in very much the same way and he said, "The burnt child dreads the fire. We don't want to get into the same thing." But Henley went on to say, "I am for cooperation too, but cooperation, if I understand the term, implies weakness. When any one church wishes to send out an evangelist and is unable to sustain him in the field she may invite her sister congregations to cooperate with her." (*Millennial Harbinger*, 1836, pp. 333-334.) Henley then explained how it was to be done. The congregation proposing to send out the preacher would invite neighboring congregations to visit them, explain what they wished to do, how they were unable to do it financially, and invite those congregations to contribute funds. The funds would be administered by the congregation sending out the man and financial reports would be sent by that congregation to the contributing churches. And T. M. Henley said this was the scriptural alternative to the cooperation meetings.

Only a few years later, for example, I find an illustration of this being practiced in Kentucky. There were three congregations (Georgetown, Hebron and Dry Run, Kentucky) who pooled a fund of several hundred dollars which all of them had contributed for the preaching of the gospel. They were going to use this to preach the gospel. I read directly from their report, "The general plan is as follows: The fund is raised and committed to the officers of the Gerogetown congregation. These officers are to meet and make all the necessary arrangements of the expenditure agreeable to the design of the donors. Reports are to be submitted regularly to the respective congregations." (*Millennial Harbinger*, 1842, p. 187) The funds were contributed by a number of congregations, committed to the care of the elders of the Georgetown church, and used in the preaching of the gospel. The very first gospel preacher who was sent out under this plan was brother John T. Johnson, one of the great early pioneer preachers and who, probably, more than any man, brought the Stone and Campbell movements together. This was his scriptural alternative to the missionary society.

Tolbert Fanning probably did more than any other man in history to convince churches all over the south that the missionary society was wrong and to turn them in a conservative direction in their understanding of the restoration plea. In 1859 Tolbert Fanning addressed the missionary society at its national meeting in Cincinnati. He explained why the southern brethren believed that it was wrong and he explained how a number of congregations were working through the Franklin College church to support J. J. Trott in missionary work among the Cherokee Indians west of the Mississippi River.

For Tolbert Fanning, for John T. Johnson, for a host of others who opposed the missionary society, cooperation through the eldership of a local congregation was the scriptural alternative to the missionary society. These are additional facts of history that need to be in the record.

## Co-operation of Churches

### Roy E. Cogdill

I am sorry that it will be necessary for me to miss the last session of this meeting. I will leave for Pampa, Texas early Thursday morning. It has been good to be here. I have enjoyed hearing every speech that has been made. I think it has been profitable to me in more ways than one. Some of the ideas I had concerning what some of you taught and what you believed were not just exactly in line with what I have heard you express here and I am glad to have these corrected. I do not like to have a misconception of any man's convictions or his position about anything because that often leads to misrepresentation and it often leads to misunderstanding. So some things have been clarified and I am grateful.

If emphasis has been placed upon the importance of the continued study of these matters and everything relative to them in the light of the Word of God, then it has helped us all, because, that is the only solution to the problem. I am sure all of us recognize this. I do not suppose anybody present or anybody who has been present, feels that he knows all about every-

---

ROY E. COGDILL—*Author of several perennial best sellers in the field of Bible study books; debater; evangelist for the Par Avenue congregation in Orlando, Florida; special lecturer at Florida College, Temple Terrace, Florida; widely used in gospel meetings throughout the nation.*

thing connected with this theme or any other. So it behooves us to continue to study and, as we study, when we learn more truth, we ought not to be either ashamed or afraid to modify our position. Personally I will change my position on anything I believe when the Word of God brings that change about in conviction and I do it without any apology except for the fact that I have been wrong and that I have taught that which the truth does not teach and that I would correct. I am sure that has been in general the attitude of all our hearts. My prayer is that we have been motivated, activated, and encouraged to recognize our need of further study of the Word of God and that we will continue to engage in such study and if we do so, there is only one end result that can come. If you continue to study God's word and I continue to study it, with open and honest hearts, the more we learn about it the closer together we are going to be. That is the only thing that is going to bring us together. We can lay down our approaches to this and that and our concepts and our ideas and that won't bring us any nearer together but the teaching of the Word of God ought to do it. I hope that this has been emphasized in this meeting in a very full measure.

Now, I am going to start my time. I am going to rub this (Greek on Board) out. I have to take somebody's word for what it means and I don't like for my faith to be in the word of man. I like for it to be in what I can read in the Word of God for myself. I am not belittling the Greek—I wish I knew more about it, but I do not believe there is any truth that has anything to do with the salvation of anybody's soul that depends on it. If it does, I never will get to Heaven. I studied it one year and finally learned the alphabet. So back to our English Bible is the necessary thing.

Now, one thing I want to mention before I get into what I want to put on the board. Brother Lanier quoted from my book *Walking by Faith*. I had not mentioned the book—I failed to get in the commercials that I might have been able to put in, but in that book *Walking by Faith*, Pg. 51 I believe—I have not checked the reference—the quotation had to do with the church selecting messengers and that those messengers were individual messengers and he seemed to think that I was contending that the messengers always had to be individuals and could not be the United States Post Office Service. Well, now the context of the statement that he quoted—if he would study that a little bit in connection with it—was distinguishing between individuals as messengers and churches as messengers and emphasizing the fact that in no instance did any church ever select any other church as its messenger. This would involve subordination of one church to another, and subordination destroys equality, so that is the point I made in the book and the whole lesson will show that is the point of it. The idea that the church should be forced to send by some individual across the country or across the world rather than the United States Government does not give a man credit for much intelligence and neither is it a very fair and honest representation of the actual intent and purpose which, of course, he may not have discerned. I am not questioning his intent in that regard, but I mean, if he got the point I was making, he could not assign or attribute that sort of a context to it.

Now, autonomy is one thing that characterized the New Testament Churches. They were characterized by *sufficiency*. They were characterized by *independence*. They were characterized by *equality*. They were characterized by *autonomy*. We need to recognize that autonomy can be violated, perhaps, even more easily than we think it can. When it is argued that it is impossible for autonomy to be violated when one church sends to another church voluntarily, this I think, is not as conclusive as some seem to think it is.

You have here (Illustration on Board) a local church and that local church is under elders. Those elders have responsibility for its oversight. They are over the members of that church. They are over the resources of it. They have the oversight of its work. They have the oversight of its worship, its edification. They have the oversight of its discipline or its fellowship, if you want to put it that way. And, as Tom Warren or Roy Deaver would say, these are the constituent elements—the component parts of the total situation. This is the total situation so far as the oversight of an eldersip is concerned.

Now, we have over here a sponsoring church or, as brother Lanier would say, a promoting church. They have promoted a work that they are unable to pay for and they want this congregation over here to send to them some of their resources and let them do a part of their work. This business of determining when a work is a church's own work has given a lot of difficulty. It has given a lot of difficulty to the folks who operate the Herald of Truth. They came out with a statement, and I still have a copy of it, in which they said, "This is our work, it isn't anybody else's work, it belongs to us, we have not delegated any part of it to anybody else." This was their first position but when, in debate, they saw that that was going to involve difficulty, certain of our brethren shifted their position on that and in the first speech on the Herald of Truth down in Birmingham, Alabama—this is in print, brother Guy Woods read a number of letters in which some of the churches, some of the major churches, which contribute to the Herald of Truth said, "When we send our money to Abilene we are not doing the work of Highland Church, we are not sending it out there for Highland's work to be done but when we send our money we are doing our own work." "We consider this to be our work."

So, there is a little ambiguity, a difficulty in making clear and plain whose work it is. Does it belong exclusively to the church supervising and controlling it, or is it the work of the churches contributing to it? If it is the work of the contributing churches, and that is what they are saying about it now, unless they have changed their position again, then you have a church delegating a part of its work to the Highland church by sending a part of its resources to do that work. Now, I have been taught all my life that *it takes all of the parts of anything to constitute the whole.* The whole is made up of the sum of its parts, and when you give some of the parts away you do not have the whole remaining. Now, here is the whole situation, the elders oversee their worship and edification and oversee their discipline and their fellowship. When they send a part of their money to the Highland church at Abilene for the Herald of Truth they are delegating a part of their oversight; they are losing a part of their autonomy. They do not have control of it any more.

Brother Harper said and the elders at Highland said "this is our money." You remember in the *Harper—Tant Debate* brother Harper said, "when Yater Tant sends me a dollar it becomes my dollar; it isn't anybody else's dollar. It is mine. Of course, if he sends it for a particular purpose I'm obligated to use it for that purpose but it isn't Tant's any more, it is mine."

So the resources are sent over here and the work is to be done over here and yet they say "it is our work." They do not have any oversight of the work. They do not have the control of their resources any more. They have lost control of their resources. They no longer can oversee this part of their resources or work. They have no selection or choice or oversight. They might remonstrate or have objections and criticisms about the way the resources are used and the work is done, but they do not control the situation. The whole point is that when they do not retain all of their constituent elements, they do not have the whole situation. They cannot send some to another eldership and still retain all of their oversight over either their resources or their work.

My contention, by the same illustration, is that elders of a congregation have just as much right to delegate the oversight of some of the local members to the Herald of Truth or to the elders of the Highland church; delegate the oversight of some of their teacher training, or their edification, or their worship, and let them control and direct it, or ask them to exercise the direction of the discipline of the church. If they can delegate one part, they can delegate any part, and if they can delegate any part, then they can delegate all of every part and it would be justifiable then for the elders of any local church to just turn the oversight of their congregation over to the Herald of Truth.

Now, the fact of the whole matter is that the Herald of Truth is another organization. This is not a church sending to a church. If you could prove that a church could send money to another church to preach the Gospel of Christ, you still would not justify the Herald of Truth. The money is not sent to the Highland church. It isn't deposited to the bank account of the Highland church. The financial statement is not the financial statement of the Highland church. It is not even run by all of the elders of the Highland church directly. It is another organization. They have their own employees, their own offices, their own bank account, their own name. They even had their own mailing permit for a long time. They give out their own financial statement, separate and apart from the Highland church, and anybody would be rather foolish, in my judgment, to argue that the Herald of Truth is the same as the Highland church. It is not even the work of the Highland church. These brethren would not agree with that. It is the work of the contributing churches, they say now, so you do not send money to the church. The church does not send its money to a church when it sends to the Herald of Truth.

One of the peculiar things, to me, about the whole situation is that if there are not two patterns—and a lot has been said about this—if there are not two patterns, one in evangelism and one in benevolence, why do they not incorporate the Herald of Truth like they incorporate their benevolent organizations? Why not do it? What would be wrong with it, brethren? And if you can incorporate the Herald of Truth and put it under a general board like you do Boles Orphan Home, then I want to know how on earth are you going to condemn the missionary society?

You know we have talked a lot about generics and specifics. Brother Hamilton's point is well taken. If you have a generic teach and a generic relieve, and you have both, the New Testament certainly teaches both, and I believe that both terms are generic. But they are gradually brought to a focus in some specific matters. If the generic relieve includes another organization than the local church, then the generic teach by all logic and by every right and reason would include another organization than the local church.

In the matter of when is an example binding, we need, I think, to clarify. We have only muddied the waters about that. This charge that anybody believes that only *uniformity makes an example binding* is just not so. I do not know of anybody that has contended that the uniformity of an example makes it binding. Now, brethren, if you want to honestly represent us from now on out, you ought to leave that charge off because it is not so. It never has been made. I never have made it. There are a number of things that have to go into the binding force of examples. I am not only interested in the binding force of an example, I am interested in what it teaches. Examples ought to teach something and whatever they did in the examples is permissible now.

I know that it is right for a church to send money directly to the preacher. I can read that in the New Testament. Now, if you can show me a passage where the church ever sent money to another church to pay the preacher I will preach that there are two ways to do it. Brother Lanier said it does not make any difference. Well, the difference it makes with me is,

*I find one of them in the New Testament; I have not seen anybody produce the other one from the New Testament.* Now, brethren, if one is in the Word of God, I do not care whether you call it a binding example or not, if one is in the Word of God and was done in the New Testament day and you cannot read, in language clear and plain, where the other was done, then it ought to make a lot of difference to all of us, if we have the regard for the Word of God that we think we do. That is the whole point and if it doesn't make any difference when one is in the New Testament and the other is not, then I want to suggest to you that we need to reexamine our attitude toward the Word of God.

The term relieve, they say includes a benevolent organization. Well, if it does, because it is generic, then teach, as a generic, includes the same sort of a missionary organization. Brother Hamilton made the point and I do not believe there is anybody who can deal with it. If you can incorporate the one, put it under a general board, then you can incorporate the other but, of course, brother Lanier does not, and brother Lemmon does not believe in a general board as the directors of a benevolent corporation. Neither do I. I have as much in common with him as some of you have with him. I could come as near claiming him as you can, because we are in agreement on this matter—exactly so. However, he thinks it is all right for the elders to incorporate like they have up at Tipton and I question that. He wants to, and leaves the inference, that we are like the anti-Sunday School folk. But he would not be willing for the Tipton church to incorporate their Sunday school classes like they have the home. Why, the only authority they have to direct the affairs of that home is the authority that the corporate charter gives them. They are directors of the Tipton Orphan Home by right of corporate law in the state of Oklahoma, not as elders of the church, but as directors of the home, and the charter will show that. He would not be willing to set up that kind of a corporation for their evangelism. He would not be willing to set up that kind of a corporation for their Sunday school work. *He believes in two patterns.* He believes in two patterns, because he would not be willing—and I am certain that he would not be—to have the same kind of a corporate set-up to control the Bibles classes and control the preaching of the Tipton church as that which controls the orphan home.

I think I could add another difference in his two patterns for benevolence and evangelism. He would not want that corporate Bible school organization to engage in business for the purpose of making money to buy their literature and he would not want them to engage in business for the purpose of making money to support their preacher. But if they can do it for the caring of orphans, why can't they do it for other purposes, unless, there are two patterns, unless you recognize a difference in benevolence and evangelism? Now, in evangelism *they sent the money to the preacher; never to the church.* Brother Hamilton is right about that, and the way to prove that he is wrong is for somebody to get up here and put on the board the passage where a church sent money to a church to support a preacher. If you, any of you, know of such a passage, produce it, brethren, so we can all study it. They did not send to Corinth church to support Paul. Why, you just have to read the Corinthian letters to find out that is so. Paul did not receive anything from the Corinthian brethren. Brethren from other churches, Macedonia in particular, (2 Cor. 11:7-11) supplied his needs. It was evidently by divine direction or by divine overruling Providence. He said that he did not exercise his right to be supported by the Corinthians, not because the Corinthian church was not able to support him, but he did it for the sake of the Gospel. (I Cor. 9:12) He did it to protect himself against the charge that false teachers were going to make that he was preaching for their money. That is the reason Paul did not let the Corintnian church give him anything and that is what your Bible teaches about it. The ability of the Corinthian church had nothing to do with it. Others came along and said "He is just preaching for your money." Paul had the best defense on earth. He said, "Oh no, I did not take any of it. That cannot be so."

## *How to Attain and Maintain Fellowship*

### Bryan Vinson

Though a theme of enduring worth and ever-present utility, this is one also of intense interest and current urgency. No subject, not only warrants but, demands examination of its truth and acceptance of its injunctions above this one. At no time within the lifetime of those now here has there been afforded the opportunity to exemplify in their lives the teaching of God's Word on this theme above the present hour. This is true because we are the victims of the results attending the breech of the instructions God has given us as bearing on the unity and fellowship of the saints. Ours is an hour of grave tragedy, and one of our own making.

There are many questions which yield to the inquiring a clearer answer when the issues of self-interest are not immediate; we can exercise a greater measure of objectivity, and thus secure a better balanced and fuller comprehension of the truth. When the Nation is at war the climate is unfavorable for resolving the issue of a Christian's relation to Civil government as related to the bearing of arms, yet just such times

---

BRYAN VINSON SR.—*Resident of Longview, Texas; evangelist for the*

*Timpson, Texas congregation; conducts meetings over a wide area; formerly preached in Houston, Denton and Dallas, Texas and in Oklahoma; stock farmer; businessman.*

are the only ones when we discuss and study it. Would it not be better to thoroughly search for the truth, and test every position in the fire of controversy, when men's passions are calm, and when they are not immediately involved? Even so, the discussion of this subject at this time presents not the most advantageous moment for success because of the influence exerted by a partisan spirit on our study. It would, then, be well for us to call into action our full powers of recollection, to exert our faculty of memory to the fullest, and in memory live again the point of our reception of lessons learned in other years on the subject of the unity of the church. Recall the appeals so fervently made by those who launched the Restoration Movement a hundred and fifty years ago. Review in our minds the provocation which gave birth to this movement. Was it not the disconcerting and distressing observation by these men that religious division was both contrary to the teaching of God's Word and self-defeating as related to the objective of saving the lost? Was it not the concern they felt over this state of division which led to the formulation of that platform capable of removing this blight?

They clearly saw that unity among professed believers was attainable only through the utter abandonment of human creeds, the renunciation of denominational parties, and the complete restoration of the New Testament order of faith and practice, of teaching and worship. In the debate with N. L. Rice, Campbell assailed human creeds as bonds of union and communion affirming them to be heretical and schismatical. Why? Because they prescribed as terms of union and communion human opinions, and thus refused their fellowship to those who didn't subscribe to them. Rice contended that among the orthodox denominations there was a unity in the fundamentals and essentials, and the creeds simply let it be known to all that those subscribing to any particular one not only held to these fundamentals in common with others, but the distinctive views held were expressed as setting forth their own interpretation of the scriptures, so that those who believed accordingly, agreeably united with others on this particular creed. Thus can be clearly seen that the utility of creeds is that of building up and giving distinctiveness to parties and sects.

That which I wish to suggest in this connection is that this discussion was born of a climate of religious discord and division, and was designed by Campbell to set forth a divinely approved means of correcting and ameliorating the then existing condition. I think it can safely be assumed that the position taken by him and his coadjutors finds a hearty response and cordial approval by all of us here. Shall we, then, be agreeable to prescribing for ourselves the same remedy to heal a similar affliction which besets us? Or, on the other hand, are we wise enough to see its applicability and efficacy when applied to others and not wise enough to see the force of its principles as applicable to ourselves? A little over forty years ago a historic discussion was held in Nashville between Ira M. Boswell and N. B. Hardeman on the issue of instrumental music in the worship. This grew out of the Tabernacle meetings of Hardeman in the Ryman Auditorium, and exchanges in the *Gospel Advocate* between J. B. Cowden and F. B. Srygley, resulting in this debate, with others tentatively to follow. These others never materialized. Your attention is directed to this as designed to refresh your memories of that debate which was published, and how the keynote appeal and fervent refrain of brother Hardeman was for the unity of all of God's people. As a youth I read this debate and thrilled at the nobility of the appeal by him as addressed to Boswell and his brethren. He was addressed as a brother, and appealed to as a brother, and the appeal was to discard that which had driven the wedge between brethren, and thus effect the restoration of that oneness which theretofore had obtained.

Along about that time I visited services one night during a meeting at the First Christian church in Longview, and heard a sermon on unity. I have never forgotten, and shall not forget, the appeal the speaker on that occasion made for the unity and fellowship of all professed believers in Christ. He made the very familiar approach with which we are all acquainted as follows: the seeking and occupying of common ground, that upon which all can stand in all good conscience. For instance, on the action of baptism the thought was suggested that whereas we have the choice of sprinkling, pouring and immersion many could not accept the first and second, but all could accept the third, immersion, in all good conscience. This principle of unity was extended to creeds and names, and possibly other points. Afterward I asked him why he didn't apply this principle to the point of difference in the worship, that as he and his brethren claim to be able to worship God without the instrument as well as with it, and there are brethren who can worship only without it, and violate their conscience in worshipping with it, the common ground is without it. Unhappily, he displayed no interest in taking his own prescription. Neither did brother Boswell and his brethren in Nashville respond to the safe, sensible and scriptural appeal of brother Hardeman. Their failure has ever been construed by those of us who cannot worship with the instrument as but indicative of a greater affection for the instrument than they entertain for the fellowship of their dissenting brethren. True, they were and are agreeable to exercising full fellowship with us, but only if we will accept the instrument, and, today, a host of other things. This attitude and appraisal is tantamount to regarding the employment of an instrument of music in the worship being mandatory to pleasing God, for on what principle of reasoning can sincere and pious people require as a term of communion that which God hasn't? When any body of people incorporate *as terms of fellowship* that doctrine or practice, whatever it may be, the very fact they so do invests such a teaching or practice with the quality and character of an item of faith. It is inconceivable that one can hold a thing as an opinion and enjoin subscription to it as a condition of acceptance and fellowship.

This very distinction gave force and attraction to the Restoration Movement: In matters of faith unity; in matters of opinion liberty; in all things charity. We are, therefore, on this principle of thought, and the distinction it makes, bound to hold in abeyance our opinions, never forcing them on others, and making them terms of communion, but rather striving together with one mind for the faith of the gospel. This suggests to me the utility, even the imperative necessity, of determining the character of this one body, this fellowship. I am not talking of any human organization but of the body of Christ, the family of God. There is a passage which has been variously exegeted and frequently cited in the discussions among brethren to which attention is invited. Not to discuss the contribution it makes to the resolving of the issue in dispute, but rather to impress upon our attention the expression it embodies. I refer to Galatians 6:10—the "household of faith." Surely no one is in doubt as to the import of this term. It is in its identity one with the "household of God" in Ephesians 2:19. In the latter it reflects the thought of those referred to as constituting the family of God, his household. Thus it embodies all of God's children, and we are concerned here exclusively and most intensely with the children of God as bearing on their proper relation to God and to one another. In this statement in Galatians the household of faith is descriptive and definitive of those thus distinguished from the generality of men.

As thus identified this family is defined as the household of faith; that is, it is a family which derives its peculiar character from the quality of faith. Faith permeates the lives and motives, the behavior of this family. One is a member of this family by virtue of being a child of God, and so becomes by faith. We are all the children of God by faith, and being the children of God we walk by faith. Is it, then, conceivable that, consistent with this high principle of sonship and fraternal relations, this family can *tolerably* be fractured into fractions and alienated one from the other? Whenever division has beset this family, feelings between brethren become estranged, motives are impugned and the cleavage is widened. This is sadly the condition now existing among us. To deny it is neither manly nor salutary; to acknowledge it and lament it provides the only basis to work for its relief.

The particular design of this effort is directed toward the *attaining* and *maintaining* of the unity and fellowship of the people of God, brethren in Christ. Certainly, in this hour before this can be maintained it must be attained, for it does not presently exist. I believe those responsible for this gathering here are to be commended for the efforts they have made in bringing us together with such a high and noble design as this. It reflects a recognition of the lamentable conditions now obtaining, and an anxious desire to see it remedied. Men moved by such motives cannot but be blessed by their heavenly Father in such a venture, and only those with honest hearts can ever merit His favor. We can here but speak for ourselves, severally, but the fruit which may be borne of this effort can reach out and set in motion events and further efforts that can be immeasurably salutary in the results ultimately attained.

One hundred years ago Moses Lard wrote in his *Quarterly* an article headed with the question: "Can We Divide?" His reasoning and contention was that we will not divide, but on the assumption that division did occur, then those responsible for the division through their departure from the Word of God would cease to be God's people and thus, in reality, the church would not be dividing, and, hence, the element remaining faithful to the Lord would constitute the church. I appreciate the logic of his reasoning, and find no occasion to dissent from his conclusions. However, in this present crisis there has been evidenced a too great a readiness by some on each side to act and speak precipitately on the point of whether the other contingent are the children of God and members of the Lord's church. I wish to instance a case or two on this. A brother whom I have known more than thirty years, and with whom I enjoyed a cordial and even intimate relationship as brothers in the Lord made this remark to me: "How do your churches do mission work?" as distinguished from how the churches with whom he enjoys recognition. To me this revealed that in his mind he was in one church and I am in another. I'm not speaking of the local congregation sense. The scriptures are clearly distinct and severely strict on the matter of the Lord having but one church, and I am of the persuasion that if he and I are in different churches, both of us are not in the Lord's church. Frankly, I do not so appraise the matter as presently existing. However, except the course currently being pursued shall be arrested and reversed, it is inevitable that two bodies shall exist where formerly only one did.

On the other hand, I heard a brother express the view that those who are proponents of these practices in dispute are not in covenant relation with God. I asked him where he got his information to such an effect, which is equal to saying they are not God's children. For several years preceding the break of fellowship brethren of divergent views, and who freely expressed them, recognized one another as brethren, and one's position on the church support of Orphan Homes and the Herald of Truth was not esteemed as grounds for marking and proscribing. Then we had the recommendation of a tag of quarantine being placed on those who were known to oppose such support. I doubt that there is a brother here who can preach in many congregations where formerly he was welcomed. Not only so, but his presence in the assembly would cause eye brows to be raised, and the thought of his being asked to word a prayer unthinkable by many! Too, to attend a service in a congregation of the contrary persuasion in these matters brings on him the charge of being of questionable soundness! Such is the sorry and tragic spectacle which confronts us.

It is my judgment that those devoted to the advocacy of these practices are responsible for the creation of this condition, simply by making a test of fellowship one's belief in these practices that are in dispute. Unfortunately, this action on their part has, in some instances, wrought a reaction of a similar course of proscription by those against whom they have inveighed. Consequently, the chasm has been deepened and widened by the spirit and demeanor on both sides. Only recently I noted an account of the preacher in a congregation branding as rank apostates some of the members within that congregation whose conscience dictated a withholding of their contribution because they could not conscientiously support these institutions through the church.

However, no good end would be served by extending remarks as descriptive of the conditions presently existing and allusion has been made only to bring into focus that which this gathering is designed to give thought toward its improvement, and, hopefully, its correction ultimately. Viewing things as they are, and looking to conditions as they once were, and thus concerned about a recovery of them, we need to give a great deal of thought, prayerfully, to what can and should be done of a rectifying nature. I wish, therefore, to mention a number of steps that are vital to any salutary results being realized.

First, there must be a rebirth in the hearts of many of God's children of a genuine love for one another, and that it find a practical application in our lives, in relation to each other, of doing unto others as we would have them do unto us. I cannot conceive of a situation in life where the force of this directive from our Savior is not legitimate and obligatory and, certainly, none where it is of greater utility than in instances such as presently exist between brethren. Can one rightly lay claim to having the spirit of Christ apart from a becoming respect for and obedience to His Word? Can men who viciously inveigh against their brethren with whom they differ possess the mind of Christ? Listen: "The rash decision of the party leaders to pursue such a determined course of deliberate division stems from frustration and desperation—an obdurant course of action by egocentric men who will not turn back from diabolical designs to wreck the churches." This is but a brief sample from the pen of one who has written his analysis of conditions, and who hesitates not to impugn motives and excoriate in terms of severe harshness those whose opposition to these institutions he once shared, his labored and vain protestations of innocence to the contrary notwithstanding. Such vituperative language does not change the convictions of anyone, nor assuage the pains of anguish occasioned by the rift among us. The only conceivable effect they can have is one of worsening relations between those estranged.

The next advance toward the improvement of the existing situation is the establishment of communication between those who presently refuse to countenance such with those of the contrary persuasion. The rank and file of the members of the congregations have been influenced by their leaders to look upon those on the other side as unfit to have any sort of contact with. Friends of many years were taken to task by a good sister for sitting at the same table in a public eating place with me and my wife, on the grounds that we had left the church, and thus with us they were not to eat! It has been my painful lot to meet brethren of years' association, and have them refuse to speak. This never contributes toward the recovery of one who has defected from the faith, but "if one do err from the truth let him know that he who converts the sinner from the error of his way shall save a soul from death and cover a multitude of sins." I conceive the upright and honorable attitude to be that of recognizing one another as brethren, but as touching the points of difference as being brethren in error. There is a wide difference in holding a brother to be in error, and in denying him to be a brother because you conceive him to be in error. Certainly I regard those who differ from the position I hold to be in error in that respect and to that degree; otherwise I would have to believe that truth can attach to different and contrary positions and contentions. Certainly this occasion wherein brethren of contrary views have consented to meet together and talk frankly and fraternally, as we have been doing, commends the advisability and demonstrates the practicality of such communication. A conciliatory spirit must be exemplified without the admixture of a compromise of convictions.

Pervading all such contacts, whether between two individuals or groups, a love of the truth must supremely prevail and possess every heart. This love of the truth must repress every impulse of self will, and wholly suppress all pride. "What saith the scriptures?" must be the searching and testing question of all discussion, without any partiality as to what the answer shall be.

A clear distinction must always be made and accepted between matters of faith and matters of opinion, with a firm attachment to those and a holding as one's own private possession these. This distinction not only embraces the point of what is properly a matter of faith and that which is rightly an opinion, but also the relative merit of each. We are saved by faith, the just shall live by faith, and we are to walk by faith and not by sight. Such is not predicated of any opinion. We must have the spirit of faith, according as it is written "I believe, therefore I speak." No one is under any necessity to teach an opinion, but a firm fidelity to the truth requires that it be affirmed and taught.

The fellowship of the saints involves more than a state or condition, as has been affirmed by some. Rather the relation of the unity of God's people constitutes the state of condition wherein the exercise of fellowship may be experienced and enjoyed. There are those today who have moved a hundred and eighty degrees from the position of severe restrictiveness formerly held to one of embracing within their fellowship all who profess to believe that Jesus is the Christ, and have been immersed. I fully anticipate they will remove the second condition ere long, and ultimately the first one. Their initial premise is that these two conditions being met constitutes one a child of God regardless of what else they may believe, teach and practice, and, hence, are to be fellowshipped. In conversation with one of the leading lights of this new approach to matters several years ago, he told me that fellowship was solely a matter of state and relationship. To him I said, and to you I say, this isn't true. Fellowship means joint participation, and yields in application to that which we *do* and that which we *receive*— it is active. The unity of God's people is germane to their fellowship, and its disruption renders their continued fellowship impractical and substantially impossible. The measure, therefore, of their fellowship is restricted within the confines of the degree of the unity existing.

The question of old of "How can two walk together except they be agreed?" is of force at this point. The walking would be the acting, and thus acting together, and the question poses the point of such being dependent on an antecedent state of agreement or unity. It is a rhetorical question, one which carries its answer in the asking. If God could, as He did, bring the dissident elements of the human race together, the Jews and the Gentiles, into one body, and as so constituted to be fitly framed together in the Lord, and thus worthily become the tabernacle of God, and holy temple of the Lord, can we not see the grim consequences of the rupture which has been wrought among us? God's acceptance of men is in this pattern of oneness, and woe be unto those who lightly esteem its preservation.

This initial effort toward reviving, a bringing back to life, this love of a fraternal warmth, and affectionate esteem becoming a reality, then a program of communication can be inaugurated, but without that this is impossible, and if sought would be wholly abortive of any worthy results. To love as brethren surely carries the import of esteeming one another as redeemed children of God, and thus of imperishable worth in the estimation of Him who died for them. I believe every one born again is a child of God by reason of this birth, and is to be so esteemed by me. And, as thus esteemed, I am to be considerate of his feelings and the best interest of his soul; I must not despise him for whom Christ died.

The more immediate results of this sort of approach and effort by all should lead to and embrace as a practical matter the recognition by congregations of other congregations as being the Lord's church, and extend such recognition to the full limits of all areas of agreement. We are all one in so many vital areas that it ill-behooves us to anathematize each other in those as yet unresolved ones. Rather, from this posture of vital oneness, extensively existing, there should in the consciousness of it be generated and encouraged and settlement of these issues of present concern. Pending any full agreement on them we should "take heed how we bite and devour one another, lest we be consumed one of another." This recognition should embody the announcement of particular meetings of neighboring congregations, and the freedom felt to visit such gatherings.

This very procedure exists between brethren who differ on a closely related issue to the Orphan Home one. I have in mind the subject of congregations contributing to colleges. As a matter of fact, the present issue which crystalized over the home grew out of a controversy over the college. We who are here can, and I trust do, clearly recall heated controversy between brethren N. B. Hardeman and Foy E. Wallace, Jr. over the church support of colleges, in which Hardeman said, in defense of such support, that the College and the Orphan Home "stand or fall together." This very statement and the discussion revolving around it is what precipitated the extended discussions over the orphan homes being supported by the church. Now, may I address you who believe congregations can support the home but not the college. If brethren insisted on pressing the support of colleges from the congregation's treasury, would you go along to get along, or would you refuse to violate your consciences by so doing?

I recall quite distinctly talking to brother Hardeman in private conversation several years before the eruption of his controversy with brother Wallace, in which he avowed as his persuasion that such support of the college was right. My reply was that I didn't believe so. It created no rift then or later between us. But had he pressed it to the point of forming an issue in which a brother's or a congregation's acceptance and recognition was suspended on believing as he did, and so practicing, then this would have created a rift. This is exactly what has happened with respect to the orphan home question. Also, among the proponents of this support of the homes there is a distinct and fundamental difference, to the degree that each contends the other is unscriptural, as instanced in the respective views of those who say such homes to be right under the elders of a local congregation, and others avowing that this is wrong, since they would as elders be over a human institution favoring a board like the board of directors of a bank. If, then, these differences have not warranted a rivening of the churches, why have brethren been subjected to the necessity of participating in the support of these homes by the church, or be forced out? I earnestly beseech you to place yourselves in our position, substituting the college for the home, and determine in the deep searching of your conscience what you would do?

No branding as "antis", as "hobbyists", or as "extremists" will ever change the conviction of the conscientious, but only the shedding of further light from the Word of God can effect the change. If we are "weak in the faith", you, as the strong are to bear with us, while trying to strengthen our faith. If with you the whole matter is mere difference of opinion, then out of deference to the prayer of Jesus that all who believe in Him shall be one you should not press your opinion on us. Should you reply that we are pressing our opinion of opping the church support of orphan homes on you I reply, I am not guilty. If you are of the opinion that such is all right, I would never mark and disfellowship you for thinking so. In fact, I would be strongly opposed to branding and withdrawing from a brother who holds the opinion that the use of instrumental music is all right. But should he press his persuasion to the point of insisting that I worship with it, and if I do not I cannot worship, I would be forced to refuse his demands of compliance. Correspondingly, as long as brethren do not force on others the violation of their consciences in this practice of the church supporting homes and/or colleges, we can be at peace, and for years we were.

The subject before us now is twofold: namely, how to *attain* and *maintain* the unity and fellowship of the saints. I believe that had we all exercised a better understanding and respect for the teaching of the scriptures as bearing on this subject, we would not be now in the painful and deplorable condition of division and disfellowship. There must be a re-assertion of those divinely prescribed principles of consideration and behavior that are designed to keep the unity of the Spirit in the bond of peace in order to effect its restoration in our time. Paul, the prisoner, besought the Ephesian saints to walk worthy of the vocation to which they had been called, and if such an appeal was of force and virtue to them it is equally so to us. The implication is inescapable that any attitude and conduct at variance with his instructions shall involve those so doing as walking unworthily. That one can go to heaven who so does is, to say the least, highly doubtful. What constitutes this worthy walk as, in this connection, Paul delineates it, involves the heart condition as basically influencing one's conduct toward his brethren. There must be that lowliness and meekness enabling one to be long-suffering in the exercise of forebearance in love. The object being to keep, by such an endeavor, the unity of the Spirit in the bond of peace. The unity of the Spirit must be a unity that is founded on what the Spirit teaches, and by no means can a oneness wrought and maintained by any other means, or as resting on any other basis than the revealed Word of Christ be the unity the Lord requires and will be pleased with. Hence, any state of unity and condition of peace existing in consequence of any corruption or compromise of the truth is not that for which the apostle pleaded, or which faithful Christians will be a party to.

Several years ago a brother, in teaching a Bible class, allegedly said that, had he been present when the instrument of music was an issue, he would have accepted it in preference to the church dividing. As painful and tragic as division is, I think it is less so than accepting a course of departure from the truth which would forfeit the blessings and pleasure of God, attending one. A broken fellowship with brethren is more grievous than, perhaps, any of us can appreciate, but a broken fellowship with Christ, the Father and the Holy Spirit is eternally catastrophic. When two or more act together they have fellowship with each other in that which they do. And when two or more jointly receive something, there is fellowship between them as thus related to the object received. We, severally, received the blessings of forgiveness, and we individually rendered that obedience as expressive of our faith which was conditional to receiving this forgiveness. But it needs to be constantly borne in mind that ours is a common salvation; that is, though individually secured it is a salvation common to all of us. We have common faith, though each one does his own believing. Peter addressed those who had obtained a like precious faith, and Paul addressed the young preacher as his son after the common faith. The faith of Christ is not the exclusive possession of anyone or group of God's children. We have one God, our common Father, one Lord, our common King, one Spirit, our common guide, one baptism to which we each have submitted, one body of which we each are members, one faith by which we were enlightened, saved and are kept and one hope which we cherish and unceasingly should rejoice in. Can one of these seven unities be destroyed without adversely affecting each of the others as bearing on our relation thereto? I fear not, and certainly so with respect to those responsible for rending this one body. No coalescing virtue either inheres in or adheres to an opinion.

I am confident that you believe as I do that the prayer of Jesus in John 17 was answered in the early church, as exemplified in the statement that the "multitude of them that believed were of one heart and soul"; and in perfect consonance therewith Paul exhorted the Philippians to "stand in one spirit, with one soul striving for the faith of the gospel." Can one strive against his brethren when striving for that which is not clearly embraced within the faith of the gospel, in contending for that which at best is regarded by its advocates as a dispensable expediency, and act in harmony with this apostolic appeal?

In the physical body the healing of a wound is promoted by the closing of the opened wound, and, correspondingly, the healing of the wound afflicting spiritual Zion can only be expedited by each striving to come closer to the other. This healing, however, depends on the healthy attitude of each, the sincerity of purpose and the intensity of the desire to please the Lord in all that we do. Any unsanitary binding can create an infectious situation which can worsen the condition. But rather than trying to magnify our differences and proliferate them, we should strive to reduce them and ultimately eliminate them altogether.

It lies within the power of God's children today to bring about a complete restoration of the peace and unity which was ours a few years ago, and principally within the power of the preachers and the elders in the churches. The rupture has been largely if not wholly wrought through their influence, and through them alone can the remedy be prescribed and applied. I wish to suggest to you the alternative is only a continued state of division and broken fellowship, with consequences too dire to foresee fully. The generality of God's people are not possessed of an understanding of the principles involved in the points of issue, and will remain "by and large" aligned as they now are, so long as a concerted and sincere effort is lacking on the part of leaders to improve the situation.

Past history reveals the existence of an understanding of the proper distinction between the character and influence of matters of faith and matters of opinion by some, and an absence of this understanding by others. I wish to point out instances of this by citing statements which reflect both, and in the persuasion that the same distinction presently exists. From the pen of David Lipscomb I read:

> Of late years, this unity of faith and harmony of action have been much disturbed. Divisions and discords, threatening the disruption of church and Christian fellowship, have entered in and have well nigh destroyed the peace, and much weakened the effort of those seeking to unite all worshipers of God in the unity of the faith, and in the bonds of love. This is a dire and fatal disaster to befall an effort so full of promise of good to man, and of honor to the Lord and Master.
>
> From the beginning there have been two classes in the church. One disposed to strictly construe the Bible and cling close to its teaching. This class, in all questions that arise, asks "What does the Word of God require?" And they restrain their practices and service within the requirements of the Divine Word. The other class, interpreting the word of God more liberally or loosely, asks "Is it forbidden?" What is not forbidden they claim the right to practice. A little thought will show the one class walks by the requirements of the Bible. The other walks in the wisdom of men. These do the things suggested by that wisdom, unless it is specifically forbidden by the Word of God. The practices of one class necessarily spring from God and His holy word. No practice can be accepted with this class that does not come from God and that is not required by His holy word. God is the author of all religious service with this class. The other class looks largely to its own wisdom, and the wisdom of men for authority and for guidance in things of religion, and anything man's wisdom approves may be used in religion unless specifically forbidden in the word of God. These paths rapidly diverge. And those walking in these diverging paths cannot walk together. They cannot live in unity and harmony.
>
> These diverse ways of regarding the services of religion led to the first division among Christians. They have in all the ages of the church led to divisions. In the days of Luther the question of infant baptism was raised. He asked, "Where is it forbidden?" and because not forbidden he retained it. The same question came up with the Camp-

bells, father and son. They adopted the rule to practice only what was required. The son said to the father, "Infant baptism is not required in the scriptures." He responded, "It must go then." Under Luther's rule he and Melanethon were forced to advise Philip of Hesse that bigamy is allowed, because not specifically prohibited.

Under this rule many gross and hurtful perversions of the truth, as well as many sinful and corrupting practices may be brought into the church because they are not specifically prohibited in the scriptures. This principle of interpretation releases men from a close adherence to the will of God as revealed in the Bible, and gives wide license to the introduction of human wisdom as the rule in the church and the life of a Christian. The substitution of human wisdom for the will of God subverts the church from the ends for which it was instituted.

Following this language Lipscomb introduced a quotation from what he styled as a "prominent paper among the disciples." I wish to read that quotation in full:

What a violent contrast to the simple but comprehensive condition of Christian fellowship enunciated by Alexander Campbell and his coadjutors and taught in the New Testament, in the Plymouthian and Sand Creek efforts, based on the same false and foolish philosophy, to forge men together in the bonds of identical opinions, mostly if not entirely about matters of no vital importance! If the fathers of this reformation emphasized one thing more than another it was the importance of the distinction between faith and opinion. They pointed out to their contemporaries that faith united men to God and to one another, but that opinions, when substituted for faith, severed them from both, and became the occasion of endless strife and bitterness. The New Testament teaches that faith in Christ and its manifestation in obedience to his commandments are the terms of Christian fellowship, and that nothing else is to be insisted on as necessary to salvation or the enjoyment of Christian privileges. Additions to these simple conditions of church membership and Christian fellowship, by insisting on the speculations of creed-makers and the crochets of egotisitc dogmatists, and that everybody shall act and think as they do in regard to all the secondary questions of church politics, have ever been the sources of sectarian strife and division in the church of God.

It seems like the irony of fate that men should arise claiming to be the loyal successors of these reformers, who are planting themselves squarely on the Plymouthian ground of opinionism and externalism, in absolute reversal of the most fundamental distinction of these reformers; and in defiance of "the book" with which they profess to be supremely "satisfied" are fomenting strife and counseling division over questions of opinion—yes, opinion—nothing but opinions—not one of which stands vitally related to the Christian faith—opinions about expedients and methods and things incidental and circumstantial and wholly external to the kingdom of God—fads and fancies and preferences about suppers and organs and pastors and missionary societies—things which under the head of ways and means have their practical value, but in comparison with the fundamental principles of the kingdom of heaven scarcely rise to the dignity of decent importance—about such matters as these or opinions concerning them, it is proposed to disrupt the churches and to build up a new denomination on the old creed of opinionism! We are not yet prepared to go back to the sectarian flesh-pots from which we have been delivered, and every effort to Plymouthize this movement by making opinions tests of fellowship will prove a disastrous failure.

Brother Lipscomb had quite a bit to say in response to this piece. Should one disregard the source of the language, and its identity with a defense of things for which it constitutes an apology, intermingled with a condemnation of those against whom the writer is writing, he could say much favorable to its contents. In essence, those whose opinions were adverse to the suppers, organs and societies were esteemed as egotistic dogmatists who were making much ado over little. The anomalous feature is that these things are to be esteemed as small and inconsequential when viewed from the point of opposition, but esteemed as very dear and vital opinions when entertained as favoring them. And the responsibility for the disrupturing and dividing of churches is ascribed to the opposers rather than to those who advocated and agitated these practices, which admittedly were matters of opinion rather than matters of faith.

They were, by this writer deemed as compared with the fundamental principles of the kingdom of heaven unworthy to rise to the dignity of decent importance!

Now, I wish to give you the advantage of hearing and considering a sample of the considerable amount of response Lipscomb gave to this piece:

> The position of the writer clearly is that the fads, fancies and preferences based wholly on opinion are to be tolerated in the churches of God, in the worship, the organism and the work of the church. It instances fairs and festivals, the organ, the pastor, the missionary society, and rightly calls them "fads, fancies, preferences based wholly on opinion." He says these are all outside of the church and its scriptural provisions, and are based upon the opinions and nothing but the opinions of those introducing them, and are to be admitted on the ground that they are mere matters of opinion and liberty of opinion must be tolerated. It is the opinion of others that these are all wrong. These must be allowed the same liberty to act on their opinion as those who think them right. Those holding antagonistic opinions cannot act harmoniously while each is acting on his own opinion. One person has an opinion that the fair or festival is a legitimate way of raising money for the church. Another has an opinion that it is not, but to raise money in that way and to bring it into the church is to set aside the law of God, it is, to bring that which is unclean in the sight of God into, and to profane, His sacred temple. Liberty of opinion as advocated, says we must let the former of these hold his festivals and bring his money into the church of God. But all principles of justice demand the other must be equally entitled to liberty of opinion, and be equally authorized to act on his opinion, and his opinion requires him to oppose bringing that into the church of God which he believed is offensive to God and which desecrates and profanes the temple of God and corrupts the church of which he is a member. He would sin to stand and see the church corrupted without an earnest effort to save it. Contention and strife unending must result. The organ is introduced under plea of liberty of opinion, no one who fellowships the church using it, and especially no one who engages in the

song service of the church, can otherwise than worship with and countenance the organ. A man has an opinion that it is a sin to introduce and use it. Its introduction deprives him of his liberty of opinion, and deprives him of his right of serving the Lord in his appointments . . . . Both cannot have liberty of opinion, in the sense that they make their opinions the basis of action for themselves or for the church. One will have his opinions tyrannized over by the other. It will be none the less tyranny of opinion that a majority, great or small, imposes its opinion on the minority. One man has as much right to liberty of opinion as any other or number of others. And this doctrine that liberty involves the right to act on those opinions where our actions come in contact with, or affects the actions and opinions of others is the very thing that will continually gender causes and occasions of discord and division.

Brother Lipscomb devoted considerable space to delivering Alexander Campbell from the imputations of this piece he reviewed. He showed conclusively that the Campbells held to the principle that one's opinions are to be held as private property, and are not to be imposed on anyone. He instanced the case of Aylette Rains, who entertained the opinion that all men would eventually be happy; that is, the doctrine of Universalism. He was received into the fellowship of Campbell and others on the ground that he would hold this as his own opinion, and simply be content with teaching and preaching what the scriptures plainly and simply taught. This he did, and in time through the mere process of not teaching and advocating this opinion it passed from his mind, a sort of atrophy or perishing through disuse was the result. Lipscomb said:

"Mr. Campbell declares everyone who introduces an opinion or preference based on an opinion is by the decisions of the Bible a factionist. Yet our writer says those who oppose the making of these opinions the basis of action, are the factionists. Mr. Campbell was then the prince of factionists. Yet he is quoted to condemn those who oppose the introduction of opinions as the basis of actions that affect the whole church."

He quotes from Mr Campbell:

"Anyone who feels himself conscientiously obliged to utter opinions, must regard them of permanent value—as equal to Divine Oracles. It is a grand mistake.—Zeal for an opinion, then, when brought to the touchstone of truth and the Bible, is mere self-love, operating in the form of pride. It may be yet made evident that this peculiar pride of opinion or understanding, enters into the very essence of all partyism amongest men, nay that itself is the very spirit of discord, the soul of the sectary, and the demon of religious persecution. Its name is legion, the first born of Satan, and its brood are emulation, strife, wrath, sedition, treason, heresy. All the contentions and divisions, all the sects and parties in Christendom, are as certainly and indisputably the effects of opinionism as the love of money is the root of all evil."

If time permitted, much more could, I think with profit, be extracted from the writings of these good and great men, and others among the notable worthies of their contemporaries. But these must be sufficient to impress on each of us how extremely vital it is that we exercise our senses to discern between faith and opinion, between what God's Word unmistakably teaches, and what we may think, or appear to us to be acceptable with Him. It is because of the long-existing disposition of men to commit the sin of presumption, the great transgression, that we need to ever be on guard lest we fall victim to it ourselves. "Happy is the man that condemns not himself in that which he alloweth." The context of this statement bears out the thought that in doing that which we allow, or approve, we may thereby bring on ourselves condemnation in consequence of the ill-effects attaching to another. We are to follow after the things which make for peace and things whereby we may edify one another.

Unless I am the victim of grievous self-deception, if I believed that these practices which are in dispute were scripturally expedient, I would, in good conscience, be compelled to forego them out of deference to those who with equal conscience believe them to be a digression from the revealed will of God. In 1870, Isaac Errett wrote in the *Standard:* "Our own course is clear. We shall advise our brethren everywhere, for the sake of peace and from a reverential regard to one of the noblest lessons of Christian Brotherhood, to discard the use of instruments in the churches. At the same time we set ourselves most decidedly against all attempts to create divisions in churches on the ground of differences in regard to an expedient. The law which binds it on us to please our neighbor for his good is no more imperative than that which forbids us to judge our brother in regard to such matters. Let a sacred regard to the conscience of others possess us and we shall master the difficulties of this question."

I have not sought to speak for any other or others, which I have no right to, but I have so spoken as prompted by my own conscience and convictions on this subject. I yield to no man in respect to the intensity and pain of my anguish over the conditions which presently envelope us. Nothing within my life has created and sustained such heaviness and sorrow in my heart as has, and does, these conditions. I am both willing and anxious to surrender every personal preference and opinion for the peace and unity of God's children, and I could not appeal to another to do so except I should be willing to thus do. In conversation with a prominent brother on the other side, I appealed to him to use his influence toward having brethren separate these institutions from the churches, and, as he teaches in theory, but doesn't practice, let them "buy their services" as they do utility companies, and other service institutions, and thereby promote the reunification of the brotherhood. His only reply was that they—meaning us— would not agree to such.

Brethren, in conclusion, may I be permitted to emphasize the truth that the church is built upon the foundation of the apostles and prophets, and upon no other basis can it exist and remain the Lord's church; and that those, and only those, who so are built together for an habitation of God through the Spirit can safely and securely be and remain His children. This building is wrought solely on the foundation of their teaching, we can never safely depart from it. To go beyond the word of God is to move off of this apostolic foundation, and to cease walking in the light and be imperiously provoked thereby to try and test the ground upon which you stand and every step you take, that it is within the light of God's Word.

I have not cited or referred to many passages of scriptures bearing upon this theme, because I have spoken on the assumption you are familiar with them. My effort has not been primarily to instruct but to exhort. May God's Grace and Mercy be with and ever attend us as we strive to do, not our will but, His.

## How to Attain and Maintain Unity

Jimmy Allen

Thank you, brother Stevens. We have just heard a presentation from brother Vinson which should be considered a classic. There is so much in his address with which I am in full agreement.

Brethren, it is a great honor for me to participate in this meeting. I count it even a greater honor to speak upon the subject of fellowship. Other than Roy Cogdill and Dudley Spears, there is no one on the other team whom I knew personally prior to this association. It has certainly been a pleasure to be with all of you. I have come to love and appreciate brethren Wharton, Vinson, Thompson and others. This has been a real experience for me and I will not soon forget it.

Several years ago I studied these issues carefully and prayerfully. I don't mean I studied them for a day or two but for weeks and weeks. However, I will have to admit that I haven't given much thought or study to these matters over the past few years. It has been worthwhile for me to re-think the issues over which we are divided. We have had a great time together this week.

I was almost moved to tears a couple of times by brother Vinson's address. I don't mean to take away from the fine spirit which has characterized the meeting tonight, however, I must say I feel like a one inch firecracker following a stick of dynamite. Likely, my feeling of inadequacy is not based on humility but on inferiority. With these things in mind, I am now ready to deal with the subject of how we can attain and maintain unity.

---

JIMMY H. ALLEN—*Professor of Bible, Harding College, Searcy, Arkansas; preacher for one of the congregations in Searcy; widely known as a speaker in cooperating evangelistic campaigns throughout the nation.*

## IS UNITY POSSIBLE?

First, we need to determine whether unity is possible or not. There are 250 to 300 denominations in the United States this evening. Furthermore, the Restoration Movement is fragmented. Recently, I heard brother H. A. Dixon on the Harding College lectureship. He said there are more than twenty divisions in the Restoration Movement. Brother Norvel Young, president of George Pepperdine College, wrote the same thing in a *Gospel Advocate* article. Just a few days ago brother Reuel Lemmons, editor of the *Firm Foundation*, said there are about twenty-five divisions in the Restoration Movement. With little difficulty, I can count seven divisions among what all of us would consider as brethren.

A number of our people are beginning to seriously question the possibility of unity in the religious world. I have heard some say and I have read others who contend that by unity our people have meant everyone else must accept "our" interpretations of Scripture. Many are embarrassed to teach about unity because of our own divisions. Robert Marshall wrote: "How can we explain the need for unity to victims of a fragmented society in a schizoid denominationalism when we are disunity personified?" *(Mission*, January, 1968)

## UNITY IS POSSIBLE

Although I have painted a rather bleak picture, I would like now to offer reasons for believing that unity is a distinct possibility. First, unity is possible for it is desirable. Men of good will everywhere say they want to be united. At Vatican Council II, on October 11, 1962, the pope addressed 2800 prelates, representing a half billion people, for thirty-seven minutes urging them to work actively for Christian unity. Recently, Dr. Carl Henry, editor of *Christianity Today,* wrote an article entitled "Somehow Let's Get Together." Not long ago G. B. Shelburne, a preacher of the gospel, presented a speech entitled "American's Oldest Ecumenical Movement" to a group of denominational ministers in Amarillo. Unity meetings are taking place among various groups within the Restoration Movement. In 1966, during the campaign in Amarillo, five conservative independent Christian Church preachers invited a number of us to meet with them to discuss the possibility of our being united. I have heard that our people in New Mexico have been meeting with Christian Church people under similar circumstances. The same type meetings are occurring in Brazil. A publication called *Communion Quester* is carrying articles written by brethren who differ on the question of instrumental music in the worship. The paper is from Brazil. Divided brethren in that nation are seeking unity.

In the second place, I believe unity is possible for the early church had it. At Eph. 4:3 Paul said, "endeavoring to keep the unity of the Spirit in the bond of peace." You can't maintain what you don't have. The Ephesian brethren had unity and were urged to keep it. Chester E. Tulga wrote: "In the early centuries of the church, denominations did not exist, consequently there is no New Testament basis for denominationalism. In the larger sense, there was unity, and heresy and heretics played only a minor part in the church life of those early centuries. The seeds of division, however, are seen in the New Testament . . ." *(The Doctrine of the Church in These Times,* p. 46). According to Acts 4:32, "the multitudes of them that believed were of one heart and one soul."

Third, unity is possible for it is commanded. In I Cor 1:10 Paul said, "Now, I beseech you, brethren by the name of our Lord Jesus Christ, that ye all speak the same thing. and that there be no divisions among you; but that ye be perfectly joined together in the same mind and in the same judgment." Surely, God did not command that which cannot be obeyed.

Fourth, I think we can have unity because Jesus prayed for it. According to John 17:20-21, Jesus, in His prayer to the Father, said, "Neither pray I for these alone, but for them also which shall believe on me through their word; That they may be one; as thou, Father, art in me, and I in thee, that they also may be one in us: that the world may believe that thou hast sent me."

Fifth, it seems that unity is possible for it is set before us in the Bible as an ideal. David wrote: "Behold, how good and how pleasant it is for brethren to dwell together in unity" (Psa 133:1).

In fairness to truth and reality, I must add that I do not believe religious unity will ever exist among all those who profess faith in the Lord Jesus Christ. Of course, I believe in unity as an idealistic possibility. However, because of human depravity and sinfulness, I do not think such will ever occur among all those who say they are following Jesus. Some of you may feel this is contradictory to my foregoing statements but, really, there is a consistency between this and earlier remarks. To illustrate: is it possible for the entire world to be Christian? Ideally, yes. If every man would surrender his heart to the Christ, then the whole world would be saved. Practically, no. Men, because of stubbornness and rebellion, will not submit to the Lord and His way. Some say that Christianity has failed because the world has not accepted it. Has soap failed? Everyone could be clean but there are plenty of dirty people today. Does this mean that soap has failed? It simply means it has not been used. Christianity has not failed; it simply has not been accepted. To my knowledge, there is no New Testament doctrine which has been received universally by people claiming to be Christians. We should not be surprised if the same thing happens with reference to the Bible doctrine of unity.

## HOW TO HAVE UNITY—THEORY

Now to the question, how can we have unity? First, I shall discuss some of the theories which have been advocated in seeking unity. All of us are acquainted with the Roman Catholic approach. They say we are to unite under papal direction. Pius XII, in an address given from Vatican City, December 31, 1952, said, "Today when the powers of evil fight in serried ranks and the need for concord among those who are on the side of God is more imperious, we make bold to call on even the separated brethren . . . Let the division cease. To you the house is open which the Lord in unmistakable words built on the rock of Peter and his successors." At least one episcopalian bishop in our country, the man who succeeded Pike, has advocated union on the terms of Catholicism.

While in Brisbane, Australia during 1965, I had opportunity to talk with a Canon in the Church of England. At that time, he and eleven other Anglican clergymen composed the Ecumenical Committee for the Church of England in Australia. I was granted permission to talk with him because of my interest in ecumenism. In the course of our discussion, I asked how he could conceive of unity between the Anglican and Roman churches in the light of their opposing concepts concerning papal infallibility. In reply, he said the Catholic problem is how to change without changing. He added that the Roman church would not change what it has written about the pope but the time will come when it will act as though such statements do not exist. At that time the pope will be accepted as simply a bishop among bishops and the two communions will be united. Personally, I felt he was being somewhat naive.

The Protestant platform for unity in times past has been creeds. Creeds were written to so clearly define doctrine that differences would be resolved. However, instead of settling differences, they created divisions and erected more barriers. In a word, creeds failed.

A different approach was taken in the Stockholm Conference of 1925. It was attended by ninety-one churches from thirty-three countries. Their motto was "Doctrine divides; service unites." In response to that, I offer the following. If doctrine divides, then attempts at unity without considering the basis for division certainly cannot unite. That which causes division must be dealt with if divisions are to be resolved. Furthermore, this overlooks the approach of the inspired Paul. In his epistles, Paul first laid a doctrinal foundation and then followed with practical admonition. In Romans he wrote eleven chapters on doctrine followed with five on practice. In Galatians there are four on doctrine and two on practice. In Ephesians there are three on doctrine and three on practice. Colossians is evenly divided with two on doctrine and two on practice. Paul dealt with doctrine before discussing practice or service. He did it in such a way that the first century church had unity.

If I correctly understand the situation, the modern ecumenical movement is striving for unity upon the least common denominator. Apparently, all that is necessary for a group to be in this union movement is to profess its belief in Jesus Christ as the Son of God *without further definition.* All admit that this is not the unity of the apostolic church. The serious differences between them still exist; they just act as though they don't. Surely, it is seen that this is simply a crossing of party lines and not an abolition of those lines.

Then, there is the approach offered by the men of the Restoration Movement. For the past several weeks I have lived in fear and trembling. Preparing this presentation has been no easy task. Through extensive reading, I have lived with the Restoration leaders in getting ready to speak tonight. In my judgment, one of the greatest uninspired papers on unity is the

Declaration and Address by Thomas Campbell in 1809. That address is summed up in thirteen propositions, five of which I shall now read.

Number 4—"That although the Scriptures of the Old and New Testaments are inseparably connected, making together but one perfect and entire revelation of the Divine will, for the edification and salvation of the Church, and therefore in that respect cannot be separated; yet as to what directly and properly belongs to their immediate object, the New Testament is as perfect a constitution for the worship, discipline, and government of the New Testament Church, and as perfect a rule for the particular duties of its members as the Old Testament was for the worship, discipline, and government of the Old Testament Church, and the particular duties of its members."

Number 3—"That in order to do this (i.e. have unity, JA), nothing ought to be inculcated upon Christians as articles of faith; nor required of them as terms of communion, but what is expressly taught and enjoined upon them in the word of God. Nor ought anything to be admitted, as of Divine obligation, in their Church constitution and managements, but what is expressly enjoined by the authority of our Lord Jesus Christ and his apostles upon the New Testament Church; either in express terms or by approved precedent."

Number 5—"That with respect to the commands and ordinances of our Lord Jesus Christ, where the Scriptures are silent as to the express time or manner of performance, if any such there be, no human authority has power to interfere in order to supply the supposed deficiency by making laws for the Church; nor can anything more be required of Christians in such cases but only that they so observe these commands and ordinances as will evidently answer the declared and obvious end of their institution. Much less has any human authority power to impose new commands or ordinances upon the Church, which our Lord Jesus Christ has not enjoined. Nothing ought to be received into the faith or worship of the Church, or be made a term of communion among Christians, that is not as old as the New Testament."

Number 6—"That although inferences and deductions from Scripture premises when fairly inferred, may be truly called the doctrine of God's holy word, yet are they not formally binding upon the consciences of Christians farther than they perceive the connection, and evidently see that they are so; for their faith must not stand in the wisdom of men, but in the power and veracity of God. Therefore, no such deductions can be made terms of communion, but do properly belong to the after and progressive edification of the Church. Hence, it is evident that no such deductions or inferential truths ought to have any place in the Church's confession."

Number 7—"That although doctrinal exhibitions of the great system of Divine truths, and defensive testimonies in opposition to prevailing errors, be highly expedient, and the more full and explicit they be for those purposes, the better; yet, as these must be in a great measure the effect of human reasoning, and of course must contain many inferential truths, they ought not to be made terms of Christian communion; unless we suppose, what is contrary to fact, that none have a right to the communion of the Church, but such as possess a very clear and decisive judgment, or are come to a very high degree of doctrinal information; whereas the Church from the beginning did, and ever will, consist of little children and young men, as well as fathers."

Here is a brief summary of those propositions. We must accept the authority and all sufficiency of the New Testament. We are to bind upon another only what is expressly taught in the word of God. Every Christian should respect the silence of God's word and no attempt should be made to bind anything upon another which is younger than the New Testament. Inferences drawn from debating and human reasoning, although they may contain many inferential truths, are not to be bound upon the consciences of others due to the fact that there are varying stages of spiritual development among the disciples of Christ.

## HOW TO HAVE UNITY—PRACTICE

Now, how can we have unity from the viewpoint of practice? My brethren, let me here state that this is more than a plea for getting along with each other. I am discussing how to please God Almighty! First, if we are to have unity, we must mortify the flesh. Paul said it is by the Spirit that we put to death the deeds of the flesh (Rom 8:13). We are not to fulfill the lusts of the flesh (Gal 5:16). We are not to walk after the flesh (Rom 8:1, 4). We are not to serve the flesh (Gal 6:7-8).

Since division is a work of the flesh (Gal 5:9-21), we must be delivered from the flesh to have unity.

Second, we must sacrifice worldly wisdom. Many think the church at Corinth was divided because brethren followed men. Really, the Corinthian division was based upon a worldly wisdom which manifested itself in the following of men. In the latter part of First Corinthians one, after having denounced the sin of partisan loyalty to men, Paul discussed the contrast between worldly wisdom and God's wisdom. In chapter two, he defined God's wisdom as Jesus Christ and Him crucified. He then set forth the fact that God's wisdom is revealed by the Holy Spirit. In concluding the chapter, Paul pointed out why the wisdom of God was accepted by some and rejected by others. A good summary of this is found in I Cor 3:18. There, we read: "If any man among you seemeth to be wise in this world, let him become a fool that he may be wise." If one is wise from a worldly point of view, he is a fool in the eyes of God. Such a person ought to give up worldly wisdom. In doing this, he will be a fool to the world and a wise man to God. Obviously, in the light of the first four chapters in First Corinthians, we must give up worldly wisdom to attain the unity we are seeking.

Third, each of us must yield to the Lord Jesus Christ. Paul said, "Other foundation can no man lay than that is laid, which is Jesus Christ" (I Cor 3:11). That statement is written on the front of the Bible Building at Harding College. At Phil. 1:21 Paul said, "For to me to live is Christ." He also declared that we are to have the mind of Christ (Phil 2:5). Alex Proctor wrote: "Put Christ in your temple, and whatever ought not to be there will depart at his bidding. Is your congregation disturbed by the presence of birds or beasts that defile it? Open the door to Him and give Him full possession, for He alone has the power to drive them out. Is the temple of your heart infested with the beasts of selfishness, which show their presence in the works of the flesh? You cannot expel them by your will alone. Put Christ in your temple."

Fourth, the Bible is our guide. Brethren, I am going to spend more time on this point than might be absolutely necessary for our group because I want this material in the book which is to be published. I now believe and always have believed in the plenary, verbal inspiration of the Scriptures. "Inspiration" appears only one time in the New Testament. According to 2 Tim. 3:16, "All scripture is given by inspiration of God." The expression, "inspiration of God" is a translation of the Greek word "theopneustos." It literally means "God breathed." In other words the message of the Bible resulted from God's breathing. He breathed His word into the minds of the inspired writers. They, in turn, faithfully set down upon the sacred pages of the Bible the will of the Almighty.

"Plenary" is from the Latin "plenus" and it means "full." The Scripture is fully, equally and completely inspired of God. *All* Scripture is given by inspiration. According to the American Standard Translation, 2 Tim. 3:16 states that "every scripture inspired of God is also profitable." Personally, I do not believe that is a correct rendition of the verse. "Scripture," as it appears in the New Testament, can always be equated with the word of God. But, if the ASV is correct, there is some uninspired scripture. Incidentally, the new ASV has been corrected so that it now agrees with the King James Version. However, it still carries the old rendition in a footnote.

"Verbal" has to do with words. Peter said, "Know this first, that no prophecy of the scripture is of any private interpretation. For the prophecy came not in the old time by the will of man: but holy men of God spake as they were moved by the Holy Ghost" (2 Pet 1:20-21). B. B. Warfield, that grand old conservative warhorse who taught for so many years at Princeton Theological Seminary, in his classic work *Inspiration and Authority of the Bible*, p. 137, wrote: "The men who spoke from God are here declared, therefore, to have been taken up by the Holy Spirit and brought by His power to the goal of His choosing. The things which they spoke under this operation of the Spirit were therefore His things, not theirs." I Cor 2:12-13 states, "Now we have received, not the spirit of the world, but the spirit which is of God; that we might know the things that are freely given to us of God. Which things also we speak, not in the words which man's wisdom teacheth, but which the Holy Ghost teacheth; comparing spiritual things with spiritual." Weymouth translated I Cor 2:13 this way: "This we also utter, not in language which man's wisdom teaches, but in that which the Spirit teaches, adapting spiritual words to the spiritual truths." Brother J. W. McGarvey, prince of Bible scholars, wrote: "Here again we have a clear claim to inspiration, and not only so, but verbal inspiration. Paul did not reason after the manner of worldly philosophers, but imparted his truth under the guidance of the Spirit, who taught him the words to use, so that he taught spiritual truths with spiritual words, a fitting combination" *(Commentary on Thessalonians, Corinthians, Galatians and Romans,* p. 61). There is one other aspect of Biblical inspiration which needs emphasis at this point. The inspired writers set forth only truth. Jesus said the Spirit would guide them into all truth (Jno. 16:13). That means the New Testament manuscripts were free from all error. The Scriptures are inerrant and infallible.

Here is a definition of inspiration, according to B. B. Warfield: "The church, then has held from the beginning that the Bible is the Word of God in such a sense that its words, though written by men and bearing indelibly impressed upon them the marks of their human origin, were written, nevertheless, under such an influence of the Holy Ghost as to be also the words of God, the adequate expression of His mind and will. It has always recognized that this conception of co-authorship implies that the Spirit's superintendence extends to the choice of the words of the human authors (verbal inspiration), and preserves its product from everything inconsistent with a divine authorship—thus securing, among other things that entire truthfulness which is everywhere presupposed in and asserted for Scripture by the Biblical writers (inerrancy)" *Inspiration and Authority of Bible,* p. 173).

My brethren, this does not mean that any translation is inspired of God. Recently, a brother wrote: "I believe that our King James and American Standard Versions of the Bible are verbally inspired and that they contain the whole counsel of God." H. C. Thiessen, who plainly set forth his belief in the verbal inspiration of the Bible, added: ". . . the definition ascribes inspiration only to the autographs of Holy Scripture. It does not, as some ignorantly suppose, affirm inspiration of any of the existing versions, either modern or ancient . . . It does, however, assert that the original documents, and they alone, were verbally inspired" *(Introduction to the New Testament,* p. 80). We have the inspired message or whole counsel of God. About that, there is no doubt. However, the message has been transmitted to us by uninspired textual critics and translators. Across the years I have heard brethren say that a man can take any translation of the Bible and learn what to do to be saved and how to live the Christian life. Of course, some translations are safer than others. All memory work done by my students at Harding College is based on the ASV, KJV or the RSV. In my judgment, the TEV is rather wild in places. Brother Cogdill, I was delighted to hear you read a passage from the RSV the first night of this meeting. You see, I use the RSV a great deal myself. I have never heard brother Cogdill accused of being a modernist, yet he uses the RSV.

Since the Bible is the verbally inspired message of God, it should be studied. We are to let the word of Christ dwell in us richly (Col 3:16). The word gets into us not by inspiration but by perspiration. The Bible is to be read. Paul said, "Till I come, give attendance to reading, to exhortation, to doctrine" (I Tim 4:13). That refers to the public reading of the Scripture. The word of God is to be preached. Paul taught that since all Scripture is given by inspiration of God, it should be preached (2 Tim 3:16, 4:2). God's word or the truth is to be obeyed (I Pet 1:22-25). The Bible is to be bound as the infallible authority of God for the Scripture cannot be broken (Jno 10:34). The Bible contains all the truth (Jno 16:13). It contains the whole counsel of God (Acts 20:27). It contains all things which pertain to life and godliness (2 Pet 1:3). It thoroughly furnishes us to every good work (2 Tim 3:17). It is the faith once and for all delivered to the saints (Jude 3).

I believe a practice must be authorized by the word of God or be abandoned. We should not be critical of one asking for Bible authority unless he has already proved himself to be a supercilious crank more interested in his own opinions than the word of God. Undenominational Christianity is first and foremost the religion of the Bible and the Bible alone. "To the law and to the testimony: if they speak not according to this word, it is because there is no light in them" (Isa. 8:20). In "The Last Will and Testament of the Springfield Presbytery," a document signed by Barton W. Stone and others, the following appears: "We will, that the people henceforth take the Bible as the only sure guide to heaven; and as many as are offended with other books, which stand in competition with it, may cast them into the fire if they choose; for it is better to enter into life having one book, than having many to be cast into hell." John Garnell wrote: "When a decision must be made between unity and truth, unity must yield to truth; for it is better to be divided by truth than to be united by error. We test the church by the truth, not truth by the church. The apostles judged the Christian community by the norm of divine revelation" *(Religion and Life,* Spring, 1957, p. 195). Alexander Campbell said, "We take the Bible, the whole Bible, and nothing but the Bible, as the foundation of all Christian union and communion. Those who do not like this will please show us a more excellent way" *(Christian System,* p. xvii).

Fifth, we must not bind our opinions upon others. In the apostolic church the Jewish opinion concerning circumcision was not bound upon the Gentiles. It is true that Paul circumcised Timothy as a matter of expediency (Acts 16: 1-3). However, when the Judaizers attempted to make circumcision a matter of faith, Paul refused to be in subjection to them (Gal 2: 3). The letter written under the superintendence of the Holy Spirit and sent to the Gentiles bound only those necessary things upon them. Circumcision was not one of those "necessary things" (Acts 15: 28). Thomas Campbell, in the "Declaration and Address," wrote: "No man can relinquish his opinions or practices till once convinced that they are wrong; and this he may not be immediately, even supposing they were so. One thing, however, he may do: when not bound by an express command, he need not impose them upon others, by anywise requiring their approbation; and when this is done, the things, to them, are as good as dead, yea, as good as buried, too, being thus removed out of the way." Brother Vinson gave an illustration of that a moment ago. The brother who believed in universalism quit expressing his views on the matter and eventually that concept departed from his thinking.

Alexander Campbell wrote: "We were not, indeed, at first apprized of the havoc which our principles would make upon our opinions. We soon, however, found our principles and opinions at war on some points; and the question immediately arose, Whether shall we sacrifice our principles to our opinions, or our opinions to our principles? We need not say that we are compelled to the latter judging that our principles were better than our opinions" *(Christian System,* p. xiii). According to Louis Cochran's report, in his debate with Nathan Rice, Campbell said, "My opponent is confusing religion with theology. A man's essential religion consists of his faith in what is revealed in the New Testament; his theology, on the other hand, consists of his opinions of what is only partly revealed or not revealed at all. I did not come to debate opinions! I am entitled to mine; you are entitled to yours. It is only upon such ground that we can ever achieve Christian unity . . . We preach the Gospel only as promulgated by the Apostles in Jerusalem. We use the exact words of inspiration. We command all men to believe, repent, and bring forth fruits worthy of reformation. It is not the object of our efforts to make men think alike on a thousand themes. Let them think as they like on any matters of human opinion, provided only they hold the head to be Christ, and keep His commandments" *(The Fool of God*, pp. 336-337).

Brethren, we must not attempt to bind even a true opinion upon another. I think Campbell was right when he said, "Our opposition to creeds arose from a conviction that, whether the opinion in them were true or false, they were hostile to the union, peace, harmony, purity and joy of Christians, and adverse to the conversion of the world to Jesus Christ" *(Christian System*, p. xiii).

Let us not bind inferences upon fellow disciples further than they can see them. By inference, I do not mean a necessary inference. As an aside, let me frankly say that I have some difficulty with what is a necessary inference. So many things have been set forth as necessary inferences which to me were not necessarily inferred. Of course, if a matter is necessarily inferred, in the full import of that expression, it is to be bound. If it does not meet this qualification, it is not to be bound. I feel we should seek unamimity even in this area but it must not be forced.

Traditions must not be bound. It is all right to follow a tradition provided it does not conflict with God's revelation and it is not bound upon others as the very word of the Lord. To illustrate, there is no pattern in the New Testament as to what should be said aloud when one is being baptized. For the first few years of my ministry, in baptizing, I simply said, "In the name of the Father, Son and Holy Spirit." One night I heard a man add "for the remission of sins." I thought that sounded good so I began to do the same thing. I am still saying it and will likely continue to do so. However, we have reached the point where some think that "for the remission of sins" must be said over every baptismal candidate or else his baptism is invalid. More than a hundred people were baptized the last night of the Memphis campaign. The brother who did the baptizing did not say the same thing over each person. Can you imagine how boring it would be to hear "in the name of the Father, Son and Holy Spirit and for the remission of sins" more than a hundred times? He used such expressions as "I baptize you into the name of the Father, Son and Holy Spirit," "I baptize you in the name of Jesus Christ for the remission of sins," "I baptize you into the Lord Jesus Christ," etc. After the meeting, one brother seriously suggested that those over whom he had not said "for the remission of sins" ought to be dipped again! One night in El Paso a nervous brother was doing the baptizing. Instead of saying what we normally say, he said, "I baptize you in the name of the Father and the Holy Spirit." Because he left out the word "Son," a brother came to me after the services and said, "He didn't say it right. Do you think we should baptize that one again?" When we baptize, we can say all the Bible says about baptism, we can say a part of what the Bible says about baptism or we can say nothing. The Lord has not told us what to say; He has told us what to do. Ten or twelve years from now I don't want a brother to point a finger in my face and say I am unsound because I don't have the same baptismal formula used by a fellow preacher. A "Church of Christ" tradition bound upon others as the word of God is as obnoxious as anyone else's tradition.

Furthermore, we should be willing to forego expressing an opinion when it gives offense to others. This does not mean it is wrong to express an opinion. We are to refrain from such only when it is offensive to our brethren. We do not have to repudiate the opinion as being sinful to achieve unity. Thomas Campbell discussed this point in the following language: "And here let it be noted, that it is not the renunciation of an opinion or practice as sinful that is proposed or intended, but merely a cessation from the publishing or practicing it, so as to give offense; a thing men are in the habit of doing every day for their private comfort or secular emolument, where the advantage is of infinitely less importance" *(Declaration and Address)*.

We are not to bind an expedient upon others in violation of their consciences. According to Paul, some things which are lawful might not be expedient (I Cor. 6:12). Paul also said, "Wherefore, if meat make my brother to offend, I will eat no flesh while the world standeth, lest I make my brother to offend" (I Cor 8:13). Now, I want to direct our attention to a study of Rom 14:1-15:13. I entitle this section as "Strong and Weak Brethren." First, who were the weak? Those who ate vegetables (14:2), who could not eat meat or drink wine (14:2), and who esteemed one day above another (14:5). That could refer to Jews who esteemed some days above others or it could refer to Gentiles who had scruples about eating certain meats. Second, who were the strong? Those who could eat anything (14:2) and who regarded all days alike (14:5). Third, what was the teaching to the weak? Do not judge your brother for he is the servant of another (14:3-4) and refrain from doing what you think is wrong (14:22-23). Fourth, the instruction to the strong. In essence, Paul said their views were correct (14:14, 20). The strong are not to despise the weak (14:3). The strong must not put a stumbling block in the path of the weak (14:13-16, 20). This does not mean we are to give up something simply because another does not like it. However, we are to sacrifice it if a brother engages in such because of us and violates his conscience in so doing. The strong are urged to keep their faith to themselves (14:22). That, obviously, is not the "faith" which comes by the word of God (Rom. 10:17) for that faith is to be shared with the whole world (Mk. 16:15). "Faith" there refers to one's personal conviction or opinion. In my judgment, the writer was not saying it is wrong to express an opinion to another. In the light of Rom 14:1, it seems that he was saying brethren should not get into verbal warfare about their opinions. The strong brethren were told to bear the infirmities of the weak (15:1). The two reasons given for that point of view are: We are not to please ourselves (15:1), and we are to please Jesus Christ (15:2). Now, the teaching to both groups. Honor the Lord by practice or abstinence (14:6). Pursue peace and edification (14:19). Learn to live in harmony with one another (15:5-6). Receive or welcome one another (15:7). Remember the judgment (14:11-12).

In teaching this material in my Romans class at Harding College, the question always arises as to how to distinguish between a dedicated Christian and a crank. I suppose you brethren have cranks among you as we do. There are three statements in this section which will help us to tell the difference between the two. The devoted child of God is seeking for peace and edification (14:19). He is also striving to please Jesus (15:1-3) and his brethren (15:1-3).

Now, to the application of what has been learned. A moment ago I referred to the meeting we had with the conservative Christian Church brethren in Amarillo. Following our meal together, I said, "Brethren, in the interest of our discussion, I will take the position that I am a weak brother. In the light of Romans, chapters fourteen and fifteen, I ask that you cease using instrumental music in the worship out of respect for my conscience." Here is Dudley Spears. I have known him for almost twenty years. He and I were fellow students at Harding College. We were also the very best of friends. Although Dudley is a member of the other team in these discussions, I can honestly say I love him more than any man on my team. I have prayed for him by name more than for any other man in this room. Let us suppose that Dudley places membership with the college church in Searcy where I am a member. Brethren, what I am about to say I mean with all of my heart. If contributing to Southern Christian Home from the general fund of the church is offensive to Dudley's conscience, I am ready to take up a special collection for that work. One can jump on that box in vestibule idea if he wants to do it but out of deference to Dudley's conscience, I am willing to have the box. I am speaking as only one man but that is my feeling. Of course, if I am willing to do that, he must keep quiet and cause no trouble in the congregation.

Let us bind only what is expressly stated in the word of God. This is what is meant by "Speak where the Bible speaks and remain silent where the Bible is silent." When we argue that something is a matter of faith, we should give a "thus saith the Lord" to uphold our contention. Alexander Campbell and Barton W. Stone were attempting to unite their two groups. They differed on the Godhead. Campbell was a trinitarian and Stone was a monist. Brother Stone held about the same view concerning the Godhead as is held by the oneness Holiness people today. The two of them had some controversy. It looked as though the two groups would not be united. Brother Raccoon John Smith, although not as learned as Campbell and Stone, was the master of the occasion. He said. "Brethren, let us speak the language of the Scripture." Obviously, neither a trinitarian nor a monist is going to be offended if only scriptural language is used in reference to God. Smith's advice was accepted and Campbell and Stone were united.

Last year I was invited to conduct a cooperative tent meeting in northern Arkansas. One of the finest churches in the area was asked to participate in that effort, however, the leaders of the congregation were not sure of my views concerning the Holy Spirit so they asked me to meet with them for a discussion of the matter. For about three hours I was grilled by those brethren. Finally, one of them asked, "Jim, are you willing to conduct the meeting and not set forth your views on the Holy Spirit?" In reply, I said, "Brethren, I am willing to do the preaching and use only the language of the Scripture concerning the Holy Spirit." The preacher for that church stood and said. "Brother Allen, that won't work. When a Baptist preacher quotes John 3:16 we all know what he means by it. When you quote the passages on the Holy Spirit we will understand what you mean by them." I said, "If a Baptist doesn't do anything but quote John 3:16, I will amen it." I added, "Brethren, you have tied my hands so that I can't even refer to the Holy Spirit in the language of the Bible! Surely, I couldn't work with you under such circumstances."

What I am advocating will mean a unity in diversity. We will have unity in faith (i.e. what is expressly stated in the word of God) and diversity in opinion. Such was done in the apostolic church concerning the taking of vows. Paul took a vow at Cenchrea and Jerusalem (Acts 18:18; 21:17-26). Paul said, "For though I be free from all men, yet have I made myself servant unto all, that I might gain the more. And unto the Jews I became as a Jew, that I might gain the Jews; to them that are under the law, as under the law, that I might gain them that are under the law; To them that are without law, as without law, (being not without law to God, but under the law to Christ,) that I might gain them that are without law. To the weak became I as weak, that I might gain the weak: I am made all things to all men, that I might by all means save some. And this I do for the gospel's sake, that I might be partaker thereof with you" (I Cor 9:19-23). Paul never compromised the faith but in matters of opinion he made adjustments to fit differing situations.

In some areas, we have been perfectly willing to practice that for which I am now contending. Take the question of the indwelling of the Holy Spirit, for example. There are three distinct positions advocated on this subject by men who are members of my team in these discussions. Reuel Lemmons and Buster Dobbs hold a position to which I do not subscribe. Brother Gus Nichols has a view which differs only slightly from the one I hold. The point of view advocated by brother J. D. Thomas in his *Firm Foundation* series is the one which I believe is in harmony with Biblical teaching. Although we have three different positions, we love one another and intend to maintain our unity and fellowship.

Consider the war question as another example. Although I have been in the armed forces and would be willing to serve as a medic now, I cannot conscientiously take human life for my country in time of war. The men on my team do not all share my conviction, however, we are not advocating division on the matter. I imagine you brethren on the other team are also divided in sentiment concerning a Christian's responsibility to his government.

Now, getting to an issue which is more pertinent to our discussion. Brethren Lemmons and Lanier believe that a children's home must be under an eldership to be scriptural. I don't hold that position. I think a home under elders is scriptural. I also believe a home under a board is scriptural. The church where I have membership sends a monthly donation to Southern Christian Home which is directed by a board. Reuel and brother Lanier believe this arrangement is an improper one, however, neither of them have drawn lines of fellowship against me. Of course, I haven't drawn any lines of fellowship against them. You brethren on the other team are divided on the question of saints only. You may feel otherwise, but from my point of view, all of the talk about homes and organizations is beside the point. The church in my part of the country, organizationally speaking, is today precisely what it was in 1949 when I became a Christian. We have elders, deacons, evangelists, teachers and members. The organization of the local church has not changed one iota. If I am wrong in what I am doing, it is not in church organization; it is simply a misappropriation of funds. Now, you brethren differ on this question of saints only. I am not trying to drive the shaft of division deeper between you, as God is my witness. If you are wrong in helping non-Christian people from the church treasury, you are simply misappropriating funds. If you can fellowship one another when some of you are misappropriating funds, why can't you fellowship us although we misappropriate funds? If you can't do this, please explain why. I want to know why it can't be done! You might say that Reuel is inconsistent in his treatment of me. Well, he must either be inconsistent or initiate another division in the body of Christ. Which is worse? Foolish consistency is a hobgoblin of little minds. Brethren, I am inconsistent with myself. I think you probably have a similar difficulty. I have listened to you talk for the past three days. I have tried to understand each of you, however, a lot of the intricate reasoning which has taken place has lost me. Imagine going to the jungles of Africa to teach a savage what has been said during this meeting! If the gospel of our Lord is that complicated, he could never become a child of God. He wouldn't be able to see it. Brethren, we are involved in a lot of stuff that just isn't in the gospel.

What I am upholding will also mean less debating among brethren. We have emphasized the good in debating. We have talked about how the truth shines more brightly when rubbed. All of this is true but we have failed to say that debating builds parties. That means if we engage in debate the resulting parties must be essential to our pleasing God. Paul taught that we are not to strive about words to no profit which subvert hearers (2 Tim 2:14). In "The Last Will and Testament of the Springfield Presbytery," I read: "We will, that preachers and people, cultivate a spirit of mutual forbearance; pray more and dispute less . . ." In his debate with Rice, Campbell said, "I have learned not only the theory but the fact, that if you wish opinionism to cease, you must not call up and debate everything that men think or say. You may debate anything into consequence, or you may, by a dignified silence, waste it into oblivion" *(Fool of God,* p. 337). Public debate is not the way to handle every problem which arises among us. Sometimes great good is accomplished by saying, "Let's not talk about it." One can talk himself into feeling badly. In some instances we can debate ourselves into nonessential divisions. There are matters which ought not to be debated.

The advice I have offered tonight is difficult because most of us are opinionated. I have heard film strip and slides knocked. I have heard criticism of prayer cells. Some have hit the ceiling because others are using the word "witness." Incidentally, that word is sometimes used in the original language concerning the giving of testimony. It does not always mean "eye witness." Church buildings, promotion of meetings and a hundred other things have been criticized by our people. Naturally, it is all right for one to have opinions on all these things, however, we must learn to keep our mouths shut about personal opinions if we want to have the unity for which Jesus prayed. The one who is overly critical of all opinions which differ with his is possessed with the spirit which eventually leads to factionalism. A factionist is basically an opinionated person. The root meaning of heresy has to do with the making of a choice. It is all right to make a choice or to have an opinion but when we begin to press it upon others as God's truth, we become heretics. A factionist is a grievous sinner (Tit 3:10).

In the sixth place, we must love the brotherhood (I Pet 2: 17). Paul wrote: "Charity suffereth long, and is kind; charity envieth not; charity vaunteth not itself, is not puffed up, Doth not behave itself unseemly, seeketh not her own, is not easily provoked, thinketh no evil; rejoiceth not in iniquity, but rejoiceth in the truth; Beareth all things, believeth all things, hopeth all things, endureth all things" (I Cor. 13:4-7). We, then, are to be patient, kind, generous, humble, polite, unselfish, even-tempered, believing and optimistic toward one another.

Brother Vinson made some applications of these principles a moment ago. I will now add a few more. First, if we love one another, we must learn the meaning of tolerance. Our problem has to do with the tension between truth and tolerance. Every mean, evil, ungodly thing under the sun has been committed in the name of soundness. People have been tortured, put on the rack and burned at the stake by those who based their actions on supposed loyalty to truth. Some feel they are extremely tolerant toward people with whom they differ, yet, if the truth were known, they just don't have any real conviction. It is easy to tolerate others when you are indifferent concerning their beliefs. It is difficult to be tolerant toward others while deeply and strongly differing with them. However, we must learn this art. Thomas Campbell felt that where there is the least amount of difference, there is sometimes the greatest vehemence. Consider how mean some of us have been in debating. I am not trying to single out anyone here. I used to do a little debating and what a struggle I had with my flesh during those discussions. I made a public apology to a Baptist preacher one night because I felt I had mistreated him.

Second, if we love the brotherhood, we must cease our misrepresentation of each other. I have heard brethren, who believe as I do about orphan homes, say of you, "They just don't care anything about orphans." Brethren, I don't believe that about you. I have never believed it. However, some who stand identified with you, in describing us, have said, "They have gone liberal and abandoned the Bible as their authority." Now, that doesn't fairly describe me or any man on my team. Let us cease such misrepresentation.

Third, we need to get out of the witch hunting business. Love is not suspicious. It is all right to collect material in preparation for debate, but how about the man who keeps a file on others in the hope of being able to find something with which to destroy them? I don't have a file on any of you. God just didn't make a scavenger of me. A spirit like that would destroy me. I cannot be constantly looking for a failure or weakness in the life of another.

Listen to this carefully. The other night, about three in the morning, I was awakened from my sleep by a voice which said, "Get out of bed, put on your clothes and drive to the airport." I got out of bed, put on my clothes, drove to the airport and met a Christian who needed a ride to Searcy. Oh, I failed to tell you that the voice I heard came to me over the telephone! Brethren, be honest, how many of you began to wonder if I was off my rocker? Did you have the idea that the Holiness had taken full control of me? What was the first thing to hit you? Did you give me the benefit of the doubt? I have made it a point across the years to never believe a bad story about a fellow preacher until forced by the facts to accept it as true. Why? Because I have had so many lies told on me. Furthermore, if it is true that a brother minister has grievously sinned, I should not be happy about it. Love doesn't rejoice in iniquity. My heart should be broken because he was overtaken in a fault.

Fourth, love demands that we learn the art of personal communication. According to Matt 18:15-17, we are to talk to one another about our differences. Some circumvent that by saying, "Since he said it publicly, I have the right to deal with it in the same way." Sometimes what was reported as having been said publicly wasn't said at all. I have seen things attributed to me in the newspapers which I never said. With all due respect to the members of the Fourth Estate, I must say that some reporters are more interested in a story than the facts. Why not get in touch with another rather than rushing into print without contacting him? If you find a statement which looks bad to you, write the brother and ask for his explanation. Surely, that is the least we can do.

Fifth, if we love one another, it would seem that we could do some crossing of party lines. Thomas Campbell wrote: "Until you associate, consult, and advise together, and in a friendly and Christian manner explore the subject, nothing can be done. We would therefore, with all due deference and submission, call the attention of our brethren to the obvious duty of association" *(Declaration and Address)*. Party lines must be crossed before they can be abolished. Otherwise, we are simply talking to ourselves. "Come, let us reason together" (Isa 1:18) has application for us today. We have done some crossing of party lines in this meeting. None of us has compromised what he believes the word of God to teach.

Some men have been criticized for engaging in dialogue. Personally, I think I can engage in dialogue with anyone without compromising God's truth. Others are criticized for speaking in denominational churches. Paul spoke in the synagogues. Restoration leaders spoke for sectarian groups. I have held two meetings for inter-denominational churches. In each instance I was invited. I asked that instrumental music not be used and that I not be restricted concerning my preaching. Those conditions were met. In those meetings, I didn't blast the people out of the house the first, second and third nights. However, before the efforts concluded, I discussed faith, repentance, baptism and the New Testament church. Eight men were baptized in one of those meetings. There were three responses in the other one. Surely, we can do some crossing of party lines without knocking one another cold and without compromising the word of the Lord.

Let us emphasize our areas of agreement. We are 99% in agreement. It is that one percent which is dealing us the difficulty. Let us seek to please one another (I Cor. 10:33). But, one will say, "We are to please the Lord." Of course, that is right (Gal 1:6-12). However, to please the Lord, I must please my brother for that is what the Lord teaches. In our past discussions we have simply overlooked this truth. Can't we implement the Bible teaching about pleasing one another? Let us pray for unity among the brethren. I haven't really prayed for unity until the past few weeks. When I began working on this assignment, it dawned on me that I should begin praying about our divided condition. May God help us to somehow resolve our differences.

A long time ago, J. H. Garrison wrote: "Alas! how few of us have the faith, the patience, the love of truth and the forbearance to treat with proper respect the man who dares to differ from us! Than this there is scarcely any greater obstacle to the ascertainment of truth. Let us hear with patience and with brotherly respect the honest convictions of everyone who believes he has a new truth, or a new view of an old truth, to communicate to us . . . This is not to be lenient to error, it is to be loyal to truth. Have we the catholicity of spirit, the love of truth, and the moral heroism and independence, to face the new and living questions of our day, in the same untrammeled way our reformatory fathers faced the questions of their day? On our ability to bear this supreme test, depends the question as to whether ours shall be a living and progressive Reformation, or a mere crystallization of past achievements" *(Historical Documents Advocating Christian Union,* pp. 363-364).

Oh, God, speed the day when thy people will be one.

## How to Attain and Maintain Fellowship

### Franklin T. Puckett

Before I begin my remarks I should like to join with others in expressing appreciation for having been invited to participate in these deliberations. I want all of you with whom I have had little or no contact before to know I am grateful for the privilege of becoming acquainted with you. I shall have a different feeling, perhaps not so much toward your position, but toward you as a result of these associations together. It has been good to be here and I truly hope nothing I have said before and nothing I shall say now will in any way be a hindrance to the development of true Christian unity. It is difficult for me to decide what I want to say in this last speech. After I get home no doubt I shall think of many things I should have said and some things I should not have said, but then it will be too late to do anything about it.

Last night brother Starling asked me to make a list of some areas of agreement where we stand on common ground and from which we can move toward the resolution of our differences. There may be more things on which we agree than I

FRANKLIN T. PUCKETT—*Writer; debater; well known evangelist — presently working with a congregation in Florence, Alabama; formerly special Bible lecturer in Florida College, conducts numerous meetings yearly throughout the nation.*

have listed, but I think all who are here will agree on the following propositions:
(1) The Bible is a verbally inspired revelation of God's will for men.
(2) Biblical authority must be established for our faith and practice in all religious matters.
(3) Such Biblical authority is established by express command or precise statement, approved example, or necessary inference.
(4) Unity is both desirable and essential and we should labor diligently to attain and maintain it.
(5) I am confident we would all agree with the motto of the Restoration Movement: "In faith, unity; in opinion, liberty; and in all things, love." Our problem lies in the application of this rule.
(6) We all agree on the importance and necessity of preaching the gospel both at home and abroad.
(7) We agree that Christians have a responsibility to provide for and take care of destitute people, and especially those "who are of the household of faith."
(8) In view of the grave differences between us, I believe all will agree there is need for greater communication between us, more diligent study of the issues before us, and more fair, honorable, and objective discussion of the things that divide us.

We disagree on what the Bible teaches concerning the work of individual Christians and local congregations, but we agree that what is done must be authorized by the Bible. Here we have a foundation on which to build. Since all recognize the Bible is the standard of authority, it now remains for us to settle down to the task of finding out exactly what it authorizes. We agree that Biblical authority can only be established by express command, approved example, or necessary inference, but we disagree on what constitutes a binding example and on what inferences are necessarily and logically drawn. Here are areas in which much work must be done before we can have unity. The discussion between brethren Cogdill and Thomas on how to establish Biblical authority was certainly in order and a correct understanding and common agreement on this matter is essential to reconciling of the issues that divide us. By Scriptural truth and logical deduction we must learn where that "wavy line" should be drawn in order to determine what is authorized. As we seek to know God's will, all must adhere tenaciously to the divine injunction: "If any man speak, let him speak as the oracles of God." (1 Pet. 4:11). The old motto: "Where the Bible speaks, we speak; where the Bible is silent, we are silent!" is still worthy of all acceptance.

Furthermore, we should be fair and honorable in our dealings with one another. I am not too surprised that division has come, but I am surprised at the rapidity with which it developed and the bitterness that has sometimes characterized it. I suspect that all of us will admit some things have been wrongly said and done by brethren on both sides of this controversy. These have contributed to widening the gap between us instead of closing the breach. Sometime cutting wounds have been needlessly given when the oil of healing should have been tenderly applied.

Unfounded accusations and blanket charges should be avoided. A position assumed and advocated by certain ones does not necessarily represent the thinking of an entire group. It is evident that there are diverse views to be found in each group here today. It would be unfair for me to take a particular position of any one of you and charge that same position against all of you. It is equally unfair for you to take some extreme statement or unfounded conclusion made by someone opposed to your institutional practices and charge that this same extreme position is held by all of us. I am no more responsible for or obligated to defend every extreme position and radical conclusion assumed by some individual among us than you are responsible for and obligated to defend every social concept and promotional scheme hatched out by some loose-thinking modernist among you. On the other hand, the fact that all do not hold a certain position does not mean that none hold it. Consequently, a position may and should be dealt with, but no one should be charged with holding that position unless he avows or acquiescently approves it. If by word or deed one gives endorsement to a false position, he may be correctly charged with it and should not feel he is being mistreated when he is challenged concerning it.

Since we have assembled here some of you have said, "Do not charge us with preaching the social gospel." Now, I do not charge you with holding to the social gospel since you deny it, but there are brethren among you, endorsed and used by churches of Christ, who certainly have embraced whole-heartedly the basic concepts underlying that philosophy. Because some hold to the principles of the social gospel, you think it would be unfair of me to make a blanket charge that all of you do. So, while I stand unalterably opposed to the social gospel philosophy, I should charge as guilty of advocating that system only those who teach it or bid God speed to it. Some have said, "Do not charge us with denying the necessity for Scriptural authority in religious matters." We differ on what is authorized by the Scriptures, but you think it unfair for someone to make the blanket charge that you do not believe there is need for Scriptural authority. Our difference then is over what is authorized rather than over the necessity of authority. Again it has been said, "Do not charge us with holding and endorsing all the views and practices which are developing among us." You do not want to be held responsible for all the extreme positions and way-out schemes of others. I do not blame you, but I would like to hear you speak out against them.

Brethren, I think it is just as unfair for you or those with whom you stand associated to charge me and my brethren with being law makers and trying to bind our opinions on others because we challenge the Scripturalness of some things you practice. All I want is the Scripture clearly and logically set forth which teaches you to do the things you are doing. If I know my own heart, I am as far from wanting to make a law for God's people as any of you. I only want to preach and practice what the Bible teaches and I do not want to preach or practice anything it does not teach. Insofar as I am able to discern it, I want and intend to have scriptural authority for what I believe and practice. Beyond that I do not intend knowingly to go. You may think I have reached a conclusion and made an application which in your judgment is unfounded, but I assure you it has not been my intention or purpose to make a law for or to bind anything upon anybody! As a matter of fact I do not try to force even the truth on anybody. I preach that which I believe to be the truth and condemn that which I believe to be wrong, but I do not try to force anything on anybody. To the extent that what I preach is the truth, the Lord will require it of everybody, but to the extent that what I preach is personal opinion, it is bound upon nobody. It is left entirely with each hearer to decide for himself in the light of what he can read in the Bible whether what I preach is truth or not. This is not legislating for the Lord or binding opinions upon men. If I am in error, show me by the word of the Lord where I am wrong and it will be appreciated, but do not make the unfounded and prejudicial charge that I seek to make laws where God has not legislated and to bind my personal opinions where He has not bound. It is not so! Such a charge impugns my motives and reflects upon my character. This I resent!

Though we disagree, we should refrain from making derogatory remarks about each other which reflect against the honesty, honor, or sincerity of one another. Name calling and title giving contribute nothing toward a better understanding. My brethren and I have been derogatorily dubbed "Antis" by some of you. The term "anti" simply means against. I confess there are a number of things which I believe to be wrong, and concerning those things, it can be correctly said that I am anti such things. But, brethren, you also are opposed to certain things, and concerning those things you are anti. So, in this sense we can all be designated "antis." When, however, the term "anti" is used without further definition and as a term of reproach belittling those to whom it is applied, such use is slanderous and contributes to further alienation. This is the use at least some brethren make of it when they apply it to us.

Some time ago I read an article which was entitled " 'Antis' of the Testament." It began as follows: "It is declared by those that decry the term 'Anti' which carries a mark of infamy, that Paul and Barnabas were 'Anti' when opposing doctrines of error as in Acts 15 where they contended with Judaizing teachers. The proper use of the term 'Anti' as used today does not carry the idea of being opposed to error as these brethren would have us to believe, but rather is attached to those who oppose Truth." *(Childhaven News,* May 1962, Vol. 12, No. 8, p. 1) These brethren say that "Anti" is a "mark of infamy" and "attached to those who oppose the Truth." This is what they mean by it today. When these brethren call us "Antis" they certainly do not mean to correctly identify us, but rather to belittle us and to pin upon us the badge of infamy. Look up the definition of infamy. I do not charge that everyone applying the term to us is so motivated, but these brethren are and have so stated.

This kind of spirit is no different from that of rabid denominationalists who find themselves unable to uphold their position by the word of God and seek to cover up their failure by calling us "Campbellites!" In this way they hope to attach some kind of stigma so that people will not listen to anything we have to say. The argument runs like this: "These people are 'Campbellites,' and a 'Campbellite' is someone who is bad, so, do not have anything to do with 'Campbellites.' Do not believe anything these people say and do not even let them be heard!" No effort is made to prove the charge, but they can close doors of opportunity against us by their implications and insinuations. This is the same device used by the Catholics when they seek to destroy those who oppose their schemes. Instead of furnishing Scriptural authority for their practices, or ceasing their practices when they are unable to do so, they endeavor to destroy all opposition by charging those who oppose them with "bigotry." "That man is a bigot, and a bigot is someone bad, so, do not pay any attention to anything he has to say." Instead of meeting you fairly, they shoot you down by calling you a prejudicial name. This is an argument (?) that cannot be answered with Scripture, reason, or logic. The door is closed before you can present your side of the issue. This same tactic was employed by our brethren a hundred years ago when those who wanted Scriptural authority for the Missionary Society and instrumental music were dubbed "non-progressives, church-splitters," etc. I charge that it is the same tactic and motivated by the same spirit when you brethren prejudice people against us by naming us "Antis." I do not object to being designated anti with proper definition of what I am against, but I resent being named "Anti" as a "term of reproach," "a badge of infamy," and "an opposer of truth." Of course the same principles will apply to me and to those with whom I stand identified. We have no right to use derogatory names and terms of reproach to belittle and vilify you. This is not a one-way street. We have no right to ask you to be more charitable or respectful in such matters than we are. All of us should manifest a better spirit than that of name calling, bitter denunciation, slanderous vilification, etc., etc. I hope we can all do a little better.

Now I have some questions in my mind which have not been answered to my satisfaction. I am still unable to justify by the word of God some of the things you brethren are doing. Until it can be shown by the Scriptures that these things are right, I cannot conscientiously endorse them. However, I am willing to listen. If you can present God's word showing they are divinely authorized, I will accept them.

What about drawing lines of fellowship? Who is responsible for it? It has been said, "Disagree with us if you must, but do not draw lines of fellowship." Brethren, I am confident some things have been done on both sides of these issues which should not have been done, but as to who has been drawing lines of fellowship over these matters, all of us can do a little talking. I have a file full of letters canceling meetings for no reason in the world except that I do not endorse your benevolent institutions and sponsoring church arrangements—arrangements which you yourselves say are matters of judgment and optional expedients. Now, who is pressing opinions to the point of division? I did not cancel the meetings. Your brethren canceled them over your optional expedients. If you want to get into that kind of thing, I can present numbers of instances where people drew lines of fellowship on me, and I doubt not that others can do the same thing.

I held a meeting at a place some years ago where certain preachers tried to get the meeting canceled. Failing in this, they or their friends were on the grounds every night trying to persuade people not to attend. They had that little church so confused and disturbed they did not know what to do. The people in whose home I was to have stayed were told no one would have anything to do with them if they kept me. Under this pressure they withdrew the invitation, but later told me the whole story. I held the meeting, but never did unpack my car. I did not know from night to night what was going to happen. Probably many of you have had similar experiences. When it comes to drawing lines of fellowship, do not imply that it has all been our side. You have been doing a lot of it yourselves. I suspect a little patience, fairness, and tolerance on the part of all of us while diligently searching the Scriptures to see what is taught on these issues might have saved many a congregation from division.

Who caused the division? The answer to that question is going to depend on who is right. If what you brethren teach and practice is right, then, our objections are groundless and we are responsible for the division that has come as a direct consequence of them. On the other hand, if our objections are valid and you cannot furnish Scriptural authority for your teaching and practice, you are responsible for the division because of your innovations. Who is right will be determined by what the Scriptures teach and God will be the judge. What is right will not be determined by human judgment, brotherhood practice, ancient custom, or longstanding tradition, but by what is revealed in God's book. To the law and the testimony let us go that we may see what is taught therein.

We have been charged with failing to agree among ourselves. Well, we do have some differences among us on some points, but does that prove us wrong on the issues before us? You also are seriously divided among yourselves on many points as can be seen right here. For you to make an argument along this line will do you no good, for the accusations made against us fly right back to perch on your shoulders. I have not always agreed with my brethren on every argument made or conclusion drawn, but in the overall picture I think we are pretty well united. I am not a party man lining up with whatever seems to be the consensus of opinion. I reserve the right to think for myself and grant the same privilege unto others. Consequently, we may find ourselves in disagreement on some particular point, but completely in agreement on the conclusions drawn.

For example, I believe the benevolent activities of the local church as a church are limited in scope. I have never read in the word of God where local churches were authorized either by precept, example, or necessary inference, to use funds from their treasuries to render benevolent aid to anybody other than saints. And, if I may say so, I do not believe you have ever read it in the Bible either. I must confess, however, that I have a little different view from some of my brethren concerning the meaning and possible application of the word translated saint. I believe that the word *hagios*, when used with reference to people, may be applied to those who are "pure," "consecrated," "sanctified," and "devoted to God." With this view, I have believed that a local church may under proper circumstances render benevolent aid to a destitute, innocent child who is certainly "clean," "pure," "set apart," and "devoted to God." This does not mean, however, that a local church becomes responsible for the care of destitute orphan children everywhere anymore than it is responsible for the relief of destitute members of the church everywhere. The same circumstances that limit one will also limit the other. In no sense is a local congregation authorized to get into the field of general benevolence. Both the people served and the scope of the operation are limited to the local church in the fulfillment of its responsibility. My position in no way lends approval to the creation and maintenance of these institutional benevolent homes involved in our discussions nor to the position you brethren hold. So, while there may be minor differences among us on some points, there is general agreement on the pattern of local church responsibility. We are agreed that the benevolent aid given from local church treasuries was to saints, or "holy ones," and I do not believe you can find in the Bible where such funds were ever used for anyone else. Now, we as individual Christians may relieve anyone as we have opportunity (Gal. 6:10), and if we will fulfill our personal duty and quit trying to pitch everything off on the church there will be no need of going beyond the divinely revealed pattern.

Furthermore, there may be some different viewpoints concerning this so-called "two-pattern" business. I have never taken the position that under no circumstances could one local church give aid to another local church in a matter that might be classified as evangelism. But in the New Testament when New Testament churches supported New Testament preachers, they sent that support directly to the preachers (2 Cor. 11:8, 9; Phil. 4:10-18). I know it is safe to do it this way. And as old brother Benjamin Franklin used to say: "It would be strikingly strange if that which is infallibly safe was not also infallibly right." I want to be both right and safe, so I propose to do it that way. Now, if some poor, destitute church is unable to provide for its own use New Testaments or songbooks, I believe that another local church could provide it with these necessities. These things provided might be used in a program of evangelism and edification. Someone says, "You have admitted that one church can help another church in evangelism, and if one church can do it, many churches can do it, therefore, many churches can pool their resources under the eldership of a sponsoring church and let them oversee a great program of general evangelism. Now we can have our area-wide campaigns, our nation-wide mail programs, and our world-wide TV and radio shows provided they are under a sponsoring church." Now really, brethren, does all this logically follow? It is argued that if we allow one church to send another church a New Testament, it follows that we must also allow all these sponsoring church progams, but if we deny that these sponsoring church programs are Scriptural, we must oppose one church sending another church a New Testament under any circumstances. That just is not so!!

The help given in the case mentioned was to supply the need of a destitute church. The need was local and genuine, and when the need was supplied the assistance ceased. While the materials might be used in evangelism, they were sent to supply a need resulting from destitution. The assistance given was in reality benevolence bestowed. To be parallel with these sponsoring church arrangements, the receiving church would not be in need of New Testaments and songbooks at all. It could buy all that it needed for its own use, but it would assume the role of collecting funds from contributing churches so that it could oversee an area-wide, or nation-wide, or world-wide program of furnishing Bibles and songbooks to other destitute churches. Thus it would become the distributing agent of the contributing churches going between them and the receiving churches who are in need. For this kind of arrangement there is no divine authority. I have never found in the word of God where a multiplicity of churches ever pooled their resources under a centralized oversight, whether that oversight was composed of the elders of a sponsoring church or of a board made up of representatives of many churches, to do a work of any kind which was common to all the churches involved, whether that work be in the field of evangelism, edification or benevolence. I have found where a church, or churches, assisted another church in fulfilling its own responsibility and meeting its own need. This I endorse and support. But I have not found where a church, or churches, turned their funds over to a sponsoring church for it to oversee in the expediting a general program of any kind. Until such an arrangement is established by the word of God, I cannot accept or endorse it.

There are a lot of other things I would like to say, but my time is about up. Brother Bill Humble and I have been good friends for many years. I recognize and appreciate him as one of the finest students of the Restoration Movement among us.

With reference to his use of Campbell's Rule of Ambiguity and Examples, may I quote another well established rule of Biblical interpretation and application: "No important teaching or practice is to be based upon doubtful or ambiguous Scriptures." (Dr. Carroll Kendrick, *Rules of Bible Study*, Ch. IX, p. 90). I do not believe, however, that all Bible examples are quite as ambiguous as has been suggested. I appreciate having had the opportunity of speaking to you, and I sincerely hope something good can come from all of this.

## How to Attain and Maintain Fellowship

Eldred Stevens

This week has certainly been a mountain-peak experience. I shall never forget it. There is probably nobody here that is more interested in the subject we have for consideration this morning than I. The love that I have for the church is great and the grief that I suffer because of the division that has occurred among us, the ill will that has developed, is almost unbearable. When I see brethren whom I have loved as dearly as I have loved some of you and realize that you regard me as unworthy of fellowship or at least a bad influence in the church, and when I see families, some of the most wonderful families on the face of God's earth, torn asunder by the questions we have talked about here, it literally cuts my heart out. Nobody is more interested in the subject we have under consideration and yet none of you, I suppose, feels as poorly qualified to speak. Nonetheless, I do want to say a few things this morning.

May I first suggest that we must never forget that divisions have always existed among us and that they always will

ELDRED STEVENS—*Evangelist for the Preston Road congregation in Dallas, Texas; formerly teacher of Bible in Oklahoma State University. Former preacher of College congregation, David Lipscomb, Nashville, Tennessee and Southside in Fort Worth, Texas.*

exist among us. The idea of rigid regimentation, of a non-varying uniformity, is a sort of a foolish pipe dream. Such uniformity could not be maintained during the time of the inspired apostles of Jesus Christ; it cannot be maintained in our day. We need to be realistic enough to face this fact. Perhaps we are. However, many of us are such idealists and romanticists that we can envision a quality of uniformity and regimentation that just is beyond the realm of reasonable possibility. In the first century there were many divisions that existed, and they involved problems, I feel, that were more serious than many of the things we have talked about here this week. I know that you will regard many of those things as matters of opinion or of indifference and would not classify them with the problems we have discussed here. However, I am reasonably sure that in their setting and among the people involved they were as serious as any question that has entered our consideration this week.

I think, for instance, of such things as the question of circumcision among the churches of the first century. I think of such things as the eating of meat considered "unclean", and the eating of meats that had been sacrificed to idols as discussed in I Corinthians 8. You reply that all these were matters of indifference, matters of opinion. Well, a large segment of people would classify the bulk of the things that we have argued about this week in the same way. Is it possible that they could be? Consider Paul's discussion of the keeping of days in Romans 14. We recall also the apostle Paul's visit to Jerusalem and the concessions, it seems to me, that he made in connection with the keeping of parts of the law. I've always been somewhat disturbed about that, as I suspect many of you have been. Recall the statement that was made to him by the elders of the church at Jerusalem urging him to do certain things to show that he walked orderly and kept the law. We also think of the divisions over preachers in the first century, over questions about the resurrection of the dead as discussed in I Corinthians 15, over the wearing of the covering in I Corinthians 11, over the observance of the Lord's Supper, and over the order of public worship as discussed in I Corinthians 14.

On and on we might go in mentioning such things. These are recalled for two reasons. The first is to argue realistically that since such divisions existed then, we're going to have our differences now. Human personality is such that there is no way on this earth to make everyone of us goose-step just exactly alike and have identical convictions and feelings about all of those matters and/or the matters that we have discussed this week. There is no way for this to be done, I honestly believe.

My second reason is sort of a confession. I had a debate with a Catholic priest some years ago. I studied then as I have never studied before or since because I was afraid. I read volume after volume of Catholic literature in which authors sought to establish what they conceive to be the inadequacy of the scriptures as an authority in religion, and the necessity for an infallible interpreter in religion. They parade page after page of historical division in an effort to show that men cannot understand the Bible and that thus the idea of using the Bible alone as the supreme court in religion is the height of folly. I never did believe it but let me tell you, brethren I definitely was pushed to face some historical and practical facts. I came to feel that if I must convince everybody on this earth that he has to agree with me on all details, I'll just never make it! I definitely had my views with reference to some of these things changed at that time. Maybe I should make public acknowledgement of this! I guess I do.

Before leaving my reference to the debate, may I venture one other observation concerning fellowship. I don't know why it is, brethren, that when we get to fighting among ourselves, we devour one another and have uglier feelings toward one another than we do toward anybody else on this earth. During that debate the Catholic priest said that one of my preaching brethren had called him on the telephone during the day and had suggested that since I claimed that the scriptures contain all authority, I should be asked for scriptural authority for using women to teach Bible classes. Now, imagine a Christian brother having more fellowship in the cause of a Catholic priest than that of a brother who disagreed with him! I say that to suggest that some of the feelings that we allow to develop in our own hearts toward our own people are more vicious than those we have toward anybody else on this earth. Brethren, these things ought not so to be! This can be explained psychologically but I know these things ought not to be.

We had divisions then in the first century and we have had many more since. I jotted down once a list of things that seemed to me to be serious questions about which we have had major controversy through the years. I had almost 100 items on that list. Many of those items in my judgment are fully as serious if not more serious than anything we have talked about during these three days. Yet we have somehow or other managed to maintain a feeling of fellowship and have stayed within the general boundaries of what we consider a single fellowship. Now why, oh why do these current questions have to be magnified out of what I conceive to be reasonable proportions and made tests of fellowship? Please don't think I am rebuking here only those who oppose cooperative work or orphans homes. When I speak of such things I am talking to all of us. I have said many times, brethren, and I am glad to say this to you publicly, that I think I know of as many churches, if not more, that have been split by "anti-antis" (pardon such!) as have been split by "antis." I have said that I have seen as much viciousness and as many ugly spirits displayed on the part of those who agree with me as I have on the part of others. So it isn't a matter of trying to be ugly with my charges here.

My time is getting away from me—too rapidly. In thinking about these issues, I have jotted down about twenty principles to keep constantly before me in guiding my own thinking in the confusion that exists among us today. Let me mention some of these quickly. (1) We must never forget that the scriptures furnish us completely unto every good work (2 Timothy 3:16-17). (2) We must never forget that there are only four means of establishing the scripturalness of any doctrine or practice. Those have been already mentioned. (3) We must never forget that there is a realm of expediency, a realm of opinion or of liberty, in which we must tolerate great variations of practice (Romans 14:2-6). (4) We must never bind where the Lord loosed, and never loose where the Lord bound. (5) We must always be conscious of the danger in *trends* (Genesis 13:12). Nobody here is more conscious of that than I am. I've studied too much of early church history not to be. We must not pitch our tents toward Sodom. (6) We must always remember the lessons of history. We must keep ourselves informed about historical data which show what has happened in the past and remember that that which has been probably will be (Ecclesiastes 1:9). (7) We must never be pollyannas who stick their heads in the sand, so determined to see no evil, hear no evil, speak no evil that in their judgment everything is good and the negative note is never to be raised. (8) We must always remember the danger of attachment to *tradition* (Matthew 15:3, 6). (9) We must always guard against the tendency to want to be like the nations round about us (I Samuel 8:5), copying the things of the world. (10) We must constantly guard against the tendency to think that the Lord did not set up His organization in a way that will work as efficiently as something else of our own making. We must never try to improve the Lord's arrangement (2 Samuel 6:7). (11) We must always exalt and make glorious the church of Jesus Christ, the body of our Lord (Ephesians 3:21). I don't like to see the church covered up as I think it is by some of the programs and organizations that have robbed it of its distinctive honor and drawn glory to themselves. (12) We must guard against what I call the "jumboitis", the tendency to build a tower to Babel (Genesis 11), or proudly to impress people with our own power and bigness. We must not put our confidence in numbers as did David on a tragic occasion (2 Samuel 24). (13) We must watch what I call "the projection principle." I honestly believe that the bulk of the troubles which exist in the church of our Lord today exist because of the projection of twisted or warped personalities (Proverbs 26:21). Please be careful in making personal applications! I believe that the bulk of the difficulties that exist among us today exist because of the personal problems which some of us have deep within our souls. (14) We must guard against the tendency to make merchandise of the truth of our Lord (2 Peter 2:3). Many of the problems that exist in the Lord's church today exist because of the desire on the part of some people to "feather their own nests" from a materialistic or financial point of view. (15) We must guard against human ambitions and watch those who seem to be motivated too much by a desire to make a name for themselves or to gain power for themselves (Matthew 18:1). (16) We must cultivate consistency (Romans 14:22). I have found myself frequently condemning in others that which I allow in myself. I think this is true of many who stand identified with me and many of you who do not stand identified with me. (17) We must guard against the tendency to be completely overwhelmed by human leadership (I Corinthians 1:12). I have always been a great admirer of great men. Some of you in this assembly are men whom I grew up almost adoring and I must guard against the tendency to allow the convictions of some such "idol" to influence me unduly. (18) We must remember the evil of division (Galatians 5:20). There is nothing on this earth worse than division. (19) We must not offend our own conscience (Romans 14:23). (20) We dare not cause another person to violate his conscience (I Corinthians 8; Romans 14:1-15:3). (21) Last and most important of all, we must remember the importance of having within our hearts love for people (Romans 12:10). Jesus Christ placed upon us the responsibility of loving not only our brothers, but even our enemies. He certainly placed upon me the responsibility of loving you, even though you differ from me as you do.

I'm praying with all the fervor of my soul that somehow or other, brethren, as a result of our meditations this week, we can love one another more and perhaps be like Jacob and Esau in running to throw ourselves upon the others' necks for a bit of weeping and some "holy kisses"! May God help us to love one another in spite of our differences and, as well suggested several times this week, have unity and love in spite of our diversities.

# HOW TO ATTAIN AND MAINTAIN FELLOWSHIP

Harry Pickup, Jr.

I want to add my genuine expression of appreciation to those of all the other brethren for being invited to attend this meeting to listen, to talk and to study. I think there is one primary thing which has contributed to the congeniality of this meeting: the expression of common courtesy. There is something about people being together and dealing courteously with each other which contributes to the proper atmosphere and climate. Good manners are never a sign of weakness or lack of conviction.

In I Peter chapter three Peter wrote: "Finally, brethren, be ye like minded, compassionate, loving as brethren and humble minded." William Barclay says a synonym for being "humble-minded" is "courtesy." Young men should treat older men with a great deal of respect and older men should demonstrate regard for younger men. Such is extremely important in times of controversy.

With this in mind I want to offer some criticism of matters presented in a previous speech. I wish to call in question

HARRY PICKUP JR.—*Evangelist for congregation in St. Petersburg, Florida; associated with the department of publications in Florida College, Temple Terrace, Florida; writer for* **THE PRECEPTOR**; *widely used throughout the nation in gospel meetings.*

some things which have been suggested as a basis for determining whether or not certain things are scriptural.

First of all, the pragmatic approach in solving problems; i.e. a thing is right because it works. Something is thought to be right—good and wholesome—because what is being done appears to be successful.

Bro. Lanier and I—a while back—attended some meetings in Denver in which the pragmatic principle was offered as proof that a thing is scriptural. There is an element of truth in this approach. The truth does "work." But not everything that "works" is true. I am not insulted when a sincere brother questions my principle because he judges my practice to be less than successful. But to affirm that a thing is right and scriptural simply because of its apparent success is to build on sand.

Bro. Briney *(Otey-Briney Debate)* made this same argument in support of the missionary society. With a great deal of emotion he appealed to brother Otey to look at the great work which he and his brethren had done throughout the North and in many foreign countries. Obviously, the missionary society had succeeded in spreading the gospel in those places. In Briney's mind this made the society scriptural. Of course, brother Otey denied that the conclusion followed from the premise stated.

Several years ago I heard a brother defend himself on this same ground when other brethren were seriously calling in question a practice in which they had cooperated with him. He appealed to them not to make the change lest they destroy all of the apparent success of the past. The pragmatic approach to scripture is not sound.

An apparent limited success should cause "us" (and by "us" I mean those who are referred to as "conservatives." I use that term only for purposes of accommodation.) to investigate the reason for less than full success. On the other hand, apparent success is not justification simply because of what it appears to be. I'm not insulted when you tell me, "Look, you're not doing all that you ought to be doing." I'm aware of that; I'm well aware of it. I believe that every group of people, every preacher, who teaches as I do on the institutional question ought to be willing to take a long hard look at our principles and practices.

But it is not my plan or your plan—it's God's plan. The New Testament teaches us to "work the work of God." The work of God is revealed in New Testament scriptures and is an incontestable basis for determining what is and is not scriptural. Pragmatism is a questionable basis.

To question our failures in working the works of God should serve two purposes. It should, first of all, stimulate us (I am talking about those who are commonly called "conservatives" or "antis") to greater efforts to glorify God and to benefit men. By the same token another's failure never becomes the basis for something being determined to be right. If we have failed, if we have failed in what we are trying to do, this is not the right basis upon which other brethren ought to work.

A second false premise is deciding that unity cannot be produced through the scriptures, because of the complications involved in Bible study. Let me read that again. I don't know whether it's precisely stated or not. But it is as well as I could do in the short time that I have had from last night to this morning. Ruling out the Scriptures as a means toward unity is a serious mistake.

A while back I sat in a number of meetings in which many brethren were present. I will refer to them as the "neo-unity brethren." I listened to either 19 or 21 speeches in which again and again the Scriptures were ruled out as a means toward unity.

The point was made that our arguments over scriptures become too involved and complicated. In discussing whether mechanical instruments of music in worship are right the arguments do not become complicated because of what the Bible teaches on the subject. Arguments tend to appear complicated, for example, when someone argues the organ is scriptural because the tuning fork is scriptural. Complications do not arise in showing that one is led to become a Christian through the power of the Gospel. The matter may appear to become complicated in trying to refute the man who claims that the Holy Spirit apart from the Gospel leads one to become a Christian and remain such. It is not complicated to show one that the church does something distributively which it does not do collectively. The application of this teaching may appear to become complicated.

The third basis that I think is in error is to decide that the true application lies equal distance between extremes. (Notice I didn't say "truth." I believe "truth" is a noun and Christ is the "truth." What we say is "true" only as we judge it by the "truth." There is more than a syntactical distinction between the noun "truth" and the adjective "true.")

Does the truth lie *equal* distance between extremes? I think not. Many years ago when I was a "Christian-wild cat"—and I like to think, a less perceptive young man—in one of my classes I spent a great deal of time trying to balance a pencil on my finger. Becoming wise and sagacious I finally came to the conclusion that because the pencil was heavier on one end than on the other the balance point would be away from the center. What I am saying is this: while the truth does lie between extremes, it doesn't lie equal distance between them. It is a mistake to try to find the truth by trying to locate the median point between two opposite errors.

The before mentioned points are negative in their nature. I don't know if they will contribute to our discussion or not. However, I hope they will.

I would like now to suggest something in a positive manner which I believe will make a contribution to our desire to be of "one mind." I believe the Bible suggests a genuine basis for fellowship. I believe a statement of this basis is found in I John 1:1-4. John says that his purpose in writing this book is to declare the basis for fellowship. This "declaration" includes both the persons of God and the truth of God. Fellowship necessarily involves association with persons. To consider Bible fellowship apart from the divine persons is meaningless.

We must emphasize the fellowship of persons. While God is not a human person, none the less He is a person. The personal quality in fellowship needs to be clearly recognized and strongly emphasized. On the other hand, fellowship with God apart from His word is impossible. These matters are clearly affirmed and delineated in this epistle.

Ephesians 4:1-6 suggests the divine program for unity. (a.) There is the plea for the preservation of unity. "Endeavoring to keep the unity of the Spirit." This passage is not commanding us to work out ways and means either for the beginning or the maintaining of unity. Rather he pleads for us to preserve that wnich the Spirit has already made possible.

(b.) In the seven "ones" we are told the platform for unity—the fundamental basis upon which it rests. There is one God whom we worship. One Lord whom we serve as master. One Spirit who leads and guides us. One body in which we are all members and are thus members one of another. One faith which we all believe. One baptism with which each is baptized. One hope which sustains us.

(c.) There is the divine provision for unity. "He gave gifts unto men . . . for the perfecting of the saints." The "gifts" were the "apostles, prophets, evangelists, pastors, and teachers." These men, miraculously endowed, implemented unity in Christ's body.

(d.) There is the perfection of unity as each member holds to the head and personally fulfills his individual service. This leads to the growth and unity of the body.

May the Lord bless us and enrich us in every good thing is my prayer honestly and sincerely in Jesus' name.

## How to Attain and Maintain Fellowship

Alan E. Highers

I believe that all of us are very conscious of the need for unity and, more than ever, of the desire for unity. But there are some conditions that exist that make unity imperative if there is any scriptural way in which it may be brought about.

All of us are already aware of the passages in the Bible on unity—how good and how pleasant it is to dwell together in unity. We already know and we have already had examples given of how unpleasant it is when there is not unity. We know the prayer of our Lord in the very shadow of the cross when he prayed that we might be one because through this the world would come to believe on him. We are aware of the fact that much of our effectiveness has been quenched because we do not have the unity for which Christ prayed, and that, doubtless, there are souls that will be lost eternally because of the divisions among us. In fact, most of us could probably cite cases where there are those who have been lost, who are lost, and unless something is done, will be eternally lost because of the divisions among us. We are aware of the statement of the apostle Paul in I Cor. 1:10 in which he beseeches us to have unity and in which he not only says we should speak the same thing, but that we should be of the same mind and of the same judgment.

Consider the world conditions at the present time. Think about communism overtaking the world. It is a Godless force. When we think about the atheistic philosophies that are current, when we think about the threat facing all of us even within the church, the threat of modernism; and when we consider that even though there are differences between us, it has been conceded that every man in this meeting, regardless of

---

ALAN E. HIGHERS—*Evangelist Getwell congregation, Memphis, Tennessee; debater; soon to become a practicing attorney.*

where he stands on the issues that we have discussed, believes in the plenary, verbal inspiration of the word of God, its inerrancy and the fact that it is *the* authority, it becomes especially imperative that we seek greater areas of cooperation, if possible, in harmony with the word of God. We are facing a common enemy and we are facing philosophies, feelings, dangers, and threats to the purity of the church and to the salvation not only of those who are members of the body of Christ but also of those outside the body of Christ who are being influenced by the philosophies in the world.

We have the "new morality"—the idea of situational ethics, that nothing is right or wrong within itself, everything is relevant and what is wrong in one situation may be right in another situation. I am not denying that principle is sometimes true, but not in regard to absolutes. I recognize that I am so close to some of you brethren on some matters, in fact on some of the matters that count the most, and that we would stand together on all of the matters I have mentioned just now—the atheistic philosophies, modernism, liberalism (and I am using that in its classic sense, not in its accommodative sense; I am talking about a denial of the scriptures, rejection of the Bible as inspired and as our authority). I realize we would stand together against the new morality which has claimed so many young people, and that we all believe in the verbal inspiration of the word of God.

I do *not* cite these matters as a basis for unity. I am not saying that because we do face common enemies and because we are mutually concerned about it, we may, therefore, unite. I simply cite these matters as expressive of the *need* for unity, that if there is any way in which it might be achieved, these crucial matters demand that we search out the ways and seek those avenues where unity and fellowship might be possible.

I believe the basic questions that we have discussed during this series have been these:

(1) When is a New Testament example binding? This is one of the truly significant questions discussed. We agree that Bible authority is necessary, we have agreed largely as to how Bible authority is established. There was some criticism yesterday of brother Humble's statement concerning ambiguity in example. I do not believe brother Humble meant by his use of that quotation, or that brother Campbell meant by ambiguity,

that we cannot find authority. But the ambiguity is just what we have found, brethren; all of us know that some examples show what we are at liberty to do, some examples, however, show what we are bound to do. The great difficulty is to learn how to determine when we are being shown merely what we can do and when we are being shown what we must do. It is my conviction that an example in itself is not binding, but that there must be an indication of some background requirement that the example itself is setting out, and that this is the determining factor of when a New Testament example is binding.

(2) Another serious question is the application of generic and specific authority, or explicit and implicit authority. We agree about generic and specific authority; in fact, even in the discussion about whether there is a law of exclusion we all agree in the final analysis with the results. I believe this is a sound principle. I do not believe that it is hair-splitting or drawing fine and technical distinctions to speak of generic and specific authority. I believe the principles that were set down in brother Kurfee's book on instrumental music many years ago regarding generic and specific authority are just as sound and vital today as they were then, and that we are on safe ground in affirming these principles. The difficulty is in the application of generic and specific authority. I believe in generic and specific authority, brethren, and I even believe there is a law of exclusion. Whether you express it that way or not, you agree with the conclusion. The difficulty here is in the application of generic and specific authority.

(3) In regard to this matter of fellowship, there is a question as to how far we may go in fellowshipping those who are in error. It has been set out, for example, in brother Puckett's address that he believes some of those identified with him are in error on certain points, yet fellowship exists. I am not trying to draw an analogy, brother Adams, to say that these questions are all on the same basis. I know you stated that you plan to deal with that in your address. I am not drawing an analogy here. In this address I am simply raising the question: How far may we go in fellowshipping those who are in error? To what extent may we go? All of us have fellowship with some who are in error because no one agrees with me on every point! Everyone of us would have to say that. We believe that every-

one is in error on some point, but fellowship exists. It is a very basic question as to how far we may go in fellowshipping those who are in error.

(4) Then, what is the basis of fellowship? I John 1:7 says, "If we walk in the light (and light is a synonym for truth as darkness is for error), as he is in the light then we have fellowship one with another and the blood of Jesus Christ his son cleanses us from all sin." The basis of our fellowship with one another is our fellowship with Christ. If we are in fellowship with Christ, we are in fellowship with one another. Fellowship with one another is based, first, on fellowship with Christ. I do not exclude anyone from my fellowship if he is in fellowship with Christ.

Now, this leads me to the primary questions that I would like to propound. It has been stated repeatedly through the Restoration Movement that nothing should be made a test of fellowship that is not a matter of salvation. That is in harmony with I John 1:7. It is also reasonable and logical because if it is not to cost one's soul, there is no reason why I should not extend fellowship. If it is something that does not take one out of fellowship with God, then it certainly should not take one out of my fellowship or your fellowship. Therefore, that gives rise to the question: Are these matters that we have been discussing matters of salvation? Is it a matter of salvation with those of you who are opposed to these things we support? Can I have fellowship with Christ and support these things to which you object? If my support of these matters is a matter of salvation, could you have fellowship with me even though I did not require you to support them? That suggestion was made in both speeches last night—that special contributions might be taken for some of these projects. But, if I continue to support them even by sending a contribution to a congregation where these things are done, if it is a matter of salvation, does that cut off my fellowship with Christ and would it, therefore, cut off my fellowship with my brethren?

It is not a question of whether you must support these things, but whether it is necessary for me to cease supporting them before we can have fellowship. I do not believe you must support orphan homes through the church treasury or that you must support the Herald of Truth in order to enjoy fellowship with us. Neither do I believe we must have baptisteries in order to carry out the command of God. I do not believe it is necessary. Some brethren have objected to Bible classes and cups. We have some brethren who believe that debating is sinful. We do not have to have debates. So, the question I raise is this: Is it a requirement that all of these things must be given up before fellowship may be a reality? I do not believe you must support them; you could have my fellowship without it, and even believe it is wrong to contribute. But the question is: In order for you to fellowship me, is it mandatory for me to cease my support of these matters under discussion?

## How to Attain and Maintain Fellowship

James W. Adams

There are so many things mentioned to which I should like to reply and concerning which I have made notes that I can see now I am not going to be able to get to all of it. Brother Stevens mentioned the matter of viciousness among brethren, you and us. I wish to make a confession concerning this. The most vicious letter I have ever received in more than thirty-four years of gospel preaching was not from a Baptist, a Methodist, some other kind of sectarian, or from what we sometimes call "liberal" brethren, but it was from one of my "conservative" brethren. Viciousness is not therefore necessarily confined to the relationship between you brethren and us. It is sometimes among us and, perhaps, among you.

Most of you present have probably received letters of this kind, or have had vicious statements made about you. Viciousness is all about us. Brother Stevens said that he could give a psychological explanation of viciousness among brethren. The explanation I have for this is found in the word of God. The Wise Man said, "A brother offended is harder to be won than

JAMES W. ADAMS—*Evangelist Mound and Starr congregation, Nacogdoches, Texas. Front page writer for* THE PRECEPTOR.

a strong city: and their contentions are like the bars of a castle." (Proverbs 18:19.) This is the Divine explanation; namely, the closeness of the relationship which we sustain to one another. An illustration of this is the fact that there is nothing more vicious than a family fight. We all know this to be true.

Brother Highers mentioned the fact that you and we have a common foe in theological "liberalism" among the churches. He said he was not urging this fact as a basis for disregarding vital differences between us, but simply to emphasize the need for a settlement of our differences. I understand his point and consider it completely valid. During this discussion the book, *We Be Brethren*, has been mentioned several times. The title of this book is taken from a statement made by Abraham of Old Testament times as he pleaded for the necessity for a settlement of the difficulties between his herdsmen and Lot's. Mentioned in the context of this statement is another fact that unquestionably made urgent such a settlement; namely, "the Canaanite and the Perizzite dwelled then in the land." (Genesis 13:7, 8.)

I wish also to say a word concerning brother Higher's statements with regard to complicated preaching. Lately, this has become almost a fetish with me. I am being made to realize more and more that brethren on both sides of current controversies are confusing the minds of the brethren on both sides by the minute and technical distinctions which we make and the complicated reasoning in which we engage. This is not to be regarded as a personal criticism of anyone, and I certainly agree that we should all study and that we should not encourage anyone to be dense. But I have tried lately to simplify my preaching and writing on these subjects, and this shall be my policy from this time forward. I am trying to reduce my teaching on these issues to basics and to discuss these fundamental principles so that people can understand them. I do not know how successful I am. Others may be more successful than I, but because the gospel is for the generality of mankind, I want to keep my discussion of these matters as uncomplicated as possible. If reasoning is too difficult for the comprehension of the average man, he will conclude, "If I am required to understand that to go to heaven, then I might as well forget about the whole matter." This is a danger we risk in getting too complicated in our study. Of course, we all understand that when sophistry is employed against a position we occupy, we necessarily become involved in technicalities. But I believe all of us have been guilty of making these matters entirely too technical in our discussion of them. In studying some of this argument, I freely admit that my own mind gets in a whirl. I get on the merry-go-round and cannot seem to get off. It is that confusing.

Brother Stevens mentioned the fact that he does not believe there must be unvarying uniformity in order for there to be scriptural unity. I do not believe that I and the brethren with whom I am associated believe there must be. We have been charged with so believing, but such is not the case. However, I would not say there are none who so believe. I can say that I have never accepted such an idea. I believe there can be unity in diversity up to a point. Here is the crux of the whole matter—*deciding where that point is*. Deciding where unvarying uniformity ends and diversity begins occasions our difficulties. Because we believe there must be unvarying uniformity in some matters where others believe there may be diversity, we are charged with believing there must be unvarying uniformity in *all* matters. Do we believe in regimentation? No, indeed! Do we believe that all must walk to the same tune in all matters? No, indeed! There is ample room for diversity among the people of God. We come from every strata of human society. All of us have different backgrounds. Therefore, it would be utterly unreasonable to suppose that God would require of human beings so diverse an unvarying uniformity in all things. This would certainly be legalistic. We do not accept any such concept nor make any such demand.

At this point, I should like to reemphasize a fact which has previously been stated; namely, *unity is not an end within itself*. I believe this was one of the mistakes made in the so-called "restoration movement." Brethren, if they did not believe it, often preached and wrote so as to give the impression that they considered unity an end within itself. I believe that many of us today regard unity as an end within itself. As I have grown older as a preacher of the gospel, I have become more concerned with getting men to whom I preach to *do the will of God*. If all of us conform our lives and teaching to the will of God, we will have unity. Hence I am more concerned about this than I am about unity. This does not mean I am not concerned about unity. I would not be here today if I were not. But I am more concerned about getting men to do the will of God. This is an end within itself. Unity is a by-product of this, hence I am more interested in the cause than in the effect.

I believe there are two extremes which one may occupy in seeking for unity, or in trying to create a climate conducive to unity. *First,* I believe we can abdicate to crankdom if we are not careful. Such could result from overestimating the value of unity, or underestimating the value of truth. It could grow out of a misconception of the true nature of "the love of the brethren" enjoined by the New Testament. I believe that we should love the brethren, but I also believe we could place a construction on what the love of the brethren demands so as to result in an abdication to crankdom. I would not accept a premise of this kind nor do I practice it. Furthermore, I do not demand this of you brethren who differ from me on the issues which we have been discussing. *Second,* there could be an adamant adherence to non-essentials which would drive wedges of division among God's people. This could grow out of egotism, selfishness, and a refusal to recognize the demand's of God's law of love. These are the two extremes. I may not be wise enough to know exactly where to find the precisely correct ground on which to

| YOU vs. YOU | YOU vs. US | US vs. US |
|---|---|---|
| 1. SUPPORT OF THE COLLEGE BY THE CHURCH. | 1. INSTITUTIONAL ORPHAN HOMES ETC. SUPPORTED BY CHURCHES. | 1. SAINTS ONLY. |
| 2. THE ORPHAN HOME ORGANIZATION. | 2. CHURCH-SUPPORTED RECREATION. | 2. INDIVIDUAL SUPPORT OF THE COLLEGES. |
| 3. CHURCH-SUPPORTED RECREATION. | 3. CHURCH-SUPPORTED COLLEGES. | 3. THE HOLY SPIRIT. |
| 4. HOW TO DETERMINE CHURCH ACTION AND INDIVIDUAL ACTION. | 4. THE SPONSORING CHURCH. | 4. HOW TO DETERMINE CHURCH ACTION AND INDIVIDUAL ACTION. |
| 5. THE HOLY SPIRIT. | | |

stand between these two extremes, but I know that here is where the ground for scriptural unity must be found. We cannot assume either of these extremes and attain unity. The basis for unity must be found between them.

Now let us notice Brother Hardeman Nichols' question: "Why don't you fellowship us when you fellowship one another since you differ with one another as well as with us?" The only exception I took to Brother Nichols having asked this question when he did was the fact that he failed to emphasize the fact that there are an *equal number of divisions among you*. Please note my chart.

The word "you" and "us" which you will note at the top are very probably sectarian and factious, but we use them accommodatively. There are other terms which we so use. For instance, the term "liberal" which we apply to you brethren. You brethren have indicated in this meeting and at the Buchanan Dam meeting that you resent our so labeling you. Brother Thomas particularly has expressed his displeasure relative to this matter. Brother Thomas equates this term with neo-orthodoxy and other forms of modern, sectarian, theological liberalism. I have never used the term in this sense when referring to you brethren. When I say "liberal" and "conservative," I mean only that we have a more conservative attitude with reference to what the word of God allows in our faith and practice than do you. But since the term is offensive to you and since it does have bad connotations as does the term "anti" which you apply to us, I wish to make a pledge here and now to you brethren. I am going to try to quit calling you *liberal*. I am going to make this pledge whether you brethren call me *anti* or not. I am not asking anything of you. I am simply going to quit calling you liberal.

Now, back to our chart. Note the fact that there are three columns. At the head of the columns, we have placed *"You vs. You," "You vs. Us,"* and *"Us vs. Us"* respectively. I shall begin with "us" first. Please observe the right hand column. Number 1 in this column is *"Saints Only."* With reference to the subjects of benevolence, the "saints only" proposition, there is a difference among us, but it is not as serious as you brethren seem to think. It poses no problem with reference to fellowship among us. It could if it is pressed far enough. This would depend upon the attitude of the individual, the applications that he makes, whether or not he trys to attend to a church's business of which he is not a part, or such like.

Brother Puckett has expressed himself on this point. My personal attitude is this: I believe in limited benevolence; I do not believe any man on earth can prove that the church is a general benevolent organization; if anyone wishes to affirm in debate that the church is a general benevolent organization, I will certainly challenge him; but I have from the beginning of the discussion of these matters opposed the affirmation of a universal negative relative to the subjects of benevolence. From the beginning I have advised the brethren with whom I am associated not to affirm the universal negative proposition relative to "saints only" in debate. They have not taken my advice in many cases, but I do not personally endorse the discussion of this proposition in this manner. I would not so discuss it because it is prejudicial of the issue. But, may I repeat, it poses no threat to our fellowship of one another because it has not been pressed among us up to this time by men among us holding either point of view to the extent that a rupture of fellowship would be demanded. If an individual should press this matter and cause division where it is not justified, this could necessitate a different attitude, but it presently poses no problem among us relative to our fellowshipping one another.

Item number 2 on the chart in the right hand column is: INDIVIDUAL SUPPORT OF THE COLLEGE. This involves another area of difference among us. Some very prominent men among us differ as to whether an *individual* can or cannot scripturally support a college operated by the brethren in which the Bible is taught as a regular part of the curriculum of that school. We are united on the question of the support of the college by the churches. We are all opposed to it—one hundred percent opposed to it. Perhaps I should qualify that statement as it is a universal affirmative. Universal propositions are seldom true. However, I will affirm a universal proposition, but I will never affirm a universal negative. So it will not do any of you brethren any good to present me with a challenge to debate in which I am expected to affirm a universal negative on the subject of benevolence, or any other for that matter. We do our cause in any realm untold damage when we affirm universal negatives. All competent debaters know this. Brother John S. Sweeney's observations concerning debating *(Sweeney's Sermons,* pp. 50-62.) impart considerable enlightenment on this point. But, back to our chart.

The difference among us relative to individual support of the college poses no threat to our fellowshipping one another. Our difference has to do with what an *individual* can do, not what *a church* can do. This, therefore, cannot affect our fellowship in the church unless some person assumes the attitude of trying to force his views in the congregation where it has no rightful place. This could cause a rupture of fellowship and division.

Now, let us note number 3 on our chart in the right hand column: THE HOLY SPIRIT. There are some among us who believe in the personal indwelling of the Holy Spirit. They do not believe in the direct operation of the Holy Spirit. Others among us repudiate the idea of a direct indwelling. Men connected with the "Restoration Movement" have always had this difference. I would not refuse to fellowship a Christian simply because he believes the Spirit dwells in him personally. I believe he is wrong—as wrong as he can be. I believe his position is not only untenable but inconsistent with his position on the operation of the Holy Spirit on the alien sinner, yet I see no reason for our divergent views to disrupt fellowship between us. We do not have any tongue-speakers—yet!

Now note number 4 in the right hand column on our chart: HOW TO DETERMINE CHURCH ACTION AND INDIVIDUAL ACTION. Some of us are not in complete agreement on this point, but it has occasioned nothing that would justify a breach of fellowship.

This brings us to *YOU vs. YOU* in the left hand column on our chart. *There are divisions among you.* You are divided on the question (number 1 on the chart) of the SUPPORT OF THE COLLEGE BY THE CHURCH. Brother Reuel Lemmons thinks this is a serious matter which could divide the church. Observe that the church is involved in this matter. It therefore becomes a brotherhood matter and constitutes a serious division among you people, and *you know it is.* Number 2 in the left hand column on the chart is THE ORPHAN HOME ORGANIZATION. Brother Lanier has expressed himself concerning his point of view on this matter. He believes it must be under the elders of a local church. I agree with Brother Cogdill who affirmed his agreement with Brother Lanier's opposition to such homes under institutional boards. You are divided on this point, and the division could be serious. One group of you says an orphan home *cannot* be under the elders as elders and the other group says that it *must*. I do not know just how you resolve this matter and maintain fellowship. I am not necessarily try to find out, but I know there is great contradiction here. I confess there are some things you do about it that I do not understand. You are divided in reference to CHURCH SUPPORTED RECREATION (number 3 in the left hand column on the chart). You are divided on HOW TO DETERMINE CHURCH ACTION AND INDIVIDUAL ACTION (number 4 in the left hand column on the chart). You are divided on the HOLY SPIRIT (number 5 in the left hand column on the chart). There are tongue-speakers among you. These are all serious differences involving the churches as contrasted with individuals, and you are divided on all of them.

Brother Hardeman Nichols said, "There are differences among you and you fellowship one another despite those differences; why then do you not fellowship us despite our differences?" This brings us to the center column on our chart entitled YOU vs. US. Listed in this column are five distinct areas of difference between you and us: (1) INSTITUTIONAL ORPHAN HOMES/ETC. SUPPORTED BY CHURCHES; (2) CHURCH SUPPORTED RECREATION; (3) CHURCH SUPPORTED COLLEGE; (4) THE SPONSORING CHURCH. These are the differences to which Brother Nichols refers. In answer to his question, may I say that I have never made these matters a test of fellowship. From the beginning of this controversy, I have tried to stay away from the question of fellowship. There is not a man here who can lay his finger on the place or time where I have said or written or done anything to make these differences a question of fellowship. I have been in some tense situations too, particularly while laboring with the 10th and Francis congregation in Oklahoma City. From my point of view, Brother Nichols' question is beside the point, for I have not made these matters a test of fellowship. I have urged all the brethren to stay away from the question of fellowship. It has been my conviction that fellowship would take care of itself. (At this point the speaker's time ran out. Brother Reuel Lemmons asked that he be allowed to continue until he was through. He said, "Let him take part of my time. He is saying some awfully good things." The request was granted and the speaker continued.)

I am sorry about this, but my failing is always to have more material than I can use in my time limit. May I repeat; I have never made these matters a test of fellowship. Some of my "conservative" brethren do not feel about this as do I. They think I am a little "soft" on this point. They believe that the question of fellowship should be "pressed." I do not. I believe that we should keep away from the question of fellowship as long as we can.

Fellowship is a sharing in things which we *do*. There is a sense in which we all have fellowship in Jesus Christ because we are saved people. But there is also the kind of fellowship which involves a sharing or participation mutually in things which *are done*. There are some things (center column of the chart) you brethren do in which I cannot share or participate because I believe them to be wrong. This does not mean that I write you off as Christians and brethren and send you down the river to the ocean. This is not it. I just cannot have fellowship with you when I am placed in the position of having to participate in things I believe to be wrong. When such is demanded of me, I must withdraw myself even if it requires me to start a new congregation. I must get away from this demand that my conscience be violated. I cannot violate my conscience to preserve "unity." If I did so, I would not be true to God. You would not want me to do this, nor would I want you to do so. I have never asked one of you to do this, nor will I ever do so. I deny the charge that I have ever made these matters a test of fellowship. My record is uniform relative to my pleading with those with whom I stand identified on these issues, "Let's stay away from the question of fellowship."

Relative to this matter of fellowship, there have been unguarded and unfortunate statements made. They were not intended to mean exactly what you brethren have interpreted them to mean. However, in the heat of controversy all of us are looking for something from our opponents that we can use against them. Consequently, we often use them wrongly. In such cases, men among us have tried to say that such was not intended (a call for breach of fellowship), but their explanation has not been accepted.

Let us now go back to the chart. We are against CHURCH SUPPORTED RECREATION. This is a real issue between you and us. Relative to ORPHAN HOMES, it must be recognized that there are two kinds: (1) the SPONSORING CHURCH variety under an eldership doing a general work of benevolence for other churches; and (2) an orphan home under an INSTITUTIONAL BOARD operating as a distinct and independent entity doing benevolent work for the churches. This is how we regard the matter, and we are opposed to both kinds. *We are not opposed to a church taking care of orphans which are her legitimate responsibility.*

This brings us back to the so-called "saints only" proposition. I am not opposed to a church taking care of little children. Let this be understood.

Another area of difference between *you and us* is THE CHURCH SUPPORTED COLLEGE. I recognize the fact that this does not involve all of you. As we said, there is division among you on this point. I cannot fellowship brethren in this activity, hence I must be versus some of you. In fact I cannot have fellowship with you in any of the four things listed in the center column of the chart. I believe they are wrong (without scriptural warrant) and I cannot mutually share or participate with you in any of them.

Brother Jimmy Allen brought up a matter with which I must deal before I sit down. He used Dudley Spears as an example. His point had to do with the matter of conscience. Brother Allen said that he personally would be willing to make a concession to the conscience of Dudley Spears if Dudley were a member of the church he serves as preacher. In other words, he would be willing to leave off church-support of the matters to which Dudley objected. (There are a great many men among you brethren who would not be willing to do this. I think Brother Allen knew this when he made the statement, but this is all right because I have probably made some statements with which brethren among whom I move would not agree.) Brother Allen further said if he made such a concession to Brother Spears, Dudley must keep quiet about his views. This sounds all right, Brother Allen, and I will accept this as a possible way to work out some of our troubles if you will be willing to keep quiet on the other side of the matter. I would have Brother Allen look at this thing as we see it. We sincerely believe the things in the center column of our chart to be wrong. With all of our hearts, we are opposed to them. Suppose we get ourselves into a position where day after day we must hear the promotion of these things and contention for them as scriptural activities, and we must sit quietly in this environment and say nothing, yet be expected to worship and serve God. Such would become one of the "impossible demands" about which Brother Roy Lanier Sr. talked. Don't you see that? It would be impossible for you and impossible for us. Brother Gus Nichols proposed the same thing in effect. I love Brother Nichols. He is a good man and has done a great deal of good in the world. But Brother Nichols would have us not preach our convictions for the sake of unity, simply because he regards the things in the center column of our chart as matters of opinion. But we do not regard them as matters of opinion. Don't you see that? Hence, these matters will have to be resolved on the basis of reaching common ground in our convictions regarding these matters that are at issue. This does not mean that we can jump from here to there in one step. Between now and the time when we arrive at this common understanding of truth there must be the manifestation of right attitudes and a willingness to create and work together in ameliorating conditions such as this discussion in which we are here engaged at this time.

(Brother Gus Nichols asks a question: "Brother Adams, we used to be united in spite of all these things. Were we Christians then and on the way to heaven? If so, why not be united now?")

I will answer this question. It was also brought up by Brother Alan Highers. The question involves the matter of making a test of fellowship nothing which is not a condition of salvation. Brother Nichols, I do not know how far a person must digress from truth before he ceases to be a Christian. L. R. Riley, a Baptist debater in Western Kentucky, used to make this argument when debating the brethren. He would demand that his opponent specify how much error a person or church must accept before he or it ceased to be a Christian or a church of Christ. Brother Nichols and Highers are posing the same sort of question. I do not know when a man ceases to be a Christian. I do not know when a church ceases to be a church of Christ. This is a problem which I cannot solve.

But, back to Brother Nichols' question about why things cannot be as they used to be. Some current differences existed back then and some did not. Some of us tolerated things then which we now regard as having been inconsistent on our part. If two men differ concerning a matter on which they hold specific convictions, the difference in their convictions will have to be resolved before there can be absolute unity (if the matter be regarded as an essential by both of them). I do not believe we can have fellowship and complete unity without this.

(Brother Nichols: "We used to.")

Well, not under the same circumstances, I believe.

## *How to Attain and Maintain Fellowship*

Reuel Lemmons

Brother Jackson, I am truly humbled by your remarks. I'd like to say one word before my time starts. This has become standard procedure. Brother Norman Starling, more than anybody else in this room, is responsible for the Buchanan meeting and for this one. Norman has had a burning desire to see something definite and concrete done to help fill the gap that is getting a little wider all the time. He approached me on it, and I told him that I had so many irons in the fire that I couldn't work at it, but that if he would do the leg work I would join him in trying to get the Buchanan meeting together. Norman did about 98% of the work and I got part of the credit for it, and in this meeting he has done just about all the leg work, all the correspondence and everything, and has worked behind the scenes as hard as any man could to make these meetings a success.

Following the Buchanan meeting James (Adams) entered in with us to help us plan this meeting. James has had a great

---

REUEL G. LEMMONS—*Editor of the* FIRM FOUNDATION; *evangelist for one of the churches of Austin, Texas; widely known radio speaker on an international hook-up; used extensively as a lecturer and speaker in gospel meetings throughout the nation.*

hand in planning this meeting so I think we all owe to Norman and James a debt of gratitude.

Now, whatever time is left . . . James was saying some things which I could not have said as well, and so he didn't take any of my time at all. Because of the things that he was saying right at the time that he was to stop I thought it would be tragic for him to stop there and leave some of those things unsaid. And before he turns off the projector I want to refer to the chart because, James, I am as sincere as you or anybody in the belief that #4 in the center column is the only difference between you and me that is of any import, and that pretty well pinpoints this whole field of controversy.

These discussions have been wonderful. They have certainly helped me. They have humbled me in many ways. They have clarified my thinking. I have not given the study to these issues that some of you brethren who are experts in the field have given and so I could come as a student and to learn as much as possible. So all of you—every man that has spoken—has contributed some good thing to me and, whether you realize it or not, my personal sense of unity with all the different shades of all of you is much greater than it was prior to this meeting.

The prayer of Jesus in John 17 makes unity so imperative that we ought to go to almost any extreme to maintain it. We ought to allow everything within the bounds of reason, and we ought to study with acute diligence and carefulness every passage, and the application of every passage, and make as much latitude for diversity as we possibly can, drawing the lines of fellowship as broad as we can rather than as narrow as we can.

The grounds for breach of fellowship ought to be reduced to an absolute minimum, and that after every effort has been exhausted to remove any differences.

I appreciate deeply brother Adams' statement of his own feelings that in the future he felt to remove the complications and to increase the simplicity of approach to these things was wise. I share that conviction entirely.

There are some valid grounds for disfellowship. (1) Doctrines which vitally affect one's faith in Jesus Christ are valid grounds for disfellowship (2 John 9); (2) Sowers of discord among brethren must be disfellowshiped (Romans 16:17); (3) Those who walk disorderly (and I'm taking it out of its context)

2 Thessalonians 3:6-7. Now, brethren, if there are any other grounds for disfellowship, I don't know it. You can subhead several things under these three general headings, but when you reduce the grounds for disfellowship—(Note: At this point someone asked him to repeat these grounds.) When you reduce the causes to an absolute bare minimum, and cut out all the subheads, I feel that there are these three valid grounds. First, doctrines false enough to affect one's faith in Jesus Christ. The whole book of 2 John clarifies that, verse 9 pinpoints it. Second, sowers of discord; in other words, troublemakers, pinpoined in Romans 16:7 and those who walk disorderly— that gets the man in incest; that gets all kinds of immorality; lovers of the world to the extent that they have to be disfellowshipped. The reference is 2 Thessalonians 3:6-7. It seems to me that when you reduce the grounds for disfellowship to the simplest terms this is what you have.

These discussions have brought out the fact that the basis of all our lack of fellowship, whatever it may be, springs from differing methods of establishing Bible authority. When you reduce all our differences to a single head, this is about it. It boils down to differences existing in our different minds about where to draw the wavy line.

About all our divisions can be equated with the differences existing in our minds on where to draw a wavy line. That is just about how flimsy I feel that the basis is for our disfellowshiping actions.

And the line *is* wavy. It has to be wavy so that it will go above or below anything that I want to allow or disallow.

I have listened closely to the three ways of establishing authority —command, example, inference. And I am persuaded that this needs closer examination. I believe that Bible authority rests solely on the revelationary nature of the scriptures, and that dealing with necessary inference and approved examples involves the use of the human mind and, therefore, interpretation.

> *Since no scripture is given for private interpretation, there is actually no Biblical ground for disfellowship in differences that are centered either in necessary inference or in approved example.*

Differences exist, certainly, but not *disfellowshiping dif-*

*ferences*; because both the degree of the necessity of the inference and the degree of the bindingness of the example are things that exist in our minds.

Authority itself does not rest in the human mind or the human mind's application of Biblical principles. Authority rests in the revelationary nature of scripture only. This is borne out, I believe, in the difficulty all of us have found, and brother Adams expressed so eloquently, in understanding some of these matters and knowing, for instance, at exactly what point a church ceases to be a church of Christ. There isn't any man living who can answer that question.

And, really, bound up in this is the degree of necessity of inference and the degree of bindingness of example. The matter is not yet so clear cut as to disrupt fellowship.

The fact that good minds—and we have some of the best here, hand picked from both groups because of your ability to reason and think things through—cannot resolve these matters, indicates the lack of any grounds for disfellowship. Your very presence here is a compliment to every one of you in the matter of your reasoning ability. And the very fact that these matters cannot be resolved in four days between us in such a clear cut manner as to remove all doubt demonstrates the fact that they are not explicit enough to warrant a disruption of fellowship. Can we cease fellowship when these basic principles are still up in the air? I don't believe we can do it, and I was happy to hear James say that in his heart and mind he has never drawn this line of fellowship. If it had not been a demonstration of bias I would have said "amen." That was ruled out by the ground rules, you know. But that describes my sentiment exactly.

I differ with some of you brethren as thoroughly as you differ with me and I don't think you have a corner on the understanding of the Bible. I think, at least at this point, that my understanding is as likely to be right as yours. I have never had, and do not now have, any feeling of disfellowship toward any one of you and I think I can live and die that way. As long as these conditions remain unresolved on the basis of the revelationary nature of the scriptures, I believe that we can pull the fringes of fellowship back together and mend the wound rather than making it deeper.

There will always be tensions in the body of Christ, "they exist between truth and tolerance," as someone has said. Bearing with this tension on the part of everyone of us is mandatory. These differences must be kept from causing a rupture.

You cannot justify some of the projects in the brotherhood;—and the brotherhood still includes you. I don't agree with some of your views and you do not agree with some of mine. You do not have to agree with me to have my fellowship, and I hope I will not have to agree with you to have yours, for I will forego it rather than surrender to your views. If, by the scriptures, the righteousness of your views can be demonstrated to me to the point that my faith changes as a result of conviction, based on understanding the scriptures, then I'll join you without pressure.

There are some points that I would like to have you consider as this meeting comes to a close. Following this meeting I would like for us to have fellowship in this much at least;—and I do believe in degrees of fellowship because I think there are degrees of agreement. Following this meeting each one of us can fellowship the other in giving the time and publicity to this meeting, and the kind of comment about what has gone on here, that will encourage those who were not fortunate enough to attend to move toward unity rather than toward disunity.

Second, each one of us can give a prayerful study to the notes taken, and to the written discussion which will probably be published, in a re-examination of the validity of his grounds and of his belief. Let not pride and prejudice keep us from ever moving closer to that divine body of truth we find in the scriptures.

Third, we can stay in communication. Most of our differences have arisen because of a lack of communication. I think each one of you has been surprised to find that the other was not nearly as heretical as you thought and many of our differences come because we do not sit down like this often enough. We can stay in communication and we can seek opportunities to promote better feelings among us, better understanding.

Fourth, we can discourage dogmatic pronouncements concerning a fractured fellowship and the finality of it.

Fifth, you brethren have something the brotherhood needs and we feel we have something you need. We would rather— I would much rather—see these needs expressed subjectively among ourselves rather than objectively from an outside, detached, intangible position. We need to be workers together with Him and to this I plead your very best efforts. May the Lord bless every one of us and give to us a spirit that will please Him and not alienate each other.

www.ingramcontent.com/pod-product-compliance
Lightning Source LLC
Chambersburg PA
CBHW072231240426
43670CB00040B/2407